Handbooks on Library Practice

COLLEGE LIBRARIANSHIP
The Objectives and the Practice

EDITED BY
A RENNIE McELROY

THE LIBRARY
ASSOCIATION
LONDON

© Library Association Publishing Limited 1984.
Published by Library Association Publishing Limited,
7 Ridgmount Street, London WC1E 7AE.
Phototypeset in Linotron Garamond by Input Typesetting Limited,
London
and printed in Great Britain by the Pitman Press, Bath.

First published 1984

British Library Cataloguing in Publication Data

College Librarianship. — (Handbooks in library practice).
1. Libraries, University and college — Great Britain — Management.
I. McElroy, A Rennie   II. Series
025.1'977'0941   Z675.U5

ISBN 0 85365 785 8

123487868584

College Librarianship

Contents

v

PART 2 COLLEGES AND THEIR LIBRARIES

PART 3 THE LIBRARIANSHIP

vii

Editor and Contributors

EDITOR

A Rennie McElroy MA ALA MIInfSc MBIM
Depute Librarian; Napier College

CONTRIBUTORS

Marie Adams BA ALA
Tutor-Librarian; Barnet College of Further Education

Douglas Anderson MSc MIInfSc ALA
Senior Lecturer; School of Librarianship and Information Studies;
Robert Gordon's Institute of Technology

K G B Bakewell MA MBIM FLA
Principal Lecturer; School of Librarianship and Information
Studies; Liverpool Polytechnic

John Bate MBE MA DipEd FLA
Chief Librarian; Napier College

Charles H Bleasdale MA ALA AIRT
Head of Department of Library and Learning Resources; Bolton
Institute of Higher Education

Editor and Contributors

Simon R Bradford BA ALA
Audio-visual Librarian; Middlesex Polytechnic

J Gordon Brewer MA ALA MIInfSc
Head of Learning Resources; Bedford College of Higher Education

Paul F Burton BA MA ALA
Chief Librarian; Leith Nautical College

Jean Cinnamond ALA
Librarian; Lowlands Sixth Form College

John Cowley BA FLA
Head of Library Services; Middlesex Polytechnic

Donald Davinson BSc(Econ) DPA FLA
Head of School of Librarianship; Leeds Polytechnic

Alan Day MA MPhil FRGS FLA
Head of Department of Library and Information Studies;
Manchester Polytechnic

J Dunning CBE BSc DEd MEd MA AMCT CEng MIM FEIS
Formerly Principal; Napier College

Nigel Ford MA BA ALA
Lecturer; Department of Information Studies; University of
Sheffield

Gordon Harris BSocSc ALA AIInfSc
Librarian; Westhill College

Colin T Harrison ALA FRSA
Head of School of Information Resources; Chelmer-Essex Institute
of Higher Education

Dennis Klappersack BA MSLIS ABD
Director, Learning Resources Center; Houston Community
College System, Texas, USA

Mary H Lakie MPS ALA MIInfSc
Project Manager; Syntex Research Scotland

John Lubans Jr BA MALS MA (PubAd)
Assistant University Librarian for Public Services; Duke University, Durham, North Carolina, USA

A Rennie McElroy MA ALA MIInfSc MBIM
Depute Librarian; Napier College

Ian Malley MA BSc
British Library Information Officer for User Education; Loughborough University of Technology

A Maltby BA MA(Econ) FLA
Scottish Education Department

Hilary A Rees BA ALA
Librarian; The College of Further Education, Plymouth

Edward R Reid-Smith BA DipAdultEd MEd FLA ALAA
Principal Lecturer; Riverina College of Advanced Education, New South Wales, Australia

D H Revill BSc(Econ) AdvDipEdTech FLA
Polytechnic Librarian; Liverpool Polytechnic

Margaret J Sked BA ALA
Principal Education Resource Librarian; Strathclyde Region Education Department, Lanark Division

C M Turner MA ALA
Head of Educational Resources; Worthing College of Technology and West Sussex College of Design

Acknowledgements

No work of this nature owes much more than the initial idea, the outline, and the team selection to its editor. The work, the inspiration, and any success achieved all belong to the authors of the individual contributions.

It is my privilege to thank all these colleagues and friends, busy people all of them, who yielded to my blandishments and agreed to write, and who have since then interpreted remits in which they had little choice with thought, professionalism, hard work, and wit. Readers should note that the views expressed are those of the authors themselves and should not be interpreted as the official views of their institutions.

College Librarianship is the product of its authors, and I am grateful to them for their efforts and their support.

Other tributes are due:

Greeba Thomson, of Napier College, contributed greatly to preparing the typescript on her word-processor, and accomplished what at times must have seemed endless re-editings and reformattings. Her labours as always, have made my task, and I trust that of the printer, much easier.

Finally, my thanks to David Pratt, Ann Corry and Maureen Keyser at Library Association Publishing for their encouragement and assistance in planning, writing, editing and producing the book.

Acknowledgements

The faults that remain, and the sins of omission, are mine. I hope that they do not detract from the reader's pleasure.

A Rennie McElroy
Napier College
Edinburgh
1983

Introduction

Any introduction should offer the reader some focussing elements, some definitions, and some vocabulary.

Volumes in the *Handbooks on Library Practice* series have sought to provide a practical guide to those aspects of librarianship which they address. Some have described and commented on the profession's bibliographic tools; others have discussed case histories, explaining problems which have arisen in the management of libraries; others again have offered readers a guide to specialisms within the profession.

If *College Librarianship* is to be likened to any of these, it must be to the last, but the match is an uncomfortable one. *College Librarianship* is, for the most part, philosophical rather than practical in the day-to-day, 'how-to-do-it-good' sense. Which is emphatically not to suggest that it is an impractical book! It seeks to identify and comment upon the principal issues and objectives which drive colleges, their libraries, and their librarians, rather than to recount the daily routine of running the library.

The book does not advise on setting up specific procedures, but tries to identify policy and its underlying issues, and objectives and their implications for librarians' behaviour, tactics and strategy. It offers comment and opinion on professional, personal, and managerial style. Thus readers who approach the work seeking a description of college administrative structures, a list of headings to be used in preparing estimates, or advice on the choice of issue systems and cataloguing practices will be disappointed. These are not present.

Instead, there are discussions of tertiary education's place in society, of the forces acting upon it, of the tertiary education library's objectives, and of how the librarian may best meet these through his policies and his use of resources. College libraries are very emphatically the children of their colleges, individuals shaped by their parent organizations rather than by the profession of librarianship alone.

What is a college? For the purposes of *College Librarianship*, a college is defined loosely as any non-university institution of tertiary education. That said, it is perhaps wisest to add as little as possible. The polytechnics are included, as are local and regional further education colleges, colleges and institutes of higher education, the specialist monotechnics, and the schools of education. The most adequate short descriptions of the sector are perhaps the contents list of Part 2 of this book and the rather untidy phrase 'all formal educational establishments which are neither schools nor universities'! It is easier and more appropriate to define colleges by what they do than what they are, and this issue is addressed by several contributors.

The institutions covered by the term 'college' are so diverse in size and scope that no single useful description can be given of their operating structures. Some large, mature institutions have all the organizational paraphernalia (the word is not used pejoratively) of the traditional university: academic board, faculty boards, boards of study, and research, library, computing, resources etc committees supporting the departmental structure. Other colleges have a simple, primarily executive, non-deliberative structure based on the authority of the Principal. Predictably, most lie somewhere in between! Where a complex structure exists, the librarian must participate in it. Where it does not, he must seek the pressure points and direct his efforts towards these. In neither can he afford to sit in his library shuffling books. That is one main thesis of this book.

It is a truism that librarianship is as much about people as books.

Introduction

Unfortunately, it is less emphatically held that librarianship's and the senior professional librarian's responsibilities are as much about managing as about doing. A library must provide good service: the right books, the right information, informed professional advice and guidance. It can only do these things if it is properly organized internally and highly regarded externally, ie by its (invariably non-librarian) paymasters and controllers. This last is vital, but is all too often ignored or shunned by professional practitioners who, perhaps understandably, wish to remain snug within their bibliographic expertise. It is as much a part of professional librarianship to fight the library's corner in the resource allocation committee as it is to carry out a literature search. The corner can be fought successfully only from a standpoint of knowledge, understanding, and sympathy with the objectives of the parent body, and the forces and constraints acting upon it. That is another main thesis of this book.

Librarians hold as acts of faith that 'reading is good for you' and that 'information permits better learning and decision making'. That is, other things being broadly equal, students and lecturers who read, use the library, keep up to date, seek and use information, are likely to do their jobs better than those who do not. But the old, rosy picture of students avid for knowledge, craving books, hardly holds in most colleges (if indeed it ever did hold, anywhere!). Students are hard-working young people with a job to do; get a degree, diploma, whatever. Not improperly, they wish to do that job at as low an energy cost as possible: an entirely reasonable principle, managerially sound. If they perceive the library, its services and collections as lessening, rather than increasing their workload, they will use them and thus expose their minds to a range of information and ideas. If not, they may chew the cud of lecture notes quite contentedly till the end of their course. And probably regret it later. It is the librarian's job to ensure that this does not happen, that people have an informed view of the library and its uses, that they use it and benefit therefrom, enriching their education. That is the third main thesis of this book.

The three theses may be summarized very simply: contribute to the management of the parent body; understand the parent body's needs, wishes, and problems; sell the library to users.

With the possible exception of the last, these are rarely seen as core topics in textbooks on librarianship, which tend, perhaps necessarily, to be rather inward-looking, focussing on the library's systems and techniques. Yet it is the experience of many college librarians that if one fails in these three areas, there is little need to worry about the other 'traditional' areas, because there are few users, fewer resources, and precious little library!

College Librarianship has concentrated on the external forces that shape college librarianship. The day to day internal administration of the library is amply treated elsewhere. The emphasis is on the management of the library; its identification and eventual solution of user needs, its interpretation and management of its parent body's operating situation, its relationship to the parent body's executive and decision-making structure, and its marrying of professional skills to institutional requirements. *College Librarianship* then, is about the *objectives* and *policies*, rather than the day to day *practice* of college librarianship.

Part 1 sets the scene by describing and analysing colleges' and college libraries' operating environment: the structure and objectives of the maintained tertiary institutions and their libraries; the examining and course validating bodies with whom they work; the schools and the companies which provide their students and employ their output.

Part 2 examines the institutions themselves more carefully, examining the nature, responsibilities, and objectives of the different categories of college, and the character and activities of their libraries.

Part 3 discusses the librarianship practised in the college sector. The 'traditional' divisions of librarianship are represented here: staff, stock, readers, finance, services. All of these are examined, as far as possible, through the filter of the needs and characteristics of the reader population. Part 3 concludes with reviews of college librarianship in other countries, and a prospect of some of the issues which may face tertiary education and its libraries in the near future.

It has been suggested that there is no such entity as college librarianship, that college librarianship provides only an artificial, institutionally-based focus for a book of this nature, that colleges are of so diverse a nature, ranging as they do from polytechnics with 7,000 full time equivalent (FTE) students offering degrees and professional qualifications to local further education colleges with 300 FTEs enrolled on a variety of general education and craft courses, that it is not useful to seek to address their collective librarianship and their libraries in a single volume.

The argument is interesting; the answer lies in the contributions to this book. The contributors were invited to write on open remits, only the broad area of their papers being specified, no themes being imposed upon them within the broad subject area. That being so, the degree of consensus that has emerged from a wide ranging group of contributors is remarkable. Librarians from polytechnics, further education colleges, industry, secondary education, and library schools, and educationists from outside the library profession, have pondered on a sector of librarianship and education individually, and have pronounced a common judgment. Perhaps the editor may be permitted to suggest some of the themes mentioned by many of the contributors which seem to establish the collective identity of college librarianship, and which the reader may care to look for in *College Librarianship*. Without comment or adornment, these are:

1 The role of the librarian as educationist and college manager, contributing to the students' life skills and to the development of the institution and its courses.
2 The need for the librarian to promote his library actively both to readers and to college management, and to convince each group that libraries have a contribution to offer; to convince them to use and support their library.
3 The desirability of developing multimedia collections and of providing via the library an interface with information technology amd the information society.
4 A concern that current political developments in the UK may take educational management away from educationists, to its long-term detriment.
5 A conviction that, in colleges at least, the chief librarian must do much important work for his library outside his library.

It is invidious to select; these themes are only some of many;

but they recur with remarkable and unorchestrated regularity from chapter to chapter, and are worthy of note.

In view of these considerations, no apology is offered for the amount of space given over to topics that some may consider to fall outside the bounds of 'librarianship' in the stricter and narrower sense. I have said elsewhere (Chapter 3) that good librarianship derives as much from a proper understanding of the library's parent body and its users, as from anything else. Nowhere is this more true than in colleges.

It is a common experience of librarians entering further education that they must acquaint themselves intimately with their college's workings and environment, with their colleagues' and their superiors' objectives, and with the aims and practices of education. Yet consideration of these issues remains rare in our professional literature, while treatments of the internal mechanics of the library and its administration abound.

I hope that *College Librarianship* may partly redress this balance. The book is only occasionally concerned with *how* college libraries are run, more attention is paid to considering *why* they are run as they are. Its foci are the objectives of the parent colleges and the students, the resultant objectives of the librarians, and some of the means which experience has suggested are best fitted to the achievement of these objectives. The book is as much about education as about librarianship, for in colleges, to separate these two is to fail.

I hope that these contributions will provide colleagues in colleges with food for thought; confirmation and/or challenge to things they do, or are considering; analysis of the views and objectives of colleagues; consideration of priorities, problems, and opportunities. I hope the book will give an overview of the aims and activities of college libraries, and help explain a sometimes idiosyncratic, even wilful, sector of the profession to other librarians. I hope the book may be read by some college managers and educationists to help them understand what makes their librarians tick. Finally, I hope that those considering a post or, better, a career in college libraries may find here analysis of the job and the institutions, a clear indication of professional challenges and satisfactions, and confirmation that college librarianship offers exacting opportunity in librarianship, and a job worth doing well.

There is some duplication of material from chapter to chapter. *College Librarianship* is a book of readings, and I felt therefore that it was more appropriate that as editor I should allow each author's paper to stand on 'its own feet', a statement in its own right on the subject it addresses, than that I should be overly concerned with excluding all overlap from the book as a whole to the possible detriment of individual contributions. This decision was mine, if there is error, that too is mine.

A Rennie McElroy
Napier College
Edinburgh
1983

Part 1

THE EDUCATIONAL ENVIRONMENT

1

The Maintained Sector of Further and Higher Education in the United Kingdom: an Overview

J Dunning

Is not a Patron, my Lord, one who looks with unconcern on a man struggling for life in the water, and, when he has reached ground, encumbers him with help?

Samuel Johnson
Letter to Lord Chesterfield 7 February 1755

The objectives of this chapter are to consider the ways in which the provision of further education has changed and is changing, and to speculate on the locus of the college in the future scheme of mass higher education. It is not the intention to present a statistical picture of events but rather to muse on the strengths and weaknesses of a system that has been well tried.

Post-compulsory education manifests itself in many forms; the universities, be they financed through the University Grants Committee or privately, be they 'traditional' or 'Open', the polytechnics (the Central Institutions and certain designated colleges in Scotland), the colleges of education, the colleges of further education and their links with the many forms of 'Training Initiative',[1] and finally the overlaps that exist between the 'upper' end of secondary education and the 'lower' end of tertiary education, in whatever way 'upper' and 'lower' are defined.

While higher education is usually associated with degree-level courses, it has a far wider connotation outside the university. Indeed, all full-time, sandwich, or part-time courses of a standard higher than GCE 'A' level (SCE 'Highers' in Scotland) are defined as advanced courses, and include research, degree-level courses, higher diplomas and certificates, and courses providing for a wide variety of professional qualifications. These many and widely varying opportunities have led to the boast that the United Kingdom has one of the most comprehensive and flexible systems of tertiary education in the world. Nevertheless, it is costly, it is complex and difficult to comprehend, and it gives rise to duplication.

The college has never enjoyed the same degree of patronage, and therefore esteem, as that afforded to the university. Why is this so? Could it be the mode by which universities have evolved, the early influence of the church, the presence from the earliest times of law and medicine, with their strong socio-moral influence, the fact that universities were the first in the field and were research institutions while the colleges were, essentially, teaching institutions? Could it be that the colleges have not sought, nor have been encouraged to seek, such patronage?

Samuel Johnson, in his letter to Lord Chesterfield, continues:

. . . the notice which you have been pleased to take of my labours, had it been early, had it been kind; but it has been delayed till I am indifferent and cannot enjoy it; till I am solitary and cannot impart it; till I am known and do not want it.

The 1944 (Butler) Education Act,[2] for the first time, placed a statutory responsibility on local education authorities in respect of further education. Section 41 stated:

Subject as hereinafter provided, it shall be the duty of every local education authority to secure the provision, for their area, of adequate facilities for further education. . . .

4

This provided for full- and part-time study for persons over compulsory school age and for recreation and leisure education. It did not mean that every local authority had, itself, to provide the full range of further education opportunity, but each had to secure provision. The principles embodied in the Act were excellent, for they allowed arrangements to be made for exchange between neighbouring authorities, the provision of regional schemes for advanced courses, and for cooperation with voluntary bodies.

Although long overdue, mainly because of the intervention of the Second World War, the introduction of the new Act was seen, by the discerning teacher, as an opportunity to establish and build a college system that could lead to the provision of mass further and higher education in the public sector. Others, who had become frustrated by the lack of development and of resources, took too much comfort in their new-found security and financial support. In the event, and bearing in mind that the development of further education seemed almost imperceptible to the public, the climate never seemed to be quite right in which to canvas or bestow patronage.

The college, born out of the Mechanics' Institute, is identifiable with specific social and educational groupings. Traditionally the college has been regarded as the institution to provide education for the less academic and the more practical. It has been developed to meet the aspirations of those who have not had the privilege, at the outset of tertiary education, of attending university. Indeed, it may well be the college's own ethos that has led to its 'second-tier' rating in the scheme of provision. As laudable as it may be to identify and remedy educational deficiencies, the college has been so devoted to the cause of providing a general education from which students might advance their knowledge of science and technology that it has itself accentuated the differences that exist between colleges of further and higher education and universities. Add to this the intensity of study needed to gain a career qualification by part-time study (the mode of study by which the majority of college students learn) and the extension of time (often 'private' time) needed to gain a qualification, and it is understandable why many become disenchanted with this form of learning. Equally, it may be argued that those who succeed have reached not only a high degree of proficiency, but have displayed such determination as to warrant additional merit. It is noteworthy that the college has been the instrument whereby many students have gained their passport to universities and to graduate courses in polytechnics and designated colleges.

The successful evolution of the college has been a function of:

1 the intensity of input made by both students and staff;
2 the determination of teaching staff to provide the widest possible range of educational opportunties;
3 the innovation of those who administer;
4 the unqualified support given by the college to industry and commerce.

Throughout the post-Second World War period the college has been subjected to continuous reorganization. As demographic trends have modulated, as course provision has changed with the advance of technology, and as the academic drift of each generation of college staffs moved upwards, constraints or relaxations were applied by successive governments to maintain balance. One can identify such milestones as Administrative Memorandum 545[3] whereby the Regional Advisory Councils regulated the provision of advanced courses, the development in the 1950s of the Colleges of Advanced Technology (CATs) with their degree-equivalent qualification, Diploma in Technology (from 1958), the establishment of the new universities in the mid-1960s, the translation of the CATs and other approved institutions into polytechnics between 1967 and 1972, and the establishment of degree courses through the Council for National Academic Awards, formed in 1964. More recently the important publication *Higher Education into the 1990s*,[4] has been debated, and the Tertiary Council in Scotland (1979), and the National Advisory Body in England (1982) have been established.

Increasingly, dialogue has been encouraged between the college and the university. The issue of cooperation becomes a little more sensitive, a little more difficult, when both are trying to maintain their positions in a contracting scenario. Nevertheless there have been cases of close collaboration, perhaps the most notable example being the relationship between colleges and the University of

London in the fostering of London University external degrees. Now that CNAA degree courses have replaced almost all external degree work, and so long as university and college vie for support from virtually the same exchequer, there is no reason why closer cooperation should not be achieved, certainly in the fields of post-graduate research and taught higher degrees.

At sub-degree level close attention has been paid to developments in Europe, and in 1964 the Industrial Training Act introduced radical changes in craft and technician courses. The establishment of TEC and BEC (SCOTEC and SCOTBEC in Scotland) in 1973 and 1974 led to an overhaul of the well-tried National Certificate and Diploma courses and their replacement with Technician Courses.

Currently the Manpower Services Commission of the Department of Industry is making inroads into technical education, all with good intent, all with much needed resources, and with a lot of new names! Could it be also with the reintroduction of many old ideas? Is there greater motivation to be gained through a 'work' situation rather than an educational presence? Has the point been reached where the Department of Industry will take over from the Department of Education and of Science? Is the Manpower Services Commission devising for the 16–18 year-olds anything markedly different from the pre-apprenticeship courses of the 'fifties and 'sixties? It would seem that the provision for small groups of young people to receive short-term vocational training will be of cosmetic value only; it does not make up for the permanancy of job security. Perhaps these are the beginnings from which the Manpower Services Commission will develop training schemes of three and four years duration! Already, there are those operating on behalf of MSC who are of the opinion that the present time-span is not long enough, and there are those who ask, somewhat cynically, if this is not a cheap way of doing things that the colleges have done in the past.

Once again therefore, the college is vulnerable. It is under pressure from several quarters; from the secondary sector with its increasing overlaps with further and vocational education; from overlapping demands of the community educators; from the training services, and from within because of the constant reorganizing

7

that is taking place. In the future more attention will be paid to the preparation of young people for working life in the final years of compulsory education, an issue which has been the subject of debate throughout the European Community since the Commission's Progress Report of 1976–77.[5] The demographic trends of the nation will influence developments in colleges. The National Advisory Body (NAB) and the Tertiary Council in Scotland will, through cooperation with the forthcoming Business and Technician Education Council (B/TEC), the forthcoming Scottish Vocational Education Council (SCOTVEC), and CNAA, be involved in the translation of courses to their appropriate location.

STRUCTURE OF FURTHER AND HIGHER EDUCATION IN THE PUBLIC SECTOR

Against this background it is pertinent to examine the structure of further and higher education. The diagram (Figure 1) was prepared for a college in Scotland, not a Central Institution, but a college offering CNAA degrees and controlled by a regional authority, and therefore not dissimilar from a polytechnic. An attempt has been made to identify, both vertically and horizontally, the main interacting components of the academic and managerial process. Obviously, the model will vary according to the internal structure of the college and its relationship with its parent body, that is to say, whether it is funded directly by central government, or by the regional authority.

In the case of direct funding, the vertical components of the model concerned with the regional authority would be eliminated altogether. Would this be desirable? Currently, the control of public sector higher education through the regional authority ensures that a given local authority can judge its provision for higher education against the provision for all education within that region, against supply and demand, the relationship of non-advanced to advanced courses, and can therefore assess the appropriate level of college and the disbursement of resources. Close working arrangements between regional authority officers and college staff provide a confidence base from which mutual trust

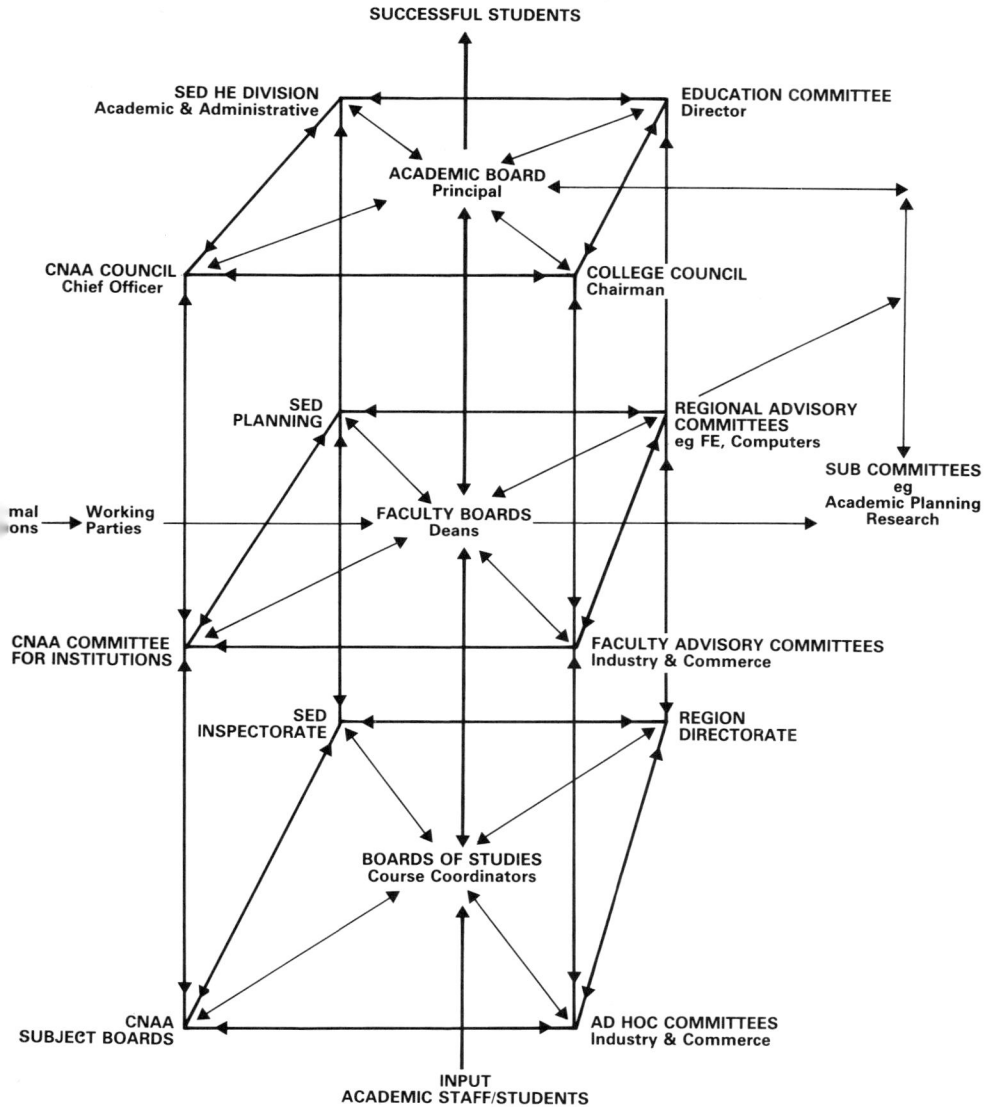

Figure 1: A model of the course educational management system.

and cooperative development can grow, an important contribution in the planning of education for future generations. Above all, it brings the staff of the advanced college into the orbit of all other sectors of education within the authority, a factor that soon loses force once the college and its administration become divorced from the region. The establishment of a balance between the personalizing of educational provision and the nation's requirement will need finer tuning.

Undoubtedly, a prime responsibility of the college is to be responsive to public demands and this implies that there are advantages to be gained from having central involvement. The major concern of the 'eighties will be the decline of the 18–21 years age group. It is important, therefore, to ensure that the national provision is not subject to wide fluctuations as a result of local variations. The nation's need for a supply of skilled manpower must be matched by provision. A corollary of such provision is the oversight of resource distribution to meet emerging needs. Central control should ensure excellence with cost-effectiveness; it must give greater continuity of planning with faster turn-around times.

The original arrangements for 'pooled' expenditure on higher education meant that those authorities offering advanced courses received considerable financial support at the expense of those who, through default or design, did not have advanced colleges. This was acceptable in a period of expansion, but once the cuts in public spending had begun to take effect, the system became questionable in terms of accountability, financial control, and good housekeeping. In the 1980 Education Act,[6] the government modified the arrangements for the pooling of expenditure and tightened up the criteria by which new advanced courses were to be approved. The innovation of new courses is, in the main, college based. The current practice of course approval is therefore not only reactive and detached, but worse, the time delay and the critical path leading to approval is so tortuous as to set the college at a great disadvantage when compared with the autonomous arrangements which exist for the universities.

What then of the future? Undoubtedly, emphasis will be placed on vocational education, whether it be concerned with the development of basic skills, or the exploration of scientific and technological thought. At the extremes, one could speculate that the non-advanced work could be rationalized as training under the Department of Industry and the advanced work, small by comparison with the non-advanced courses, could be financed through a body similar to the University Grants Committee. And if that is possible, why not through the UGC itself?

In truth, one expects the outcome to be one of compromise. The non-advanced colleges will continue to supply the in-fill of education for the various training initiatives, and the new arrangements being developed through the National Advisory Body will lead to greater central control of higher education outside the universities. Unless it is recognized that polytechnics and similar designated colleges have reached that maturity which entitles them to the autonomy enjoyed by universities, the reasons for central funding may not be realized. Were that to be so, it would be wise to take the ultimate step of controlling all higher education through one body. Some colleges might do well to establish a federation with their neighbouring university now!

REFERENCES

1 Department of Employment *A new training initiative: a programme for action*. Cmnd 8455, HMSO, 1981.
2 *Education Act*, (7 & 8 Geo VI c. 31) HMSO, 1944.
3 Department of Education and Science *Approval of courses in establishments of further education (including the report of the working party on further education courses)*. Administrative Memorandum 545. The Department, 1957.
4 Department of Education and Science *and* Scottish Education Department *Higher education into the 1990s. A discussion document*. The Departments, 1978.
5 Commission of the European Communities 'From education to working life. Resolution of the Council and of the Ministers of Education. Report of the Education Committee' in *Bulletin of the European Communities. Supplement 12/76*.
6 *Education Act*. (28 Eliz II c. 20) HMSO, 1980.

2

The Educational Role of the College Library

A Maltby

Since the objectives here are to provide both a broad overview of the potential of the college library in support of the curriculum and the way in which it can help provide a springboard for lifelong education, this chapter falls naturally into two parts. Although distinct, these are by no means mutually exclusive.

It is right to consider first of all the question of learning resources in relation to the curriculum, for this must be the basic reason for providing, for staff and students alike, a library within the college. It must be said at the outset that, whether it is single or multi-site, whatever the hierarchy, traditions, or management structure, the library is there for the service of all. Whenever any knowledgeable person looks critically at college libraries, the size and scope of which generally mirror quite closely that of their parent institution, it is possible to find within the various sectors of non-university higher and further education both good and bad practice. No attempt has been made here to identify individual institutions which may be considered exemplars in this respect, yet clearly there are several factors which can help promote good practice. An obvious one concerns reasonable levels of spending, staffing, and accommodation in relation to acknowledged standards. Less obvious, but very important, are a healthy library tradition within the college and a high degree of perception by the college principal, heads of departments, and chief librarian, of what can be achieved. Obvious to relatively few is the crucial need to incorporate the library service within a total planned strategy for the management of print and other 'software' resources within college. Resources-based learning must be properly integrated with the curriculum. Aspects of this last theme, which leads into areas essentially bound up with pedagogy and choice of teaching methodologies, are among the topics explored briefly below.

College librarians, in reviewing the expressed or suspected resources needs of their lecturing (and indeed administrative) colleagues are, at the outset of such a review, in the same position as any library service to a clearly definable and easily counted clientele. As far as the lecturers' requirements are concerned certain basic questions can be asked:

1 Which departments use the library most for curriculum purposes?
2 Which individuals are the heaviest users?
3 Are student assignments, involving reading or other resource-based follow-up, set to add depth and understanding to a theme introduced in a lecture?
4 Is curricular material for the library recommended and used by each department?
5 What are the reasons for non-use?
6 Can further use be encouraged?
7 Is there a library or resources committee for the college?
8 Is the librarian alerted early to curricular developments with resources provision implications?

Problems arise, of course, even with these fundamental considerations, concerned largely with the quantity of use. In most colleges, large or small, there are some members of staff who are easily persuaded to become active library users; some who can, with more difficulty, be so persuaded; and some few who remain obdurate or uninterested. To some limited extent, the quantity of use is affected by subject area. It is, however, affected far more by attitudes – persons who have enjoyed, or begun to get, a good service will quickly develop a keen appreciation of how the library can help their work. This perception affects, in turn, student use – many students are frankly wary of reading curricular support items which have not been mentioned, perhaps not even read, by their lecturers. These books, reports, or journal articles may even offer alternative, thought-provoking opinions! Other factors affecting the use of the books (and indeed college audio-visual resources for curricular ends) are real or imagined examination constraints, a high number of class contact hours for lecturers and students, and a teaching mode which concentrates too heavily on a didactic 'chalk and talk' role for the lecturer. Yet, if we use textbooks as an example, it must surely be true that many such give an account of their subject which is superior to the lecturer's notes. The intent here is certainly not to disparage or underrate the latter, but to encourage balance in the choice of learning methods and some increase in two-way communication. Good, in qualitative terms, resources use by a lecturer and some, suitably directed and supervised, resources-based learning for students must be valuable in terms of variety, and beneficial as an educational experience. It should yield opportunity for lecturer and students to spend rather more class time discussing problems or opinions arising from, say, reading, and this can be just as productive as equivalent time spent by students in listening and note-taking. To some degree, this is true at school level. But it is dramatically so in a higher or further education environment, where student pressures for a positive, participatory rather than passive, role are understandably greater. But Carl Sagan's justly famous passage in *Cosmos*, in which he notes not only the tremendous educative power of books, but also offers a caveat about limited time and the importance of selecting the right books to read, is sound advice here.

The college library service must take pains to ascertain and keep up to date with lecturers' needs for learning material. Thus a current awareness service, directing staff to new books, articles, educational records or cassettes, government publications etc of potential relevance is, whether computerized or not, an important ingredient in encouraging staff use. Obviously, to do this, librarians need to know the work and specialist leanings of the lecturing staff. They must also command the confidence of academic staff and be able to ascertain, often through informal conversation, how they can best be served. Today's college contains broadcast and other audio-visual items, computer applications software, and worksheets or other lecturer-generated learning materials in addition to the various printed resources traditionally associated with libraries. Frequently, some of these materials are held departmentally, but, whether or not this is so, the multimedia potential of the college library must be recognized. All these items, notwithstanding their variation in format, are susceptible to the same selection, organization, and retrieval problems as books. It is thus sad to note that a recent publication from the Council for Educational Technology which has much to say that is helpful in terms of support staff and an overall system for the management of learning resources, nevertheless – in further education at least – lists the activity of a librarian as being concerned with 'management and service functions relating to books'.[1] It is not necessary here to introduce at any length a well-aired debate on the merits or otherwise of the phrases 'college library' and 'college librarian'. Yet they do seem, however unfairly, to inhibit resources use and appreciation in some quarters. Sound alternatives are not too easily found. But, as novelist Anthony Burgess put it as long ago as the late 1960s:[2]

> . . . in the major field of information, the very term 'library' must become a misnomer, since new facts will not wait on the snail-trail that stretches from author's typewriter to book publisher's warehouse. This is the day of journals, xeroxed monographs, the immediate transmission of ideas and their immediate supercession.

Well, at least we may concede that it is not the only inadequate term in use. The word 'computer', for example, if strictly interpreted, fails to give a proper picture of the range of abilities and services on offer, but its attractions are so self-evident that there is no question of inhibition or misunderstandings arising! This may be as good a place as any to note the impact of electronic publishing and similar matters on college libraries, as discussed, for example, very ably by Stirling.[3]

One area of library activity which always needs to be taken up concerns resources advice and coordination in their various aspects. Thus, for example, the librarian should be a source of (perhaps not always welcome) advice on copyright regulations. Likewise, the usual library activities of borrowing books from various external sources and conducting, if need be, online searching and reference retrieval may be naturally extended so that the library is the point of contact with a plethora of local and national resources agencies. Indeed, although the present writer's statement of a few years ago[4] that librarians perhaps 'put too much emphasis on possession and not enough on availability', did not seem wholly acceptable at the time, this partial shift from a holdings strategy to one of access has recently been authoritatively endorsed,[5] provided of course that a due sense of realism is preserved. Links with the outside world are no substitute for an adequate basic stock, but they can be very important in rapidly augmenting it. If duly publicized within the college they can be psychologically valuable too, stressing the role of the service and its staff as being not merely concerned with the immediately tangible, but as information brokers and gatherers. Another aspect of coordination is that the library should hold a record of any audio-visual software resources or printed material held by individual subject departments. Even if these are rather jealously preserved, in certain instances, as departmental property, it does no harm to have them centrally indexed. There have been some unfortunate examples of the borrowing or hiring of items which, quite unknown to the requester, were already held by another department in the institution!

Reference has been made to the need for the planned management of print and audio-visual resources. The larger or more complex the college, the greater this need becomes. The library in many colleges will be a strong and well-recognized unit, often a department in its own right. Even so, it needs links with any college work associated with educational technology. This is a theme which goes further than equipment and software, for it encompasses attempts to encourage a systematic approach to the use and appraisal of learning resources. In colleges where the library is small and not so strong, it may be helpful to look for an educational technology framework, or its beginnings, and try to build the curricular support role of the library into an emerging strategy for the management of learning. Some elaboration of, and commentary upon, the type of framework envisaged in such instances might be helpful here. The suggestion that any kind of coordinated college resources strategy is needed sometimes meets with lecturers' resist-

ance because it is feared that what is envisaged will interfere with
their choice of teaching methodology and basic independence. It
is, however, undeniable that the college should strive to receive
the best possible return, in qualitative terms, from the resources
purchased for curricular support. This suggests scrutiny and a
constructive lead from a person of appropriate knowledge and
status who will be concerned to see that resources are used with
due regard for their curricular intent and their impact monitored
and appraised. In the effort to avoid mismatch, we quite clearly
enter the arena of the technology of education. This wider interpretation of technology to embrace strategy and system, with its
concern for the effectiveness of the learning experience, its implications for the consideration of possible alternative teaching methodologies, and its concept of a situation in which resources use is
monitored and managed, needs to be put to many lecturers with
due care and discretion. It requires the understanding and full
support of the college principal and his deputy. In fact, the 'person
of appropriate knowledge and status' mentioned above must be
either a Head of Department (Resources) or someone of Vice Principal rank if due impact is to be made. Yet without some organized
strategy for the management and evaluation of resources in support
of the curriculum, there can so easily be much desultory or
haphazard resources use. Indeed, in thinking of this theme, a phrase
from Shakespeare came unbidden to the mind:

'. . . set at liberty imprison'd angels.' (*King John* 3, III, 8.)

Books, journals, slide-sets, records, broadcasts, computer applications software must all be assessed, matched with their curricular
objective, and their effects later evaluated and noted if the
'imprisonment' of their learning potential is to be avoided.

The resources management adviser will be concerned with other
matters too, such as the range and availability of audio-visual equipment and the role of specialist technicians, but these do not concern
us here. Indeed, as it is customary to equate 'technology' with the
use of equipment, we might give it a capital 'T' whenever it is
employed to denote a concern for a resources strategy which
includes the qualitative aspects of resources use within the
curriculum. In this context, the adviser might ask certain questions,

which dovetail quite well with the ones envisaged earlier for the college librarian. Thus:

1 How do library resources and any departmentally held items 'interface' for curricular ends?
2 Which departments use the resources they hold most . . . and least?
3 Which departmental resources are most used . . . and least used?
4 Do lecturers, as part of a process of self-evaluation, note the effectiveness of any resource or resources combination used during a lecture?
5 There is also the question of achieving balance in an essentially limited amount of time. This might lead to questions such as: how much exposure to various types of resources do particular groups of students receive over a term's teaching?
6 Are individual students getting the right back-up and encouragement in terms of stimulus for further reading and learning?
7 Have lecturers and librarians been introduced to the idea of a Technological approach to the use of curricular resources?

The exact nature of any strategy chosen must depend, *inter alia*, upon the nature, size, and management structure of the college. But the overseer visualized may well be the person to chair the resources committee in colleges where there is one, and if a separate library committee exists, he must be on it.

Some librarians may see much of the preceding two paragraphs as an irrelevancy. To such it must be said that they are professionals with a professional contribution to make to any total resources management strategy. In several cases they will be closely bound up in the teaching process as tutor-librarians. But, particularly where they are not, there is a danger that lecturers will not appreciate the knowledge and skills complementary to his own that the librarian (very much a minority profession in the college environment) represents. Even well-developed college libraries sometimes run parallel to educational technology departments or learning resources units. Coordination and cooperation then become essential: the library is, itself, above all else, an enormous learning resource. It is important that the less established, but aspiring college library services in particular, seek out ways to 'get inside the educator's skin'. Thus appropriate aspects of an educational Technology system (and we shall return briefly to the qualitative factors implied here by giving 'technology' a capital 'T') as outlined above, should not be feared. The development of an analytical, informed view of the library's achievement and potential in support of each syllabus can only be healthy. It is by being visibly bound up with the curriculum rather than seeming to some lecturers to exist in a vacuum, and by demonstrating librarian concern for the effectiveness of total resources use that library-held curricular support materials, many of them at least potential 'angels', will escape the risk of imprisonment and make their just contribution to the learning process.

Along with its essential role in curriculum support, the college library has another, overlapping, task. This, if not equally essential in immediate formal education terms, is equally valuable. It is nothing less than a major share in any work done within the college to encourage the concept of learning as a potentially enjoyable lifelong process – that concept the French call *éducation permanente*. From the students' point of view, there are perhaps two facets of this. They need, first of all, *to be persuaded that continuing learning is worthwhile*, that education is not a restrictive coil to be shuffled off, with considerable relief, as the ink dries on the final examination paper. Within our infinitely elaborate, necessarily enormously expensive, total educational system, it is sobering to reflect that college or university is the last formally presented chance – for those who get that far – to receive encouragement and stimulus to go on learning, at their own pace, what, when, and hopefully where, they wish. The second facet is that *the students must be given the means and confidence to come of age as learners and stand on their own feet* – to possess autonomy for the selection and direction of future study experiences. The inculcation of the necessary knowledge, skills, and assurance for this is certainly not easy within an already crowded curriculum, especially in the case of day release or other part-time students. Both securing time for this work, and the capturing and holding of students' interest present real challenges for the lecturing staff. But, provided lecturers and librarians are working well together, the college library can offer much in the way of material which goes beyond the immediate or anticipated needs of the curriculum, but is wisely selected to provide the necessary liberal, but appropriate, complement to curriculum orientated stock. Instances where this goal is achieved, or where good progress has been made, all underline the need for planning and partnership, not only between the Head of General Studies (or equivalent) and the Principal Librarian, but between various members of their staff. For the library, there is an accommodation implication too: every college library should ideally have a study area and a further, more informal, area designed to encourage leisure reading or other comparable and compatible activities related to education in the widest sense. Hand in hand with this goes a welcoming, comfortable, and relaxed atmosphere.

The material provided must once again involve a variety of media. Certain selected educational games may, for example, very well have a place in the library environment. The presence of some microcomputers provides the opportunity for self-supervised, 'hands-on', experience available at such times as lunch hours and evenings. Here the concept of balance in the learning experience, and the thought that variety in media and method may itself stimulate the learning process, are again relevant. Yet, at the risk of riding a personal hobby-horse, it should be said that balance implies not merely the elimination of the risk of over-exposure to print, video, computers, or whatever, as implied above, but also an understanding of the potential strengths and weaknesses of various media in the provision of information or educational experiences. Whatever new technology gives us, we are not going to get additional hours in the day. Thus a place for books, which some educationalists now seem to consider 'old hat', to be used with other media in a suitably objective way, is reasonable enough. Films and videocassettes may be particularly valuable for the illustration of many practical tasks. The strength of books, in the mass, may well lie in the encouragement they give to dip, dig, and delve, or – especially when we are faced with a complex theme having many shades of opinion – to consider, weigh, and review. One can then reach a viewpoint with the knowledge that alternative attitudes and their causes have at least had a fair hearing. By saving us from reliance on the pictorial alone, books contribute their own unique stimulus to the imagination. What is more, while text on the screen is a marvellous way of transmitting and updating a variety of concise, mostly current, facts, it may tend to promote a form of intellectual laziness in some – a reliance on headline information achievable by pushing a button. Certain other people, although not lazy, also seem to want this. They know that, to be informed in today's world, one must cover much factual terrain in a short time. But, if we seek to rely on the result of, say, a sporting event, transmitted by a single line, 'Coe flops in Athens' (Teletext: Summer 1982), or expect to grasp the problems of, say, modern Zimbabwe from a single screened page or two of information, we do ourselves grave disservice. The secret is surely to know some subjects well, via several media, including books, and to know a little about others via a concise message. Above all, as to these two classes of knowledge, we need the wisdom to know the difference! It might be argued, of course, that book collections could be replaced by video discs, each holding content equivalent to a few thousand volumes. But, while these will certainly have their uses, anyone who has obtained benefit and pleasure from browsing, at any level, could feel that the offering of a disc as a total pre-selected subject package usurps his research rights – however academic, however humble – or reduces opportunities for serendipity. To do some themes justice, especially inter-disciplinary ones, we may need access to a wider collection of material, even to several libraries. Lacey, posing as an enemy of some of the newer media, makes the point a little differently:[6]

> Libraries are, above all, social systems: a teaching-learning milieu in which retrieval of information is only a part. If the new technology destroys this environment, it will also destroy what it is trying to maintain and improve.

But this is a partial digression. How do we encourage college students to go on learning when they are college students no more? Clearly, to achieve this, learning must be seen to be interesting and, although it cannot, alas, guarantee employment, relevant to day-to-day living. As Philip Coggin in a short and stimulating article argues:[7]

Life and learning, so often pulling in opposite directions, require an inner compulsion if they are to interact and be mutually beneficial. The starting point is wonder, curiosity and the joy of discovery. . . .

He adds:

. . . the academic approach should become part of the Technological [*my capital*] approach, which is an open-ended, disciplined, problem-solving methodology applicable to all areas of life and learning, and the key to learning how to learn.

Many years before, that great benefactor of libraries, Andrew Carnegie, had put it much more starkly:[8]

We have called them [our young people] educated. They have been 'educated' as if they were destined for life upon some other planet than this.

Interactions between learning and life must bear in mind new technological possibilities and an enforced increase in leisure, whether the latter is determined by uncertain employment prospects or a shorter total working life. The 'joy of discovery' should have the chance to prosper in such a climate. It may be aroused by a good lecturer. Clearly it can be encouraged through knowledge of how to get the best out of print and non-print resources. Yet the sad truth is that even many of our most academically gifted students seem to lose interest in their specialism when full time education ends. Coggin suggests this is because our system leads to a situation where 'the compulsion to be qualified replaces the love of learning'.[7]

Perhaps so, but there are other factors. It is admittedly easier to continue college or university work by further study for pleasure in certain disciplines than it would be in others. Yet the *malaise* strikes even several specialists in, say, history or English, some of whom never seem to read beyond the set higher education syllabus at a later date. Somewhere, disenchantment sets in and their plight is essentially summed up by borrowing a quotation from the poet, Philip Larkin, coincidentally also an academic librarian, and asking, in the name of true education, what is the consequence if disbelief in the continuing value of and need for education comes during college days:

> And what remains when disbelief is gone?
> Grass, weedy pavement, brambles, buttress, sky,
> A shape less recognisable each week,
> A purpose more obscure. . . .

Of course, continuing education may not relate to a past further or higher education course specialism, but can involve other themes of practical or intellectual worth. It cannot be said that the implanting of a desire to go on learning with, among other matters, its considerable boost for pleasure and morale at the time of retirement, which otherwise can be an occasion of real dread, can be simply solved by the college library, however excellent. It must be said, however, that if the latter is presented and used aright it will make a very considerable contribution to a solution. What is more, part of the problem may reside in the lack of information gathering skills, a learning experience for which the multimedia library is an ideal laboratory.

This brings in the other facet stressed at the outset – an acquisition of those skills which can facilitate present and future self-directed learning – knowing how to find out. Many college librarians design, or participate in, extensive programmes in this area. Absolute fundamentals concern a knowledge of the range of library facilities, learning how to use catalogues and reference books, and how to trace journal articles. To these things must be added proficiency in using various audio-visual media. In the case of degree-level work especially, the fundamentals need to be developed by planned study of sources of information relating to the chosen specialism. The contribution of information gathering and handling techniques to the learner's attainment of self-sufficiency, or something approaching it, for future exploration can scarcely be overestimated. College of education students certainly need such skills. They will have little chance to acquire them later, and the greater status they achieve as teachers, the more likely they are to experience reluctance with regard to the admission of the lack of such knowledge. They may well be also reluctant to concede their pupils' need for it! In an entirely different area of college work, the teaching of such skills, at an appropriate level and with carefully chosen emphasis, is extremely valuable as a complementary studies element in many Business Education Council (BEC), Technician Education Council (TEC), or City and Guilds (CGLI) courses. The exact programme of instruction will vary greatly from college to college and may include such diverse elements as knowing how to find simple current facts, how to use PRESTEL, how to trace scientific information in patents or report literature, or how to extract and summarize the information found. Notwithstanding the differences in the time allocated and the nature of needs from college to college, the present writer, if asked advice on achieving success, would say:

1   Involve both specialist lecturers and library staff.
2   Cover audio-visual items, videotext, simple computing knowledge, as well as printed information sources – and show how to trace agencies which can be contacted to advise or to enhance available resources.
3   Integrate this work with the college curriculum as much as possible. However, do not neglect ways of showing how to gather information on hobbies (eg from popular periodicals) and local studies or local community information.

Active recreation in adult life, stemming from the pursuit of individually selected aims, demands specialist skills and (almost always) some qualities of self-reliance, with the ability to 'go it alone' if absolutely necessary. Selected aims will not, in every case, involve a programme of academic study, but will draw on locally available resources including of course, to use a phrase rather deliciously introduced into one 19th-century novel, 'certain phenomena called books'. That a large section of society hungers for second-chance learning as mature students is readily evident from the enormous increase in, and work on behalf of, open and distance learning systems. It is quite possible that the response to these increasing pressures will lead to the setting up of new (and expensive!) alternative learning modes. This most assuredly should not be done for the sake of innovation to the neglect of existing resources which could be adapted to meet the need. Adult education students should be directed to local libraries and resources centres, including the college library if this is available as a community education facility. College and public libraries are not in competition, but one large advantage of the former is their wealth of back-up teaching expertise to help via the introduction of such flexible arrangements as 'learning by appointment' and 'computer assisted learning'. At worst, provided the would-be learner has the determination and the rudiments of study skills, he may manage without a teacher since access to knowledge, without a mediator, is always one possibility in a truly open learning situation. But it is generally most undesirable, most especially in scientific or technical subject areas, and indeed there is much to be said against it in social as well as purely educational terms. The absence of both class and teacher is a big loss with regard to opportunities for the interchange of ideas. But, as a last resort, this do-it-yourself approach can be followed if the will and some basic information gathering skills are both present. In such situations, which still exist, resource-based learning is all. But usually it will be employed to enhance a structured, lecturer-directed, course.

Even someone who may feel that some of the comments above are sweeping or subjective will hardly deny the need to encourage the attitude that life should be a continual act of enjoyable, varied, and profitable learning; the need to provide each individual with the basic skills and confidence to initiate, in adult life, some further experiences to promote such learning and self-development; the need to make the best possible use of existing resources and opportunity. The college libraries, despite great differences in size and emphasis, with their stocks of recorded knowledge and access to supportive outside educational and information providers, must surely be central to the tackling of these needs. Subject-wise they both span and transcend the formal curriculum. Whatever the college departmental structure, the library must be seen as a service applicable to all disciplines and one from which lecturers from all disciplines can, working with librarians, both use resources as a valuable curriculum support and provide the impetus for post-college learning. Argument on these lines concludes fittingly with a reference to a personal favourite writer, now largely neglected. John Mackinnon Robertson (1856–1933), a self-educated man and an open learner long before the concept was officially recognized, became a prolific author on Elizabethan literature, religion and free thought, and economics. On the theme of this chapter, he has this message to give:[9]

> . . . the achievement of a mind worth having in old age must be the product of *all* [my italics] one's preceding years.

and:

> Whatever the nations of the world lack, be they rich or poor . . . they all have one thing in common . . . too many blockheads to the square mile.

What is significant is that these words occur in his one mono-graph on libraries[9] – he saw the remedy was to be found in wide, wise, selective reading. Three quarters of a century later there are still too many blockheads, and, without the necessary means and encouragement for educating themselves wisely, increased leisure can only intensify their problems. It may be reiterated that we now need to use many other resources in addition to books and journals. Near total preoccupation with any one medium may well merely develop a new variety of blockhead. Key words and phrases here again include perception, balance, selectivity, appraisal, limited time and, of course, a 'Technological' approach to the whole matter. As an Elizabethan scholar, Robertson would have been interested in the choice of the Shakespearean quotation earlier in this chapter. But he might have argued that the 'imprisoned angels' are not simply the bottled-up or mismatched resources but, even more so, those denied young people who never achieve the encouragement or skills to become active and independent lifelong learners.

REFERENCES

1   Willis, N (ed) *Teaching and learning support services. Based on an investigation by Gerald Collier. 1. Higher education: task and activity details at professional and managerial levels. 2. Further education.* Council for Education Technology, 1981.
2   Burgess, A *Urgent copy: Literary studies.* Cape, 1968.

3   Stirling, J F 'Technological developments in information transfer: some implications for academic libraries'. *Journal of Librarianship*, 14 (4) October 1982. 235–246.
4   Maltby, A 'A philosophy for all seasons'. in McAdams, F (ed) *Of one accord: essays in honour of W. B. Paton.* Scottish Library Association, 1977. 44–56.
5   Department of Education and Science and Office of Arts and Libraries *The future development of libraries and information services.* HMSO, 1982.
6   Lacey, P A 'Views of a Luddite'. *College and Research Libraries* 43 (2) March 1982. 110–118.
7   Coggin, P 'The British disease'. *Times Educational Supplement (Scotland)* 739 19 December 1980. 12.
8   Wilson, M B *A Carnegie anthology.* New York, 1915. (privately published).
9   Robertson, J M *What to read: suggestions for the better utilisation of . . . libraries.* Watts & Co., 1906.

3

The Library in the College: Working in Education

A Rennie McElroy

Collage librarianship is different from other forms of librarianship. At least, so college librarians think!
What makes it different? What does 'different' mean in this context? Is 'different' merely a shorthand, perhaps chauvinist synonym for 'interesting, demanding, satisfying, challenging'? Possibly. Indeed, probably. But there is more; there is genuine 'difference' too; genuine identity. This chapter presents a view of college librarianship and of the relationships between college, education, teachers, students, and librarians, and tries to identify the contribution that college librarianship has made to the profession of librarianship as a whole.

Good librarianship is more a product of its environment than of its techniques and systems. It is, or should be, more influenced by the institutions and the users it serves than by its tools and by those specialisms – cataloguing, classification, bibliography – which are claimed by some to be the only unique, identifying features of professional librarianship and the Chartered Librarian. Study of the attitudes and professional preferences expressed by librarians in the last 30 years prompts one to the conclusion that today's librarian is more immediately concerned with, and more influenced by, his working environment and his parent organization's objectives and problems than before. With a few important exceptions, today's library serves first, and collects, stores, and guards afterwards. This is certainly so in the colleges.

Little apology is offered therefore, for looking again, with many other contributors to this book, at the colleges themselves, to draw out their collective character and to consider their attitudes to libraries, learning, and indeed to resource allocation in general. These attitudes, as much as the efforts and views of college librarians, have shaped college libraries and library services.

What then, is 'different' about college librarianship? What characteristics, activities, and philosophies give it its distinctive identity?

The first and most important factor governing all college libraries is that they are academic, educative libraries. This affects all that they and their librarians do. It will be said, of course, that all libraries have an educative function; this is so, but only libraries in schools, colleges and, to a lesser extent, universities, are ruled by that function to the extent that the parent body's educational and academic objectives may at times be pursued even to the shorter term detriment of the library's collections.

The college librarian believes himself to be an educationist, and believes that a good college library can contribute to a better educational experience for the student. By profession and by inclination, he is committed to education as well as to the library. The college principal is also committed to education, and to his college as a whole, but rarely to particular parts of that whole for their own sakes. The Principal's main objective, properly, is to maximize the benefit to his college (expressed in terms of student successes) from the total resources available to him. While it overstates the case to suggest that a college principal need give nothing at all to the library, it certainly is true that most principals will only allocate resources to the library in excess of a 'decent minimum' if they are satisfied that good use will be made of them, and that benefit will accrue to staff and students.

How then can the librarian prove himself as a professional in the college? How can he prove the worth of his library, in order to obtain for it the resources he needs to develop it to the point where it can be a power for academic advancement in the college? He must first be a college man, rather than, narrowly, a library man.

He must be academic and educationist first and proactively, and librarian only after he has secured his basic position through successful achievement in this prior phase. This apparently paradoxical requirement, for the librarian to prove himself and his library outside the library itself in the wide sphere of the whole college and its broad academic objectives, is central to the concept of college librarianship.

This academic, educative theme has influences more far-reaching than their impact on the manner of obtaining a proper share of resources. It gives the librarian the opportunity and responsibility of contributing, not simply to a student's reading, but to his future life success. It requires the librarian to recognize that user requests express *needs* rather than *wants*. This single factor, more than any other, influences the librarian's attitude to book selection, enquiry handling, and inter-library cooperation. Too often, the reader's request is classified as a desire, over which the librarian may exercise control, rather than a need, which should be sacrosanct. This interpretation of reader demand as need rather than want, more than any other single issue, moves college libraries firmly along the collection/service spectrum of librarianship towards a special library approach referred to later.

To enter a reasoned and fruitful dialogue with academic users, the college librarian requires certain knowledge, skills, understanding, and sympathies which are not automatically part of the professional librarian's tool kit given the present structure and content of much professional education.

Harris expressed dissatisfaction, if a little mischievously, with the academic librarian's education and qualifications.[1] Though the primacy of subject specialization claimed by Harris remains open to challenge, it is certainly the case that the college librarian and his staff must be able to communicate meaningfully, in subject terms, with a wide range of staff and students, and must have a deep understanding of the contemporary developmental interests of all subjects taught in their colleges. Above all, they must have a deep understanding of education itself. The librarian requires a detailed understanding of staff and student needs, motivations, and pressures. This can be derived only from intimate involvement in course development, teaching, and indeed the whole educative process. In this concern lies the stimulus for colleges' concentration on user education and other college (rather than library) oriented activities.

The college librarian will often spend as much time working in his college as in his library. User education, course planning, academic board, research, college management; all are areas to which he must contribute. He must demonstrate to other college managers that he can fill a *college* role. Only then will he be given resources and opportunity to develop the library *per se*; only then will he have provided for the security and viability of the library. This point is made again by Don Revill in his contribution to this book (Chapter 17), and at greater length in an unpublished policy document developed for the information units of the pharmaceutical industry.[2]

The majority of the 600 plus institutions making up the 'maintained sector' (*sic*) of tertiary education (how do the universities survive – if they are not *maintained*?!) are relatively recent foundations, having existed in their present form only for some 35 years; many are even younger.

The further education 'boom' of the late 1950s and 1960s was accompanied by a definite and deliberate drive to recruit into teaching and senior college management people with extensive and recent industrial and commercial experience. This had an enormous impact on college development and helped to determine the philosophies and attitudes which were to shape the youthful institutions, and which indeed are still important features of colleges in the 1980s. Attitudes to resource allocation were particularly influenced, particularly in technical education: things had to 'show a return', in fairly concrete and immediate terms, or go to the wall. In essence, there was little wrong with this, indeed performance measurement is now, belatedly, a major interest in our profession. Here though, was a major influence on the librarian, and the first nudge that would help shape college librarianship.

This factor could be accompanied by a consciously 'brass-tacks' approach to education management which, coupled with the nature and level of the courses offered, the type of student attracted, and the attitudes of these students, accentuated the pressure exerted on librarians to 'show a return', to prove themselves useful members of the college community, and to demonstrate above all that financial, spatial, and personnel resources expended on the library do indeed return a benefit to the college in terms of its academic progress, and are not 'money down the drain'.

But none of this is to suggest that all college libraries and librarians are unwanted, unregarded, ill-funded, and unused. There are problems aplenty, as perusal of Part 2 of this book in particular will show, but college librarianship has, by and large, sought and found its opportunities in its difficulties. The particular flavour and pattern of this sector of the profession has been developed by stressing services and activities designed to meet, satisfy, and if necessary combat the objections and drawbacks which may arise from the attitudes described above. The strategy has been successful. Libraries are important to our colleges; although their collections and services prosper slowly (too slowly for those working in them), they make a meaningful contribution to the quality of further education and to local commerce and industry; they offer a challenging, satisfying, and now clearly identifiable and distinctive career pattern. What is more, and this is the real measure of college librarianship's collective success, major features of college librarianship, professional activities and themes which college librarians can properly claim to have developed, are now accepted features of library service in other sectors of the profession.

The longer one looks, the more features 'unique to colleges' emerge – inevitably. But the 'we are unqiue' syndrome belongs to most professionals, often coexisting happily with the 'I am indispensable' theme! Any attempt therefore, to ascertain that which is genuinely different about college libraries may well be best rewarded by insisting on quick, tip-of-the-tongue responses, and refining these. On this basis, this writer believes there would be considerable support amongst college librarians for the following principal characteristics:

1 The attitudes of college teaching staff, management, and students towards libraries and the literature in general. These in themselves have generated:

2 Relatively small libraries able and required to concentrate on service provision rather than collection management.

3 A desire and a need amongst college librarians to demonstrate unequivocally the benefit that may be derived from the effective and efficient use of libraries, and the development of a professional style which has pursued this as a primary aim.

4 A concerted effort by college librarians to identify as closely as possible with education and to participate in course management and college management.

5 A willingness and ability, born in part of small size and institutional sympathy, to test the new.

There is no single, definitively typical college library. There are probably as many views of college librarianship as there are college libraries – if not college librarians! Despite this, there is a remarkable degree of consensus amongst college librarians as to what is 'good – desirable' and what is 'bad – undesirable' with regard to what one tries to do as a college librarian and what one should avoid. The remarkable, yet quite unorchestrated expression of common interest and priorities demonstrated by the contributors to this volume is testimony to this. Differences of detail notwithstanding, most features of college librarianship can be traced to the five principal factors identified above. On these a fairly thorough picture of the college librarian's credo may be based.

College librarianship traditionally requires considerable flexibility of library management, a willingness to experiment with significant changes in major aspects of the service, and the frequent absence of the librarian from his library, this last in an institution where the professional complement of the library may be small, even only a single person. Above all, it requires that one provide a high quality library-information service from a very limited resource base in terms of stock, staff, finance, and space, and that one be devoted first and foremost to educational objectives.

That these demanding conditions can be met is due in part at least to the fact that, with the exception of the larger polytechnics and the older colleges of education, libraries in colleges tend to be small, most would say too small, in comparison with the libraries of the universities and the central libraries of the major public library authorities. To a considerable extent, that smallness, which in one sense is one of the shortcomings of many college libraries, has at the same time been one of their strengths.

Relatively small size has meant that the vital options of major change, relocation, restructuring, and fairly large scale experimentation have often been available. Furthermore, when these options are taken up, when major change and/or experimentation is instituted, the results, favourable or otherwise, may be seen fairly quickly. The libraries themselves have relatively little inertia; change has a rapid effect. To take the happiest case: a college library which complains successfully of unsatisfactory stock and funding levels and which is given a large, once and for all injection of capital can show an almost immediate improvement on the shelves, one which is apparent to the most casual browser. Similarly, special collections can, with a little labour and a lot of thought, be put together quickly to satisfy a special need, and later redistributed. Change and improvement can be made, given the will and some money, and can be demonstrated quickly.

A further effect of relatively small size is that the libraries are easier to use and understand, are less intimidating to the user. An important consideration in any library, this feature is particularly vital in further education and throughout the college sector, where students may turn less readily than some to books and to reading. Colleges are teaching institutions; the classic phrase 'reading a subject' is little heard. There is a considerable movement towards student-based learning, as there is throughout the educational world, but the college student still relies primarily on his teachers to provide him with material or to guide him towards it; he may often be quite tentative in approaching libraries and the literature on his own. Small may be beautiful in such a situation.

Smallness has liberated college libraries to a very considerable extent from much of the administrative minutiae of librarianship. Systems, whether of classification, cataloguing, acquisition, or charging, may be relatively informal and undemanding of time when compared with the more sophisticated demands placed on the library manager by very large collections, some at least of which may be of considerable age and intrinsic value.

Finally, smallness has been of assistance in permitting college libraries to adopt and adapt new technology, both in the bibliographic and the housekeeping modes. Douglas Anderson deals more fully with this topic in Chapter 21; only the briefest outline is given here. Small journal collections and smaller ranges of abstracting and indexing journals cry out for the support offered by services like DIALOG and Euronet DIANE. Small reference collections could benefit enormously from the directory replacement possibilities offered by PRESTEL, if only that service ever manages to make its performance equal to its potential. Small order, issue, and reservation files lend themselves to microcomputer based in-house automation via Pet, Apple, and Horizon. The attendant disadvantage is that only a few of the larger colleges, polytechnics and the like, have to date found it advantageous or cost-effective to join the automated cooperatives, eg SCOLCAP and BLCMP. The record-handling facilities offered by these bodies are, generally speaking, beyond the reach of medium to small libraries on the grounds of cost; at present, despite regular protestations of interest in small libraries on the part of some of the cooperatives, there seems little real chance of improvement. It will be a pity if cooperation, logically the saviour and friend of smaller libraries, is in its automated form priced out of their reach and remains a big boys' club.

Not all college libraries are micros, or even minis. Some are now quite large libraries, even in the academic libraries' league. The crux of the matter however, is that nearly all have been small at some time, and nearly all have staff who had experience of them when they were small. This influences the attitudes and directions of college library work.

The traditions then, are flexibility, change, development, and service, coupled with a close understanding of and contribution to the parent institution and its objectives. The college librarian may feel more closely wedded to his institution and to education than to librarianship in the narrower sense. That this may be so without undue damage to the library is due in part to the nature, size and objectives of the libraries.

Perhaps the principal distinguishing feature of college librarianship however, is the teaching role. Teaching is a major part of the college librarian's life. User education forms one leg of a classroom *troika* which is completed by contribution to non-professional education for librarianship and the teaching of subject bibliography and information science and technology.

The originating stimuli of user education and other library-based teaching are several. Perhaps the most powerful of these is the simple professional belief that the library-information service can serve the professional person, whether scientific, technical, or commercial, both in his academic career and in his later work. That is, it contributes towards making the individual a more efficient and effective student while he is in college, and it adds, like everything else in the parent course, to his permanent, lifelong professional competence, enabling him to solve work problems by resorting to published and other sources of information, and to keep up to date. The library and the literature can only contribute towards these objectives if the student is taught how to make proper use of them and led to appreciate their problem-solving qualities.

This theme is supported by the equally simple professional belief, common to all librarians, that libraries and reading are 'a good thing'. This factor has been of particular impetus to user education in those courses whose students may be rather reluctant readers.

All in education wish to offer students a wider range of studies and educational experience than might lie within the strictly technical, scientific, or commercial confines of the parent course, particularly if latter is mono-disciplinary. This aim has been furthered by the policies of discipline integration pursued by the Council for National Academic Awards (CNAA), the Technician Education Council (TEC), the Business Education Council (BEC), and their Scottish equivalents, SCOTEC and SCOTBEC, and goes far beyond the now dated and simplistic concept of 'liberal studies'.

The college librarian wishes and needs to prove the worth of his library to the college, to show that it is of value to and is used by staff and students. User education programmes, aimed at demonstrating the potential performance of libraries' contents as well as at instructing students in their use, have played an important part in increasing the use made of libraries, and thereby increasing the return on the resources invested in them.

Another aspect of college librarians' teaching is involvement in education for the profession of librarianship itself, especially at sub-professional level. With few exceptions, the tutor librarians in the colleges, rather than the lecturers in the library schools, have developed the syllabuses and taught the courses for the Library Assistants' Certificate, the Business Education Council's national award in librarianship, and in Scotland, the Scottish Technical Education Council's (SCOTEC) Scottish Certificate in Information Science, Certificate in Library and Information Science, and most recently, the Higher Certificate in Library and Information Science. This last, incidentally, puts Scotland well in the lead in developing the sub-professional course structure envisaged for librarianship by the Paulin Report.[3] In this connection, the Scottish Library Association adopted a policy statement in support of these educational developments in 1979[4] stating forthrightly that the (Ordinary) Certificate should be a fundamental qualification for working in libraries to which all library assistants should be given opportunity to aspire. Would that librarians as individual managers would follow their professional body's corporate example, and use the courses fully for the proper development of their library assistant staff.

The teaching of library assistants is a job-enrichment factor mentioned with favour and evident enjoyment by many college librarians, who value the contact it gives them with a wide range of library problems and solutions. The teaching brings an immediacy of contact with the grass roots of library service provision, the value of which it is difficult to overstate. Perhaps however, it is unfortunate that so many library schools restrict themselves to professional, now undergraduate and postgraduate, education, thus contributing further to academic drift in the institution and in the profession at large, and denying the academically able but inexperienced would-be professionals contact with a cadre of library assistant staff case-hardened by extensive experience of the daily library round. Similarly, it is disappointing to note that relatively few library schools contribute to the user education programmes offered to students in disciplines other than librarianship. Though this distancing may on the one hand leave opportunity open for 'practising' librarians, it is difficult to believe that student librarians would not benefit from receiving the experience of teachers who had continuing contact with, and knowledge of, the information problems experienced by subject specialist library and information users.

Finally in the teaching vein, librarians are becoming more involved in teaching students something of the resources, potential, and methodology of information technology: the nature of data bases; the operations and services of DIALOG, PRESTEL and the rest; the structuring of information of all types for incorporation in a data base; simple information retrieval techniques; communications technology actual and potential.

Teaching has given a strong educational ethic to college librarians: in most it carries at least equal weight with their original librarianship ethic. The typical college librarian will feel himself to be as much of education as he is of librarianship. Many librarians have sought further development of their interest in education *per se*, and have been encouraged in doing so by their colleges through membership of academic boards, course development working parties, boards of study, and teaching teams. In these fora, they play a fully developed role ranging over the multifarious activities inherent in course development, validation, management, and assessment. They emphatically do not play a limited bibliographic-consultant's role, checking references and producing book lists on demand. (This is not to diminish the importance of these tasks.) That such involvement should now find explicit advocacy in the Library Association's own recent policy statement on college libraries[5] bears eloquent witness to the degree of acceptance that this role has achieved in this sector of the profession.

Deriving from this activity, and vitally supported by it, is the librarian's contribution to the management councils of his college. Faculty boards, resources committee, academic planning, and above all academic board, are bodies to which he must have access, and where his voice must carry weight and be heard with respect if the library is to prosper.

In their gut reaction, teachers tend to view education as a battle; the battleground is the classroom; if one is not in the classroom, one is not truly in education, not truly of the college. So runs the argument. It is manifestly incomplete and unsatisfactory, yet it has truth enough in it to command recognition and a positive response.

38

This is the experience of college librarians. Only when he teaches, contributes to the academic ends of the college in this narrowest, as well as in the wider sense, shares the working and educational experience of his colleagues, is the librarian (and therefore his library), fully accepted. Acceptance at this level is vitally important, not for petty reasons of personal status and pride, but because that acceptance and recognition bring with it access for the librarian to decision making, policy formulation, and resource allocation in the college. This is essential to the favourable development of the library.

The desirability of not trying to make the library a special case for consideration (a tactic that invariably rebounds upon the perpetrator sooner rather than later) and the fairly competitive and 'political' atmosphere obtaining in some colleges, where a principal may often seek to motivate departments by sanctioning or indeed promoting open competition for resources between them, combine to make it essential for the librarian to develop the fullest and most sensitive understanding of his college's objectives and motivations. Quite properly, these are academic, teaching, and student oriented. Colleges and their principals are not interested in libraries and books for their own sake. They are interested in them only in as much as they contribute to the achievement of overall college objectives, to the raising of academic standards (and pass rates), and to the improvement of the quality of the student's educational experience. The librarian can develop his library only through the fulfilment of these aims. This he can achieve only by involving himself fully in the work problems and work experiences of his colleagues.

It is significant that the most searching role analysis yet carried out on college librarians explored this issue and was undertaken by an educationist, Whitworth.[6] Whitworth discovered that, the more highly motivated and job orientated the librarian, the more likely he was to contribute to the broad educational ethic and college-wide activity. Later work by librarians draws heavily on this analysis. Revill[7] and McElroy et al[8] also concluded that libraries were better funded and staffed, more highly developed and more highly regarded, in institutions where the librarians had sought and filled the wider role of educationist and college-wide manager.

All of this is interesting and challenging, but it demands that the college librarian develop new skills: how to teach, design a syllabus, assess a piece of work, think through his professional expertise and pass on only that part of it which is of value to others. This last is particularly important and is the key to successful user education. The librarian must explain the library and the literature only sufficiently to satisfy the student's need to be able to use these tools, and emphatically must not offer to students the much greater detail that would be required to satisfy a fellow professional. In essence, it is a simple exercise in subtraction. But the arithmetic of many is found wanting.

The college library then, is first and foremost a department of its institution. The college librarian is first and foremost an educationist who works through books, and a resource manager. He is, in the non-pejorative sense of the term, an organization man. He must identify with his organization and its objectives, and must fully understand its operating environment.

College libraries try to offer their institution a quality service, and they put the emphasis on service. Lacking the very large collections and more generous funding of libraries in the university sector, and perhaps making a virtue out of necessity, college librarians have stressed the quality and range of professional services that professional staff can offer in interpreting in-house collections and in exploiting the published literature through bibliographic guides. There are few colleges which do not spend more on library staff salaries than on library materials. Half of a college's library service walks about on legs, and is there to be questioned.

Many college libraries regard themselves as special libraries, and aim at special library standards of service. Information retrieval, specific enquiry answering, user education, current awareness and SDI services, albeit at times unsophisticated, are common features, as are a wide range of special document collections catering for specific needs in the individual institution: company reports, college prospectuses, product literature etc.

To further support the service approach, as distinct from the collection building philosophy of librarianship, college libraries have given a considerable lead in the development of multimedia collections and in the provision of integrated indexes providing access to these. To quote another contributor to this volume, Marie Adams: 'My library is in the business of buying and providing information, in whatever form.'[9] That it is now accepted that libraries of all types should offer their users both print-based and other types of material is due in large part to the efforts of libraries in the tertiary sector, and their creation, 20 and more years ago, of collections of slides, tapes, films, programmed material etc, and the integration of these with the traditional collections of books and journals.

The trend is still strong and is still gathering strength, to the extent that many libraries now retain a technician force to help them create their own packages of material, rather than relying solely on published products. Some college librarians now bear a title such as 'Director of Learning Resources' emphasizing the multimedia trend. For an attempt to list the full extent of a multimedia collection, the reader is referred to the Library Association's *College Libraries*.[5]

Their long experience of handling non-book media eased the transition of colleges into electronic information. For a library already handling tapes, slides, records, videos and the rest, the step to online information retrieval was relatively small and not one, strangely, that the often ambitious computer personnel cared to make in the colleges. As a result, many college libraries offered online information retrieval services to their users from an early period in their availability. They came second only to the special libraries of industry and the research associations in exploiting the enormous potential of this technology. That they were allowed and encouraged to do so by institutions who had been taught to value and invest, not in *libraries*, but in *information service from libraries*, is tribute to the effectiveness of librarians' policies and to the standards of service they have tried to offer. Once again, college libraries' size, or lack of it, played an important part in the development. One may more readily embrace online services if one's in-house collections of abstracting services and primary journals are relatively restricted. By contrast, larger libraries, with large sums invested in their journal collections, might reasonably take the initial view that users should exploit the resources already provided, before seeking greener grass across a telecommunications divide.

All academic libraries serve students and teaching staff; all are aware, perhaps more than the users themselves, of these readers' information needs. Until recently, however, only colleges and their libraries had extensive experience of students with widely varying attendance patterns. Elsewhere in education, full-time attendance is still overwhelmingly the norm. In colleges, full-time, day release, evening, block release, and distance learning students are all present in substantial numbers. Not only that, but all are present, in most institutions, in many and varying disciplines, and over a wide range of academic levels which may range from GCE 'O' and 'A' level to degree standard and beyond.

Clearly this presents special problems in the allocation of resources and the design of services. The needs of part-time students are particularly urgent and present special difficulties. They have, if anything, a greater need for books than their full-time colleagues, yet are less able to visit the library to compete at the shelf for scarce resources. How to resolve this? There are perhaps as many attempted solutions as there are colleges; all demand an intimate knowledge of courses, a flexible approach to stock management and selection, a willingness to create special short-term collections, and a deep commitment to the concept of service.

In addition to serving students and staff in their learning and teaching roles however, college librarians have made specific and successful efforts to serve college management – directorate, administration, heads of department – in its endeavours to run and develop the institution. Such activity embraces information retrieval in the educational literature and in official publications, statistics, regulations, guidelines etc, and requires of the librarian an intimate knowledge of the workings of the country's educational system and the roles played by its many constituent bodies. It offers the librarian a unique insight into the college's strategic planning, the problems with which its management is currently grappling, and its likely future development. It is a dull librarian who cannot receive a request for information, discuss it with the enquirer, and infer the likely development issue from the enquiry! Dull indeed if he cannot do so given the involvement he already has (or should have!) in other academic areas.

The value is obvious: he derives, through his work and the service he provides, two great complementary and synergistic benefits. First, he provides information to management to help solve a problem, and the library's stock rises for his having done so. Second, he learns something of likely college developments from his work on the enquiry, and is able to tailor his library service and prepare his stock in advance to meet changing circumstances. Thus he is credited with being a good resource manager and so is given a better share of resources. Again, the library and its users can only benefit.

This picture, however rosy, is not overpainted. Things do happen in this way; the user satisfaction/increased resources spiral does exist. But one must beware the vicious downward trend of dissatisfaction and falling resources. The responsibility and the opportunity both belong to the librarian. He neglects them at his peril: if he accepts them, the rewards to him and all his users can be great.

Book selection has been one of the most neglected aspects of librarianship in recent years. That it is so is a considerable indictment of the priorities of professional librarians, and of their willingness (ability?) to make value judgments about books. It is many years since Ranganathan taught us that libraries are not merely collections of books; they are the right books, brought together to serve a specific group of people, and interpreted by caring professionals. Ashworth[10] and Spiller[11, 12] are amongst the few who have contributed meaningfully to the recent literature on this theme. The first of these, in a searching analysis, throws down the gauntlet to the profession. Select, he says, in a paper that should be required reading for all of us,[10] cease to collect and preserve uncritically: make judgments, and be prepared to defend them: or fail in the professional's responsibility to his community.

Too often, and particularly in former days of easy financial pickings, book rejection, rather than selection, was practised. Occasionally no doubt, some colleges have been as guilty of this as others. But in one particular area, cooperative selection (with users) of stock, the record is good. By and large, the bickering about who selects the books, subject specialist or librarian, is noticeable in colleges by its absence. In most, there is a genuine partnership between a librarian who knows his college's courses from the inside and a subject specialist teacher who recognizes this and is prepared to back and supplement the librarian's judgment accordingly. Trust and cooperation, springing from course involvement, add strength and quality to library collections.

It was noted at the beginning of this chapter that many colleges are recent foundations. An inestimably valuable result of this is that colleges have few long-standing traditional concepts of what their departments ought to do, and how they ought to do it. There is still room for innovation.

This factor has one perhaps undesirable effect: colleges do not regard their libraries as prestigious establishments and do not afford them special protection. But do we wish to be a protected species, with all the dangers of fragility and imminent extinction that are implied by such status? Hopefully, not.

The counterbalancing benefit and opportunity, which can be found in almost any situation if one looks with a free mind, is that librarians in colleges have, by and large, been free to develop library services and collections as they see fit, under resource constraints that have often been severe, certainly, but in an atmosphere generally conducive to professional drive, imagination, and dynamic innovation. Furthermore, they have been given opportunity to prove the worth of books and libraries to a body of students, staff, and management who, perhaps more than some in post-compulsory education, needed convincing.

At their foundation, all colleges were given libraries; some wanted them. While many college libraries remain small, they nevertheless exhibit, as a sector of professional librarianship, a group of collections, services, and librarians very closely integrated with the objectives and activities of their parent bodies and their users. By developing services of genuine benefit to the college, by proactive participation in the college's management and its academic development, by emphasizing service from librarians rather than collections in libraries, by a willingness to change and innovate, by teaching, and by embracing varied educational media, college librarianship makes a valuable and meaningful contribution to college education and to professional librarianship in the widest sense.

REFERENCES

1 Harris, K G E 'Do library schools really understand academic needs?' *Library Association Record*, 84 (10) October 1982. 351–2.

2 Lakie, M H *The managerial and organizational orientation of library-information staff*. (in preparation) 1983.

3 Library Association working party on the future of professional quali-fications *Recommendations and Implementation* (Paulin Report) Library Association, 1977.

4 Scottish Library Association 'Recruitment, education and training for librarianship'. Scottish Library Association, 1979. in *Scottish Library Association News*, 155 January–February 1980. 15–22.

5 Library Association *College Libraries: guidelines for professional service and resource provision* Third edition. Library Association, 1982.

6 Whitworth, T A *The role of the technical college librarian*. The author, 1969.

7 Revill, D H 'Academic librarians in colleges of further and higher education'. *Journal of Librarianship*, 13 (2) April 1981. 104–18.

8 McElroy, A R, Swallow, K B, and Harrison, C T 'Realistic (that is, academic) gradings mean better libraries'. *Library Association Record*, 83 (3) March 1981. 136–9.

9 Adams, M F *Personal communication*. 1981.

10 Ashworth, W 'Future perfect'. *Aslib Proceedings*, 31 (4) April 1979. 158–69.

11 Spiller, D *Book selection*. Bingley, third edition, 1980.

12 Spiller, D 'Book selection in hard times – a sadly neglected science?' *Library Association Record*, 84 (9) September 1982. 297.

4

Validating and Examining Bodies and the College Library

Donald Davinson

'Fictitious status' is a term employed by sociologists to denote a condition in which certain individuals or institutions are invested with the outward trappings of prestige without actually possessing or commanding the power, authority, and rights associated with a true place of honour in a social system. Libraries and librarians have shared with others in the service industries the frustrations of being accorded a fictitious status which has not always been translated into real recognition and high rank on a scale of achieved or ascribed social prestige. Libraries and librarians have frequently been held to be indispensable to society, but have often proved eminently dispensable, or at least deflatable, in hard times.

The library was characterized as the heart of a university in 1921 by an early University Grants Committee annual report. For many years thereafter the centrality of the role of the library was hardly to be seen reflected in the behaviour of the Committee when it came to the disbursement of resources in support of the function they had seen as so vital. Nevertheless, the nature of university teaching and its associated research activity ensured that the value of the library's role in the achievement of the educational objectives of the university was never entirely overlooked. Material support by way of substantial starting grants for basic acquisitions for those new universities established in the 1950s and 1960s indicated a certain continuity of interest and added some tangible form to the status ascribed to the role of the university library.

Early appointment at a very senior level of experienced chief librarians for the emergent new universities added to the visible evidence of the importance of the university library. It is now nearly half a century since the last honorific appointment in a university of a 'Librarian' who was in reality an academic – a professor of Greek, Latin, or Theology perhaps – not conspicuously overloaded with teaching duties. Teaching and learning patterns which stressed self-organization of study and independent reading had been a well-recognized pattern in universities since well before the University Grants Committee's 1921 statement. There was, in other words, always some sort of a constituency providing a boost to the status of the university library. The huge expansion in the size of universities and the numbers of them which took place in the 1950s and 1960s added semi-automatically to the nature of their recognition and the acquisition of a real status.

By contrast to the university situation it is difficult to recognize any natural tendency to regard the libraries of public sector colleges as having a constituency interested in their creation, survival, and growth. Until relatively recent times, the library was regarded as the responsibility of the college registrar along with the other elements of stationery, material and physical plant. The typing pool provided the rudiments of staffing. 'Librarian' was not usually considered a title invested with such honour that it could be used to further distinguish a senior academic in the institution. Sometimes however, it could fit up a less senior, broken-down one with a sort of sinecure to await retirement.

Teaching patterns in the public sector emphasized description and prescription rather than induction and self-organization. There was no obvious evidence of, or focus for, a powerful constituency encouraging the development of college libraries from within colleges or, indeed, without. Very few colleges until the 1960s had a library of any size and many colleges did not have professionally qualified librarians. As Gordon Wright indicated,[1] there was little need for large libraries or for many librarians in the typical college because 'students were rarely entrusted with free study periods' so they could not use a library even if one was provided, and the lecturer, who used it sporadically as a source of lecture notes, had a vested interested in not encouraging its use by students!

The first substantial evidence of a clique in support of the idea of a sound college library was a joint committee report[2] which pointed out the need for students to be so equipped whilst students that they are able, thereafter, to find information for themselves in order to keep up to date. The beginnings of a serious effort to improve quality were there to be seen, but this report was, as were many later activities, exhortatory and carried little weight in places where the will was not present. The Ministry of Education's Circular 322 of 1957[3] was a stronger instrument, clearly relating the need for curriculum revision in favour of more student self-organized study, with more effective libraries. A constituency was now in being and it is a matter of record that there were great improvements in some colleges. The so-called Weaver Report,[4] again Government inspired, and relating to the colleges of education (the, then, new name for teacher training colleges), emphasized the value of libraries and encouraged the presence of the college librarian on the college's academic board. This happened not only in colleges of education but also in many other colleges using the example thus before them.

The problem in all of this accumulated activity has already been hinted at. It was that the development of college libraries was uneven. The more enlightened college authorities made spectacular progress, the less dedicated were still in the 'typing-pool-and-locked-when-not-in-use-as-a-lecture-room' era. Exhortation only works on the enthusiastic or on those willing to be convinced. Sticks or carrots or both are required to move the unconvinced.

THE COUNCIL FOR NATIONAL ACADEMIC AWARDS

Fortunately for a part of the public sector further education sphere, there emerged in the mid-1960s a body concerned for quality in academic standards which had teeth it could and would use when necessary. The Council for National Academic Awards (CNAA) was the body so equipped. It had the inestimable advantage of having something valuable to offer colleges. There is nothing quite like self-interest for encouraging conviction. The CNAA is but one of a number of bodies interested in the development of quality in education – various professional associations, the Business Education Council (BEC), the Technician Education Council (TEC) and their Scottish counterparts SCOTBEC and SCOTEC are similarly engaged – but for a 10 to 12 year period in the lives of the most advanced end of the public sector higher education market, CNAA was the predominant influence. Apart from mere influence it carried a substantial punch which, in the early days at least, also had backing from the DES and the Scottish Education Department, in the sense that money and facilities were often found for the improvement of support services – most notably perhaps, computer facilities – but also on occasion, libraries, following CNAA pressure.

The circumstances found by CNAA when it began its visits to colleges were very varied. The Council's Royal Charter embodied a statement requiring it to ensure that the standards of its awards were equivalent in academic terms to those of the British universities. Naturally, a condition upon which the equivalence of standards might be based was that the teaching and study structures employed might be more in accordance with traditional university models than traditional technical college models, where classroom teaching, rote learning, and highly structured work patterns predominated. CNAA recognized very early that the encouragement of more open learning structures had consequences for academic support services such as libraries. In many colleges however, the mid-1960s situation was that comparing their libraries facilities with those of the universities was rather like matching a stunted gnome with a ball and chain fastened to his feet with the heavyweight boxing champion of the world. Some colleges even then had excellent facilities, but in general the situation was as Gordon Wright described it.[1] The library was a teaching staff facility in the main and therefore in terms of size and range of stock, and indeed of accommodation and facilities, was not equipped to deal with a large influx of students.

The aim of the CNAA-based effort was to develop a substantial new growth of first and higher degree studies and to do it quickly. The previous burst of activity in this field had been the new university foundations in the late 1950s whose growth had been slower than hoped for and very, very expensive. The colleges using CNAA as their basis for development of degree studies had none of the advantages available to the new university planners. Not for them the remit to turn a green field into a plate glass student menagerie with relatively unlimited funds. Colleges often had clapped-out plant originally designed as Methodist chapels, primary schools, and the like, and needed to evolve new structures alongside the old, keeping the teaching of the old going whilst developing and negotiating the new. Specifically for the library situation, the problem was that somehow inadequate space and resources had to be turned into a decent working environment for the growth of the new modes of teaching and learning now being introduced. The requirement was to do it quickly and without the huge initial capital injections which had been available to the new universities for stock building and background material.

That a very large number of colleges were indeed able to meet the very heavy financial requirements of building respectable academic libraries is now a matter of visible fact in all parts of the country. A great deal of ingenuity, a lot of hard work and, most importantly, a strong initial push from CNAA, have been responsible for the exciting development of the 1970s. It must be eternally to the credit of the CNAA that it interpreted the remit to maintain standards equivalent to those of the universities widely.

It was not necessarily obvious to all parties to the new CNAA deal in 1964 that a legitimate interpretation of the remit was that which included inspection of, comment on, or even refusal to validate a degree, because of inadequacy in the library provision of the institution. When in 1967 CNAA began to undertake formal inspection of college libraries as part of its validation powers for degree courses, the effect was immediate and immediately beneficial for the libraries of those colleges involved.

The early history of the manner in which the CNAA's interest developed in the inclusion of library quality in its consideration of institutions' fitness to use the Council's 'licence' as a means of offering degree awards is given in Davinson's 1976 paper.[5] There

50

is little doubt that the situation of the libraries in many such institutions would not have been so secure or so relatively well resourced without the vigorous policy pursued by CNAA in the late 1960s and early 1970s. Those were heady days, and the gains made were real ones in conditions which, although they never seemed affluent at the time, now seem so by relative measurement. It is to be doubted whether ten years later anything like so much could have been achieved so quickly. The problems so many of the less advanced colleges are experiencing in building up effective support for BEC and TEC courses is that they have lacked such a lively and powerful constituency. The times were not right for a CNAA-like finesse by these two councils. Anyway, every action created reaction, to misquote Newton, and library validation is not the heady thing it was. There are too many people, institutions, and local authorities around alerted by bruising contact with CNAA in its days of maximum clout to let other would-be validatory hares run loose.

It was not simply that the plug was pulled in the economy bath in the mid-1970s which produced a hardening of attitudes towards letting CNAA (or any other validating mechanism, come to that) have a free hit at the colleges and their libraries, however. The very success of the CNAA in extending its umbrella over a wide range of courses and institutions in both subject and size of college created problems for coherence and consistency of treatment which caused many problems in the 1970s. The somewhat amateurish involvement of individual members of CNAA's Librarianship Board on a totally uncoordinated basis worked well enough when the council was dealing with only 40 to 50 colleges, mainly of a similar pattern, size, and scope, but it began to show cracks in its casually derived and uncertainly erected edifice with the expansion of the Council's activities consequent upon the colleges of education being brought under its notice in the 1972–3 period. Subsequent later extension into colleges of art and other, often small and specialized colleges, exacerbated the problems, as did the trend in some institutions towards the establishment of combined learning resource collections.

A series of examinations of the consequences of the changes taking place – a Colleges of Education Libraries Working Party, a

Libraries and Related Resources Working Party, and a Learning Resources Working Party, all in the 1974–7 period, brought about considerable alteration in the way CNAA looked at libraries. Most tangible was the splitting off of library investigation functions from the primarily course validation responsibilities of the Librarianship Board. Most intangible was the continuation of concern for having the right instruments for measuring effectiveness of the library contribution to the institution/validatory body debate. The intangibility concerns the desire to strike a balance between the purely quantitative aspects of assessment and the need to gauge also the quality of the service provided and its interaction with the teaching process.

STANDARDS AND OTHER CRITERIA

The problem in assessment of library performance is that it is beguilingly simple to draw up statistical criteria representing some form of 'standards' but much less easy to determine whether such statistical measures result in effective service on the ground. A statistically adequate library might be a practical disaster area. Many essays in statistical delineation of presumed quality have been undertaken by various organizations, most notably the Library Association,[6] the National Association of Teachers in Further and Higher Education (NATFHE),[7] and indeed CNAA itself, which in 1969 had a brief flirtation with the production of quantitative standards. The problem with quantitative standards is that they can take the initiative for creating library facilities out of the hands of the professional librarians and the teaching staff and place it in those of the accountant. If the standard calls for 500 reader spaces and these are provided, what does it matter, the accountant would say, that 350 of them are in a converted warehouse next to a sawmill distant from the college's main lecture room provision. Qualitative considerations, of the sort graphically portrayed by Revill for his mythical Granilash College,[8] are major factors in the creation of a really effective service, and might not be present in a library considered on the basis of sheer statistics to be inadequate.

The discussion of modes of library validation and evaluation within CNAA have revolved around the quantitative/qualitative issue with strong pressure coming from the senior managements of colleges and from local education authorities for the production of 'CNAA standards'. Thus far, the Libraries Panel of the Council, a body established in 1979 to replace the part-time inputs of the Librarianship Board with a full-time and specialist college library visiting panel, has resisted the call. It has been felt that the over-emphasis upon quantities of books/periodicals/reader places per head of student population militates against really significant issues of a qualitative nature, such as involvement of library staff in the academic and resource debates in the college, library user education, the introduction of new technology, and the interaction of classroom teaching and library and learning resource support services generally. The validatory activity of CNAA so far has materially assisted the growth of awareness of the full role of libraries in academic institutions, most especially through emphasis upon qualitative issues. Pressure continues however, for the generation of checklists of ideal or average quantitative standards, and there is no doubt that something will have to be done about this pressure soon.

It is fair to say that most of the pressure has come from three principal areas. It has come from senior management and local education authorities who have been irritated by the success of CNAA in promoting the growth and development of college libraries, sometimes by fairly crude methods. It has come from the weaker and less able college librarians looking for convenient external sticks to beat their colleges with rather than, themselves, become involved in hard and perhaps acrimonious debate. Lastly it has come from people, often the same people as in the first case above, who have become aware of inconsistency of approach and conflicting advice or requirement from CNAA in respect of library regulation. In large and complex colleges with visits from a wide range of different boards and visiting parties from CNAA, the growth of inconsistency of approval in library matters is a serious one which CNAA must tackle, and is now tackling. Obviously a confused message is a weaker one than is ideal.

The call from librarians for a cosy system of quantities to be read off to senior administrators as a mandate reveals another serious problem for CNAA or, indeed, any other validation process. It is possible for the validatory bodies to go too quickly for the underlying ancient culture of the librarian as conservator and passive supplier of materials on demand to catch up with the new conditions. Libraries these days are expensive operations no longer defensible as 'good things' beyond question, yet some librarians still have to be persuaded that the fight is theirs to fight. In the cut-throat world of higher education only the fittest survive. The validatory bodies can supply the basic tools but it is up to the librarians to use them. Curiously, it is the pressure of CNAA and other bodies to regard their behaviour as academic rather than administrative which has caused the problem for some librarians. Culturally, they are unprepared for the obligations which go along with the rights and privileges of academic status. Whilst many librarians have thriven mightily, others have been bewildered and upset by the heat in the academic kitchen, where heads of departments tend to fight each other hard for the resources they want. These librarians who have been calling for the production of quantitative standards and yardsticks are often the ones who cannot stand the competition, cannot muster and advance the managerial arguments, and want, subconsciously, to return to the womb of the registrar's administrative protection. But they want to keep their academic status! That said however, there remains the problem of inconsistent application of regulations and accompanying comment in CNAA library matters. It is something which needs tackling and it is not a problem confined to CNAA. Other bodies, especially the various professional bodies, uncoordinated and uncoordinatable, also run the risk of losing credibility if their messages conflict. This is a matter to be returned to later in a discussion of possible codes of good practice for validators.

TEC, BEC, AND THEIR SCOTTISH EQUIVALENTS, SCOTEC AND SCOTBEC

If the libraries of institutions whose levels of academic work fell below that taken under notice by CNAA thought that the evolution of the various Education Councils to take over and develop the confusing mass of professional and industrial qualifications would provide them with similar sticks with which to beat their colleges over library improvements, they have been disappointed. The times were not right economically, nor were the circumstances of the new councils' necessary range of activities and concerns. The cynic might also argue that having been once bitten by a superordinate validating body – CNAA – local education authorities were twice shy of allowing it to happen again!

Generally speaking, TEC, BEC etc were taking over administrative responsibility for pre-existing course structures for the former national committees. Their initial concerns were for a smooth takeover of the reins of government, to clear lines of communication, to agree changes in course structures and the functions of courses, and to encourage the wider spread of their course opportunities. Opportunities to spend time considering the means of influencing resource issues such as library provision were necessarily limited. Whilst not disinterested in influencing resource issues, the new councils would clearly have had difficulty in waving big sticks over colleges who had been running effective courses quite successfully for many years without having had their resources too closely questioned. The early Business Education Council documents[9, 10] made only passing reference to matters which could, by extension, be interpreted as bearing upon library matters – the need for reading lists to be attached to course submissions and the statement that 'approval procedures' would provide opportunity to 'review resources and [the] experience of potential centres'.

For the new councils to have jumped in with both feet, closing courses here, giving severe warnings there, would not only have been contrary to the style they were attempting to adopt, it would have rebounded upon them. The HND/C, OND/C programmes which the new councils were initially replacing were well-respected, old-established, and affectionately regarded, both in the colleges and in industry and commerce. Had the councils overplayed their hands on resource issues, particularly in such 'academic' areas as library resources, their already tenuous grasp on the imaginations of employers and colleges would have been seriously loosened. The position of CNAA in the late 1960s had been different. It was selling a product that the colleges needed, and knew they needed, possession of which led to substantial gains in prestige. CNAA was in the position of being able to impose standards of excellence in all things on their supplicants. It was easy to assert that quality in library provision was a live issue in these circumstances.

If this analysis is correct it postulates the rather gloomy hypothesis that it is only under the lash of covetousness that a college authority will be moved to develop its support services, and only then if it can see no alternative. It has not been too evident that, in the absence of real validatory teeth in the councils over the library issue, colleges have voluntarily come to the conclusion that they must inject massive resources into their library services in support of BEC and TEC courses.

The principal difference of the 1977 BEC/TEC/SCOTEC/ SCOTBEC situation as compared to that of CNAA in 1967 was that the economic climate was much less favourable to an insistence upon growth. CNAA laid down its benchmarks in more prosperous times, a period of what must now be seen as near profligacy in support of higher education. It made policy and achieved standards which would not have been possible ten years later. CNAA's problem now is to sustain standards to which the other councils have not been in a position even to aspire. Neither situation is a happy one when times are hard.

As the initial flurry of the councils' basic administrative concerns has settled, a more sober look can be taken at the process of validation and the procedures for ensuring that standards are maintained, and more notice can be taken of the resource implications of course proposals. Many institutions new to the business of externally validated proposals for courses based upon the institution's own ideas and resources have been drawn into the BEC/TEC net, such as schools and the smaller further education institutions. In these circumstances it has been in the realm of practical politics for the councils to draw attention to resource deficiencies; in a few cases it has been indicated by BEC, and especially by TEC, that resources are inadequate to support aspirations. It is true that it has usually been computer resource inadequacy which has attracted attention but, nevertheless, it has focussed attention on support services generally in some colleges.

The difficulty with which the various Education Councils began is that which CNAA encountered later in its activities. In assessing library adequacy they now have problems in drawing up guidelines simply because of the wide range of sizes, natures and conditions of the institutions with which they are in partnership. More awkward still, it is in the nature of the courses offered that simple quantitative standards do not serve. Nor do some of the qualitative judgments, based for example upon the availability of library tuition. So much of the work of students involves, not formal academic study of published texts (though there are serious inadequacies regarding the availability of suitable material in this area), so much as the use of project materials based upon local resources and local knowledge. Files of data on local industry, business, and commerce often form the basis of project work, especially in the BEC/SCOTBEC areas, and it would be difficult, if not impossible, to assess the effectiveness of libraries in such areas.

PROFESSIONAL BODIES AS VALIDATORS

Various professional bodies have begun to take an interest in examination of college library facilities as part of their procedures for assessing the viability of college programmes for exemptions and other measures of recognition of academic qualifications or sandwich course placements. It is difficult to think that the push in such matters has come from anything other than the experience of members of various professional bodies on CNAA visits over the years. One of the happy, though unlooked for, benefits of the seriousness of CNAA interest has been the educational force for good upon such people in regard to the value of a good library service. Nevertheless, there must be serious cause for concern that professional bodies are exceeding their authority and even overplaying their hand in undertaking such assessment. By no means all professional bodies have taken up the business of assessment of library services and many of those who have, have done so out of a somewhat misguided enthusiasm unqualified by expert advice.

So vital is professional recognition of college courses in times of recession and mass unemployment that colleges are perhaps often more supine than they ought to be in respect of professional association validations. Their tendency to exceed their brief goes unchecked by colleges unwilling to offend powerful interests. Nevertheless, the piecemeal evaluation against variable criteria by a large number of professional bodies could create serious problems for college libraries, who could be on a hiding to nothing. To be identified as the reason why a major course or a strong department was not accorded professional recognition could do untold damage to personal relationships and, more to the point, to the future influence of the library. If, as is beginning to happen, there is a veritable rash of professional body evaluation uncontrolled by any overall appraisal mechanism such as, theoretically at least, is available through CNAA's Council and its Committee for Institutions, then college libraries could be pulled in all directions by competing claims on funds, for it is typically upon the mere absence of specific periodical titles, texts, or reference books that professional body evaluators have focussed. CNAA subject boards have also done this sort of thing in the past and have caused much irritation in doing so, but their need to become more sensitive to moods, climates, and approaches has moderated the nuisance somewhat. Professional bodies may become involved in an individual sectarian protection racket possessing power but with no necessity to exercise it responsibly, being unmoderated in the manner of the Education Councils and CNAA by DES and/or SED officials. Their interest is necessarily and understandably in squeezing out the best deal for themselves. It is not always a basis for coherent library development but unfortunately there is little opportunity for the library to make its appeal against a possibly unwarrantable intrusion and against 'stick-'em-up' diktats from the professional body and their college counterparts.

This is not to say that all, or even most, professional body evaluation is irresponsible or uncontrolled, but some is, and all of it possesses the possibilities of abuse and over-zealous pursuit of limited objectives. It must be questioned too, whether much professional body evaluation of library services has anything to do with these bodies' real purposes.

Some of the abuse of the system may come from librarians themselves, through their recognition that here may be the means of making bullets for others to fire at the competent authorities. Manipulation of CNAA visiting parties in this way is, after all, not unknown! Unlike CNAA however, professional bodies rarely have available competent library advisers able to mediate between the various interests and place them in context with sober possibilities and realities. Without competent advice, it is also likely that professional bodies will sooner or later make a mistake which seriously compromises their reputation within a college and does damage at second hand to the course or department with which it deals. Some kind of regulation is vital to the conduct of some activities but it is difficult to see how it might be done.

A CODE OF PRACTICE FOR LIBRARY VALIDATORS?

It has been suggested from time to time that it would not be inappropriate for the Library Association or some other competent body having professional library expertise to evolve a code of practice for validators. It is an interesting idea. Whilst obviously there would be no means of enforcing such a code across all of the various parties possibly interested in library assessment, there could be powerful advantages in having such a code. It could, for example, provide a means whereby a body interested in undertaking library validation for its own purpose could obtain guidance as to how it might be done fairly and professionally. A code could also provide protection for a college librarian in the sense that a damaging report from a body which had not been sensitive to 'good practice' might be mitigated by reference to a standard produced by a reputable body and, perhaps, used by other bodies undertaking assessments. A college librarian's position might be much strengthened by such a code and, of course, so could that of the college generally in dealing with a professional body which had been overbearing or irresponsible.

Such a code of practice might lay down the headings needed for a statement from the college librarian on the condition and content of the library. It might incidentally insist that such a statement is in fact drawn up by the librarian and not by an administrator concerned to whitewash the position, as has happened in some colleges in the past. It might therefore define the ideal status of the college librarian in the institution, and underline the value of the participation of library staff in all aspects of validation, including preparation for it. An important aspect of a code would be to define what is regarded as appropriate and good practice by the validatory body in terms of the range of questions they might legitimately ask, the issues they might usefully explore, and the need to agree an agenda in advance, rather than spring themselves unprepared and uncontrolled upon the library and indeed the college. How the body writes a report, uses it, publicizes it and requires responses to it might be the most valuable part of such a code, avoiding the kind of nasty incident wherein great play is made of information subsequently proved to be misrepresented, misheard, or illegitimately obtained.

In association with the production of such a code, it is possible that the availability of expert advice and consultancy from experienced librarians might be made mention of to bodies wishing to include an assessment of library adequacy in their deliberations over colleges and courses. It might take years to propagate such a code successfully but its availability would be a boon to the responsible and mild chastisement to those less so.

CONCLUSION

Just how valuable is outside assessment of college library fitness for purpose is uncertain. What is certain is that there is a poignancy about the relationships between validator and validated which is akin to a parent/child relationship. In the early days of a relationship, a college can be very dependent upon the validator for additional muscle in sorting out problems. The validating body is a safe haven to turn to in time of trouble; the college librarian will enlist its support at every opportunity in pressing home messages about the efficiency and usefulness of the library to his institutional paymasters. Advice will be earnestly sought, gratefully received, and bullets placed in the validatory rifle to be carefully aimed and fired. In adolescence the relationship changes somewhat. Advice is not sought and will be mildly resented if given. What the college librarian wants now are expressions of satisfaction with the way things are going. In maturity the library follows its institutional lead and thoroughly resents any comment, even supportive, thinking it an intrusion and patronizing or even, as in family relationships, evidence of senility beyond the boundaries of wisdom and experience.

REFERENCES

1 Wright, G H (ed) *The library in colleges of commerce and technology.* Deutsch, 1966. 16.

2 Association of Technicians' Institutions, and Association of Principals in Technical Institutions, and Association of Teachers in Technical Institutions *Report: Libraries in technical institutions.* The Associations, 1938.

3 Ministry of Education *Libraries in technical colleges.* (Circular 322/1957) HMSO, 1957.

4 Department of Education and Science *Report of the study group on the government of colleges.* HMSO, 1966.

5 Davinson, D E 'The Librarianship Board of the Council for National Academic Awards'. *Journal of Librarianship* 8 (2) April 1976. 79–95.

6 Library Association *College libraries: guidelines for professional service and resource provision.* Third edition, Library Association, 1982.

7 National Association of Teachers in Further and Higher Education *College libraries: policy statements.* NATFHE, 1982.

8 Revill, D H *Use and abuse of college libraries.* The Association of Colleges of Further and Higher Education, 1979.

9 Business Education Council *Approval and procedure.* (BEC Circular 1/77) Business Education Council, 1977.

10 Business Education Council *Notes of guidance to colleges on BEC Higher National Awards.* (Circular 3/77) Business Education Council, 1977.

5

Tertiary and Employment: Liaison with Industry

Mary H Lakie

The relationships explored in this chapter will be those between colleges and the industrial sector in general rather than simply that between industrial libraries and college libraries. Having proposed that each library exists to support the overall objectives of its parent body it will be clear that all aspects of the relationships between organizations must then have implications for that between their libraries. Each librarian should see his function in the context of the whole organization, not that of the library alone – he must also see his institution in the context of the community in which it is located, in terms, for example, of people, education, local government, industry and commerce.

It is important to recognize that in many companies there is no clear distinction between the provision of library and of information services, either from the senior management or the users' viewpoint, or in the way in which services are provided. Requirements within any one organization will range from those which can best be met by user access to a good collection and reading/study facilities, to those more effectively filled by the librarian's selection, evaluation, and active dissemination of relevant information; that is, they range from the traditional library service to a proactive information service. For this reason the terms 'librarian', 'information scientist' and 'information specialist' tend to be interchangeable in industry and are so regarded by this author. The term 'librarian' in this chapter is therefore deemed to include information scientists and information specialists.

For simplicity, the term 'industry' is taken to encompass, in addition to manufacturing, commerce, trade and research associations, public corporations, professional firms, eg architects, surveyors, lawyers, and service industries, eg banking, insurance. It includes all organizations whose libraries may be described as 'special libraries' to distinguish them from public libraries and libraries in education.

THE INDUSTRIAL LIBRARY ENVIRONMENT

The functions of the librarian or information specialist in industry may be summarized conveniently as follows:

Professional/Technical

1 To plan, organize, and supervise the work of a special library or information department.
2 To select, organize, and evaluate sources of information, printed and non-printed.
3 To plan, implement, and evaluate services and systems.
4 To provide a reference/advisory service for all types of users.
5 To provide SDI/current awareness services based on user interest profiles.
6 To understand and exploit information transfer and document use patterns exhibited by the learned world, and by governmental, industrial, and commercial organizations.
7 To ensure personal professional development.

Managerial

8 To understand and exploit information technology.
9 To plan and allocate resources.
10 To be responsible for the training, motivation, supervision,

and professional and technical development of subordinate staff.

11 To develop 1 to 10 with due regard to the parent organization's interests and to developments in librarianship and information science.

12 To participate in the management and development of the parent organization.

Provision of relevant library and information services depends on a sound knowledge and understanding of the objectives of the organization. What is the nature of the business? How is it funded? What are the economic, ethical, and technical constraints on its development? Who are the competitors? How successful are they? What are the internal organizational and political realities of the company? What are the specific current projects or operations and the medium- and long-term plans? The requirement to participate in management, and to develop the professional, technical, and managerial functions with due regard to the company's changing needs and to developments in librarianship and information science, are of prime importance, yet appear to be the least well understood responsibilities of librarians, not only in the industrial/commercial sector.

A subject specialist with a good understanding of and experience in general management is required. In some companies, or parts of large companies, the most important criteria for appointment are a specific scientific, commercial or perhaps language expertise, and intimate knowledge of the company. Should the right candidate also have a qualification in librarianship or information science that would be ideal, but neither wins the day alone. For this reason, together with the less creditable and hopefully now less frequent one of moving a poor scientific or commercial performer into a post in which 'he can do no harm' industry has a large proportion of librarians having no qualification, and sometimes no previous experience, in librarianship or information science. Provided that they are good managers, a few are, nevertheless, just the type of librarian most organizations would value, and which one would hope to find as products of education for librarianship.

In addition to providing current awareness services and problem solving support, the librarian may be a member of an interdisciplinary team responsible for the planning, progression, and evaluation of a particular aspect of the business, eg course development committee in college, or a project or product development team in industry. Membership of such a team demands participation in many fields of interest. By filling this interactive role effectively the librarian becomes an integral and essential part of the team.

New entrants to a profession do not come as experts, nor are they expected to do so. Yet such is the nature of the librarian's job in industry that most are required to demonstrate some skill in interdisciplinary communication, and in management, from the earliest days of employment. Their general management education and/or orientation should therefore be sufficient to enable them to:

1 Understand the objectives and workings of commerce, industry, and government in general, and of the employing organization in particular.
2 Understand the objectives and principal responsibilities of management and managers.
3 Manage effectively and develop any service or activity for which they are responsible.
4 Identify, select, and apply appropriate management tools and routines.
5 Pursue continuing personal professional development.

The professional environment for which we should aim is well described by Bauer,[1] dealing at length with the integral role of the information specialist in the planning, progression, problem solving, and evaluation of the business, research, or development of the parent body. Equally important are the attitudes and approaches to evaluation of the library's contribution to the funding body argued by Bladgen.[2]

Not every institution would describe its library/information function in Bauer's terms, nor recognize it in such. Nevertheless, the highest quality service is usually welcomed by management, and can lead to varied and significant career opportunities for the librarian. It is essential that students of librarianship and information science be encouraged to achieve and put into practice the very best in management, communication, and organizational skills.

Such ideas are expressed at greater depth, but in a very readable form, by Drucker.[3]

The library-information service must inform, educate and solve problems at all levels. It must adapt readily to changing business requirements by identifying and responding to the real need of its users. It therefore requires of its participants dynamically service oriented attitudes.

The librarian must develop attitudes to employment, to colleagues, and to management which reflect a high level of professionalism, in its broadest sense, in all aspects of the job. These may be demonstrated by an analytical and objective approach to problems; an informed and proactive approach to their solution; a capacity for constructive discussion and argument, both formally and informally, without or despite acrimony. Good verbal and written communication skills are equally important. The librarian must be capable of identifying salient points, summarizing succinctly, and presenting material in an organized and intelligible fashion.

It is important that the librarian should meet user colleagues on their own and on neutral territories and should develop a rapport with interdisciplinary colleagues at all levels, based on personal and professional integrity and mutual respect.

None of this comes automatically and much of it not easily. Nevertheless, many practitioners achieve and maintain such relationships by a continuing willingness to learn, to participate, and to be alert for opportunities to promote the library and information service to the obvious benefit of the whole, or any part of the organization.

The function of the library in industry may therefore be seen to parallel that of the library in the college, being concerned with several distinct user groups. Employees generally, specialist staff, and senior management may usefully be compared in a college with students, teaching staff, and management and administration respectively, as described in the Library Association's *Guidelines* for college libraries.[4]

In addition, the concepts of academic librarianship expressed by Revill[5] are equally relevant to industrial libraries. Simply read *scientific* or *technical* for *academic* throughout his paper. To be effective in industry and commerce the librarian must fulfil a varying combination of informational, educational, advisory, and managerial roles. In scope, therefore, his role is not significantly different from that of his college librarian colleague, in that library and information provision in any organization, being a service function, must become and be seen to be, an integral and vigorous part of the whole.

Having established the industrial scene in terms relevant to college practice we may proceed to examine areas of existing and potential interaction.

SERVICE SUPPORT AND THE PROFESSIONAL NETWORK

Service support is probably the most readily recognized aspect of interaction between college libraries and those in industry, commerce, and the service industries. It is however a miserable, if essential, affair if it fails to initiate some of the longer term and more far-reaching interactions proposed in this chapter.

Libraries in industry tend to be small, often only one or two person operations. By any standards the collections are small, highly specialized, and heavily biased towards periodicals, standards, reports, grey literature, and ephemera. In general, the emphasis of the collection is on the most recent publications, with only a limited core of material more than five to ten years old. Stock tends to in-depth coverage of specialist subjects with only limited cover of peripheral subjects, but may also include a good range of directories, specialist dictionaries, maps and indexes to publications and to the collections of other libraries.

Such a library cannot satisfy all requests for document supply and problem solving from its own stock and will depend on several other libraries for support. Many requests from the industrial/commercial sector to the college library seek access to a larger, more broadly based collection, often for reference only, or to a search/enquiry-answering service. The extent to which colleges can help will depend on their subject coverage, academic levels, the attitudes and abilities of their staff, and college management's philosophy on external users.

Approaches from college to industry tend to be seeking document supply or sources in a specialist subject outside the college's expertise. Although inter-lending does occur it is not necessarily the most common example of service support.

Cooperation may extend to the exploitation of information technology. For example, there is no good reason why, at a commercial price, colleges should not consider making computing facilities available to small companies, partly as a service function but also to provide applications experience for students. Nor is it inconceivable that the reverse could be true between a large company and a small college. In this respect as in many others, the most common reason for lack of development on both sides is individual conservatism which is reluctant to explore beyond the *status quo*.

Since the mid-1950s a number of local cooperative ventures have been developed by college, university, public, and industrial/commercial libraries. Their scope ranges from union catalogues and inter-lending to provision of technical information or other specialist current awareness and problem-solving services. Factors limiting development of cooperatives encapsulated by Corbett[6] have been reinforced by the current recession. It is an unfortunate truth that in such times of greater need for efficient use of resources, the potential for cooperation is severely limited by reduced staffing resources, and indeed little real progress appears to have been made in such cooperative efforts in recent years.

Establishment of a multiplicity of informal local and national professional networks is a natural product of cooperative or supportive activities. Developing professional rapport and mutual regard strengthens the informal professional network. The effects of these networks spill over into the activities of the various professional organizations, but many librarians, for a variety of reasons, obtain most of their professional stimulus and support from these 'invisible colleges' or 'old boy networks'.

Good interaction between colleges and industry or commerce is particularly helpful in drawing young professionals and support staff into the network. Relationships between organizations may be built up from occasional telephone enquiries to a readiness to 'pull out all the stops' for each other in emergencies, to mutual encouragement to participate in professional activities and to seek and enjoy personal professional development and increased job satisfaction. This is exactly the type of support essential to those librarians both in industry and commerce, and in small colleges, who run a very small operation, sometimes single-handed, and with consequent professional isolation.

But these aspects are well known and have been so for many years. There are many other useful and fruitful fields of liaison to consider.

EMPLOYEE AND STAFF/STUDENT INTERACTION

1 Employees as Students

Employees who are also students range from technicians taking OND/C or HND/C courses on day release as basic qualifications, to postgraduate staff undertaking part-time diploma or Masters degree courses to further career development. In some companies the student group also includes full-time students in the sciences, industrial, or business studies gaining industrial experience as an integral part of their first degree course, or postgraduate students undergoing pre-registration experience for a professional qualification. The bigger the company, the greater the range of academic levels and subjects of the student group. Only a very few small companies have no students in their employment, although many have no library.

Students, whether in full- or part-time education, need library and information services which will (a) provide access to specific recommended sources of information, other than essential standard textbooks, which they should buy for themselves; (b) provide instruction on types of information source, and opportunity to gain experience in their use; (c) provide instruction in and experience of seeking, evaluating and applying information to problem solving.

Teaching and library staff in colleges aim to ensure the provision of all of these to full-time students, but often find it difficult to do so satisfactorily for part-time students whose time in college is severely limited. In many technician level courses the teaching staff aim to provide sufficient information in lectures and recommended reading material to allow the student to pass the examination. However laudable and necessary, this may not, paradoxically, be in the student's long-term best interest! Students need to be taught, at the earliest opportunity, to understand the nature and structure of sources of information, whether published or unpublished. They need to recognize and be able to use different types of guides to sources to discover information relevant to their own needs, and must also learn to evaluate different types of sources for different purposes. If lower level courses in further and higher education do not fulfil these requirements, then the student will not be fully equipped to achieve his full potential in higher level courses and in personal development. Project-based user education, as described by McElroy and McNaughton,[7] and by McElroy and Bate,[8] aims to satisfy this requirement. It is an approach which is readily acceptable to the student since it assists, literally, in his problem solving. It converts readily to problem solving in employment and is a concept which the librarian in industry can promote and support for students and staff alike.

Students may also turn to the company library for assistance. By liaising with colleagues in college to understand course structure and assignment objectives, the librarian in industry can provide advisory support and instruction in information handling to students at any level. This does not infer that all relevant sources will be or should be available within the company, but suggests that the requisite informed teaching/advisory support, a reasonable stock, a referral facility to other libraries or specialist organizations, alternative access to indexes and abstracting services, and access to the company's specialist collection can be at the student's disposal.

The librarian in industry, by creating the right opportunities, can advise students on study materials, report and essay writing, and even examination techniques. Obviously, to give informed advice and do so effectively, he must liaise with the college and with colleagues in education. In this author's company, where part of the librarian's function is 'selection, evaluation, and active dissemination of relevant information', this proposition does not appear exceptional but merely a reasonable extension of his informational/educational/advisory role.

2 Students as Employees

Many examining and professional bodies require the full-time student to undertake, as part of the course of study, a specified period of industrial experience and training which the college has an obligation to organize and supervise. The purposes of the placement are that the student should gain experience in applying his theoretical knowledge, should become proficient in some techniques, learn new ones, and gain experience of being employed. For various reasons, the right kind of industrial placement is not always easy to find. The college library, by virtue of its contacts with and service provision to local firms, may be well placed to identify likely opportunities and to initiate communication, however informally.

In most respects these students are no different from other employees in that, to contribute effectively to the work of the employing organization and to promote their own intellectual growth and technical development, they must acquire good habits of information seeking, analysis, application, and evaluation. Special library staff should aim to continue and amplify the user education provided by tutor librarians in college. This period should also introduce the student to various aspects of being employed, hopefully those indicative of a good employer and a good employee. As a specialist contribution, the librarian can introduce the student to the company as a whole, the interaction of its various functional departments, and its scientific, technical, commercial, and/or marketing objectives.

In a small company, this may be achieved most effectively by informal methods since each individual can be readily identified but it must be clear to the student that it is part of a formal induction procedure. In a larger company, a more highly structured approach is necessary. Students on industrial placement in the author's company have indicated that time spent with the library/ information staff during the first month provided a helpful and informative framework for subsequent experience. In other cases, after six months, the student lacking this contact knew a great deal about the department in which he had worked, but little of its relationship with other departments, or of the company as a whole:

not necessarily a comment on interdepartmental relationships, but obviously reflecting poor understanding of the student's need.

The librarian in industry cannot function effectively unless he is well informed as to the company's objectives and the information requirements of its staff; the combination of information updating and problem solving provides him with a privileged view of the work and interactions of the various departments, and a broader, more informed view of the company than is likely to be available elsewhere below top management level.

Indeed, whether the student is on sandwich placement, postgraduate experience, or even vacation employment, the librarian in industry has an excellent opportunity, and indeed a responsibility, to imbue him with personal updating, problem solving, and browsing habits which will stand him in good stead throughout his career, the practice of which will enable him to seek opportunity and succeed in career advancement.

Students on placements where there is no library will be dependent on whatever services are available to other employees. If the company is a successful one then he will probably meet one or more 'gatekeepers' (Allen,[9] Katz[10]) whose information gathering and dissemination habits will be worthy of examination and probably of emulation.

However brief the period of placement or employment, the student brings a new, often refreshing point of view on his subject, on employment, and on libraries and librarians! His presence and participation prompts analysis, rethinking, and evaluation of activities. Sometimes it encourages change, often it does not, but the interchange can be mutually beneficial. It challenges tradition and routine, and demands that long-cherished values and activities be re-examined in the light of current good practice and future potential. For the student it should provide opportunity to test technical/professional arguments in an interdisciplinary environment and to develop and improve communication skills at different levels.

These are not concepts which should relate only to the exceptional student and the good employer. It is important to industrial and commercial development that interaction between employers and new graduates or diplomates should be encouraged to develop in this manner. Librarians in education and in industry are well situated to identify potential opportunities and to play a full part in encouraging and supporting such interaction. They should be prepared to play this part in full.

STAFF EXCHANGE AND SECONDMENT

From college to the private sector, staff exchange may occur as industrial secondment or by consultancy agreements. Both can be invaluable to both parties but are not sufficiently common.

By industrial secondment, placing teaching staff with a company to work on an agreed project for a period of weeks or months, a college can draw on the strength of local industry to encourage the professional development of its teaching staff. Industry thereby contributes to improving the quality of the education of its own present and future employees. At the same time, the college's academic board and the senior management of the company concerned will ensure that the project proposed is a viable one likely to be mutually beneficial.

College librarians have an overall educational function to fulfil and therefore each should, from time to time, seek opportunity to gain experience in the environment for which their students are being educated. Many libraries in industry are small, even one-man operations. There is always conflict therefore, between the need to provide heavily demanded services now, and to plan and manage equally effective services for the future. The worst possible situation is for the librarian to become so engrossed in performing routine tasks as to lose sight of the organization as a whole and of its changing needs. In such cases it can be professionally stimulating and synergistic to have, for a time, the cooperation, constructive criticism and support of another librarian with a different point of view. While a consultancy might conceivably be forced upon the industrial library by management, it is most unlikely that such would be the case with a secondment, which, by the very nature of the agreement, demands cooperative preplanning. It tends therefore to be a mutually interesting and beneficial experience with significant educational and development spin-off for the industrial library's support staff.

Industrial secondment should not be ruled out simply because a company does not have a library. All institutions depend on good information provision for their development and success. Where there is no library, the secondment project might investigate the nature and scope of the information needs and the extent to which they are currently satisfied. This type of exercise would require a more experienced librarian than might otherwise be the case, but such would be valid if, for example, the college was to consider offering services to local industry. The librarian during secondment would have unequalled opportunity to identify the means by which the college library might contribute, to promote and argue these ideas during normal day-to-day interchange with industrial colleagues, and to sell the ideas and objectives of his profession to a healthily sceptical management. What greater test? What greater reward?

By consultancy, industry draws on the strength of the college to provide an expertise not otherwise available to it, or to review, independently, the recommendations of its own experts! The company specifies the subject of the investigation and agrees to pay certain fees. There is no requirement for the project to be mutually beneficial, although such is (and should be) a frequent by-product.

College staff on industrial secondment become to all intents and purposes employees of the company for a specified period of several weeks or months. The individual gets to know his industrial colleagues both formally and informally, at all levels, and will be bombarded with opinion, argument, and demand as if he were a regular member of staff. Whilst the consultant must familiarize himself with the structure and organization of the company, his relationship with employees will usually be rather more formal and the time spent on-site is inevitably fragmented. The secondment pattern offers more, both to the company and the individual, by virtue of these interpersonal advantages.

Staff exchange in the opposite direction, from industry and commerce to college, is certainly less common and usually less clearly defined. It occurs on an irregular and informal visiting lecturer basis, usually to present and discuss a particular aspect of industrial or business requirements or applications, to students of science, industrial studies, business management or (of course!)

librarianship. This opportunity is poorly exploited by many colleges, even those with a school of librarianship. It is difficult to understand why so many colleges fail to take advantage of the professional expertise available to them in industry.

Seminars may also be organized by the company rather than in college, providing an opportunity to see industrial librarianship in its proper context and to gain a more complete view of the company than is otherwise possible. More often, the college librarian may arrange for a student or students with a particular interest to visit an appropriate library or series of libraries to explore that interest. It may be part of an exercise for assessment, an exploration of career potential, or to examine a particular aspect of special librarianship. Opportunities for this level of information interchange abound but tend not to be used as freely as they might be.

Each time a special library is the subject of a seminar, presentation, or hosts a visit, the librarian should find it advisable to analyse and re-evaluate functions and services before promoting them. This inevitably has beneficial spin-off for the organization and its library staff, in that the greater their involvement, the less chance of their settling into mindless routine! If well prepared and presented, these activities are good public relations and will be welcomed as such by management. Despite possible fears that staff will be distracted by participation in such activities, it is more often the case that those professionals who are sufficiently dynamic to promote librarianship out with the company more than redeem time they give to these activities by improved job performance and high levels of energy reinvested.

Within the wide range of organizations under the industrial umbrella, it is manifestly desirable that senior staff should be highly regarded by colleagues outside the organization for their professional *savoir faire*. This may mean holding office or being a driving force in a business or professional organization, eg Chamber of Commerce, Institute of Bankers, Cement and Concrete Association, Library Association. Publication is also a significant measure of regard, and for this purpose includes presenting invited papers at conferences or seminars. The librarian who is so recognized, not only by his own profession, but by colleagues outside that group, can be much more readily recognized by and assimilated into the

interdisciplinary coterie of his institution than can he who hides
quietly amongst the books.

The college librarian should be one of the more obvious providers
of encouragement and support to anyone wishing to pursue the
route of professional participation and publication, whilst his colleague in industry is well placed to work actively on user education
and to ensure a flow of useful and constructive feedback to course
organizers.

SENIOR MANAGEMENT

Senior management in industry, like the college principal and his
management group, is concerned with planning strategy for the
continuing development and viability of the organization.

Since colleges are in the business of 'educating for employment',
interaction with industry and commerce at senior management level
ought to be frequent, and variable in scope and intent. Employers
have legitimate concerns regarding the content of courses, determination of student attendance patterns for part-time courses, and
provision of in-service courses. Involvement in these areas is an
essential prelude to determining properly the type of in-company
support which should be made available. Their greatest concern,
however, is finding appropriate means of bringing comment and
constructive criticism to the attention of college management and
academic boards.

Some colleges have excellent interactive relationships with local
industry and commerce, but many pay little more than lip service to
marketing their wares. An annual contribution to a faculty advisory
committee for example, from selected companies, with an agenda
determined by the faculty, hardly addresses these concerns. To be
effective, consultation needs to take place frequently and naturally,
at subject and activity levels, rather than solely in the boardroom.
Equally, college management needs to receive informed support
and criticism with the employment sector rather than the sporadic,
unstructured, and often biased comment which is too often the
only input available in the present non-interactive structure.

When college managements can be seen to be serious in their

intent to interact with employers, present and potential, then will they be able to draw on expertise from the senior level which makes the decisions on sandwich placements, consultancies, postgraduate experience, in-service education and training, all matters of concern and self-interest to the college, in which management might be expected to have an active and continuing interest.

CONCLUSION

The extent to which interaction can occur between colleges and the employment sector is influenced by senior management attitudes and philosophies on both sides, but the most significant factor by far is the dynamism – or inertia – of individuals. Too many individuals, particularly in librarianship, are prepared to hide behind the excuse that 'management would not approve', accepting no responsibility for influencing the management decision.

Specialists are appointed to inform, advise, educate, and to take or to influence decisions; the sooner librarians accept that opportunity, and its consequent responsibilities, the better it will be for the profession. Then and only then will the scope and variety of interaction between college and company approach its true potential.

REFERENCES

1   Bauer, C K 'Managing management'. *Special Libraries* 71 (4) 1980. 204–216.
2   Blagden, J *Do we really need libraries?* Bingley, 1980.
3   Drucker, P *The principles of management.* Pan, 1968.
4   Library Association *College Libraries: guidelines for professional service and resource provision.* Third edition, Library Association, 1982.
5   Revill, D H 'Academic libraries in colleges of further and higher education'. *Journal of Librarianship* 13 (2) 1981. 104–118.
6   Corbett, E V *Fundamentals of library organisation and administration.* Library Association, 1978. 256–257.
7   McElroy, A R and McNaughton, F C 'A project based approach to

the use of biological literature'. *Journal of Biological Education*, 13 (1) 1979. 52–57.

8 McElroy, A R and Bate, J L 'User education – for life?' *Library Review* 31 (1) Spring 1982. 3–10.

9 Allen T J *Managing the flow of technology*. MIT Press, 1977.

10 Katz, R 'An investigation into the managerial roles and career paths of gatekeepers and project supervisors in a major research and development facility'. *R&D Management* 11 (3) 1981. 103–110.

6

Tertiary and Secondary: Relationships with Schools

Margaret J Sked

There is a considerable community of interest between school and college libraries. Naturally therefore, extensive arrangements exist for cooperation in what may be called the 'traditional manner'; inter-lending, enquiry handling, visits of readers (usually from school to college), etc. Cooperation of this nature is well established throughout librarianship and will be familiar ground to most readers.

School and college libraries share a less well documented relationship, yet one which is more important to them professionally, directly related to the interests and intellectual well-being of their readers, and central to the objectives and management of the libraries themselves and of their parent institutions. It is on this aspect, which I shall term the progressive educational role of the library in school and further education, that this chapter will concentrate.

The progressive educational role is particularly expressed through selection and provision of varied information and learning resources, through teaching, guiding, and advising pupils and students in the effective use of these resources by librarians and teachers in partnership, and through the development in the pupil of life skills in information use.

The complexity of information requirements in society, amongst children and adults, in families, at work, in unemployment, and at leisure, places on education a responsibility to provide tangible evidence of the diversity of information resources available, and to provide structured learning opportunities for pupils and students to acquire skills in identifying, seeking, finding, and using information. For the individual, an ability in comprehensive information management has never been acquired readily, and although the techniques necessary are considered essential to an ordered and full life, there is little evidence, as noted in the studies by Irving and Snape,[1] and by Brake,[2] of formal educational preparation.

> The majority of pupils leave school at the end of fifth year, yet the existence of any formal preparation for using information and library resources outside school was undiscovered.[1]

> *The Need to Know* was based on the assumption that many school children, especially those who do not go on to further education, are ill equipped either to locate or evaluate information; consequently this reduces the effectiveness of their decision-making, and restricts their freedom of choice and participation within society in general.[2]

The ability to locate and evaluate information is an essential part of the acquisition of knowledge and of all learning activity. We acquire knowledge gradually in a variety of ways, building increasingly complex information upon that which has been assimilated at earlier stages. The requirement, therefore, to provide access to a variety of information resources, and to learn to use these resources efficiently, is crucial to this build-up of knowledge. The techniques of using resources must be centred on the information required and developed naturally at each learning stage. From the earliest stages in education, the child must learn to identify and define his own learning requirement; he must have opportunity to explore an appropriate variety of sources, and learn to recognize and select those which will answer his queries; he must present them efficiently for maximum communication; not least, he must learn to appraise critically, appreciate, and enjoy the form of the resource, its style and arrangement, and its content.

The importance of surrounding the child with a plentiful supply of stimulating resources in his early years at school is accepted by educationists and librarians. However, the foundations of preparation for a lifetime of independent information acquisition are less well-recognized, and the techniques needed to extract and present information are rarely practised in a structured and progressive way. The arrangement and organization of resources for the beginner in the classroom requires careful thought. A sense of the rightness of using resources should be instilled early by emphasizing feelings of security; for the young, physical comfort, for example, while reading or listening, ranks high in the promotion of resource use. In selecting books, emphasis should be placed on the communicative qualities of colour and sound, in addition to readability. At this stage the young child should be taught how to care for and handle books. The child should learn to be considerate of others using books; learn to turn pages correctly; understand page sequence; understand the principles of locating and borrowing books and other items, and of returning them to the library; identify and name the bibliographic and physical parts of a book; use a bookmark to hold for reference; identify a picture which conveys particular information; listen or observe, and relate a significant fact; enjoy listening to stories and cassettes, and looking at pictures, filmstrips, films, and video. Whilst basic, these qualities of learning form the foundation of the complex information skills necessary to befit a person to deal efficiently with the requirements of modern society. It is important in succeeding years that more advanced information needs are met in an equally structured way. The research undertaken on behalf of the Schools Council by Vera Southgate and others over ten years, and published in 1981, confirms this.[3]

> The training of children in methods of locating and extracting information from books relating to their topic work requires a detailed plan, worked out and agreed on by all members of staff – a plan which can be introduced in carefully graded stages throughout the four years of junior education.

In addition to the need to promote more successful information retrieval on given topics, educationists are aware also of the need to allow time for children to acquire better reading habits. Research suggests there is a relationship between increased individual reading and improved language ability. Facility in the use of language is crucial at all stages in the handling of information, and librarians must be aware of the educational necessity of providing opportunities during the school day for reading. Care must be taken over the selection and grading of books and other resources which may be used to promote more individual reading. Here, as at all stages of education, the less able must be nurtured. Too often in the past, the language difficulties of such children were compounded by a system of rewarding children with additional reading time only on the early completion of an exercise. Inevitably, the slow learner and the less able suffered. Another factor for consideration is that the time one child may take to read, listen, or observe may vary greatly from that taken by another child. This time factor in assimilating information has implications, not only for children in the primary school, but also in secondary and further education, and should be considered in all programmes of user education, and reflected in the degree of flexibility, and the opportunities for individual attention designed into the programme.

The primary school is often the child's first introduction to a central library collection, and the organization and arrangement of resources is important. The organizer of such a collection should be aware of the systems used for library organization in the related secondary schools, and ultimately in further education, and in the public library system. Consistency of approach is important. In the past, many primary schools have evolved systems of resource arrangement which required intricate learning patterns to cope with a series of subject indexes, colour coding, and numbered places on the library shelves. By operating an adapted and simplied version of the bibliographic schemes used in other library systems, the child will learn to transfer and extend the primary school information-tracing skills to the secondary school and to further education, a system of work based upon educationally sound principles.

Partly because of the importance of surrounding the young child with books and resources in the primary school classroom, partly because of the lack of planned library space in most primary schools, and partly because of the real accommodation difficulties experienced by many primary schools, the development of central libraries has been slow. Research suggests that where resources are dispersed throughout the school, or where they are housed in space inadequate for group use, the learning, not only of the skills related to locating resources, but also of those skills related to locating information within resources, is adversely affected.[3]

> The result was that in a number of schools, little direct training appeared to be given in the bibliographical skills, such as, for example, the use of subject and author indexes. In fact, one of the findings of this piece of research is that children in the first two years of the junior school require more specific training in the use of books, and particularly of non-fiction books.

The various difficulties encountered in organization of resources in primary schools may have considerable effect on the resource utilization and information seeking abilities of children entering secondary education. The able child who has received a structured programme of resource-based work throughout his primary school years should bring to the secondary school a confidence in resource use which can be developed into truly independent learning. For example, a child should have attained experience in using a library catalogue, identifying the information therein, and locating sources in the library; should be familiar with a number of bibliographic terms such as cross-reference, glossary, index, guide word; should be able to distinguish between the purpose of the table of contents and the index of a book; should be able to set up simple audio-visual equipment with appropriate software; should be able to take simple notes; should be able to use a variety of audio-visual equipment to record information, and extract information from a range of audio-visual resources; should be able to present information in various formats, notes, graphs, simple maps, simple bibliographies; should be able to locate and enjoy folk-tales, fantasy, historical fiction, poetry and non-fiction, in both print and non-print forms. Many children will not have attained this degree of experience, and the secondary school librarian may find it necessary to introduce children to the basic skills required for resource-based work. The child with learning difficulties, particularly if these are related to language and reading, the slow learner, and the less able, will require much individual attention in library and resource skills, and constant reinforcement of the skills learned will be necessary.

Although in primary education the ideology of education is child centred, in the secondary curriculum there is greater emphasis on subject-based learning. As a natural consequence, resource-based learning and information skills should be centred within the context of the subject. This has been generally accepted only recently by educational librarians, but the uneven implementation of the teaching of curriculum-based information skills in school libraries indicates that the initiative for development must come from the schools' senior management. It is important to realize that the innovative, enthusiastic school librarian will achieve only limited success if not supported by a 'whole school' policy for resource organization, selection of resources, and resource-based learning, centred on general curriculum planning. The skills required for retrieving information for science may differ from the skills required for retrieving information for English, and certainly sources of information will differ widely, because of the structure of a subject, and the modes of subject presentation. To teach general library skills without reference to the learning requirements of the various subjects is not helpful to pupils who may not find it easy to transfer a set of skills from one context to another, or to pupils who require frequent reinforcement of all learned activities.

> Efficient library research and study skills should be taught to secondary pupils at the earliest possible stage, but their intro- duction should be followed by continuous reinforcement vert- ically, as pupils progress through the school, and horizontally, in all curricular areas. Skills instruction should be coordinated by someone with relevant expertise and breadth of knowledge about curricular needs, and taught or reinforced by all teaching departments to ensure transferability and applicability to pupils.[1]

If the information skills learned in secondary schools are to be regarded as adequate for equipping young people for further educ- ation and life after school, the librarian's resource selection must complement the curriculum by matching resources to learning needs, and by providing for mixed ability teaching and learning requirements at all levels.

Whatever the form of organization, effective science teaching demands well equipped laboratories and a good range of suitable reference books and audio-visual aids. For mixed ability teaching it is even more important to have plenty of resources because of the need in a given lesson to provide materials suitable for more than one level of ability and because of the greater variety and amount of experience needed by some pupils.[4]

Selection of resources will be related to curricular requirements, to providing subject coverage of all levels of work undertaken, to catering for differentiation of ability, to the practical teaching and subject requirements of the teachers, to stimulating intellectual and emotional growth in young people, and to extending the requirements of the curriculum with a variety of interesting, appropriate, and recreational resources. The balance of provision of audio-visual resources in relation to that of print materials will be decided by the needs of the subject, and by learning patterns. For example, history needs to be supported by resources including photographs, models, learning packs, and facsimiles, whilst children with learning difficulties will be supported by a variety of film, video, and tape-slide productions to promote interest and sustain concentration. Resources are provided primarily to support the learning activities within the school. Clearly, on many occasions collections of resources are required in proximity to teaching. The role of the school librarian in managing resources, in gauging the pace of curricular activity, and organizing its support by the provision of resources, may be as crucial within subject departments as within the school library.

As education at the secondary level is concerned also with preparation for self-sufficiency in society and in adult life, attention should be given to methods of satisfying the wide-ranging information requirements likely to be experienced. The provision of resources useful in the learning of life skills such as simple reference tools in which to find information related to, for example, the consumer, the motorist, or the employee, is essential. The librarian should be aware of, and whenever possible involved in, pupils' expeditions into the local community. It is important that the librarian helps pupils discover the nature of resources and sources available within the community, such as public libraries, citizens' advice bureaux, post offices, and other public offices.

For young people in the 16–18 age group, there are new implications for the quality of information skills preparation provided in school. *A Basis for Choice*[5] recommends that all courses offered to this age group in further education should contain a common core. The design of such courses should foster opportunities for self-development and promote the abilities to communicate, to learn from 'study, experience and colleagues' and to understand the 'political, economic and aesthetic factors which affect their lives'. The ability to learn from study, and to grasp the concepts of politics, economics, and aesthetics requires a maturity in the individual which may be nourished by the extended provision of independent learning opportunities throughout the secondary school years.

If further education is to succeed in raising the level of achievement in literacy, and succeed in consolidating competence in a variety of study skills, it is important that further education lecturers and librarians should be assured of a structured legacy of information knowledge on which to build. Colleges should be able to anticipate that young people will bring from secondary school to further education a fundamental understanding of a subject, and learning strategies equal to coping with extended and detailed study of that subject. This implies: that the student will possess the skills of independent study, an attitude of enquiry, and a maturity in critical assessment and appraisal; that the student will be familiar with the organization of knowledge within a library; that the student will be capable of formulating a clear definition of a study assignment, and analysing a range of possible subjects and sources for investigation.

The mixture of practical training and education at the centre of learning within the further education curriculum has acquired general acceptance and success within the worlds of commerce and industry, and within society. Indeed, representatives from commerce, industry, and a variety of society's institutions are involved in an advisory capacity in the construction of further education syllabuses. Often this has led to a more economic organization and utilization of resources, as well as a more pragmatic use. In a time of economic stringency there is likely to be more emphasis on accountability in education. Parents, society, and government will seek evidence of the successful preparation of children and young people for life. Faced with a series of crises within society, unemployment, the decline of the traditional heavy industries, changes in family units, social unrest, educationists in schools have sought new ways of making teaching and learning more meaningful to modern requirements. In addition to other strategies employed, they have emulated the methodology of further education by designing courses emphasizing practical skills which complement theoretical abilities.

But, although further education examining bodies such as TEC and BEC, and SCOTEC and SCOTBEC in Scotland, have introduced elements of library centred information skills to their syllabuses, there is little evidence that secondary school curriculum bodies or examining boards have considered making similar recommendations in any structured manner. In syllabus notes, however, reference is made frequently to the qualities necessary to acquire knowledge and understanding of the concepts, themes, and terminology related to the subject studied, and to the variety of resources necessary to support such study. Despite this, the importance attached to the organization of the resources, the positive exploitation of the resources in support of the curriculum, and the role of the librarian in aiding resource-based learning appears not to be understood by school managers.

> [A librarian's] . . . expertise, as a resource, is particularly important because of a fact many educators overlook: that use of the library and its contents and services is an integral part, and often a very important part, of the learning experience of pupils and students. Libraries are not warehouses: they are learning centres. . . .[6]

The education of 16–18 year olds who have chosen to leave school is affected by the contemporary need to foster a flexible and adaptable attitude in the individual, and a readiness to cope throughout life with changing employment patterns. The White Paper *A New Training Initiative*, published in 1981,[7] outlines a scheme in which the apprenticeship training of the past is adapted to those new needs, and basic skills in the use of tools and machinery, and in office operations, are augmented by skills in numeracy, literacy, and communication. Information skills, as shown, form an important part of such a basic skills programme. Similar concern for the education of young people who are not readily stimulated by concepts and ideas, is reflected in a pilot scheme introduced by SCOTEC and SCOTBEC to further education in Scotland in 1982–3 and organized by the joint body, the Scottish Vocational Education Council (SCOTVEC) from 1984. This *Scottish Certificate in Vocational Studies* includes a core element which aims to develop skills perceived by young people to be of value to practical and real life situations.

It is, therefore, a matter of interest to educators in further education that such young people, previously not expected to follow formal further education, are given at school comprehensive opportunities to develop skills in handling information resources and in selecting and organizing information compatible with the advancement of their abilities in further education. Certainly in secondary education, there is evidence of a greater awareness to provide for differentiation of ability. In Scotland, this can be noted through two major developments: the introduction of courses in S3, based on the Munn and Dunning reports on curriculum and assessment,[8,9] in 1984–5 for all pupils at Foundation, General and Credit levels; the implementation in 1984 of *16–18s in Scotland: an action plan*,[10] in which schools will provide relevant courses in a modular system, linking directly with further education, and joining some schools and FE colleges together in consortia to provide a good choice of modules.

Another group of young people who are now encouraged to participate in further education are the physically and mentally handicapped, whose particular difficulties are discussed in *Disability and Adolescence*.[11] Problems are associated with school education being completed at special schools. A sense of insecurity results when transferring to a situation wherein the young people are expected to adjust to the normal needs of society, with very little background of experience to help. For the mentally handicapped particularly, the hurdles must seem enormous. Welcomed to further education, where, because of their particular learning difficulties, they often continue their education apart from other groups of students, they are, however, encouraged to mingle with all students in social areas, and in the library. Librarians and educators alike describe libraries in colleges as complex, possessing sophisticated information systems. Although educational librarians provide an increasing variety of stimulating and interesting resources to support the education of the mentally handicapped, there are few large centralized collections in special schools to introduce the concept of a library to such students. These young people pose special problems in the selection and provision of resources, and in user education, for the college librarian, but the presence of varied collections of learning resources throughout their years in school, a familiarity with library resource centres, and experience of the support of a librarian, would make their sustained and progressive library resource education a more attainable target for the librarian in further education.

The concepts of distance learning, and the Open Tech, will obviously have many implications for resource provision in colleges, and in public libraries. The success of the Open University is evidence of society's hunger for education. Individuals, often with few formal education qualifications, adapted to a variety of learning strategies based on text, radio, television, record, and cassette with the minimum of personal tutoring. Distance learning programmes offered by colleges and through the Open Tech will exploit similar strategies. If, during school education, pupils are equipped to handle information through library supported resource-based learning and a school librarian closely involved in curricular activity, many of the inhibitions felt about embarking upon a course of study requiring independent learning techniques may be alleviated. If the student can observe a clear connection between the information skills acquired at school and their application to independent further education and to acquiring knowledge through using the resources of local colleges and public libraries, he will approach new learning requirements with greater confidence.

The further education college library which provides a variety of user education programmes designed to encourage proficiency in information skills across a variety of courses, and in a variety of situations, is an accepted part of the further education system. The college librarian, like his lecturer colleagues, expects students to come with the ability to study and learn at more demanding levels than those experienced in school, and therefore equipped with the skills necessary for progression. The sequential nature of learning information skills and the importance of relating specific information skills to specific subjects should be recognized, and more generally accepted in school. Also, school librarians should be made more aware of the contribution they can make to the whole process of learning.

> . . . each school should draw up for itself a whole-school information skills policy, and that policy should form an integral part of the school's departmental and pastoral programmes. Such a policy would improve pupils' ability to search for and make use of information, and also greatly facilitate their learning in all areas. Learning to learn is not only part of the curriculum in its own right: given a whole-school approach it is a powerful aid to improving the effectiveness of the rest of the curriculum.[12]

Such an interpretation of the profound contribution that the librarian can make to education has implications for the education of the librarian who wishes to work in schools and colleges. That librarian needs knowledge of curriculum design and developments; of the methodology of education; of the differing learning abilities of groups of pupils, and of individual pupils; of the elements within society which shape attitudes to learning; of resources, and their appropriateness to particular learning requirements; of how to promote the use of resources in support of learning. In education, it should be accepted that librarians work with teachers and lecturers, and as a result of the teacher's guidance on subjects, learning objectives, and strategy, the librarians will provide suitable and stimulating resources. Provision of resources requires foresight and initiative in selection, qualities which are more effective if securely grounded in knowledge of the curricular and teaching methods. Inevitably, this places a responsibility upon the schools of librarianship to provide courses which befit the librarian to fulfil the requirements of the work.

An educational library is a specialist library, whose selection, organization and dissemination procedures are directed towards highly specialist purposes – educational purposes. It aims to promote the educational and research aims of its institution and clientele through every path of its work, every area of its building and by every action of its staff.[6]

The benefit of dual qualification in librarianship and education, and the absolute need for librarians working in schools and colleges to have a thorough understanding of, and sympathy with, the structure of the education system and the objectives and practices of education itself was recognized by the introduction, at Loughborough University, of a joint honours degree course. Many librarians take opportunities to study part-time to gain certificates in teaching or in educational technology, from colleges of education. Certainly many practising librarians in education are conscious of a deficiency in their training. As shown, the value of the school librarian's role in promoting resources in support of learning is not fully realized or exploited. There exists, therefore, the curious dilemma of the deficiency in education for school librarianship giving support to the deficiency in the role of the school librarian, and that deficiency in role supporting the preclusion of further developments of a specialist education for school librarians. Much of the recent research work promoted by the British Library Research and Development Department within the Inner London Education Authority[13], at the University of East Anglia[14], and at the University of Lancaster,[15] for example, confirms the value of information skills in the curriculum, and confirms the positive contribution which the librarian can make to learning. The greatest hope for professional development must lie here, and, inevitably, such development must influence the structure of courses provided in the schools of librarianship.

Nevertheless, the success of a number of school libraries, and of college libraries, owes much to the education and training of their personnel, to the attitudes of management in schools and colleges, and to the cooperative endeavours of teachers and librarians to operate a curriculum-related library information skills programme. But ultimately, success is dependent upon the quality of selection of resources, and on how closely that selection 'is directed towards highly specialist purposes'.[6] The purposes of education may be summarized as opening fields of knowledge and understanding, so that the pupil or student may develop his full potential as an individual, and as a member of society. The resources of the library should support knowledge and understanding, but it is important also, with young people, that the development of the individual should be guided by the structured provision of opportunities for appraisal, criticism, and appreciation of these resources. Only in that way will the individual develop his own strategies for independent consideration of the qualities of literature and resources, and through that, of society and of life.

The selection of resources for the library is part of a dynamic process which should include reading, viewing, listening, reviewing and discussion. The resources provided should give opportunities which will encourage in pupils an awareness of points of view other than their own, an understanding of styles of life different from their own, to develop qualities of tolerance and respect, and to evolve principles upon which life can be developed. Library resource provision within an educational system, which promotes the ideal of self-sufficiency, is not concerned simply with training for finding information. It is part of a process which helps provide the individual pupil with the means of making judgments and choices, which helps produce alternative ways of approaching problems, and which encourages the growth of a more responsive personality capable of creatively using the information which surrounds him to formulate his convictions and sculpt his life.

> Ultimately a man sets the measure of his own freedom and his own bondage by the level at which he chooses to establish his convictions. The man who orders his life in terms of many special and inflexible convictions about temporary matters makes himself the victim of circumstances. Each little prior conviction that is not open to review is a hostage he gives to fortune; it determines whether the events of tomorrow will bring happiness or misery. The man whose prior convictions encompass a broad perspective, and are cast in terms of principles rather than rules, has a much better chance of discovering those alternatives which lead eventually to his emancipation.[16]

REFERENCES

1 Irving, A and Snape, W *Educating library users in secondary schools.* (British Library Research and Development Report 5467) British Library, 1979.

2 Brake, T *The need to know; teaching the importance of information.* (British Library Research and Development Report 5511) British Library, 1980.

3 Southgate, V, Arnold, H and Johnson, S *Extending beginning reading.* Heinemann (for the Schools Council), 1981.

4 Department of Education and Science *Mixed ability work in comprehensive schools: a discussion paper by a working party of her Majesty's Inspectorate.* (HMI Series: Matters for Discussion 6) London, HMSO, 1978.

5 Further Education Curriculcum Review and Development Unit (Advisory Intelligence and Development Body for Further Education) *A basis for choice: report of a study group on post-16 pre-employment courses.* The unit, 1979.

6 Beswick, N W 'Editorial: The nature of educational librarianship'. *Education Libraries Bulletin.* 25 (1) Spring 1982.

7 Department of Employment. *A new training initiative: a programme for action.* Cmnd 8455, HMSO, 1981.

8 Scottish Education Department and Consultative Committee on the Curriculcum *The structure of the curriculum in the third and fourth years of the Scottish secondary school* (Chairman: J Munn) HMSO, 1977.

9 Scottish Education Department. *Assessment for all. Report of the committee to review assessment in the third and fourth years of secondary education in Scotland.* (Chairman: J. Dunning) HMSO, 1977.

10 *16–18s in Scotland: an action plan.* Scottish Education Department, 1983.

11 Anderson, E M, Clark, L, and Spain, B *Disability in adolescence: psychological and social adjustment of adolescents with cerebral palsy or spina bifida and hydrocephalus.* Methuen, 1982.

12 Marland, M (ed) *Information skills in the secondary curriculum: the recommendations of a working group sponsored by the British Library and the Schools Council.* Methuen, 1982. (Schools Council Curriculum Bulletin 9.)

13 Inner London Education Authority: Centre for Learning Resources Information skills in the curriculum research unit.

14 University of East Anglia *Library access and sixth form studies.* The University, nd.

15 Lancaster University: Centre for Educational Research and Development *Using books and libraries project. Information skills in the secondary curriculum.* The Centre, 1980.

Tertiary and Secondary

16 Kelly, G A *The psychology of personal constructs.* Vol 1. Norton, 1955.

Part 2

THE COLLEGES AND THEIR LIBRARIES

7

Colleges of Further Education

Marie Adams

To our sorrow, there is hardly a single generalisation that can be made about further education in England that does not require an array of reservations and exceptions before it is accurate.[1]

I can only concur with Crowther. The diversity of further education is such that it is difficult, if not impossible, to give an account of it in definitive terms. It is rare to find two identical colleges or college libraries because each college is shaped and characterized primarily by its individual response to the needs of the community it serves.

This chapter attempts to present an introduction to further education and its librarianship based on working experience of one college of further education. The references list some of the titles available which give an account of the further education system for the reader who desires more detailed historical and statistical information than is given here.[2-5]

THE COLLEGE AND THE FURTHER EDUCATION ENVIRONMENT

The first step is to identify the further education college. To many people in a local community it is affectionately known as 'the local tech' or 'night school'. College of further education, technical college, and college of technology are more or less synonymous titles. These institutions of further education are included in the official Department of Education and Science (DES) category of 'other maintained and assisted major establishments', usually abbreviated to 'other major establishments'. They provide, principally for a local community, full-time and part-time (day and evening) educational, vocational, and recreational courses for persons over the compulsory school-leaving age and are maintained or assisted by a local education authority. The latest DES statistics available indicate that in 1979 in England and Wales there were 526 'other major establishments' with a total of 1,604,837 students.[6]

There has been no overall plan or clear directive for the provision of further education. The Education Act, 1944, for example, simply requires every local authority to provide 'adequate facilities' for further education in its area.[7] In terms of funding, further education has been the Cinderella of education by comparison with universities, teacher training colleges, and polytechnics. Partly because of this, further education has developed entrepreneurial skills which have enabled it to exploit gaps in the educational system by satisfying perceived customer demand quickly and flexibly. Thus, for example, it developed (external) degree courses from the 1920s when universities could not cope; it provided full-time courses for 15–18 year-olds in the early 1950s when secondary schools could not cope, and it trained craftsmen and technicians when industry was not interested in doing so.

Now, (late 1982) with cutbacks in higher education and the fall in school rolls, further education is still the focal point for growth and innovation. It should be noted that only a small proportion of those aged 16+ take up further education and there is, therefore, an enormous potential market to tap. Working on an annual programme and budget, and with the facility to change its short courses term by term, though within the confines of that annual budget, further education is perhaps the only area of education which can adapt quickly to changing needs. Contemporary issues include new technology, open learning, remedial education, unemployment in terms of the needs of the young unemployed and adult retraining, and education for the 'Third Age' (post retirement).

Colleges of Further Education

AIMS AND OBJECTIVES

Broadly speaking, a college of further education seeks to provide the opportunity for those who have left school to continue and extend their education, to give vocational training for those who have not yet entered employment, and to enable those in employment to further their qualifications. Most colleges also seek to provide opportunity for the general public to pursue or learn a hobby, to join with others in organized classes or societies to discover new interests, to extend or practise their skills, and enjoy a shared educational experience. The wider and more general aspects of personal development and social relationships are equally important. Overall, a college seeks to be a focal point in the life of the community and to make a positive contribution towards its enrichment.

Having established the general aims, the more specific objectives may be determined broadly as follows (with acknowledgement to Barnet College):

1 To offer the community an appropriate mix of full and part-time courses.
2 To determine and respond to the changing needs of the community, to technological change and to matters of community concern.
3 To cooperate with schools in offering an alternative educational route.
4 To cooperate with institutions of higher education to provide more access to continuing education.
5 To provide vocational education and training opportunities so that individuals are equipped to contribute to industry, commerce and the public sector.
6 To exercise positive discrimination with respect to educational training for the young unemployed, women, ethnic minorities and the disadvantaged.
7 To meet the needs of those who require re-training, remedial education and coping skills.
8 To assist in increasing and developing the interaction of recreational, cultural and educational activities in the locality.

MEETING THE OBJECTIVES

It will be clear from this list of objectives that a distinctive characteristic of further education is its wide range and level of provision.
It has links with the whole of the educational system from pre-
school to higher education. It also serves industry and commerce,
leisure, and community needs.

In the following description of ways in which colleges may
achieve these objectives, it should be borne in mind that the catego-
rization is neither comprehensive nor rigid. The response to technological change, for example, spans the whole range of objectives as
suggested above.

The percentage mix of full and part-time courses will vary from
college to college. In Barnet College, for example, part-time
students as individuals outnumber the full-time students by 8:1,
although in terms of full-time equivalent (FTE) the split is more
or less equal.

One of the main aims of further education is to widen access to
education by providing a great variety of attendance patterns and
removing the limitation of full-time attendance. The analysis of the
attendance patterns of students in 1979 in Table 1 below gives a
very clear picture of the appeal of part-time education. Note the
reversal of full-time and evening attendance between advanced
further education (AFE) and non-advanced further education
(NAFE).

Table 1: Attendance patterns in further education[6]

	AFE	NAFE	All courses
Total student numbers	135,039	1,469,798	1,604,837
Full-time*	38%	20%	22%
Part-time day†	47%	42%	42%
Evening	15%	38%	36%

* Full-time, short full-time, sandwich.
† Block release, day release, and other part-time day.

One more recent innovation is that of 'open learning'. Barnet
College was the pioneer of 'FlexiStudy', which allows students to

enrol at any time of the year, to study by correspondence material at home and at their own pace, but with access to tutorial guidance and to all the facilities of a local college, including the library.[8, 9]

The Open Tech,[10, 11] initially a four year programme and part of the government's 'New Training Initiative', is to utilize open learning in the education, training, re-training and updating of adults in technician and supervisory levels of skill.[11] Recognition is given to the need to remove barriers to improve access to education and training and also to the flexibility of open learning, which allows participants to choose when and where (at home, at work, in a library, classroom, or training centre) to learn. Technology has a central role to play in the programme in terms of computer assisted learning, methods of audio-visual communication and presentation, etc. Seven or eight 'starter' projects had been commissioned by the end of 1982, including 'one or two regional consortia of colleges and industrial firms', and 'one or two based on particular colleges from amongst a range of non-engineering subjects at technician level'. Another is the 'use of information technology-based resources'.[11] Further education is well advanced along the road of open learning, much more so than any other sector of education, and it will be seen from the above that the library has a key role to play as an open resource centre.

The changing needs of the community may be looked at in terms of the retired and the unemployed.

The over 60s account for one fifth of the population in the UK. With the growth of opportunities now for early retirement, there is greater need for education in personal fulfilment without the demands and discipline of full-time employment. Pre-retirement courses offered by local colleges therefore play a vital role in assisting with adjustment to and preparation for this phase of life. Courses such as 'Health in Retirement' cater for the special needs of the more elderly and every effort is made to integrate the retired with the community and utilize their skills and experience so that they may continue to play an active part in that community.

Unemployment too, is throwing the spotlight on the use of leisure time, enforced though it may be. A considerable percentage of the work of many further education colleges (24% of the FTE in the case of Barnet College) is concerned with Adult Education.

Categorized for this purpose as recreational courses, a wide variety of subjects from antiques to yoga is offered part-time day and evening. There is an overlap here with part-time vocational courses as, of course, these are open to any student.

Since the majority of colleges are unable to accommodate all courses on the main campus, school and community halls are used as adult centres. Students are usually able to select a centre reasonably close to their homes which is another vital factor in providing access to education.

Cooperation with schools is achieved by linked courses which enable school pupils to attend a college for one day or a half day a week to use specialist facilities, eg computers, or to provide a vocational 'taster' course. Linked courses can assist with the transition from school to college or from school to work. Increasingly, courses with vocational awareness are being offered in schools, and the further education college is able to organize specialist facilities in the form of workshops etc, and with the aid of staff experienced in teaching these courses.

Cooperation with higher education includes liaison with neighbouring polytechnics and institutes of higher education through access to specialist resources and the exchange of teaching staff as well as through UCCA. While a number of colleges do offer degree-level and professional courses, the further education college more generally provides a number of routes to continuing education in the form of courses leading to entry qualifications for higher education and the professions. Best known is the GCE 'A' level certificate, further education being able to offer subject combinations and minority options not readily available elsewhere. GCE work forms 23% of the FTE student body at Barnet College. GCE 'A' level equivalent courses include Business Education Council (BEC) and Technician Education Council (TEC) full-time Diplomas and part-time Certificates, the Foundation Course in Art and Design and the Design and Art (DATEC) Diplomas. The BEC/TEC courses are vocationally based and continuously assessed as well as externally examined and/or moderated to a nationally validated standard. They provide an educational foundation for a range of careers in industry, commerce, and the public sector, and through specialist options, eg library and information work, cater for the development of vocational skills. BEC/TEC courses have placed emphasis on student-centred learning, and the degree of student assignment work involved has made a considerable impact on the college library.

The vocational education and training aspects of further education are probably familiar to most, as the 'local tech' tends to be associated with secretarial students and apprentices. However the range is very much wider. The purpose of these courses (46% of the FTE at Barnet College) is to fit students for employment and therefore involves considerable liaison with employers in terms of work requirements, assessment of course work, off-the-job training, and job placement. One particular area of development is that of computer studies, with courses being offered in engineering, programming, and word-processing, and as joint business studies/technology ventures.

To support ethnic minorities, the majority of further education colleges run courses in English as a Foreign Language and English as a Second Language.

The area of the disadvantaged and young unemployed is one of the focal points of further education at the present time, and involves considerable liaison with external bodies. Further education colleges are concerned with adult literacy provision and with taking courses to those in the community who are physically unable to attend the college. General education courses provide the opportunity for those from special schools, for those who are physically handicapped, or for secondary school leavers to improve their basic education. Work experience is an integral part of such courses. The latest provision, where students receive payment from the Manpower Services Commission (MSC) to attend approved courses in colleges, attracts resources and funding from the MSC to supplement college funding. The Training Opportunities Scheme (TOPS) is for mature students, ie those over 19 years of age. Pre-TOPS provides basic education and work-related training for the unemployed 19+ who have failed TOPS entry tests. Youth Opportunities (YOP) courses introduce the unemployed 16–19 year-olds to the world of work, or prepare them for further training. Work Experience on Employers' Premises (WEEP), offering work placement for a limited period, involves college attendance one day a week. Literacy, numeracy, social skills, vocational guidance, and work experience are vital elements of all courses.

Colleges are currently (session 1982–3) preparing for the New Training Initiative (NTI). This ten point programme, introduced in a White Paper in December 1981,[12] includes 'a new £1 billion a year Youth Training Scheme guaranteeing from September 1983 a full year's foundation training for all those leaving school at the minimum age without jobs': the full scheme is to have some 300,000 places (this is equivalent to 20% of the numbers following NAFE courses in 1979). Pilot schemes are already underway, eg a 48-week year Work Skills course for literate/numerate unemployed 16–19 year-olds to improve employment and further training opportunities. The YTS,[13] which is to succeed YOP, is also to cover employed young people. There is also an adult re-training element of NTI. The impact of this programme on colleges of further education is likely to be enormous.

The whole area of MSC funding is causing considerable concern. Many educationists feel that government is taking over the control of education and using it to keep the unemployed off the streets, off the unemployment registers, and out of the statistics. At the same time the regular funding of education is being cut back. The MSC can withdraw support from a funded course at any time. Therefore the overall planned development of education is at risk. Many college lecturers fear that their colleges will be overrun by 16–19 year-olds and that adult education will suffer in consequence. College planners have an enormous responsibility to ensure balanced provision and the maintenance of educational standards.

Many colleges encourage the interaction of community activities by making their facilities available for recreational, cultural, and educational purposes. The college hall may also be a public hall for meetings, drama productions, concerts, art exhibitions, etc, and the college may arrange such events itself as well as offering accommodation. It will also have links with other agencies, eg university extra-mural departments, the Workers' Educational Association, Women's Institutes and Townswomen's Guilds.

THE COLLEGE COMMUNITY

Further education is non-statutory, that is, its students attend voluntarily, although some may do so under moral pressure from parents and/or employers. School leavers may choose to attend a college because they are disenchanted with school and feel that a college is a more mature environment. For others the appeal is the greater flexibility and selection of subjects offered. For yet others the selection of their choice is not offered at school. For many students, further education is a second chance, whether they are in need of basic education because they did not get on well at school, or to improve their qualifications for an academic or vocational purpose. In some cases there is no alternative route, part-time and open learning providing opportunities for those who cannot study on a full-time or even regular basis. For many others further education presents the opportunity to pursue a subject from the point of view of interest or personal development and to meet other people.

The balance of students in a college, ranging in age from 16 to 80+, and through every level of ability, provides a stimulating community in which to work. Part-time students, attending college in their own time and often at their own expense, are usually highly motivated and the mature students bring with them a wealth of experience from every walk of life. But they are demanding as individuals, particularly on central services, by comparison with full-time students. The further education population is largely a shifting one; enrolment takes place annually, even termly, for the adult programme, and full-time courses are usually only one or two years in length. A college can never be sure what each year will bring in terms of the age, ability, and academic discipline mix of its student population.

With attendance patterns on a full-time, part-time day, day-release, block release, sandwich, evening, or open learning basis, and the equally wide range of the duration of courses, a college is busy from 9 am to 9 pm, with a constant changeover of students during these times. With the exception of the 48–week year off-the-job training courses, the majority of further education colleges operate a 36-week teaching year. However, the New Training

Initiative raises the issue of the extended college year and full services will now be required for 48 weeks. This development is of particular concern to central services, including the library, if it is to be put into practice within existing resource provision, as such services often operate on a skeleton staffing during vacation periods, staff being under considerable managerial, professional, and moral pressure to restrict their leave periods to 'out of term' times of the year. Staffing calculations depend on this. The 48–week year will clearly render this impossible, and will create an immediate need for extra staffing as a result.

The majority of college lecturers are highly qualified in their own field and have had work experience in industry and commerce before entering further education. Every encouragement is now being given to the acquisition of formal teaching qualifications and to staff development generally, highlighted by the NTI, through both external and internal means. A feature of further education is the large number of part-time lecturers required to support the very wide range of courses offered. Support staff, technicians, administrative, maintenance and refectory staff, play a vital role, and they too must be attuned to and kept up to date with the college's objectives and needs. Staff development is a key issue.

THE COLLEGE LIBRARY

The reader will by now have a fair idea of the complexity of the further education institution and its community. A frequent comment from colleagues in higher education is on the nature of the integration of the further education college library with its community. This high degree of integration can only be achieved if the library is seen and developed as a focal point and an essential service to the college community and if the librarians see themselves as educators. The service and staff are a part of the institution, not separate from it. Their responsibilities do not stop at the library door. The objectives of the library should respond to those of the college and as such should be concerned with preparing students not only for higher education and employment, but also for life. In addition to the traditional role of academic support there is, therefore, emphasis on life skills with implications for a very wide range of materials provision and for user education.

In the less formal atmosphere of a further education college, the library is a very real centre of community life. The library is probably the only place where all levels meet and the librarians perhaps the only members of staff who have contact with every type of student and the opportunity for liaison with the greatest number of staff across the college. This close liaison with colleagues is particularly important in a college where the tendency towards small establishments prevents the appointment of specialist subject librarians to the degree required. On a formal basis, the librarian should be a member of the academic board, provision for which is made in DES Circular 7/70,[14] and seek representation on as many committees as possible for a real understanding of and involvement with the work and needs of the college. Faculty/departmental boards of study are a particularly valuable means of two-way communication. The library committee, under whatever title, should be a subcommittee of the academic board and have representatives from every faculty/department, from management and administration, and from the student body – that is, from every sector of the college which the library serves. Informal liaison takes place in the staff room, in the refectory, and through involvement in college activities. The further education librarian needs to be outgoing and able to communicate at all levels, to go out to the community, rather than waiting for the community to come to the library.

> User education, teaching students to use libraries, their resources and the literature of their subject to provide them with a life-long skill, is one of the professional librarian's most important duties.[15]

User education is still more highly organized, developed, and integrated with the curriculum in further education than in other sectors of education. The emphasis is placed on giving the students the confidence and ability to use any library and on finding information, rather than on using a particular library's systems. Many students in further education have little background of using libraries, and every effort has to be made towards 'user-friendliness'. The ability to communicate at many levels is very important since the librarian may have to switch directly from a remedial group to a higher diploma or degree course group of students. Liaison with teaching colleagues is vital if the user education session is to be fully integrated with the teaching programme. Many colleges now have tutor librarian posts, but equally, many do not. The advent of BEC and TEC has done much to highlight the importance of user education and it is not uncommon for these courses to include an integrated library assignment.[16]

In terms of materials provision, the college of further education library should have a living stock reflecting the work of the college, and of sufficient breadth to encourage personal development. It will range in level from remedial and elementary to advanced material. Preservation of material for the long term is relatively unimportant, and can be left to public/national collections. The college library should not attempt to duplicate public library services, eg a large collection of novels, but it should offer a representative collection. It will require access to other library collections and this will involve considerable local liaison as well as use of formal inter-library loans systems. Liaison with other local agencies, eg the careers service, and with local business and industry is also important.

Reference has been made to the use of audio-visual presentations and technology. Further education has played a leading role in multimedia use and provision. Information is information whether it comes in book, periodical, tape, slide, video, or computer assisted learning (CAL) package form and one form may put over required information more effectively than another. Barnet College has adopted the policy of the centralization of audio-visual services under the library and a lecturer in educational technology is a member of the library services team. The use of non-book materials and related equipment is highly integrated with both information searching and user education. The less academic student in particular tends to respond well to non-book presentation, although the encouragement of reading is a very important aspect of the education of such students. Microfiche, PRESTEL, and microcomputer software provision has facilitated the infiltration of a number of college departments which now make regular bookings for specialist user education sessions. The advent of the computer has caused some concern in the library profession, but the librarian has to come to terms with it since the benefits of CAL packages for students, as well as its assistance in housekeeping etc are too great to be ignored. The library has a vital role to play in open learning and other college developments which will lean heavily on non-book media.

Ensuring balanced provision for the very wide range of courses in consultation with subject lecturers and that of continuous stock revision is a time-consuming business. The librarian has to encourage the majority of teaching colleagues to become involved with the library, as well as to fight, as is the case in many colleges, for acceptance of the role of the librarian in the college.

Communication with vast numbers of part-time students and lecturers, many of whom will be off-campus, is a very real problem, as is making adequate provision for them in terms of opening hours and user education, due to the heavy demands on services during the day and by full-time students. In turn, there is conflict between the use of the library as a workshop with the ever growing project centred courses, and by the less academic/library orientated students, and those who wish to use the library for private study and research. NTI courses will increase this problem, especially if they are introduced within existing resources which for many college libraries are less than adequate in terms of accommodation, funding, and staffing.

There is often conflict for the librarian whose post is on a non-teaching grade in the relationship with teaching staff in terms of status and of the decision of whether or not to undertake formal teaching. It should be recognized that work with individual students does constitute a teaching role. The whole area of the status of the college librarian has been fully discussed elsewhere,[15, 17–20] but recognition should be given to the librarian's role *qua* head of department even if the official status is denied.

Where the library staff is small, a decision has to be taken on the difficult issue of maintaining a staffed service desk to the exclusion of vital liaison work, whether on a formal or an informal, internal or external basis. Another dilemma is whether to accept responsibility for non-book provision without additional resources, or to allow it to develop separately and elsewhere in the college.

There are no 'right' answers; each librarian must find the optimum solution for his college, his library.

External activities, that is keeping in touch with current developments in librarianship and education, are always important, but even more so where there is a small staff and limited professional contact within a college. Without such activities the librarian can become introspective, disillusioned and wallow in local problems. The service suffers in consequence.

CONCLUSION

Further education is a very demanding, but also stimulating sector in which to work. It provides great variety and never stands still. The college librarian must be able to integrate his library with the college and, no less important, integrate himself with his colleagues. He must play a very positive and active role in the provision of education for the whole spectrum of the community. It is a very extended role, from shelf-tidying to representation on the decision-making panels of the college. A futher education librarian may be a jack of all trades, but must also be a master of the whole!

ACKNOWLEDGEMENT

I am grateful to Mr E Fletcher, Principal of Barnet College, for the encouragement he gave during the writing of this chapter, and for his comment and advice at various stages in the drafting. His counsel was always wise, and the faults remaining in the paper are mine alone.

REFERENCES

1   Ministry of Education *15 to 18. A report by the Central Advisory Council for Education. (England)* (Chairman: Sir Geoffrey Crowther) Vol 1, para 464. HMSO, 1959.

2   Bristow, Adrian. *Inside the college of further education*. Second edition, HMSO, 1976.

3   Cantor, L M and Roberts, I F *Further education in England and Wales*. Second edition, Routledge and Kegan Paul, 1972.

4   Cantor, L M and Roberts, I F *Further education today: a critical review*. Routledge and Kegan Paul, 1979.

5   Waitt, I (ed) *College administration: a handbook*. National Association of Teachers in Further and Higher Education (NATFHE), 1980.

6   Department of Education and Science *Statistics of education. 1979. Volume 3. Further Education*. HMSO, 1982.

7   *Education Act*, 1944. Section 41. (Sections 41–47: Further education).

8   Barnet College of Further Education *FlexiStudy: a manual for local colleges*. (NEC College Reports Series 2 Number 4). Second edition, National Extension College, 1980.

9   Adams, M 'FlexiStudy and the college library'. *Proceedings of the conference on the part-time student: from research to action*. City of London Polytechnic, 1983.

10 Manpower Services Commission *An 'Open Tech' programme: a consultative document, May 1981*. The Commission, 1981.

11 Manpower Services Commission *Open Tech task group report, June 1982*. The Commission, 1982.

12 Department of Employment *A new training initiative: a programme for action*. Cmnd. 8455. HMSO, 1981.

13 Department of Education and Science *The youth training scheme: implications for the education service* (Circular No 6/82, 8 September 1982) DES, 1982.

14 Department of Education and Science *Government and conduct of establishments of further education* (Circular No 7/70, 14 April 1970) DES, 1970.

15 Library Association *College libraries: guidelines for professional service and resource provision*. Chapter 4: 'User Education'. Third edition, Library Association, 1982.

16 Library Association: Colleges of Further and Higher Education Group *Examples of library work for TEC and BEC courses*. (Occasional publications no 5) The Group, 1980.

17 National Association of Teachers in Further and Higher education *College libraries: policy statement*. NATFHE, 1982.

18 Library Association *Recommended salaries and conditions of service for non-university academic library staff*. The Association, 1981.

19 McElroy, A R, Swallow, K B and Harrison, C T 'Realistic (that is academic) gradings mean better libraries'. *Library Association Record*, 83 (3) March 1981. 136–139.

20 Revill, D H 'Academic librarians in colleges of further and higher education'. *Journal of Librarianship*, 13 (2) April 1981. 104–118.

8

Small Libraries: Special Problems, Special Opportunities

Hilary A Rees

Other contributors to this volume discuss particular aspects of librarianship in post-compulsory education outside the universities. This chapter will attempt to relate these to work in a small college library. The operation of such a service will be examined through its resourcing, services, and stock, with the intention of demonstrating both its opportunities and challenges. Some possible future developments will also be indicated, although these may not be applicable in every small library.

The large educational libraries are in the universities and polytechnics, but there are about 600 others in colleges of further and higher education. A significant percentage of these could be considered small. For the purposes of this paper 'small' means libraries with less than 20,000 volumes and five staff, or those with substantially less than the average resourcing for the type of college. The most recent statistics of resource levels are those compiled by Lomas (see Table 1).[1]

It is necessary to use both criteria, although there is overlap, because there are two types of small library. There are those in small establishments, which are in proportion to the parent body, and in the case of colleges offering degree courses, will have received CNAA approval. The others are in larger colleges, principally in non-advanced further education where staffing and other resources are related neither to the number of full-time equivalent (FTE) students nor to the Burnham unit total.

Table 1: Average values for types of (FE) establishment, polytechnics omitted.

	Further education	Higher education	Other colleges
Number of colleges	304	53	115
Books/FTE	20	155	57
Seats/FTE	0.07	0.31	0.13
Capitation	8.26	49.10	21.28
FTE/Member of library staff	422.2	90.8	223.6

When the library's size is properly related to the number of its users, it is able to offer a good service. There are no nationally agreed standards, however, and this produces the second type of library which is unable to offer a comparable service. There can be marked discrepancies between libraries even in the same authority. In Glasgow, two adjacent colleges had, in 1980, book funds of £0.85p and £12 per FTE student respectively. There are other examples throughout the country. The situation will not alter until there is a consensus of opinion within further education on the role of its information services.

RESOURCES

In the present circumstances, the library's standing within the college closely affects its resourcing. It depends to a great extent on the position of the librarian in the college management structure. If the college does more than 20% advanced work, the librarian is a member of the statutory Academic Board, although the influence of this body varies greatly.[2]

In a college with less than 20% advanced work, and this includes many in FE, the standing of the librarian is less certain especially if the service is small. The college may not have an Academic Board, or the librarian may not be an ex-officio member. While information on the meetings can be obtained without attendance, it provides a useful forum in which the library's work can be related to that of the college and its development.

The Academic Board, or its equivalent, is not the executive arm of the college; this is made up of the Principal, Vice-Principal(s), Heads of Department and other senior managers. The Library Association recommends that the College Librarian be a head of department so that the resources and services develop in relation to its users.[3] In further education this pattern only obtains in 13 colleges, according to a 1980 survey.[4] In at least one instance, however, a librarian has been given the status without the pay or (Burnham) conditions, and this may be a way forward in some institutions.

The librarian's position determines his knowledge of the total college resources and his ability to influence their distribution. In the second edition of *College Libraries* it was recommended that 2–3% of the total college budget (excluding salaries) be allocated to the library.[5] Small libraries did not achieve this even in the halcyon days of the early seventies. In the third (current) edition[6] there are more moderate per capita calculations. These are still much higher than the averages given in Table 1.

The library's productivity is not measured in Burnham units. Where its status within the institution is uncertain, it may be particularly susceptible to cuts during financial retrenchment. Yet this is a time for radically rethinking library resourcing. B/TEC courses emphasize student centred learning and other courses are following the same path. This is in part to reduce unit costs and in part to increase the student's involvement in his own learning.

Any college library, regardless of size, may be involved in a wide range of learning methods. In distance learning courses, the library may be a student's only contact with the college apart from the course tutor. There are vocational preparation units for the learning disabled. The Youth Training Scheme part of the New Training Initiative announced by the UK government in December 1981 has begun. There was a pilot study for 100,000 youngsters in schools, skills centres, and colleges before the full scheme for 460,000 persons began in 1983. These courses include a strong element of life and social skills, subjects which have traditionally made heavy use of the library.

Financing the library can no longer be limited to an annual materials budget and a commitment to pay staff salaries. There are accommodation costs, either to expand or adapt to the new demands and to the new information resources. Audio-visual equipment may require modifications to existing facilities. New technology will require small libraries, like the large, to invest in expensive hardware, and this will need capital allocations.

Two aspects of local authority funding may cast particular burdens on the small library. Annual budgeting prevents the cost of expensive items being spread over several financial years. Capital allocations for purchasing materials must be spent within the year. This is common to all sizes of library, however, and leads to poor stock development. In subjects that are rapidly developing, this can lead to a stock which is rapidly out of date; examples are catering operations and all aspects of computing.

Distribution of the resources allocated to the library service is varied. The librarian may not have control of the funds. They can be divided between the departments with the librarian's responsibility confined to the periodicals, reference collection, and general interests. If the librarian does control the budget, and his status is uncertain, the monies must be seen to be allocated equitably. It is possible to use a formula which demonstrates that allocations are made on objective criteria. Such formulae are based on evidence of past need or size and cannot take account of all the variables. They may be used safely only in conjunction with a substantial general fund. Cowley suggests using annual estimates to explain library needs[7] and this may be helpful where the librarian is not on the executive.

STAFFING

The library's most important resource is its staff. To quote the Library Association's *Guidelines*: 'stock is a passive resource which needs good staff to enliven and exploit it'.[6]

As with other resources, there is no single level of provision common to small libraries. In some degree-level courses the influence of outside professional bodies will have set a particular standard. Many small libraries have less than the absolute minimum staff, four, proposed by the *Guidelines*, and the staff to student ratios suggested by both the Library Association and NATFHE have not been adopted by the authorities. In purely practical terms a rapid increase in staffing requires work space that many libraries, not just small ones, would be unable to provide.

Gradings of staff are also diverse. In the 1980 survey the Library Association found that 48% of librarians were on Burnham grades, the rest on local government scales. Since then Cheshire has converted academic posts to NJC. The case for Burnham gradings has been well argued by McElroy, Swallow and Harrison on the grounds of the librarian's academic functions.[8] Additionally, parity of grading with teaching staff, and a related staff:student ratio would allow library staffing to be adjusted as educational methods alter. Without this, colleges lack the flexibility to transfer resources between the different modes of learning.

Each member of staff has the opportunity to be involved in a wide range of duties and share in most aspects of the work. There cannot be a strict division of professional and non-professional duties. The features of work in a site library away from the main library of a polytechnic, described by Professor Ashworth, apply equally to a small college library:[9]

> . . . variety of duties remains characteristic of split-site librarianship. This can often be to the advantage of each individual member of staff in giving wider experience and freedom from becoming type-cast, and generally reducing the tendency to feel just a single cog in a large machine.

This may produce greater job satisfaction than the narrower band of responsibilities each staff member has in a larger system. It can also lead to inaccuracies and incompleted tasks, as Ashworth also noted:[9]

> . . . senior staff . . . tended to have more informal contact with teaching staff and students (for the exchange of information and

teaching library usage) than is usual in most university libraries. Consequently they are often interrupted for varying amounts of time in the course of more routine tasks. Though these are constructive interruptions in their contribution to the effectiveness of the institution they are destructive in relation to the performance of necessary routines.

In a small library this phenomenon is not confined to senior staff.

The work provides a good training ground for new professionals who gain knowledge of the context in which an educational library operates and avoid early specialization which might restrict their later careers. However, promotion generally involves a move to another institution because a small team offers very limited career opportunities. If there is no senior professional post, there will be more frequent transfers out of the college and the library will lack a coherent development plan.

For professional staff the small library offers the full range of duties and frequent contact, both formal and informal, with users. The close involvement in the college is balanced by professional isolation. Even the self-starter needs the fresh ideas and new perspectives which can be gained at meetings and conferences.

Through contact with his fellows the librarian keeps abreast of developments and thinking in other areas of the profession. Common problems and solutions can be discussed. Ideas begun in larger institutions can be adapted to the needs of smaller units. For example, at the end of an article by Pemberton and Clifton on the on-line ordering system installed in Buckingham College library, mention was made of a modified version being developed for smaller libraries.[10] This is an illustration, too, of the value of the oft-scorned professional press.

Some colleges are reluctant to send staff to courses outside the immediate locality, and staff may have to pay their own expenses until they can convince their superiors of the value of such gatherings. Outside the metropolitan areas, attendance may be hampered by the amount of travelling involved, and, for members of a small team, term-time meetings are very difficult, especially in the autumn term, when all are involved in inducting and instructing new users.

Non-professional staff gain satisfaction from working in a small unit because of the variety of work and the opportunities to undertake more responsibility than is normally offered in a large system. Management is inevitably participative, so library assistants and technicians are actively involved in decision making. The organizational structures are simple and the lines of communication rapid. Daily decisions can be made quickly and the chief librarian is easily accessible.

SERVICES AND USERS

The ways in which the library meets the information needs of the institution vary as much as the colleges themselves. They respond nevertheless with a selection from a common range of services. All aim to serve the students, lecturers, senior management, and administration. In a small college this may be a very closely tailored service. The smallness of the user group and the good communication and close relationship this normally engenders means the library is quickly aware of changes. Its provision can then be adapted to the new needs with the minimum of delay. The facility to do this diminishes as the institution grows, when alterations may be confined to the requirements of those users of whom the library is most aware. This biases the service in favour of those who are library-orientated, and, in a multi-site institution, those to whom the library is most accessible.

The users are divided into the four groups cited above. By far the largest of these is the students. Most small college libraries cater primarily for the 16–21 year-olds. In FE as much as 75% of the student population is in the 16–19 age band. Some 24% of this group are in non-advanced FE[11] and the new MSC courses could double this. There is a wide ability range, especially in the general technical college, which may have postgraduates on vocational courses, and ESN students on courses created by the Warnock report,[12] as well as all those in between.

As research has highlighted, adolescents prefer, as a rule, group activities to solitary pursuits like reading.[13] A small survey by Clench showed that FE students voluntarily read an average of 1.35 books per month, although they read more magazines.[14] Most have received little or no instruction at school in library use or information recovery and evaluation. Experiments like that at the Harry Carlton Comprehensive School, East Leake, Nottinghamshire, where the first three years are taught on a series of themes researched in the school library are few.[15] For this reason, colleges have a long tradition of library instruction[16] and Brake sees people who do not go into post-compulsory education to be seriously socially disadvantaged, because of their inability to use information properly in their decision making.[17]

The remainder of the student population may be any age. They may be updating or increasing their qualifications, retraining to re-enter the job market, or a new area of it. They may be following a course for personal interest, or as part of their continuing education. The size of the college, again, will not affect the range of users and learning methods with which its library must cope.

Any college library is involved directly or indirectly in many different learning modes, including lectures, tutorials, directed and independent private study, whether in the library, the college, or outside. The services offered will depend upon the resources. The *Guidelines* point out that minimum staffing will provide only minimum service,[6] and, unfortunately this must sometimes be the case. In these instances it is often the part-time students who suffer because their opportunity for access to facilities is more restricted than that of full-timers.

The very size of the unit can provide a service because it appears cosy and intimate. To a reluctant or inexperienced user, this can be more attractive than the impersonality of a larger library. The person who instructs new students in library use is seen behind the counter. Staff can offer assistance informally when research or retrieval problems are spotted. The subject specialist role in a larger system, designed, at least in part, to meet the need of users to identify with individual members of the library staff, effectively emulates the small library's persona.

The amount of user education will depend on the staffing and policies of the individual college. The librarian often has opportunity to take the initiative. A comprehensive programme may be offered at key points in a syllabus. It could be confined to an introductory talk, possibly reinforced by retrieval exercises, with a subsequent talk at the start of project work. There are numerous permutations of this. Some personal contact is essential but slide-tape presentations have been used since 1960. This is still the preferred audio-visual aid although a number of libraries have experimented with video, with varying degrees of success.

The student centred learning in B/TEC syllabi has been used to increase the library's involvement in the academic work of the college. At St Austell, for example, the librarian teaches on the 'People and Communications' module of the BEC General course and on TEC courses. At Barrow-in-Furness the tutor-librarian uses BEC sessions on filing to explain the library's files and to demonstrate library use in a way directly relevant to these students. Such involvement is not always practicable but library-based course work needs to be planned jointly by the librarians and lecturers if it is to make best use of the resources.

USER ASSISTANCE

Whatever the scale of the librarian's involvement with formal instruction, he will assist readers in their information searches. In a small college he can develop expertise over a range of courses, particularly in a specialist college, eg art or agriculture. This brings a very real sense of involvement in the work of the students. If it is not possible to have, as the *Guidelines* recommend, a professional librarian always on duty, alternatives may be sought. At Highbury for example, two tutor-librarians are at an information desk over lunch-time, normally the busiest period, to offer guidance on using the resources.

In-depth comprehensive subject knowledge cannot be offered by a small staff in a general technical college, though each member of the team may specialize. One possible division could be for professional staff to concentrate on course-related subjects, because of their liaison work with lecturers, and non-professionals on the general interest areas. Breadth of knowledge is substituted for the depth provided where staffing permits subject specialization. Gauging the type, and level of information sought has to be on an *ad hoc* basis, because, as Hutchin points out, the information needs of courses below degree level have been largely ignored as they have not been so clearly defined.[18] This is a field in which there is scope for individual enterprise.

No library, however small, can afford to neglect indirect assistance to users through guiding and leaflets. Where there are few staff, signposts, colour coding, and displays at point of use can help create independent learners and concentrate staff time on more complex enquiries.

Leaflets are a concise but under-used means of giving information according to Thorpe.[19] In the college library there must also be some question of how much they will be read! There is a greater chance of their proving useful if they are directed at particular courses of study. General guides to different aspects of the library itself may be less successful.

The Library Instruction Materials Bank (LIMB) based at Loughborough University could be used and developed by smaller libraries. It holds examples of existing library publications which it willingly distributes to enquirers to consider before drafting their own. Much of the present material has been deposited by universities and polytechnics, and contributions from other colleges are sought.

The other three user groups, teachers, management, and administration, can be offered individualized service because they are much smaller. In a well resourced small college this can be as specific as that offered by special libraries in industrial and commercial concerns. The informal relationships within such colleges give the library staff awareness of the particular interests and needs of each person whether in management, administration, or teaching.

To assist the management and operation of the college the library can provide a current awareness service of published materials relevant to its planning and organization. This may be an in-house system, especially if the staffing permits a member of the library staff to scan appropriate journals and newspapers. Without this, the library may use published services like the *Hertis Information Review*. One library subscribing to the press release service of the Central Office of Information can select and deliver copies of government press releases and associated documents within 48 hours of publication, often before senior management is aware of them.

The library's involvement in the academic work of the college is multi-faceted. Teaching and the cooperative preparation of learning materials have already been mentioned. Some librarians are part of the course planning teams, proposing materials, costings, and the extent of the library's involvement in a particular course. If the college offers a wide range of courses, the librarian's involvement will be restricted by the limited time available for this among other duties.

The interchange of information between teaching and library staff will allow the library's stock to be closely tailored to the requirements of current courses. As with the current awareness service to management it is possible to anticipate lecturers' needs when their courses and syllabi are known. This is unlikely to be a formal system but casual mention that a particular item or piece of information has arrived that may be of interest. Local reorganization of the materials in an order helpful to the students can be more readily undertaken where the stock is small and the users' needs well known or easily ascertained.

At Plymouth, a Group 9 college, such service cannot be offered to all, but certain courses do receive, because of the cooperation between the library and lecturing staff, a very specific information service. In the School of Chiropody, an initial careful analysis of the subject interests listed in *Index Medicus* together with a judicious selection by a member of the library staff has created a comprehensive collection of relevant journal articles. Another example of the effects of this liaison with college staff comes from Mid-Cornwall Technical College, and has resulted in a more efficient service to users and greater stock use. Two computer lecturers in conjunction with the librarian designed an automated circulation system suitable for small libraries and budgets. Currently they are developing a cataloguing programme which should aid information retrieval.

These information services operate most effectively in a small college where they are fostered by its intimacy and informal communications. Some measure of them may be offered, nevertheless, in large institutions. Many lecturers in further education remain unaware of the role the library can play. By taking an interest in the teaching and giving unsolicited assistance the librarian can create demand, although if he is under-resourced, it can only be met on a restricted basis.

STOCK

A small college library needs to offer a wide range of information in as many formats as possible. It should differ from larger institutions in scale, not standard of provision. Whether it is involved in audio-visual production will depend on the individual college, but all libraries should aim to develop multimedia collections.

As small libraries are frequently short of space, perhaps the best acquisitions policy is one based on the Atkinson concept of 'a self-renewing library of limited growth'. Maurice Line has pointed out that it is not the size of stock but its usefulness to the readers which is important.[20]

> Size has been one of the few measures that can be easily calculated, and unfortunately it has been seen as a measure of value; clearly a far better measure would be the level of satisfaction of potential demands on the library.

He also argues for a policy which recognizes the existence of comprehensive national collections which can be used by inter-library loan.

Increasingly, selection for the small library will also take account of other local resources. Although reduced funding may have caused this, a selective stock can be beneficial to users. Many are inexperienced, and unassisted, may select out-of-date or unhelpful material in the right subject field. A small, carefully selected stock is of more value than a large, less relevant one.

While recognizing that the majority of stock will be course-related, most small libraries, particularly in FE, also carry general interest stock. Although this may appear old-fashioned, harking back to the time when the library was an adjunct to liberal studies in aiding students' cultural development, it is still important. If the post-industrial era brings high unemployment or greater leisure for all, then individuals will need independent interests. Ruffell and Davies note the lack of public library provision for teenagers, so the colleges are often their only library resource.[21, 22]

The inter-library lending networks are surprisingly under-used by many small colleges. Although they should not be used as a substitute for adequate resources, they do allow library funds to be concentrated on material in frequent demand. Use will not be entirely one way. Small colleges, specialist or general, have stock of interest to other libraries.

AUDIO-VISUAL MATERIAL AND NEW TECHNOLOGY

Audio-visual materials are integrated into most college libraries but are a time-consuming way of transmitting information from the librarian's point of view. Viewing and listening equipment must be selected and maintained, and users taught how to operate it. Software must be kept up to date and in good repair. Smaller libraries will not necessarily have technician support to maintain a large collection, but can offer a selection.

PRESTEL and online services are not yet common in smaller libraries, but must become so if their students are not to be disadvantaged in the market place where most will be expected to be familiar with VDUs and microforms, if not with the full range of computer applications. PRESTEL can be used for a wide range of courses in providing information, and also, according to Leary, as an aid to literacy.[23] There are geographically imposed cost restrictions outside the metropolitan areas. Here the small system may well benefit from not being in the vanguard of change. If as planned, DIALOG and BLAISE are put on PRESTEL, the small library can acquire all the services in one package.

The installation of computers for independent learning need not be confined to large systems. The idea was tried at the social sciences site library in North-East London Polytechnic and was used for seven hours each day. Interest in using them extends beyond specific courses and in non-advanced FE they are often more acceptable to students than books. This can attract users into the library who will subsequently move on to printed materials.

STOCK EXPLOITATION

With a small stock the staff will have a thorough knowledge of the holdings which will assist them in directing users to the information they seek.

Full bibliographical cataloguing is not always needed, as the Anglo-American Cataloguing Rules recognized in the 2nd edition with their three levels of description. Finding lists like those used on automated systems can also be used for manual systems with the same efficacy, according to the recent findings of Seal, Bryant, and Hall.[24] While it is not possible to reduce the subject approach to the same extent, smaller libraries can consider less than full classification. Great specificity is not necessary in the smaller collection and where it involves 15 digit numbers can discourage users. If, in the future, the stock grows dramatically, it is then possible to classify more closely by adding the 'missing' numbers. It may be a large task, but no different from a larger system converting to a new edition of Dewey.

In a small library, those who process materials are also those who assist users to find them. This gives the staff an opportunity to judge the helpfulness of the classification and retrieval approaches at first hand. Reviews and modifications can then be undertaken more rapidly. In large systems, subject specialists are used who select, process, and exploit particular fields to achieve the same effect.

Automation of cataloguing as well as circulation may also improve stock use. The microprocessor has put computerized housekeeping within the financial grasp of many small college libraries. It is of particular value here, not least because of the frequent interruptions to routine duties mentioned above. It also allows staff to concentrate on services which require the personal approach, creativity and flexibility. The amount of current work in this field is shown by Burton's directory of microcomputing applications.[25]

CONCLUSION

An active team can integrate the library fully into the work of a small college. This can produce developments which will benefit not only the immediate users but also the profession as a whole. In other establishments where there is a discrepancy between the size of the library and its parent body such a high level of service is not possible. Small units can demonstrate the role the library service could play if adequately resourced. There may for either type be problems of resourcing, role definition, and staffing, a situation which is unlikely to change until the functions of college libraries have been determined and the necessary levels of provision to support these have been endorsed by both national and local authorities.

REFERENCES

1   Lomas, T 'College library statistics'. *Library Association, Colleges of Further and Higher Education Group Bulletin* 34, Summer 1982. 3–4.
2   Department of Education and Science *Government and conduct of establishments of further education.* (Circular 7/70) The Department, 1970.
3   Library Association *Recommended salaries and conditions of service for non-university academic library staff.* Library Association, 1980.
4   Library Association *Census of staff establishment and staffing in libraries in universities, higher and further academic institutions 1977–78.* Library Association, 1980.
5   Library Association *College libraries.* Second edition, Library Association, 1971.
6   Library Association *College libraries: guidelines for professional service and resource provision.* Third edition, Library Association, 1982.
7   Cowley, J 'Government and finance' in Jefferson, G and Smith-Burnett G C K (eds) *The college library.* Bingley, 1978. 60–78.
8   McElroy, A R Swallow, K B and Harrison, C T 'Realistic (that is, academic) gradings mean better libraries'. *Library Association Record* 83 (3) March 1981. 136–139.
9   Ashworth, W *Organizing multi-site libraries* (Occasional publication 1). Library Association, Colleges of Technology and Further Education Section, 1976.

10 Pemberton, J E and Clifton, B J 'Online book ordering in the college library'. *Library Association Record* 83 (1) January 1981. 15.
11 Department of Education and Science Education for 16–19 year olds: a review undertaken for the government and the Local Authority Association. The Department, 1981.
12 Committee of Enquiry into the Education of Handicapped Children and Young people *Special educational needs.* Cmnd. 7212. HMSO, 1978.
13 Heather, P *Young people's reading.* (CRUS occasional paper No 6). Centre for Research on User Studies, 1981.
14 Clench, J D 'The voluntary reading of FE students'. *The use of English* Autumn 1981. p 57–62.
15 Armstrong, A D *Resource-based learning.* Paper given at the Conference on Libraries in education held at Dartington, 4–5 January 1982.
16 Smith-Burnett, C 'The development of the college library'. in Jefferson G and Smith-Burnett C (eds) *The college library.* Bingley, 1978. 17–59.
17 Brake, T *The need to know: teaching the importance of information.* (BLR & DD Report 5511) British Library, 1982.
18 Hutchin, B D 'Libraries in colleges of higher education', *Library Association Record,* 82 (12) December 1980. 592–593.
19 Thorpe, S 'Leaflets for information'. *Library Association Record,* 83 (9) September 1981. 434–435.
20 Line, M 'Local acquisition policies in a national concept.' in *The art of the librarian.* Oriel Press, 1973.
21 Ruffell, A 'Where do all the teenagers go?' *Library Association Record* 84 (2) February 1982. 59.
22 Davies, G 'What some suspended pupils think of public libraries'. *Library Association Record,* 83 (5) May 1981. 238.
23 Leary, G 'Vast prospects for Prestel'. *Library Association Record,* 83 (9) September 1981. 417.
24 Seal, A, Bryant, P and Hall, C *Full and short entry catalogues.* (BLR & DD report 5669) Bath University Library, 1982.
25 Burton, P *Microcomputer applications in libraries and information retrieval: a directory of users.* Leith Nautical College, 1981.

9

Colleges and Institutes of Higher Education

Colin T Harrison

The Colleges and Institutes of Higher Education were created following the James Report of 1972.[1] This report was concerned with teacher education and training and made several far-reaching recommendations. Its theme was elaborated in a Department of Education and Science (DES) publication *Education: a framework for expansion*, also published in 1972.[2] In fact, the 'expansion' of the title turned into a reduction in the number of establishments offering teacher education and a reduction in the numbers entering the profession.

In March 1973, DES Circular 7/73[3] gave effect to the proposals for reorganization advocated in the earlier documents. Broadly, the proposals were to enable teachers to be educated in colleges offering a wider range of subjects than is normally found in a teacher training college. To achieve this, a number of teacher training colleges were closed completely, others were merged with universities and polytechnics; some were merged with other teaching training colleges but with a wider curriculum, and a final group were merged with colleges of technology. The colleges and institutes of higher education stem from these final two groupings.

The size and pattern of the new institutions differed widely. Some were liberal arts colleges offering a modular degree structure broadly based in the humanities, others offered a wider curriculum, developing principally the science subjects, whilst a third, smaller group had a range of subjects more akin to the mixture found in polytechnics. The first of the colleges began operating in their new form around 1976 and currently some 60 colleges remain in the group.

This new 'third force' in higher education had, at least theoretically, a golden opportunity to create a new type of institution, since they had the experience and tradition of longer established colleges, but also the freedom to devise new and exciting structures. In the event, nothing radically new developed; some opted for a structure of small schools of study, others for a departmental structure, yet others went for a faculty structure. In the early days, the overriding concern was the realignment of positions and the creating of a stable management structure to meld together the different ethoses and methods of operation of these separate colleges.

This was an exciting time in academic librarianship for few parts of the new institutions had systems that were easily compatible. This was often particularly true in the college library. Different forms of catalogue, cataloguing styles, classification schemes or editions of the same classification scheme, purchasing policies, ordering arrangements, attitudes to the role of the library within the college, all needed a great deal of careful attention to produce a workable integrated system in a relatively short space of time.

A snapshot of the institutions has been produced by Lomas of Barrow College.[4] They show (Table 1) the following outline of the *average* institute in terms of its library:

Overlaid on this mechanistic level of librarianship was a heated debate about the academic role of the professional librarian and his library in the new institution. Most librarians started from a firm position with their academic colleagues, since the instruments and articles of government approved by the DES placed them as ex-officio members of their academic board. This enabled them to be in on the ground floor of the debate about the shape and form of the new college and to establish a place within that for their developing services. It is to the credit of most of the librarians that they took this once-and-for-all opportunity to project their libraries as facing out into the institution and sought a much more dynamic role *vis-à-vis* the teaching departments than perhaps is common in some academic libraries.

Table 1: Average library statistics in the IHE sector

Number of degrees	5
FTE students	856
Total funding	£85,494
Capitation/FTE	£49.12
Book Fund	£25,404
Number of books	87,580
% capitation spent on books	67.5
Books/FTE	156
Books/library staff member	11,038
Number of journal titles	487
% capitation spent on journals	18.4
Number of staff served FT/PT	182
Number of staff:library staff	19.3
FTE students:library staff	90.8
Total area	1,052.4 m²
Number of study places	189.6
Study places:FTE	0.31
Area:FTE	1.58 m²

The first task was to establish the library firmly within the academic structure of the institute. In some colleges previous tradition made this a relatively easy task, while in others it was regarded with some suspicion, and a great deal of work was required to convince colleagues that the library should be afforded this recognition.

The arguments put forward by most of the librarians related to two areas of their work. Firstly, there was the straightforward teaching function of the library, exemplified through traditional class contact methods. Librarians could, in most cases, demonstrate that they and their more senior professional colleagues spent some proportion of their time teaching, in a classroom, the use of libraries and information relating to the subjects being studied within their colleges. The second string to the argument was the important role that the librarian could play within the course development and course monitoring activities of the college. To the committed librarian, it was obvious that this was an integral part of the job, since without it they could not provide adequate and informed support to the students in the college. To sell this to the academic board and the subject boards was a difficult task in some colleges. In a few colleges, the debate continues to this day, and librarians are not fully involved in this essential part of the academic life of the college. However in the great majority of colleges, the chief librarian and his professional staff are increasingly being drawn into the development of new courses and the modification of existing courses.

The information gained through participation in this work is of crucial importance in forward planning, enabling the library to fit its provision and staff expertise more closely to the real needs of the college. It also enables the librarian to suggest teaching strategies to course members that will enable them to produce the best package for their students. Recent developments in technician education and business education have brought home to many lecturers the fact that they can no longer teach students solidly in classrooms throughout the day. The techniques of seminars, tutorials, projects, etc are now a normal part of most courses in higher education. This change has of itself reinforced the librarian's original plea to be involved in the design and administration of courses whose students will spend a significant part of their learning lives in the library.

Inevitably, this emphasis on the academic role of the librarian has spilled over into the debate as to whether librarians should be classed as academic staff. It is beyond the brief of this chapter to explore this issue, but the debate continues and at some point will require resolution.

Regardless of their 'official' grading, all librarians within the colleges and institutes of higher education saw themselves as teachers and educators in the broadest sense. The education that they provide may be formal, as mentioned above, or informal in the sense that readers' enquiry work within their libraries is clearly educative. Perhaps in this respect, if in no other, the work of the academic librarian is different from that of his colleagues in other sectors of the profession. The academic librarian clearly sees his role as an educative one and even for the most straightforward enquiry will take pains to show the student the *structure* of the information that he is seeking and the most effective way of discovering a pathway through that information to the specific fact or idea required. In this way, together with formal lectures, the academic librarian adds to the education of the student, so that a qualification, once gained, can be continually updated throughout the working life of the individual. Government and educators talk glibly about education for life. The librarian gives reality to this concept.

Overlaid upon the librarian's academic role, *vis-à-vis* his library and the user, is the contribution that the librarian can and should make to the general academic management of the institution. Through membership of the academic board and other senior committees, the librarian is in a position to influence the general direction and style of the institution. In most colleges he has not shrunk from this task. It is an interesting irony that in many colleges it is quite acceptable for colleagues in one subject discipline to comment on the worth and techniques of another, when, if the librarian offered similar comment, he would be reminded that his brief was to talk about library matters. This mould has been broken in many colleges, and it is the responsibility of all librarians to take full part in the life and management of their colleges. No longer can they afford to sit on the touch-lines and watch the game progress, they must be full members of the team, participate in *all* the difficult decisions that have to be made in education, not just those normally and obviously related to the library. Nor may they opt out, and then carp about the results of decisions made by others, having defaulted themselves.

Just as the institution as a whole was reviewing its structures, so the merging libraries reviewed theirs. It is not possible to give a single answer to the question of how the libraries are organized. There are so many variations on the theme that one would suggest that there are as many solutions as there are colleges in the sector. There are, however, some points of commonality. Most of the colleges appear to have chosen a structure which, at least in part, involves the appointment of what are called subject librarians. In an ideal world these would have been people with first degrees in the subject of their specialism together with a postgraduate library qualification. The reality of the situation is that the new librarians had to manipulate existing staff, and in most colleges staff found themselves undertaking new roles with a minimum of training or subject qualification. At least the effort has been made, and in many colleges made successfully, and the principle of the subject librarian has now been accepted by the colleges. As posts become vacant it is increasingly easier to recruit staff with the most appropriate qualifications for particular posts. Inevitably, given the overall staffing levels of the libraries, any specialization is necessarily broad. This has not of itself been a great deterrent to becoming involved in the academic work of the subjects covered.

The subject librarians should be members of appropriate boards of study, faculty boards, and course development teams, etc. In this way they are able to create outward facing links between the library, the teachers and the students. Some of their time will be spent in classrooms working with students, the rest will be devoted to working within the library, mainly with the students of their discipline. This concept of taking the library out to the student is an important aspect of librarianship for the colleges and institutes of higher education, who regard their libraries as integral parts of the learning environment.

The other principal function of the subject librarian is the selection and, in many cases, cataloguing and classification of materials to support the courses. This selection process is undertaken in close cooperation with other teaching staff and with students. It is interesting to observe the occasional imbalance between the material recommended by teachers and that requested by students. The difference in level is often quite significant, and it is often the students who request the more 'advanced' material. It is only by close cooperation with both groups of users that the subject librarian can develop a balanced and exploitable stock of materials.

As the subject librarians necessarily spend part of their lives outside the library on this specialist work, it is essential to maintain a level of staffing within the library to handle the day-to-day administration, processing, request services, and all the other support services that the students have a right to expect. The procedures for doing this vary tremendously, from the employment of a dedicated staff whose sole function is to provide in-library service, to the use of subject librarians on a rotated timetable basis within the library.

The other dimension to library organization relates to the multi-site operation common to many of the colleges in this sector. It is not uncommon for similar or related subjects to be taught on several sites of the college. In some cases it is practicable to give the librarian a roving commission across all sites within his subject, in others it is more cost-effective to have teams of subject librarians operating from individual sites.

The acquisition, distribution, and control of the library budget occupies a significant portion of the time of most of the chief librarians in the institutes of higher education. Most of them look for the provision of funds on the basis of the number of full-time student equivalents (FTE) within their institutions. In recent years (ie since late 1980), the 'going rate' per FTE has been about £50 per annum (1980 prices). In addition to this, librarians have sought special funds for the replacement of equipment, extension or redevelopment of buildings, and the development of brand new courses for which no existing course has been withdrawn to release funds. In reality, in most colleges financial pressures have reduced the creation of genuine estimates to the level of 'what you had last year plus or minus an agreed percentage'. Nevertheless, in a number of institutions, the librarian has been able to make a case for an overall increase in the library budget by arguing the central role of the library as a learning tool and demonstrating the cost-effectiveness of using the library in this way. It is important that the librarian demonstrates to the institution that there is a 'pay off' in terms of better support for the learning process when real additional monies are voted for the library budget.

The internal redistribution of library funds is a complex business in which highly structured mechanisms have often been evolved to ensure fair support to individual courses, departments or faculties. Factors that have been taken into account include the number of students, the proportion of part-time to full-time students, the average cost of library materials in specific subject areas, the essential 'bookishness' (or otherwise) of the subject, and the teaching methods employed within particular courses. It is possible to build all of these factors into a formula that will aid the librarian in the distribution of funds. It is important to recognize, however, that the existence and use of formulae will never remove from the librarian the need to exercise professional judgment based upon how the library is currently used and how he perceives the institute wanting the library to be used over the next several years. It follows that the results of any formula calculations need to be modified in the light of this judgment.

Once allocated, the librarian and his professional colleagues need not only to encourage the appropriate spending of the money but also to monitor the rate of expenditure closely to ensure that it lasts the whole of the financial year and that it does not run out towards September each year. Accelerator and brake can be applied via the librarians' work with faculty boards and subject boards, providing yet another impetus to the need for the librarian to be involved with the work of these bodies.

With the complexity of the modern academic library and the present somewhat moderate level of funding 'enjoyed' by the libraries within this group, the coordination of the purchase of library materials is vitally important. Selection procedures, while being originated by subject librarians, need to be collated and copy numbers moderated by someone in a central position. Often, this is done by the chief librarian or his depute. Occasionally, it is done through a central unit which coordinates the general ordering of library materials, together with the processing and distribution of the said materials.

The advent of the computer, microform reader/printers, photocopying machines, word processors, etc have all offered opportunities to libraries to extend and develop the range of services they have offered to their readers. Most of the libraries now offer online information retrieval services through such hosts as DIALOG, LEXIS, TEXTLINE. While at first sight the use of these services may appear to be expensive, it is usually found to be cheaper to do an electronic search than a manual search if one calculates and compares staff time, salaries and the purchase of the hardcopy materials with which to undertake the search. Since the bulk of these systems only require payment after use, the library can be a member of a large number of 'clubs' and have potential access to virtually all of the world's leading abstracting and indexing services, supported by online computer manipulation, without having to provide a large quantity of money in advance of use. Therefore the rate of expenditure on these services can be controlled by the librarian rather than having the lack of access to high quality information sources hinder the librarian, the teacher, and the student in the performance of their work.

The increasing cheapness of stand-alone microcomputers with tape or disk drives has offered the opportunity to quite small libraries of computerizing some part of their issue control system, ordering system, periodicals system, etc. Many have taken this opportunity. Some have been able to convince their colleges that membership of one of the larger cataloguing cooperatives, BLCMP, SWALCAP, OCLC, etc is cost-effective and so have been able to produce a very real breakthrough in this heavily manpower-based part of library activity.

This technological development has been proceeding in these colleges for several years. During 1982, designated by the British Government 'Information Technology Year' it became commonplace to look at all of the systems mentioned above, under the collective title of 'Information Technology'. Many colleges became excited, and for the first time began to recognize the importance of information in both print and electronic form as a selling point in their courses. This recognition was of considerable use to librarians since they were, in many cases, able to demonstrate that their own forward planning was in line with the institute's.

Being up-to-date with academic methods, with modern teaching strategies, with technological developments, and with current practice in librarianship demanded that librarians in this group looked seriously at the development of their staff. The aim was obviously to isolate within the budget a sum of money to allow a proper programme of staff development. Some were able to draw upon the institute's central staff development budget. The importance of this activity cannot be overemphasized, since the up-to-dateness of the knowledge of the librarians, and their level of motivation, both in terms of their own profession and the literature of the subjects taught in their institution, greatly affects the credibility and quality of the service that they are providing. In many cases, use has been made of courses leading to higher degrees provided within their own institution or at polytechnics or universities; some have used the Further Education Staff College, Coombe Lodge, while others have used short courses run by the Library Association, Aslib, and other organizations.

In a few instances, there has been genuine cooperation between colleges and the public library sector in mounting joint courses for in-service staff training. Nationally, this area of staff development is weak, yet, theoretically at least, offers great potential for the updating of professional skills in cooperation with larger units. Perhaps to some extent this relatively low level of activity is understandable given the frequently poor levels of staffing in the colleges and the extensive opening hours that they provide. It is often easier to send one person away on a one or two day course than to release a group of staff to attend a locally organized in-service programme.

The theme of staff development is one that the Council for National Academic Awards (CNAA) often takes up with an institution when making validation visits. The impact of the CNAA on the development of the colleges in this group is most significant. Many of them originally validated their degree courses through links with universities. In the last few years that validation has been placed with CNAA whose rigorous inspection of syllabus, teachers, and facilities has led to an improvement in the academic rigour of many of the courses offered by institutions within the group. The influence of the CNAA on library provision in particular is marked and beneficial. Visiting panels have, over the years, commented adversely on the quantity as well as the quality of library provision and have indicated ways in which colleges may improve their library services. The rigorous development needed to promote a new course submission to CNAA has also opened pathways for librarians to participate in course development, as mentioned previously in this chapter.

As the CNAA or the local university is to the validation of degree programmes, so the Business Education Council (BEC) and the Technician Education Council (TEC), now merged as B/TEC, have been to the provision of higher technician courses within the institutions. The emphasis that these two bodies have placed on learning methods has greatly increased the use made by students of library services, and this has had a direct and good influence on teaching methods within the institutions. Although validation visits by BEC and TEC are not on the rigorous scale of CNAA, their detailed guidelines have been helpful to librarians in integrating their services more fully into the learning and teaching life of the institution.

Through BEC, TEC, and CNAA, all professional validating organizations, the colleges developed their curricula, moving towards a heavy emphasis on advanced, that is to say, degree or degree-equivalent level courses. In this respect, they followed the pattern set by the polytechnics after their inception, a move which has been described in the literature as 'upwards academic drift'. It is certainly true that the major new developments from this group of institutions have been at the higher level, even in areas of technician education. While these developments were controlled and monitored by the appropriate Regional Advisory Councils and the Department of Education and Science, there was no obvious national level of planning for higher education and the entrepreneurial instincts of each institution came into play.

This state of affairs began to change in February 1982 when government established the National Advisory Body for Local Authority Higher Education (NAB) to undertake the following group of tasks:

1   For the time being and in the light of resources specified for local authority higher education in England by the Secretary of State after consultation with local authorities, to consider on the basis of recommendations from the Board for Local Authority Higher Education, the academic provision to be made in institutions in selected fields as decided by the committee.

2   To advise the Secretary of State in respect of those fields on the appropriate use of his powers with regard to the apportionment of the advanced further education pool and to the approval of advanced courses.

3   To monitor the implementation by local authorities and institu-

tions of dispositions made by the Secretary of State in the light of this advice.

4 In formulating this advice, to contribute to a coordinated approach to provision, as necessary in relevant academic fields, between the local authority and the university, voluntary and direct grant sectors of higher education.

5 To undertake or commission such studies or to seek such information as appear necessary for the determination of this advice.

Following the first meeting of the Committee, a press conference was held at which the chairman (Mr William Waldegrave, Parliamentary Under Secretary of State) drew attention to the factors which had led to the establishment of NAB. He emphasized that there was an urgent need for advice on the academic provision to be made in the local authority sector of higher education, and that central and local government were united on this point and in their desire to see NAB functioning effectively as soon as possible. He pointed to the need for NAB to have regard to the long-term development of local authority higher education as well as to the short-term problems. It was also recognized that NAB would need to establish early and effective links with the university, voluntary, and direct grant sectors as well as with the 366 local authority colleges having some advanced work.

One of the committee's first decisions was to authorize the board to set up working groups, to review provision in certain defined areas of the curriculcum: art and design, engineering, and pharmacy. The board, in addition to these subject groups, set up two operational groups: one to establish a database for NAB, and the other on the regional component of NAB's work.

The first major piece of advice from NAB to the Secretary of State related to the moratorium on the approval of new courses introduced by Circular 8/82.[5] A new Circular 5/82[6] invited proposals for new courses for a 1983 start, developed according to certain specific guidelines. The act of looking at new courses, the continuance of existing courses, and the allocation of the reduced 'Pool' were the first steps in producing a plan for the logical development of higher education. Inevitably the phrase 'logical development' became 'logical reduction' in many cases and the first public action of NAB was to write to colleges seeking reduction in expenditure and in courses.

It was perhaps inevitable that any organization set up to look broadly at higher education in the current economic crisis should start in this fashion. Perhaps, however, higher education can look forward to a more planned and cooperative future once the board has got through its initial task of coordinating national and regional provision for higher education and has sorted out the balance of students on different types of course, different subjects etc. While this 'sorting out' process is carried out, however, there will inevitably be a degree of confusion and concern in this particular sector of the educational market-place.

REFERENCES

1 Department of Education and Science *Teacher education and training* (The James Report) HMSO, 1972.
2 Department of Education and Science *Education: a framework for expansion*. Cmnd. 5174. HMSO, 1972.
3 Department of Education and Science *Development of higher education in the non-university sector*. (Circular 7/73) The Department, 1973.
4 Lomas, T *Personal communication*. 1982.
5 Department of Education and Science *Approval of advanced further education courses in England*. (Circular 1/82) The Department, 1982.
6 Department of Education and Science *Approval of advanced education courses in England (Revised arrangements)*. (Circular 5/82) The Department, 1982.

10

Polytechnics and Central Institutions

John Cowley

In the first ten years of their existence the polytechnics have become recognized as major institutions of higher education. The work in the institutions embraces higher degree and research activity, first degree studies, and a significant body of sub-degree and diploma provision. The extent of research activity in the polytechnics is small when compared with that in the universities and there has been a deliberate shedding of lower level work over the years. In consequence, the polytechnics are viewed primarily as first degree institutions with a strong emphasis on the teaching function. With the support of CNAA, the polytechnics have created a vast range of courses which present wide choice to students. The standard academic disciplines are there alongside modular courses providing the student with a great choice of options. There is also considerable emphasis on applied skills, vocational, and professional education.

From the beginning, the polytechnics aimed to meet the needs of part-time and industry-based students. Mixed mode attendance was made available in many courses and a significant commitment to the sandwich course became a feature of polytechnic life. A significant number of mature students attend polytechnic courses, attracted by the mixed mode pattern of attendance and the bridging courses, such as DipHE, which provide a second educational chance to those not successful at school or who seek a fresh entry into the educational system after being otherwise engaged with family or working commitments.

The formation of multi-site polytechnics from the merger of frequently scattered constituent colleges provided the institutions with severe management and logistics problems.[1] Inefficient buildings and surplus staff were two features of the mergers. Subsequent changes in central government policies created further change, particularly in the field of teacher education. Thus mergers became a part of life with all the attendant organizational and human problems. At the end of the first decade of activity these problems remain as further adjustments are made in response to sometimes unpredictable ministerial decisions.

Demographic change and variations in government policy towards higher education have combined to create a basically unstable educational system. The capping of the pool, changes in policy in relation to student fees, and, latterly, the creation of the National Advisory Body (NAB), suggest that the 1980s, far from being a period of consolidation and strengthening of polytechnics and their library services, will represent instead yet another decade of change and instability. From the narrow institutional point of view there can be little comfort in the situation, although it must be said that the early excesses in academic staffing and the over-provision of courses within given geographical areas could hardly be justified.

It is possible, in seeking comfort in a situation fraught with anxiety, to envisage a tidier, more cost-effective polytechnic and higher education system in operation by the 1990s, when student demand is expected to fall. Even the assumption of decline in demand in the latter part of the 1980s is now held to be suspect by many and exemplifies the prevailing uncertainties in the field of higher education.

The background as described has had enormous impact on the nature of library provision. The polytechnic libraries in the early 1970s were in a parlous state. The physical provision was generally poor and book stocks weak and unbalanced. There were few injections of capital funding with which to speed the library's development. Progress had to be made from a revenue allocation of 4–6% of total institutional funding.

Another major weakness showed itself in the lack of appreciation on the part of many teaching staff, who were still clinging to old college traditions, of the importance of the library in a first-degree institution. However, by the mid-decade, the influence of the CNAA, with its concern for the supporting infrastructure, the commitment of the first generation of polytechnic librarians and the pioneering impact of pacesetters such as Hatfield, began to create a favourable climate for library development. A considerable building programme led to the opening of several good quality libraries whose sensible, functional design owed much to excellent collaboration between librarian and architect.

The work of the library became subtly integrated with teaching activity as the new breed of subject or specialist librarians worked together with teaching staff to create carefully planned support for students. Book stocks improved as revenue resources increased and staff were able to sort out wide variations in the standard of provision partially resulting from the enforced merger of stocks and the changing emphasis on curriculum development. The students' appreciation of libraries increased with the development of user instruction and programmes of library publications. Librarians' involvement in the work of academic boards and committees involved them in everything from institutional policy making to the detail of course planning. In all, there developed a new level of confidence and consciousness which firmly placed the library and its activities at the centre of institutional activity.

It is fortunate that such a foundation had been created so effectively by the turn of the decade, as it is now evident that the next few years will be difficult and challenging. The supposition is that resources for higher education will be reduced in real terms, that a programme of 'rationalization' will be conducted and that there will be a period of contraction and amputation of selected areas of activity in designated institutions. There may well be new approaches to area or regional planning which will remove an element of decision making from the institutions who will no longer be totally free to develop from within.

Alongside these problems of authority and control, the 1980s will witness a vast change in the nature of library provision as new technology becomes increasingly influential. It seems certain that the interest generated during IT'82 will not be a thing of passing fancy but will mark a significant escalation in the application of new technology to the task of the processing, transfer and exploitation of information.

By the time this book is published, the NAB will have been in existence for more than half its initial three-year period and its deliberations will be known to those in the public sector of higher education. The indications are for a period of the ending of selected courses and the greater concentration of activity in fewer centres. It is not impossible to contemplate further enforced mergers where, for instance, a small college is adjacent to a larger institution. Whatever the outcome, the impact on libraries will be significant and disruptive.

The scenario described above suggests the creation of redundant stock as courses are closed down, and the merger of other collections. It has also to be said that it is by no means certain that library jobs can be guaranteed in such a situation. As the main objectives of the exercise are to provide greater efficiency and lower costs, the loss of staff appears to be a likely concomitant of the whole exercise. It should be noted that there have already been significant staffing losses in selected polytechnics since cuts began in 1979, but these have mainly been achieved by non-replacement and early retirement. Premature retirement compensation was also used in the early 1970s when several colleges of education were merged into the new polytechnics. Although it is not clear exactly how local authorities will deal with inevitable trades union and institutional resistance it seems that redundancies may be a feature of the rationalization programme now hanging over the polytechnics. Voluntary departures, particularly where the average age of polytechnic librarians is quite low, may not be sufficient to meet required financial targets.

The possibility of further mergers of stock probably no longer cause any deep concern, as library staff have gained considerable experience of the associated management problems during the past decade.[2] The availability of online systems has greatly speeded the task of changing records and, as can be seen from the recent COPOL publication on the subject,[3] most polytechnic libraries have sophisticated cataloguing services at their disposal. If mergers are to be in evidence again, there will remain the problem of staff time needed for associated stock editing, reclassification, and the physical handling of stock in libraries which may be short of reserve storage space and faced with declining numbers of staff.

The recent highlighting of the importance of information technology follows a period of steadily increasing commitment to automation in polytechnics and colleges. The handling of information in libraries inescapably led to a surge of interest in computer applications. Library 'housekeeping', such as financial records and control and periodicals holdings lists, proved to be ideally suited to the use of computers. Modest programming effort and low-cost hardware were able to dispense with laborious, time-consuming manual systems. From the mid-1970s cooperative schemes of cataloguing, using standard formats and benefiting from the availability of national data bases, were readily taken up by the polytechnics. Polytechnic use of computers is now well established and new technology has been applied extensively in all but a few institutions. However, it is probably true to say that the impact of these changes has so far been felt by library staff rather than the users. While IT'82 has heightened awareness of computer use in libraries, it is possible to take the view that the full potential of existing technology is not yet appreciated by some librarians and certainly not by many academic and student users. In every institution there are those who are actively engaged in programming activity and introducing computer assisted learning into their teaching activity, but there is evidence to suggest that the majority of students are not being introduced sufficiently to new technology and that conservative methods of teaching still prevail.

It is to the credit of sections of government that a national effort is being made to increase interest in the use of microcomputers and there are signs that a new generation, now attending school, will be coming through to higher education with some appreciation of computer applications.

Her Majesty's Inspectors (HMIs), CNAA and other influential groups are encouraging the greater use of computers for academic, research and administrative purposes to the extent that even the unenthusiastic are now having to face a period of significant change. Nor is it likely that we have reached a plateau of development. As

Mel Collier[4] has suggested, more and more services will cost less, storage capacity will increase, and there will be greater integration of applications. With hardware costs decreasing dramatically and commercial interest in information processing and retrieval increasing, use of the new technology is bound to develop. It is certain that electronically based services will modify the nature of library provision in higher education.[5] The range of full-text services will increase and facsimile services will become more readily available.

The local network experiment at the Polytechnic of Central London will assist the development of high quality, locally controlled computer information services. Institutional needs will be met increasingly from local systems with easier user access. It is likely that the old aims of high quality support services for academic and research staff, which have been under pressure as a result of the economic downturn, will be met by increased use of local networks. Designated information files, selective dissemination of information and current awareness services for selected groups may all find a new lease of life with the application of computer technology. As Collier puts it: '. . . we will see a reassertion of the information intermediary role of the librarian . . . with particular emphasis on user specific service . . .'[6] Collier also hints at greater user independence as increased computer facilities provide the individual with enhanced capacity for self-help and new approaches to information gathering.

The changes in levels of funding and the advent of new technology, together with the background of uncertainty engendered by likely policy and structural changes in higher education, suggest that the time has come to reappraise the function and aims of polytechnic and college libraries.

During the past decade a solid foundation of achievement has tended to produce a reasonably standard response from librarians in the higher education public sector, despite variations in local conditions. Multi-site operations, as opposed to single-site, have marginally influenced the organization and deployment of personnel, and the choice of in-house computerization as opposed to membership of cooperatives has had impact on approaches to automation of services, but, in essence, libraries have responded fairly consistently to the typical range of user needs derived mainly from first degree studies. A strong tradition of subject or course support developed in the polytechnics, not uniquely, as can be seen by the work carried out in the new universities,[7] which provided middle-grade professional staff with the opportunity to become heavily involved with a defined teaching-learning group having particular needs. The more successful subject librarians were able to offer close support in the form of literature searches, selective dissemination of information, online information retrieval, library instruction and individual tutorials, as well as initiatives and liaison activity in the fields of stock selection, stock editing and provision of student reading lists. The inherent variety of work and the immediacy of user response often provided subject librarians with a high level of motivation and job satisfaction. However, the success of this work is heavily related to the availability of a sufficient number of professional staff with appropriate qualifications and experience.

A professional librarian, with adequate support from other library staff and systems, is able to operate effectively at around a library staff:student ratio (LSSR) of 1:250 or, to put it another way, one professional member of staff could support all three years of an 80-intake course when operating within a well organized system having an adequate balance of library assistant staff and support facilities. When provision falls seriously below this level, modifications have to be made to the quality and sophistication of services on offer. It is possible to envisage some adjustment to the suggested ratio according to the degree of technical and assistant support available. Pressure on funding may well lead to a reappraisal of the desired ratio of professional to assistant strength in academic libraries. The more expensive professionals may have to operate in reduced numbers as long as favourable adjustments are made to the strength of support teams. It is common experience in polytechnics that professional work is most frequently undermined by the pressures brought about by the lack of assistants. As a consequence, professional staff are frequently diverted from their more advanced work in order to assist with routine operations. The non-replacement of staff frequently takes place in random fashion so that the crucial balance of a team is disturbed and role differentiation becomes less certain. There is some evidence to suggest that this outcome is more pronounced in a multi-site situation when teams are modest in size and particularly susceptible to imbalance. As cuts and stricter costings become more pressing it will be necessary to reconsider the balance of teams and the nature of duties to be carried out by different levels of staff. The much longer progression to full Associateship of the Library Association will require those with managerial responsibilities to consider how best to use and deploy members of a team which may be weaker in professional terms but stronger in the sense of the capabilities available in those yet to achieve full professional status. It may be that a greater measure of task evaluation, allied with the realistic appraisal of skills capability at all levels in the team, will allow for a change in the professional: non-professional balance. Needless to say, higher demands on non-professional personnel will require an associated reassessment of status and rewards.

If staff skills are to be re-examined and the potential of new technology fully harnessed the question of training and staff development will take on a new significance. The national debate on curriculum development in schools of librarianship and the associated question of post-school continuing education and training will have to be kept under review. It is already apparent that the speed and fundamental nature of change have been such as to intensify the need for in-house training. While staff absorb a good deal of new methods in the routine working situation, the introduction of radically new methods, such as online circulation control, has created the necessity for carefully planned re-training. It has also been necessary to study the impact of new systems in terms of changed capabilities and staff reactions to involvement in greatly modified styles of operations. Although much of the re-training can best be carried out within the library, perhaps with the help of cooperative teams whose great strength is in the sharing of knowledge and systems, nevertheless there appears to be a need for radical change within the schools concerned with professional education.

Curriculum change has been under investigation at several levels, and it may be that the one-year postgraduate course in its present form will be seen for what it is, merely an introduction to professional studies in general. Greater emphasis must be placed on post-qualification studies, and varied modes of attendance, in order to accommodate the requirements of those facing heavy work commitments and significant developments in working methods. It may be that new knowledge and skills required from continuing education will more effectively be obtained outside existing schools. Their relevance to the profession at large may depend on their ability to extend the range of teaching and courses, perhaps by drawing more heavily on skills already available in the institution at large.

The alternative model would seem to suggest an acceptance of dwindling resources, a concentration on the basic one-year courses and a handing over of continuing professional education to other providers. The range of management and professional skills needed now and in the future require a dedication to in-house training and team development of a level not yet achieved in most polytechnics. These will have to be extended by post-experience courses, in varied formats, provided by polytechnic departments or specialist organizations.

Since the beginning of the decade, with its economic pressures and rapidly developing technology, there have been signs of an inevitable coalescence of learning resource services. It is becoming increasingly difficult to separate the boundaries of library and information work from the teaching and learning process. While the development of electronic systems and networks, and the improvement of telecommunications, are leading both information providers and users towards the concept of distributed information services, at the same time these developments are making users more aware of the value of information and are removing much of the tedium previously involved in manual searching. The librarian's value as an intermediary has never been greater and the provision of a wide range of non-book media, with which to supplement the traditional periodical and book, has helped libraries reach out to a wider audience. The librarian's cooperation with computer and media colleagues has strengthened his ability to provide knowledge and information, in a variety of physical forms, more effectively related to developing methods of study and research. Teaching teams, numerically in decline, are making heavier and wider demands on learning resources. Research activity is regularly preceded by online searching and the increase in student project work is emphasizing the value of the library tutorial, instruction in literature searches, and the librarian as information provider. If the training capabilities and attitudes of librarians are pitched at the right level it is possible to envisage a new period of academic–librarian liaison, the value of which will be more substantial than that achieved during the first decade of polytechnic operations.

The strong government interest in library cooperation and links with the local community gives the polytechnics and colleges an opportunity to provide information and study facilities to both individuals and local organizations. Several polytechnics are involved in industrial consultancy and information provision to local firms. The Hatfield based service, Hertis, draws on the resources of the polytechnic and the county library in providing subscription-based services, but several polytechnics operate more informally and pragmatically in assisting individuals and companies with bibliographical and information searches.

While it is the case that small firms often have difficulty in defining their needs, it is likely that online links will lead to an increase in this kind of local cooperation. The typical polytechnic support embraces the use of in-house material, wider online facilities and, importantly, a good deal of academic expertise. Students drawn from local industry and commerce traditionally provide a significant proportion of polytechnic recruitment, and local information services gain in relevance as a result of these close links.

Part-time and sandwich students who operate in both the industrial and college settings come to recognize the value of information through their involvement in courses and library-based activity and return to the working environment better aware of services available. The provision of information services to small firms and the local community may well be an area ripe for further development, not least as a result of the direct interest now being shown by the Department of Industry.

The lessons of Hertis suggest that the provision of extra-mural services requires close attention to be paid to resource implications, including staffing needs. Conflicts of interest between industrial users and internal research staff may arise out of shared use of resources, and the question of confidentiality cannot be ignored. However, the extension of library and information service into the community is desirable in both utilitarian and political terms. There is still much to be done in the way of local cooperation.

It seems inevitable that in the immediate future polytechnic and college libraries will be concerned with significant technological change and new priorities. There is likely to be a shift in resource allocation away from traditional provision towards the greater use of electronic media. The importance of the book will not diminish for those engaged in first-degree studies but most students will expect to have access to a wider range of learning materials. Computer based information services, electronic publishing, computer programmed video, and collections of non-print media will be used alongside traditional stock. Library, computer, and educational technology services will grow closer together as disciplines and systems converge into an integrated learning resource. Access to these systems may become more distributed, and distance learning made more feasible, but polytechnic librarians, if alive to current developments, will continue to provide academic and student users with a crucially important service based on the printed word and its modern variants.

REFERENCES

1 Cowley, J *Personnel management in libraries.* (Chapter 9: The management of mergers) Bingley, 1982.
2 Bundy, A L *Amalgamations and libraries.* (Occasional publications no 3) Footscray Institute of Technology Library, 1981.
3 Ellard, K R *Directory of computer applications in UK polytechnic libraries.* Council of Polytechnic Librarians, 1982.
4 Collier, M 'Centralization and after: a review of the prospects for distributed processing in libraries'. *Aslib Proceedings* 34 (6/7) June/July 1982. 295–300.
5 Thompson, J *The end of libraries.* Bingley, 1982.
6 Collier, M 'Information technology and its applications in polytechnic libraries'. *Aslib Proceedings* 34 (10) October 1982. 437–444.
7 Guttsman, W L 'Subject specialization in academic libraries'. *Journal of Librarianship* 5 (1) January 1973. 1–8.

11

Education Libraries

Charles H Bleasdale

Prior to 1973 this chapter might well have been called 'Colleges of Education'. Up to this date the initial and post initial training of teachers was mainly carried out either in the university institutes of education or in monotechnic colleges of education. A variety of factors, including a decline in the national economy and a drop in the birth rate, led to a call for the reduction in the number of teachers employed in the public sector. As a result, the Secretary of State for Education issued Circular 7/73[1] which announced a cutback in the number of new teachers to be produced annually, and as a consequence, a reduction in the number of colleges needed to educate and train them. Other economic constraints caused local education authorities to take a critical look at the organization of further and higher education. Critics may say, with some justice, that their actions then and since have been concerned solely with financial inputs to the exclusion of consideration of educational outputs. This predominant concern for finance was expressed in some cases by the bringing together of institutions which had hitherto been seen as totally separate in ethos, nature of work, and type of facilities required. In fairness, it must be said that the James Report[2] had indicated some dissatisfaction with the system whereby teachers were educated in an environment totally divorced from the real world and without any significant contact with students of other disciplines.

In this situation, one of several fates befell the colleges of education. At worst they simply closed once their existing student intake had graduated. Alternatively, they merged with existing polytechnics to become schools or faculties of education. In some cases they merged with technical colleges to become colleges of higher education. A small number managed to preserve their independence by diversifying their courses into (mainly) arts fields at degree level and became colleges of higher education by osmosis rather than by absorption.

The consequences of these changes were considerable. As pointed out in works such as those edited by Platt[3] and Neal,[4] the 1960s were a time of very rapid development for these colleges. They had to build on the excellent earlier traditions of the teacher training colleges and at the same time adjust to the demands of larger numbers of students, larger libraries, and the necessity of coming to terms with quite radical changes in librarianship and in education. Librarians in these colleges were in effect a race apart from librarians who practised in other, more diffuse areas. No doubt colleagues from systems as far apart as university libraries and technical college or school libraries claim equally unique attributes. The difference lies perhaps in the related factors of institutional scale and subject specialism. Other librarians proudly proclaimed the creed of 'all things to all men' whereas the college of education librarian perforce became a specialist in the literature of education, and since student numbers were small by comparison with other colleges and universities, he perhaps developed a closer relationship both with the clients and with the theory and practice of the subject.

This period of growth is well recorded in the invaluable Shercliff report.[5] It is paradoxical that by the time this report appeared in 1973 there were already clear indications that changes were once again about to take place. The 'specialness' of these librarians was signalled by the breaking away from the University, College and Research Libraries Group (UC&R) of the Library Association of a group who were to become the Colleges, Institutes and School of Education Group (CISE) of the Library Association. This later changed its name in 1979 to the Education Librarians Group (ELG), thus re-emphasizing the particular contribution the members felt that they made to the discipline of education.

What then is this particular feature? Beswick has covered the main points.[6] It is perhaps crystallized when he says:

> An educational library is a specialist library, whose selection, organisation and dissemination procedures are directed towards highly specialist purposes – educational purposes. It aims to promote the educational and research aims of its institution and clientele through every path of its work, every area of its building and by every action of its staff.

Many other types of library would no doubt lay claim to many of these points, but they are by their nature required to serve many masters, with a consequent dilution of subject expertise. The changes brought about in the 1970s highlighted the dilemma which other types of library had already begun to recognize. The education library had been subject oriented, leading to an outward looking service seeking to anticipate the reader's needs. Diversification, merger, call it what you will, meant that these librarians now had to practise in a different, wider world of information to which they had given tacit recognition in the past but in which they now had to engage wholeheartedly.

It is of course recognized that all libraries may rightly claim to have an educational function. In the case of the libraries under discussion, there was added to this function a concern with the practice of education, or if preferred, pedagogy. Colleagues in other areas would be less likely to claim a direct professional and personal concern with the *practice* of engineering, building, or any of the many other areas reflected in their book stock and in their institutional aims. A plethora of reports and articles have made the point that the librarian of such a college should be appointed to academic scales and should have academic functions transcending mere 'introduction to the library' for new students.[7-15] Similarly, the reports drew attention to the fact that the students involved were not necessarily different from those students undergoing teacher training in the universities and that their library expectations and provision should be at the same or a similar level.

Over a relatively brief period of time there then grew up a particular ethos of education librarianship and a range of expectations for both users and practitioners. A further understanding of these developments can once again be found in Shercliff,[5] where he enunciates three prime aims of education libraries and follows these with the objectives by which these aims may be realized.

One of the most significant of these is the emphasis laid on the teaching role of the library and his outline of how this may best be achieved. Initially of course, the basic mechanics of using the college library must be explained. Following this may be courses on the organization of knowledge, and on methods of enquiry and associated practical information and guidance on how to help the student to organize his own work. This will be associated with an introduction to the bibliography of the subject, including journals, indexes, abstracts etc. Courses will be offered on learning resources other than the conventional printed book. These will include films, film strips and loops, video, television, and other non-book media presentations. In this way the education librarian opens up to the student teacher not only alternative ways of studying but also alternative ways of teaching. User education thus becomes a vital function of library service in the education field. Having the built-in advantage that student teachers may be assumed to be highly motivated in their pursuit of learning, the style of user education adopted by college of education librarians developed closely in line with the pedagogic and subject interests of the students. To this extent it became very much simpler to introduce such courses and in many cases to ensure that they featured in timetables rather than being purely *ad hoc* arrangements.

To this range of educational activity should be added the provision of children's literature and the development and management of courses in its use. These are often carried out in conjunction with colleagues in the teaching faculties and closely identify the librarian and the library with the learning role of the institution. The school practice library is perhaps unique amongst libraries in higher education, Jean Wood notes:[16]

> It should provide a variety of the best books for children, it should be an example of the best kind of school library, it should provide books for students to use in schools and for curriculum study courses within the colleges, it should enable students to observe children using books and should encourage

teachers in training in the belief that books are important in education so that they will go into the schools ready and competent to use them in the classroom. . . .

Thus the education librarian is able to influence and guide the product of his institution in a way that the author suggests relatively few other categories of librarian have opportunities to do.

These materials then provide not only for the learning activity of the student teacher but also provide examples of the range of materials used in schools. Hence the 'teaching practice' collection will at certain times of the year be virtually denuded. To fulfil its purpose the collection must at all times reflect accurately the curriculum in schools, rather than merely the curriculum in the college.

The Shercliff Report continues its discussion of the objectives of the education library service by describing the need for active programmes demonstrating the applications of periodical indexes, abstracts, and online data base facilities, along with the production of library guides, subject lists, and the development of current awareness services, at least for the staff, and probably for all users.

From this last arises the interesting question as to which element in the equation influences the other. Over a period of years much attention has been given to the presentation of information in classrooms. The belief has been propounded that one means of creating and maintaining interest amongst learners is by varying stimuli. In consequence, we have seen introduced into the classroom films, television, film strips and loops, slides, audio-cassettes, and other non-print materials. As this trend developed it exercised a considerable influence on libraries and in particular on education libraries.[17] It became a commonplace to find in such libraries a wide range of audio-visual materials, often catalogued, classified, and arranged alongside the traditional book stock. In association with these media was found the hardware by which to utilize them. A new dimension was thus introduced into the thinking of the librarian. There rapidly grew up the concept of the resource centre. Almost immediately this became a contentious area. Within the profession one school of thought believed that a parallel library should be created with the materials, equipment, catalogues, and related bibliographies housed adjacent to, but separate from, the main library. The other school held that these materials were no different from books. It was just information in a different format. The exponents of this latter philosophy often packaged the film strip or audio-cassette and similar items in book-like packages and stood them on the shelves in sequence with the books. The catalogue entries might well be integrated also. A whole new terminology entered the librarian's vocabulary. Extensive correspondence was penned on what to call the format; non-book materials, audio-visual aids, learning resources, *et al.* The genre developed its own literature, its own cataloguing rules,[18] and of course its own experts. Special posts were created, again with new titles; audio-visual librarian, media specialist, resources librarian, and many others. New elements appeared in library school syllabi, short courses proliferated and a whole new field of librarianship grew up.

To the outsider some of these preoccupations may have seemed trivial. Beneath this concern with hardware versus books lay the germ of a power struggle which has not yet been entirely resolved.

Perhaps a more fundamental concern lay in the *educational* implications of these 'new media'. Many questions were raised: how and when should they be used in teaching? did they really aid learning? are they solely teaching aids for the classroom or are they also learning aids (like books!?) for the individual? To contribute towards the resolution of these problems, teaching departments within the colleges developed courses and specialists to teach, research, and implement the new aids. In many cases new departments were set up. The staff of such departments overnight became Educational Technologists; again, a new discipline was born. The problem for the librarian was, and is: where does the library fit in? And, perhaps of equal importance: what is the effect on the librarian's status? In some cases the two departments worked in parallel. In others the library was absorbed into new departments with names like Learning Resources Department, Educational Technology, and Media Resources. Entrepreneurial, thrusting librarians, on the other hand, absorbed the staff of the teaching departments and so were obtained the Library and Learning Resources Department and other similar sounding titles. There were, and are, real problems of control, status, and salary. Today there are many combinations of personnel, function, and title, but usually all have the same aim – that of educating, training, and guiding both the student and the practising teacher.

This has been one of the major developments and preoccupations of the recent period. It afforded librarians a new dimension of professional expertise and of managerial skills. The emphasis in teaching has moved away from the teacher as provider of knowledge to the teacher as a manager of the learning situation, and the librarian in teacher training institutions has been given the choice of being in the forefront of these developments, or of being a somewhat reluctant follower.

The combined effects of developments in teaching methods, the emergence of better educated librarians through changes in the library schools' syllabuses, and staff development programmes, coupled with the degree of consultation inherent in academic board participation meant that an almost imperceptible change began to occur in the college's perception of the status of the librarian. It would be impossible to isolate the invaluable work of the Library Association and its groups together with sections of the then Association of Teachers in Technical Institutions (ATTI), later to be absorbed within the National Associations of Teachers in Further and Higher Education (NATFHE) in effecting this change. Whatever the diverse elements, it is true to say that during this period the librarian in an education library began to be increasingly recognized as an important member of the management team of the institution.

It is interesting to reflect that Donald Urquhart said that the experience and training of a librarian should fit him for higher management in many fields outside the library.[19] The late 1970s saw in some small measure the fulfilment of this observation as the librarian increasingly became seen as a manager of a major expensive resource within the institution, as well as an academic participating in the management of learning. The significance of this change perhaps lay in the fact that increasingly the librarian himself began to recognize the wider contribution he could make in management terms, and by extension the increased influence that the library department could wield.

Quite clearly many of these developments were not peculiar to the college of education librarians; similar events were taking place in other types of academic libraries. In the majority of cases however, the main developments were taking place in this type of college, and were providing case studies for other libraries who entered the field a little later. Many of the proceedings of the Windermere Conferences[20, 21, 22] highlight the concern and interest of librarians, not only in the librarianship of learning resources but also in its educational and institutional implications. Here again can be seen the involvement with the aims and objectives of the institution which, it is suggested, are the hallmark of the librarian in this kind of library. These proceedings also reflect the greater involvement that librarians were finding in the government of colleges, partly as a result of DES Circular 7/70,[23] which suggested that the college librarian should, ex officio, be a member of the academic board. This of course referred to all colleges, but as far as the colleges of education were concerned, when taken in conjunction with the other events mentioned above, even greater opportunities for influencing events were offered.

Probably the next major development in librarianship was the introduction of mini- and microcomputers at a price which small libraries could afford. Although not alone in this approach, many education librarians saw that the micro had great potential as a learning and teaching instrument and seized the opportunity to introduce them into their libraries. This was perhaps a natural extension of the idea of resource-based learning, since the micros were used not only for the housekeeping tasks, but also as an aid to student study within the library area.

It was at about this point in the decade of change that many of these libraries began either to merge with larger institutions, ie polytechnics or technical colleges, or else began to diversify into other areas of study. Those librarians faced with a straight merger were naturally apprehensive, not only for their personal futures, but also for the quality and nature of the services for which they had been responsible. It is not the purpose of this chapter to chronicle the many permutations of change that took place, save to say that in many instances the college of education library became a campus library of the merged institution and in due course found itself serving a wider range of students. In other cases the diversification of courses on the same site meant that, initially at least, the college of education library felt that it was still carrying out its prime function with others grafted onto it.

Whichever course was pursued, the point at issue could be stated simply as: 'is there a special relationship between librarians involved in the theory and practice of teacher training and the practitioners and their literature?' An over-simplified answer could be put forward by saying that in the eyes of the profession there must be, otherwise there would be no need for a specialist chapter in a book of this nature! That in itself is some justification, but needs rather more exposition.

As at present distributed, teacher training is in the main being conducted in the same premises, largely by the same staff, using the same libraries as before. Thus an entrenched position is offered to these people. Indeed, some librarians have been heard to say that apart from different control and exposure to a number of different courses, their education librarianship has not altered in any way. This situation must surely change as those practitioners who represent the colleges as they once were retire and are replaced by librarians who will represent a fresh outlook. Moreover, at the time of writing, further cuts in teacher training numbers are being announced which will involve further closures, either of institutions or of faculties.

Is there then any prospect that the special relationship referred to earlier will continue to exist whilst undergoing yet more change? The answer is almost certainly 'yes'. Whilst the numbers of teachers in training are to be reduced, there will be for a long time to come developments in the field of in-service training. Successive governments have paid lip service to this idea, some have even made notional financial provision to enable it to develop. Moreover, it is not difficult to predict that in the not too distant future the cry will once more go forth that there is a shortage of teachers, and the existing truncated trees of learning will find themselves urged once again to make good the shortfall in the quickest possible way and with the highest possible standards! Libraries, partly because of their archival function, will perhaps be enabled to present an element of continuity on which a future requirement can build. It is therefore important that this particular concern with the practice of education as well as for its literature is not lost sight of in the present general atmosphere of retrenchment, cuts, and dissolution.

Nothing in this chapter is intended to suggest that only college of education librarians have a special relationship with their users or their institutions. Subject specialists exist in every kind of library, and indeed many of the polytechnics and universities structure their libraries on these lines. The special relationship in this field of librarianship develops from the first introduction to the library through the entire course as student, librarian, lecturer, and administrator combine to develop an awareness of systems of learning and teaching that relate both to the present and the future activities of all involved. After all, it is said that we can all teach because we have been taught, and any fool can run a library. Within teacher training we attempt to put these over-simplifications together to the benefit of both of our professions. With what success we rarely find out, but those of us engaged in this work know that what we are doing is important, professionally satisfying, and best of all . . . different.

REFERENCES

1 Department of Education and Science *Development of higher education in the non-university sector.* (Circular 7/73) The Department, 1973.
2 Department of Education and Science *Teacher education and training.* (Chairman Lord James) HMSO, 1972.
3 Platt, P (ed) *Libraries in colleges of education.* Library Association, 1972.
4 Neal, K W *British academic libraries.* K W Neal, 1973.
5 Department of education and science *College of education libraries research project. Final report.* Manchester, Didsbury College of Education, 1973.
6 Beswick, N 'The nature of educational librarianship' in *Education Libraries Bulletin.* 25(1) Spring 1982.
7 Board of Education *Teachers and youth leaders.* (McNair Report) HMSO, 1944.
8 Library Association and Association of Teachers in Colleges and Departments of Education 'Training college libraries'. *Library Association Record* 60 (1) January 1958. 12–13.

9   Library Association and Association of Teachers in Colleges and Departments of Education 'Training college libraries, recommendations on their development to meet the demands of the three year training course'. *Library Association Record* 63 (12) December 1961. 419–423.

10 Ministry of Education *Libraries in training colleges.* Ministry of Education, 1961.

11 Library Association 'Recommended minimum establishment scale for training college library staff'. *Library Association Record* 66 (4) April 1964. 174–176.

12 Association of Teachers in Colleges and Departments of Education and Library Association *College of education libraries: recommended standards for their development.* ATCDE/LA, 1967.

13 Department of Education and Science *Second report of the committee on non-teaching staff in maintained colleges of education* (Odgers Report) The Department, 1968.

14 Library Association *College Libraries: recommended standards of library provision in colleges of technology and other establishments of further education.* Second edition, Library Association, 1971.

15 National Association of Teachers in Further and Higher Education *College libraries, policy statement.* NATFHE, 1982.

16 Wood, J B 'The school services library' in Platt, P (ed) *Libraries in colleges of education.* Library Association, 1972.

17 Library Association *School library resource centres: recommended standards for policy and provision.* Library Association, 1970.

18 National Council for Educational Technology and Library Association *Non-book materials cataloguing rules: integrated code of practice.* NCET, 1973.

19 Urquhart, D J 'Presidental address'. *Library Association Record* 74 (11) November 1972. 209–212.

20 Association of Teachers in Colleges and Departments of Education (ATCDE) *The developing role of the college of education librarian.* ATCDE, 1972.

21 ATCDE *College of education libraries and higher education.* ATCDE, 1973.

22 ATCDE *Learning resources in teacher education: some implications of the reorganization of higher education.* ATCDE, 1975.

23 Department of Education and Science *Government and conduct of establishments of further education.* (Circular 7/70) The Department, 1970.

12

Monotechnic Colleges: Unity in Diversity?

Paul F Burton

The monotechnic college is an expression of the need to provide specialized education and training in certain subjects. Originally and historically, this was often at a relatively low academic level (certainly, below degree level), but this is no longer true, and monotechnics now offer courses up to and beyond degree standard. Many developed either because the necessary level of education and training was not available elsewhere, or because the subject (or more exactly, the industry which the monotechnics served) perceived a need for a concentration of specialist skills, knowledge, and resources in one establishment dedicated to the provision of properly trained recruits for the industry or profession. Monotechnics were therefore established to satisfy a particular and clearly seen need, and this overall *raison d'être* can be seen as a guiding principle which continues to hold good, although, as will be suggested later, it is one which is today subject to considerable pressure.

By definition, the monotechnic is the antithesis of the polytechnic; a single-discipline institution in contrast to the multi-disciplinary. However, taken nationally it would be a mistake to regard the monotechnics as an homogeneous group. There is a wide variety of colleges which can be regarded as monotechnics and while the various types within the group have considerable formal links with one another, as a group there is little evidence of formal contact on the basis of simply being a monotechnic. There is no equivalent of the University Grants Committee for monotechnics, nor is there a SCONUL or COPOL-type body for monotechnic college librarians. As we shall see later, this individualism is at once the monotechnics' major asset and the source of their greatest weakness.

However, within the group of colleges which we are considering, the various subject groups have established formal or semi-formal links, at various levels, including the librarians of these colleges. There is, for example, an Association of Navigation Schools (ANS) and a Marine Librarians' Association (MLA), and these two examples epitomize the unique situation of the monotechnics. The ANS includes monotechnic staff (the Heads of Departments of Navigation, for example) and also staff from those polytechnics and colleges of further education where navigation is taught. Similarly, the MLA consists of librarians (and other interested individuals) from universities, polytechnics, further education, and public libraries. The point being made is that the monotechnic college identifies more closely (at least on a formal level) with the subject taught and thus with all other institutions where the subject is taught, rather than with other monotechnics *qua* monotechnics.

A little over 140 monotechnics can be identified from standard education directories, though this does not include a number of hybrid colleges resulting from amalgamations, mergers, etc, and bearing names such as College of Art and Technology, or College of Further Education and Agriculture.

Most are administered by the local education authority, although in Scotland a number of monotechnics are Central Institutions and funded directly by the Scottish Education Department. (This means that two of Scotland's nautical colleges have different authorities, as one is a Central Institution, while the other is funded by a local education authority.)

The two largest groups are the colleges of agriculture, horticulture, and forestry (disciplines which may be combined in one college), and the colleges of art or of art and design. These two together account for some 70% of the monotechnics in the United Kingdom although, as the previous sentence may suggest, it is not always easy to establish a single group by name alone. There are colleges of art, of art and design, and of art and crafts; music and drama may be combined in one institution or in separate schools; there are colleges of building, of printing, and one college of building *and* printing! The wide variety of disciplines covered by the 140+ monotechnics goes some way towards explaining why they are rarely treated as an homogeneous group (except perhaps, in books on college librarianship!). In addition to those cited above, there are colleges for nautical studies, food technology, cookery, fashion, furniture, mining, textiles, business studies, and the distributive trades.

It can, of course, be argued that, as a group, the polytechnics and colleges of further education contain an equal diversity of subjects. However, these two types of institution are designed, as it were, to provide these subjects within the unified framework of one institution. Furthermore, the historical development of the monotechnics should not be forgotten.

We have spoken thus far of the monotechnics as single-discipline colleges, but, as even a cursory glance at prospectuses and entries in the educational yearbooks will show, great variety can be found even within a monotechnic in terms both of the subjects and courses provided, and the levels to which they are taught. In addition, divisions into departments may be more specific than is the case in larger multi-disciplinary colleges. In this respect, as with other colleges, there are implications for librarianship and library provision.

For example, one London college of art and design offers honours degree courses in art and design, and the subjects taken can include ceramics, industrial design engineering, or jewellery design. Another college of art and design, however, offers a range from BA (Honours) in fashion or fine art to GCE 'O' and 'A' levels: the same college includes a department of environmental studies. Colleges of agriculture tend to be less varied, because their subject material does not embrace the same range of topics, but here too it is possible to find certificates in livestock production rubbing shoulders with farm management, turf management, and courses for greenkeepers beside ornamental horticulture. Within the nautical colleges, yachtmasters may be found in a classroom next to radio officers or masters of ocean-going tankers.

On the other hand, subjects which in a college of further educa-

tion or polytechnic would usually be provided by separate departments, such as general studies or the 'service' subjects of mathematics and science, are often subsumed within an existing department
in the monotechnics, if only for administrative convenience (otherwise known as 'for pay and rations'!). Such a situation can lead to
some strange bedfellows, though on the whole the problem is
perhaps greater for the lecturing staff involved than for the
librarian, unless the head of the department concerned consistently
fails to take account of the library needs of all sections under his
control. In addition, it will often be found that the degree to which
the total discipline is divided in monotechnics is balanced by the
presence of small numbers of lecturing staff in the individual
subdivisions.

Staffing levels in monotechnics tend to be low, not least because
student numbers are lower (being restricted to a much narrower
section of industry or the professions). Full-time staffing complements of less than 100 are not unusual, but again the variation is
so great that a college of agriculture offering only part-time City
and Guilds courses can have a full-time teaching staff of seven,
while an art college with BA degree courses can rise to over 92
part-time staff. Student numbers can show an equally wide range,
from a full-time equivalent (FTE) of 120 to 600. The nature of the
courses in some monotechnics, however, means that FTE figures
give no real indication of the actual number of students who will
cross the college threshold in an academic year. Where courses are
mainly of a higher level, they will tend to be full-time, as in the
colleges of art with degree courses and many of those with Technician Education Council (TEC) courses and their equivalent. While
agriculture also has post-degree level work, students, by the nature
of the industry, will tend to be part-time, sometimes day-release
only. Despite the fact that some monotechnics, notably some of
the colleges of art and design, have chosen to concentrate on higher
level work, this diversity in the amount of time a student spends
in college is largely due to a monotechnic's embracing (almost) all
levels of education for one discipline: they provide for many levels,
and will often include the so-called non-vocational courses, often
run during the evening for the general public, but utilizing the
specialist facilities and expertise available. What all this means in

sheer numbers is exemplified by a nautical college with a student FTE of 550, but which caters for 2,000 students (enrolments) in an academic year. Clearly, this phenomenon is not unique to the monotechnics, it is also a feature of a large number of the colleges of further education, but it is suggested that the relative impact is greater upon the monotechnic, and will be felt particularly by the library.

It was suggested at the beginning of this chapter that the principal *raison d'être* of the monotechnic colleges was their specialization in one discipline: they were, and are, intended to be centres of excellence in their particular subjects, centres where resources and expertise can be concentrated to the maximum benefit of all concerned in terms of facilities, standards, etc. Their objectives are the education and training of students in these specialisms, and it is largely because of this concentration into one establishment that the monotechnics collectively offer such a wide range of subjects at various levels.

In present-day education, specialization of this nature may lead to a precarious existence. Evolutionary biology suggests that over-specialization can lead to dead ends and extinction when conditions change rapidly, and the monotechnics are no exception to this fact of life. The colleges of education can bear witness to this in their own fashion and they also indicate the most likely route open to a monotechnic which has to succumb to such pressures, namely merger with some other institution in the area, either to become a department or faculty within that institution or to form with it a new institution. Thus, for example, the emergence of the colleges of higher education.

The phenomenon is not unknown among the smaller monotechnics. A little over ten years ago, a school of domestic science and a college of technology were merged and simultaneously transformed in a complex process which left the parent city with a new polytechnic dealing with advanced work and a new college of further education for non-advanced work. However, an existing college of art and design remained independent and does so to this day. In recent years, seven other monotechnics have merged with other institutions: in one case, this was a complex process, in that two colleges of technology and a college of art and design amalgamated to form one 'new' college of arts and technology. In practice, such amalgamations may seem to have little effect upon the former institutions, particularly if they remain geographically separated.

Despite their specialisms and individuality, the monotechnics are clearly not divorced from mainstream developments in education, and to this extent they differ little from the colleges of further education or the polytechnics. TEC and the Business Education Council (BEC) are the validating bodies for the appropriate courses (together with their Scottish equivalents SCOTEC and SCOTBEC), the Council for National Academic Awards (CNAA) validates degree-level and postgraduate courses where these are not awarded by a university, while professional bodies will take a more than passing interest in relevant courses. Nautical colleges are further influenced by the role of the Department of Trade and Industry in setting certain examinations and in maintaining standards in the education and training of marine engineers and deck officers, and a number of disciplines will have their training and educational needs overseen by Training Boards such as those for agriculture and for the merchant navy.

Clearly, a major influence on the monotechnics is the decline in student numbers caused by the falling birth rate. As one of the evolutionary pressures already mentioned, it could be said that the impact of this decline is proportionately greater, since the monotechnics generally have smaller student numbers. This has led to attempts at 'diversification', or the development of new courses which remain linked (however tenuously) to the general character of the college. Such courses may often be developed rapidly (which is not to say that they are not properly thought out!), and this can place a considerable burden upon library provision.

It is debatable whether the monotechnics can react as easily to government pressures to accept a larger intake of mature students to replace falling numbers of younger students in pursuit of their first professional qualification or to satisfy the demands for new skills caused by technology change. Because of their specialization, to follow the courses offered by the monotechnics can demand a major change of the mature individual seeking re-training, though the more technically oriented monotechnics may have more to offer and may be able to adapt more readily. They may also be involved with the Manpower Services Commission in promoting industrial training.

Changes of this kind will no doubt result, over a period of time, in a significant change in the character of the monotechnic, despite efforts to retain its essential character. It is also a fact that attempts to diversify in this way may bring the monotechnic into competition, even conflict, with local further education colleges and polytechnics.

Some at least of the monotechnics have attracted regular and significant numbers of mature students who attend, not for retraining, but as part of a continuing educational process which involves their profession through various levels of qualification or the updating of qualifications. This is certainly true of the nautical colleges, where there is a distinct series of steps on the educational ladder to the highest qualifications, and where the requirement, on legal and safety grounds, to be up to date with developments, often of an international nature, is particularly marked.

Finally, no consideration of current influences on monotechnics can ignore moves towards distance learning, open learning, Flexi-Study, and similar methods of study which endeavour to cater for the personal circumstances of the student. Any move away from 'chalk and talk' towards resource-based, student-centred learning will have an impact upon all areas of the college; this impact will be felt particularly by the library, which will be called upon to provide resources to support these learning modes, and must modify its service pattern to satisfy changing student needs.

What, then, are the effects of these influences, and of the character of the monotechnics, upon libraries and librarianship in these colleges?

Since, as we have seen, there is a range and diversity of subjects within the monotechnic, we can expect this to be reflected in the stock of the library. Though the size of the stock will tend to be small in comparison with many colleges of further education, it will aim to be comprehensive with respect to the level of courses provided by the institution. Because of the specialized nature of the collection, additional material required for general studies, service courses (mathematics, science, etc) may well constitute a larger proportion of the total than might be the case in other colleges.

This said, it must also be noted that the libraries of monotechnics exhibit the diversity we have come to expect from the group as a whole. Holdings in some typical monotechnics range from 3,500 monographs in a college of agriculture with an FTE of 450, to 28,000 in a college of art with an FTE of 600. One college of printing has a stock of 70,000 volumes. Diversity in monograph collections, however, may be as much a function of the available literature as of student numbers and course level. The effect of this upon the monotechnic library will also be proportionately greater, since a small publishing output in one area cannot be balanced by the larger output of some other subject.

It is perhaps in the area of library staffing that the monotechnics display the greatest discrepancies when compared with other academic libraries. Most can be said to be adequately staffed with regard to standard factors, in that there are full-time and part-time staff, with an element of professional library staff, even though he or she may be the only professional. (It being axiomatic that no librarian will admit to having sufficient staff – or books – the phrase 'adequately staffed' is merely intended to indicate that most monotechnic libraries do have both professional and non-professional staff in approximately correct ratio to academic staff, student population, etc!)

However, the colleges of agriculture show some exceptions to this general picture. Some few have no library at all in any formal sense; in others, the library is supervised by a member of the teaching staff, perhaps with part-time clerical assistance. This lack of adequate library provision is a symptom of a situation not unknown in other monotechnic and further education colleges, namely the status of the librarian or, more adequately, the view which the college authorities and the teaching staff have of the librarian's status, together with college attitudes towards library provision.

First of all, it must be said that the number of monotechnics without a library is extremely small indeed, and to that extent library provision is recognised as a necessity – how much of a necessity can vary and is often reflected in the position accorded to the librarian. Apart from the more intangible (but nonetheless real) factor of how the librarian is regarded by teaching staff, there is the much-exercised question of the academic status of the librarian, his or her position on such bodies as the Academic Board (however called) and course committees, boards of study, etc, and whether the chief librarian has head of department status, with the library seen as hierarchically equivalent to a teaching department.

It also remains true that many monotechnic librarians may encounter an apathy, not to say antipathy, towards library provision, particularly in those monotechnics where the education and training provided is regarded as being essentially practical. The library may be seen as an unnecessary luxury by those to whom 'practical' equals 'getting your hands dirty' and little else. An attitude such as this can quickly rub off onto students, who may vote with their feet thereafter. To encounter it requires continued effort by library staff to demonstrate the ability of the library to contribute usefully to the learning process. Sympathetic teaching staff can do much to counterbalance the negative attitudes of colleagues, particularly among students, and the librarian who cultivates such allies need feel no shame! There will come a point when it will be seen that the library does indeed have a role to play. It may not happen overnight: the most effective approach is the 'drip' principle, slowly wearing away antagonistic attitudes, not by frontal assault (which usually serves only to harden attitudes), but by daily and varied examples of library service and provision.

This problem is not unique to the monotechnics; it has exercised the minds of further education librarians for some time, and shows all the signs of continuing to do so. The situation in the monotechnics is just as varied. In a number of cases, the problem of the librarian's academic status has been resolved (to the satisfaction of the college, at least) by the creation of a tutor-librarian who, in addition to being the head of the library, has an element of teaching, which may be as much as 50% and more of the working week. All librarians expect to teach their subject, the use of the library and of information sources; the amount of such teaching and the depth to which it goes will be related to student numbers and the level of course provision. However, many tutor-librarians in monotechnics may also be teaching other subjects. Communication studies is a favourite topic, but in the monotechnics there may also be an element of mainstream teaching of a subject in which the tutor-librarian is qualified and which is a major subject in the college curriculum. An art librarian may contribute to classes on the history of art, and the college of agriculture librarian to farm management or milk testing. Known occasionally as 'extended-role librarians', tutor-librarians are, however, a minority in the monotechnics, if title alone is any criterion: a broad analysis of titles suggests a ratio of approximately 1:2.5 of tutor-librarians to librarians.

The creation of tutor-librarians simply to invest the library and library staff with academic status merely begs the question of the library's contribution to the learning process. While it is desirable to reward efforts which are additional to the professional work of the librarian, that professional work alone should be seen as equivalent and parallel to the work of teaching staff, since both serve a common end. It is regrettable that, in discussions on this topic, it is necessary constantly to refer to 'teaching staff' and 'professional library staff' since it implies some sort of opposition, when in fact, they are merely two sides of the same coin. The current trend towards student-based learning, together with distance and/or open learning and Flexi-Study, will have the added bonus of demonstrating this fact.

The ability to teach a subject other than the use of the library presupposes some formal qualification in that subject, probably, but unfortunately not always, in addition to librarianship qualifications. This latter would constitute an ideal situation, since a qualification in a relevant subject would bring with it an understanding of the teaching and learning needs of that subject, a fact which has been appreciated by university librarians for some time. While salary scales in the monotechnics may not always be of a kind to attract a graduate with library qualifications, the specialized nature of education in a monotechnic gives the holder of a subject qualification a useful advantage, as well as an enhanced status in the eyes of his or her teaching colleagues. However, the monotechnic librarian may still be called upon to provide a library and information service to areas with which he or she is unfamiliar. We have already identified the range of subjects which can be taught within the monotechnics, and it is no more likely that the librarian will be well versed in all of them in a monotechnic than he would be in a large college of further education or in a polytechnic. Take, for example, a nautical college, where the typical departments reflect the division of merchant navy personnel into engineering, radio and electronics, and deck (navigation) officers. While there are elements in common, they are at a basic level, and a qualification in one would not offer a great deal of insight into the others, although there may be an understanding of the total picture. This should not be taken as a suggestion that subject qualifications are not required of the monotechnic librarian: it is merely to indicate that the question of *which* qualification is as relevant here as it is in other areas of librarianship, schools, colleges of education etc.

If monotechnic college libraries can be compared in so many ways to those of other, multi-disciplinary colleges, it would seem appropriate to turn to those features which are most typical of the monotechnic alone.

Having relatively small libraries, monotechnics offer an opportunity for professional responsibility at an early stage, while not divorcing the librarian from contact with users. At the same time, the degree of specialization and the fact that the college, and therefore the library, is serving a clearly-identifiable section of the wider community, creates a sense of identity with that community. There is a close involvement in the discipline and the college which may be lacking in the larger multi-disciplinary establishment. It becomes possible for the librarian to establish close contacts with all levels of the college, and to offer a more personal service to staff and students. Of course, all librarians endeavour to develop such an approach; it is not suggested that large size makes this impossible, simply that the nature of the monotechnic makes it easier. It is easier too, to develop that informality which can so augment the quality of library service.

To all this, one caveat must be uttered. Specialization can lead to over-specialization, in the librarianship as well as in the college. It is therefore doubly important for the librarian to maintain contact with developments in librarianship through courses, conferences, and the professional literature, if he or she is not to succumb to narrowed vision. Such professional development is important not only on a personal level but also for the good of the monotechnic's own library service, which may benefit from new techniques and philosophies, regardless of where they originated, though these must, of course, be applied in the light of a sound knowledge and experience of what is needed for the particular library.

The monotechnic college library, along with the parent institution, is part of the total college library picture and is therefore subject to most of the pressures, problems, and opportunities which affect other areas of college librarianship. At the same time, it possesses a unique aspect of subject specialization within a relatively small establishment where responsibility is accompanied by close contact with users and the opportunity for an informal and closely involved approach to librarianship.

13

Sixth Form and Tertiary Colleges

Jean Cinnamond

Sixth form or tertiary? A much debated subject amongst educationists: what does each mean in terms of libraries and librarianship? This chapter will address this question and raise issues for discussion about an area which arguably may be considered the Cinderella of college librarianship. Before looking directly at the demand for and approach to libraries in such colleges, it is necessary to understand a little about the institutions themselves.

Sixth form and tertiary colleges are relatively new educational concepts, little more than twelve and seven years old respectively. While sixth form colleges operate under school regulations, tertiary colleges operate under regulations laid down for the further education (FE) sector. The difference is reflected in the courses offered by these institutions, and in their staffing.

Primarily a two year establishment for the 16–19 age group, the sixth form colleges stemmed from the school sixth form with much of their work revolving around the GCE 'A' level examination and preparation for university and higher education. In addition, one year courses led students towards 'O' level examinations. Under school regulations, the sixth form colleges may only offer courses of the type covered by schools, and therefore they lean to the academic rather than the vocational, although some sixth form colleges do now also offer more vocational courses, eg City and

Guilds foundation, Royal Society of Arts (RSA), business studies, pre-nursing, etc.

In contrast, the tertiary college covers both sixth form work and that normally provided in FE colleges, so that in addition to the studies previously mentioned, the tertiary college may offer many craft and vocational courses. As a result, a very broad spectrum of subjects and levels is achieved and therefore a greater variety is evident in the student population. This is accentuated by the fact that such colleges provide post-16 education on a full-time or part-time basis with no upper age limit.

The backgrounds of these two types of institutions, and the nature of courses offered, are clearly reflected in the staffing patterns they exhibit. Many of the staff in the sixth form colleges have been drawn from the schools, whereas in the tertiary colleges there is a mixture of former school teachers and further education lecturers.

Despite the differences between these two types of institution, their objective is the same: to prepare students to take their place in higher education or in a subsequent career. In order to do this certain common factors and requirements emerge; amongst these, the need for a library.

To support and assist the parent college in its main purpose of providing post-16 education, the library itself will require its own regularly revised objectives. These will normally be drawn up by the librarian in consultation with the principal. Whilst varying in detail, objectives will be broadly similar from one college to another whether sixth form or tertiary; to give assistance to the students with their studies, to help staff keep up to date, and to service the college's courses.

Although the principal objective in the sixth form and tertiary sectors of education is to assist the students with their studies, special attention must be given to factors peculiar to this type of institution.

Many students, particularly those straight from school, meet circumstances totally unfamiliar to them. Teaching is less confined to the classroom and much intellectual stimulus is provided through informal contact elsewhere. There are periods of private and independent study which they must learn to use effectively, and all students need to learn how to use the library effectively. The library therefore seeks to assist students in these areas.

College staff, whether teaching, management, or administration, also need assistance from the library: teaching staff to keep up to date with their subjects and research, the others to be able to request or find any information as required. In both types of college the library needs to service college courses: in the tertiary sector these may be very diverse, ranging from academic to vocational, postgraduate to 'O' level.

How then are the objectives met? By accommodation, stock, staff, and services offered. This is common to all libraries, but here, because of the special problems of age groups covered, the mixed ability of students, variation in course subjects and levels, they require some modifications.

Services include, in addition to the provision of suitable stock, a user education programme and library staff carefully selected, trained, and motivated to undertake the specialized duties demanded by this area of educational librarianship.

Sixth form colleges are in the school system while tertiary colleges are part of the further education sector: the Library Association's recommended standards for these libraries are in different publications.[1,2] This is wrong, for although sixth form colleges are covered by school regulations, the similarity ends there. In terms of libraries and librarianship, such establishments have far more in common with colleges than schools, and as such should be included in the college libraries group along with the tertiary sector. This is further evident from the fact that it was necessary to produce a statement[3] to the school libraries recommendations to cover sixth form colleges more fully. This is the principal work of the Sixth Form College Libraries Group (SFCLG), about which more later.

LIBRARY ACCOMMODATION

Preferably in a central position, the amount of space allocated to the library depends on the size of the college in terms of students and staff. In the LA standards,[2,3] it is recommended that this should be 16% of the teaching area in the case of a sixth form college and a minimum of 500m² for a college library. The result of a questionnaire sent out to tertiary colleges in June 1981 by the librarians of the sixth form colleges in Harrow, proved however that this is not always provided. 70% of the colleges who replied were below the recommended standard. Similar figures for sixth form colleges are not available, but informal comment from colleagues in the SFCLG suggests that many suffer from inadequate accommodation. Although some sixth form colleges have, like their tertiary counterparts, been purpose-built, many are ex-schools where already inadequate accommodation is often limited by the architectural style and age of the existing building.

The areas into which this accommodation will be divided is similar in both types of college library. Study accommodation is essential as are book stock areas, lending and reference, a periodical display area, perhaps with easy chairs for browsing, and an audio-visual or learning resources area. Space will also be required for the issue desk, catalogue, and display areas, with additional rooms for teaching, office accommodation, and storage.

With student populations ranging from 400 to 1,300 and with between 25% and 33% of these engaged on private study at any one time, a heavy load is put on library accommodation.

STOCK

Books, pamphlets, maps, periodicals and an extensive range of audio-visual materials will be common to both types of college. In a tertiary college however, the wider range of vocational courses will demand a broader range of subject coverage, as well as the inclusion of reports, standards, etc.

The sixth form college library stands on its own without the support provided by either the resources available in a tertiary college for the wider range of courses and levels or those provided for the lower forms which exist in the sixth form in a secondary school. Therefore additional items must be purchased to make up for this.

The tertiary college, by the very nature of its student population has greater problems in stock selection, for account must be taken, not only of variations in reading ability, but also of the previous education experience of students. This will mean the inclusion of a certain amount of background reading, some of it at remedial level. In contrast, at the other end of the scale there may be a demand for material for the postgraduate. This, along with the need to update the stock regularly, particularly in technical subjects where change is frequent, requires a sound book fund.

It may seem that because of the narrower subject coverage and more limited level, the sixth form college has less to worry about in the matter of book selection, but the lack of support from other areas that such a library receives is a loss that must be made good in stock. In addition, by virtue of the age group served and the frequent lack of general background knowledge and experience of life, a wide variety of non-fiction on all subjects is required together with a good fiction stock. The fact that more sixth form colleges now also offer some basic vocational courses increases the need for books for the less academic student. Such a stock requires careful and knowledgeable selection and is best undertaken by professional librarians in cooperation with teaching staff.

The size of the stock should in theory depend on the number of students and staff; in practice this is rarely the case. Pearce notes:[4] '. . . no tertiary college library should be satisfied with less than 40,000 volumes, anything less would be inadequate to fulfil the wide range of requirements'.

In the survey mentioned above, only one college reached this figure. Much remains to be done to improve book stocks. In the statement to their recommended school standards the Library Association states that a sixth form college 'of average size (360 students) should have a library of 7,000 items plus an additional 3,000–5,000 items to make up for the lack of support by lower form resources'.[3] Statistics provided by members of the SFCLG[5] again show that many colleges are understocked.

Periodicals and newspapers are of great importance to both the sixth form college and tertiary college libraries. They are required to support courses and to provide general and recreational reading to help broaden and stimulate the mind, particularly important for younger and/or less able students. A total of '150 current journal subscriptions plus appropriate indexing and abstracting services' is suggested as 'an adequate minimum level of stock in a small college' by the *Guidelines* for college libraries.[2] Pearce however, suggests a list of about 300 titles.[4] Whatever level is selected, it is unlikely that the small book funds currently afforded to the average sixth form college library can approach either figure.

In addition to the printed word, an important part of the stock in the sixth form and tertiary college library is audio-visual or 'resources' material. This encompasses cassettes, records, tapes, film strips, slides, videocassettes, wallcharts, etc. Facilities must be available for their use, including the provision of equipment and suitable study areas, some of which will need to be partially or wholly enclosed. The services of a technician are a great asset. Many libraries however, notably in the sixth form college sector, have had to forego the inclusion of audio-visual materials in their stock because the provision of such a service is too costly to be met from a small library budget: not a satisfactory situation when these materials play such an important part in modern teaching methods.

USER EDUCATION

A user education programme, serving both staff and students, is essential in both the sixth form and the tertiary college library. This will encompass both formal and informal tutorial work. All students require an introduction to the layout of the library, its resources, and how to retrieve them, along with an introduction to the use of general and particular reference books. In addition, they must be given an understanding of the value of periodicals, the bibliographical tools especially relevant to their own subject area, and instruction in the use (and care) of audio-visual collections. Those straight from school need to be taught how to employ private and independent study time effectively. In the sixth form colleges, where the libraries are sometimes smaller than their tertiary counterparts, it is necessary to give those students working towards higher education some idea of the greater resources which libraries in that sector will have to offer. Such a user education programme will need a range of teaching and self-teaching aids. Staff too may need to be educated in the use of the library.

FINANCE

In its various guidelines[1, 2] the Library Association recommends budget levels using such criteria as the number of students, current average book prices, levels and varieties of courses, number of staff, etc. Although it is usual for salaries and equipment to be budgeted separately, in most colleges the book funds must also cover many other necessary library items in addition to books; periodicals, audio-visual material, stationery, binding, etc. Having allocated money to such items, the balance must then be divided between the subjects taught in the college, with some money set aside for reference books and bibliographic material, along with an allocation for new courses.

The college librarian usually has sole responsibility for the manipulation of the library budget and in the sixth form and tertiary sectors, where budgets are often quite inadequate in relation to any standards, this is no easy task. 'Book funds in Sixth Form College Libraries are scandalous' says Pamela Wright[5] whilst Pearce[4] notes that of the total college expenditure 'the tertiary college librarian may count himself fortunate if he finds himself with more than one per cent'. It now becomes clear why book stocks and other materials are often below recommended levels.

As in all colleges, the finance for the sixth form college library comes from the parent college's per capita income. There are, however, other areas from which an additional amount of financial assistance may be derived, eg parents or, more substantially, the public library, if the institution forms part of this system.

STAFF

Staffing in tertiary and sixth form college libraries is often poor. Most are manned by one member of staff who, as college librarian, is not necessarily qualified or Chartered. In some colleges the librarian does have clerical help, usually part-time. Few boast the luxury of a full-time library assistant.

The duties of the sixth form college librarian therefore encompass everything from being responsible for and undertaking the managerial, professional, and teaching duties of the library, to such non-professional tasks as shelving and filing. In addition, the librarian may be required to supervise those students using the library for private study, often in numbers too great for one person to manage effectively.

Not only does this undermanning affect the quality and quantity of the library service that can be offered, it also means that the librarian is confined to the library area during the working day and so is unable to talk to staff and students outside the library, visit bookshops to select and buy materials, or attend professional meetings and conferences.

Salaries and conditions of service vary considerably. Most librarians are employed full-time, a few for term-time only, being appointed as 'ancillary staff' with non-academic conditions of service. Salaries range from clerical to AP grades: a few are on Burnham salary scales and conditions of service. Some are employed as part of the public library service. The problems posed by such variations in staffing, salaries and conditions of service are further highlighted elsewhere.[6]

What is being done to improve this situation? The SFCLG are preparing for the Library Association a statement on pay and conditions of service for sixth form college librarians which includes proposals for improved staffing. This recommends a minimum staffing complement of a college librarian, one assistant librarian and one full-time library assistant; the college librarian should be a Chartered Librarian at head of department level, the assistant should be professionally qualified, and both should have Burnham scales of salary and conditions of service. These proposals, if implemented, will provide a career structure for those wishing to enter this area of librarianship. Hopefully this statement will have been ratified by the time this book goes to press.

Tertiary college libraries appear to be better staffed than their sixth form college counterparts. This is partly due to evening classes which necessitate longer hours of opening in the tertiary sector with resultant staff requirements; but on closer investigation, how do they really compare?

From replies received to the Harrow survey, no college is manned by only one librarian, but there are colleges with staffs as low as two people, which considering the evening opening hours is not over generous. With the exception of two colleges, the college librarian is Chartered and all but one is on the Burnham scale of salaries in recognition of the academic role of this area of librarianship. None are employed as part of the public library system.

The Library Association *Guidelines* for college libraries[2] recommends 'a minimum of four library staff is essential'. 50% of the replies to the questionnaire show a staffing of four or more, certainly an improvement over sixth form college libraries, but indicating there is still room for improvements in the tertiary sector if the library is to play its full professional and educational role in the college.

CONCLUSION

What of the future? Whilst the educationists and local authorities continue to argue the merits or otherwise of sixth form and tertiary, some even changing from one system to another, one factor emerges. There is likely to be a move away from the sixth year in the comprehensive school to either the sixth form college or the tertiary college where a wider range of subjects is available. This in turn will mean a demand for a library in the chosen institution; it is important that the way is made clear by improving the standard of libraries and librarianship in both the sixth form and tertiary sectors.

How? The librarians already working in this area can do much although it will not be easy and progress may be slow. It is important that the Library Association, through its appropriate groups, SFCLG, and the Colleges of Further and Higher Education Group (CoFHE), is kept aware of problems and of the standards obtaining, particularly where these fall short of what is necessary for the good of the students. Both the above groups have done much to improve library standards in the colleges which they represent. SFCLG was formed in 1977 because sixth form college librarians felt that they 'belonged' neither in the existing schools nor the college libraries' groups. Publication of a monthly *Newsletter*, twice yearly meetings, representation on various committees followed, and in 1981 it became associated with the Library Association. SFCLG's aim is to improve libraries in sixth form colleges and the status of the librarians who work in them.

CoFHE needs no introduction and represents libraries in colleges of further and higher education, hence the tertiary college library. In the past, the group has been criticized for alleged neglect of the smaller, lower academic level, colleges into which the tertiary sector falls. This is no longer so. CoFHE put much hard work into its recent revision of the college libraries *Guidelines*.[2] The needs of the smaller, non-advanced colleges were given as much consideration as others in that revision of these standards, and considerable thought, debate and ingenuity went into the drafting of a document that would be relevant and helpful to all.

Librarians in both the sixth form college and tertiary sectors have a personal, collegiate responsibility: they must make the principal of their college aware of the problems and shortcomings of the library and do all in their professional power to persuade him that it is in his and his students' interests to provide a strong and viable library service. This can be done by active demonstration of the library's worth – in many spheres – and pressing for improvements and ensuring that the principals are made aware of recommended standards. It is often useful to ensure that attention is drawn to other colleges in the sector which have libraries approaching these standards: few like to be seen to lag behind!

Finally, in spite of poor accommodation, book stocks and staffing, it is in the service offered that the worthwhile educational and professional support given to the college by its library can best be demonstrated.

REFERENCES

1   Library Association *Library resource provision in schools: guidelines and recommendations*. Library Association, 1977.

2 Library Association *College libraries: guidelines for professional service and resource provision.* Third edition, Library Association, 1982.

3 'Statement on sixth form college libraries'. *Library Association Record* 81 (8) August 1979. 399.

4 Pearce, B L 'Library as learning environment' in Cotterell, A B and Heley, E W (eds) *Tertiary. A radical approach to post-compulsory education.* Stanley Thornes (Publishers) Ltd, 1981.

5 Wright, P 'The role of the sixth form college librarian' in *Sixth form college libraries: an insight.* Ian Henry Publications/Sixth Form College Libraries Group, 1982. 1–10.

6 Cinnamond, J 'The special problems and future of sixth form college libraries' in *Sixth form college libraries: an insight.* Ian Henry Publications/Sixth Form College Libraries Group, 1982. 11–22.

14

Libraries in the Polytechnic Library Schools

Alan Day

Lest any doubts or misapprehensions as to the nature and character of courses in library schools in the polytechnics and the sort of library service required linger on, certain basic facts of library school life should be acknowledged and accepted. In this way the air can be cleared, the scene set, and confusion avoided.

First, library school staff and students are no different from any other library users. In the matter of library provision they expect, to borrow a time-honoured phrase, a comprehensive and efficient service. Similarly, the students are no different from other students in higher education in that, despite what local educational authorities or the Department of Education and Science might award them in the shape of grants or bursaries, or on what basis, most of them have no intention whatsoever of buying their own textbooks.

Second, the days have long since vanished when library school libraries could satisfy their users' requirements from a reasonably comprehensive collection of books in the 020s and 650s, complemented by multiple copies of Legouis and Cazamian's *History of English Literature* and some intermittent runs of the standard professional journals. With the development of education for librarianship from a strictly narrow professional basis to much more broadly based degree courses and a concomitant extension of individual project work on the part of students, to say nothing of the research interests of academic staff, library schools' libraries are now expected to be much more evidently self-sufficient over the whole range of printed material than they were twenty years ago. Books on educational theory, research methodology, management theory, sociology, statistics, computer technology, data transmission, bibliometrics, the theory of communications, abundantly testify to the broadening of the library school curriculum and the widening horizons of today's and tomorrow's librarians and information workers, and, incidentally, go a long way to explain the deep suspicions entertained by some of yesterday's traditionally educated library staff of what present day library schools think they are up to.

Third, although the words 'polytechnic library school libraries' roll easily off the tongue, giving the facile impression that they all share a common organizational background and infrastructure, it must be remembered that the polytechnics themselves are comparatively recent institutions and that their constituent parts, the former colleges of art, commerce, and technology, in which the library schools were originally established, represented a wide diversity of internal organization, buildings, and control structures: in other words, they remain a long way from absolute standardization of procedures in any sphere of operations, and particularly in the pattern of library provision.

In fact, most library school libraries no longer operate as separate entities (many of them never did), simply because contemporary library and information science involves so many diverse disciplines that the concept of an independent departmental library has become totally unrealistic although many lecturers still hanker after their own library where students would enjoy quick access to specialized collections without interfering with other library users. Familiar arguments against the wasteful dispersal of expensive resources in staff, buildings, books, and related materials. implied in the provision of departmental or off-site libraries, rehearsed over and over again in academic library circles, could be ignored or offset on the grounds that the requirements of schools of librarianship and information science entitle them to individual consideration, but the realities of resource provision support opposing arguments, equally familiar, that library school students, especially those on first degree courses without previous library experience, gain much from the opportunity to exploit the total resources of a large integrated general library. And so, like every other department within the polytechnic, the library school, with the notable exception of Leeds, has bowed to the inevitable and accepted that to a large extent it must rely on the services of the main library.

At least one library school pressed this point hard recently when economic circumstances forced its parent institution to look long and hard at its accommodation with a view to making substantial economies. Faced with the prospect of moving away from the immediate vicinity of the main library to ostensibly more attractive premises, surrounded by green parkland, miles away from the soot and grime, graffiti, noise and confusion of the city centre, staff and students united in their opposition to the proposed move. Winding, flower-lined paths, a swimming pool, and an impressive gymnasium, were rejected in favour of remaining close to the polytechnic library which alone could offer the range of material so conspicuously lacking in even the best of outlying site libraries. This to the expressed surprise, chagrin, and initial incomprehension of the polytechnic's administrative hierarchy. Significantly, the one library school that succumbed to the attractions of sylvan surroundings insisted on retaining its own almost autonomous departmental library even though a well-stocked library awaited it on site, thus skilfully achieving the best of all possible bibliothecal and educational worlds. Most library schools are content, however, to avail themselves of the polytechnic library's resources and to continue their traditional links with the public reference libraries which, in the early days after the Second World War, generously placed their collections and premises at the disposal of the fledgling schools.

The Polytechnic of North London School of Librarianship library has experienced a more chequered history than most. In 1964 a lecturer/librarian was appointed to the staff of the school charged with the responsibility of establishing a teaching collection of sample bibliographic and reference material housed separately from the central library service which continued to provide the normal lending facilities. Three years later, when the school moved to its own premises in Essex Road, the librarianship collections from the main library were transferred and merged with the school's collections. Ultimate responsibility for the library rested with the polytechnic librarian, but the school's lecturer/librarian continued to exercise effective control. A major policy of acquiring virtually all new English language librarianship texts, including reports and pamphlet material, to enable the library to be self-sufficient in the teaching of subject bibliography and to act as a demonstration library, was funded from both main library and library school resources. Following reorganization of the polytechnic in 1971 the school's lecturer/librarian was translated to the polytechnic library service and the library became a site library of the polytechnic.

A further development came in the summer of 1983 when the school moved into a building already occupied by other departments of the faculty of social studies. The school's library also moved and is now incorporated into the social studies library and has assumed its full part in the polytechnic library services. Recognizing the individual needs of the library school, a special teaching collection of what are officially described as 'worthless' (!) books has been formed to provide raw material for the teaching of library management and cataloguing by linking with the main library's computer cataloguing and loan systems. This ingenious scheme allows students to benefit from direct interaction with modern computerized systems without interfering with the day-to-day activities of a busy site library.

Another interesting organizational variation occurs at Robert Gordon's Institute of Technology, Aberdeen, where the School of Librarianship controls a separate study and demonstration library intended, as its name would suggest, to be utilized as a convenient base for practical instruction. This features a one copy, reference only collection (short overnight loans are possible), current and immediate past issues of periodicals, pamphlets, a communications clippings service, and a library technology area, staffed by a professional librarian and an assistant librarian who come under the direction of the institute's principal librarian. The central library of the Institute is housed in the same building and holds the main lending collection of librarianship books and files of back numbers of periodicals. Here too, there is a proposal to move the School of Librarianship into different premises and it will be interesting to note how the School's library services will be accommodated if the move eventually takes place.

Because of their specialized interests, even library schools close to their main polytechnic library have built up substantial collections of their own, usually with the polytechnic librarian's connivance and acquiescence. In the recent past, more than a few pre-1964 public library staff collections have found their way to library schools and donations of superseded editions of bibliographies and reference works regularly arrive from all types of libraries, complementing the material bought with whatever exiguous funds the school can draw upon.

Manchester's Polytechnic's Department of Library and Information Studies can boast of five substantial and well-used independent book collections now coordinated into a single Learning Resources Unit. The management laboratory places its emphasis on ephemeral material unlikely to be added to main library stock or to be readily accessible in surrounding libraries: annual reports, current awareness bulletins, staff magazines, reports from the various cooperative schemes, and specimen library publications, all of which are frequently plundered by students seeking up to the minute information for their project work. In the information retrieval laboratory are housed classification schedules, thesauri, lists of subject headings, cataloguing codes, computer print-outs, holdings lists, abstracts and indexes, national bibliographies, and books on cataloguing and classification, together with general texts on the organization of knowledge and information. For teaching purposes, multiple copies of the schedules and codes are purchased from class material funds. Closely linked to this collection is the computer studies laboratory which contains essential hardware and software for the study and teaching of all aspects of computer applications to library and information work. Specimen copies and runs of a wide range of bibliographical and reference works are shelved in the bibliographical services laboratory, enlivening the teaching of what is traditionally a difficult area in which to sustain practical and theoretical interest. Four distinct categories of material comprise the stock of the children's literature laboratory: books for children and young people arranged by subject and by age range; the Woodfield collection consisting of books about children's books, authors, and illustrators; periodicals and publishers' catalogues relating to children's literature, library services to young people, and to school libraries; and the Youth Library Group (of the Library Association) collection on long loan to the Department, augmented to almost twice its original size from departmental resources.

Subject team leaders supervise and coordinate these laboratories' services, whilst their day-to-day management is in the hands of the department's technical assistant who is also responsible for the ordering and accessioning of new material and the maintenance of the author-title computer print-out catalogues.

At Newcastle, the polytechnic library's provision is supported by similar teaching collections in the School of Librarianship and Information Studies' lecture and seminar rooms. A joint historical bibliography, local history, and archives collection, designed to help in teaching these subjects in a practical way, contains a sufficient number of items of commercial value for considerations of security to be continually uppermost in the minds of responsible staff. Early specimens of children's literature, along with more current material, form a collection intensively used in project and assessment work. An information systems collection, including multiple copies of different classification schemes, prompts the skills and techniques of this arduous area of modern library science. Another collection of specimen reference and bibliographical works, turned to good account in the lecturing and tutoring of the access to information part of the curriculum, is housed in the school so that the normal routines of the main library are not disrupted. Library reports and other heavily used ephemera, not collected by the polytechnic library, are included in a management collection. Lastly a selection of relevant teaching slide sets, audio and video-tapes etc are assembled in a room devoted to audio-visual apparatus.

Notwithstanding its close proximity to the North Centre Library at Perry Barr, several important collections have been developed in the Department of Librarianship at Birmingham Polytechnic. Masquerading under the less than euphonious acronym BICBOC, the Birmingham International Children's Book Collection comprises children's books from overseas. Formed from a variety of sources, authors and publishers prominent amongst them, this research collection numbers over 2,000 items from nearly 50 countries and is particularly rich in German, Russian, and Japanese material. A rare book collection, including significant specimens of fine binding, illustrations, and typography from the sixteenth century onwards, is especially strong in books of the nineteenth century, a period now acknowledged as being of increasing importance in the history of the printed book. The Charles Knight collection, named after the nineteenth century publisher and pioneer in working-class education, also facilitates the study of publishing during this now fashionable period. This collection is important in the study of series publishing, and the progression of editions of a title over a long period. Still in its early stages is a collection devoted to the history of librarianship over the last century. All areas are covered including the changing nature of professional education and the history of reference and information work.

At present, the School of Librarianship and Information Studies of Liverpool Polytechnic relies on the nearby Thomas Gore (humanities) Library which serves the faculties of Business Management Studies, and Humanities and Social Studies. This includes a representative collection of children's books located in a separate room and a reference teaching collection which allows students to undertake practical exercises without disturbing readers in the main library.

Library facilities at Ealing College of Higher Education will be enormously improved when a major extension of the college library now in progress is completed. Here, the policy is that all schools in the college will enjoy a centralized library service but the School of Library and Information Studies will continue to maintain an information retrieval laboratory where students working on their assignments will have immediate access to cataloguing codes, classification schedules, précis manuals, etc, and also to a bibliographical collection consisting of standard texts, bibliographical society publications, and sample copies of different types of reference material.

Pride of place among library school libraries in the polytechnics must unquestionably be awarded to the School of Librarianship in Leeds. Their library has developed over the last twenty years from a rudimentary collection of books arranged in alphabetical order of authors (how else, the writer was once asked, could you find

Walford and Winchell side by side on the shelves) under the supervision of an unqualified part-time librarian to what it is today –
an integral and indispensable part of the School's activities and
operations. Under two successive 'academic librarians' the library
has survived three removals to different premises and has now
emerged on the Beckett Park site in Far Headingley, resplendently
redesignated as the School's Study and Demonstration Unit, a well-
chosen and deliberately innocuous title artfully designed to placate
the site librarian and to confuse the administrative powers that be.

Unconfirmed reports suggest that the academic staff were not
entirely convinced initially that an autonomous school library could
be wholly justified in times of economic stringency when it could
so easily be accommodated in a long established site library on the
same campus where students might enjoy all the advantages of a
large general stock shelved close to their own specialized
librarianship material. Fortunately, those of sterner mettle who
never lost sight of the crucially significant role a properly equipped
and oriented professional and demonstration library could play in
the school's comprehensive programme, prevailed over their more
conventionally minded colleagues and, much to the benefit of the
school, the continuing existence of its library was assured.

Funded by an agreed percentage of the annual polytechnic library
book fund, a sensible policy which avoids the need for tiresome
and potentially antagonistic haggling every year, and with a tolerable staff establishment comprising a full-time academic librarian
on senior lecturer grade, two qualified tutor-librarians working
two-thirds of a week each, and five part-time library assistants,
the new Study and Demonstration Unit possesses the necessary
resources to fashion and implement a six point plan of action. The
declared aims of the unit are: to support the students' prescribed
and general learning activities; to stimulate and support the educational and professional activities of staff and students, both
curricular and non-curricular; to assist staff to develop their
teaching effectiveness both in subject knowledge and teaching
methods; to support the research activities of the school; to assist
librarians in the area; and, generally and cumulatively, to integrate
with the teaching programme. In brief, all staff and students have
at their disposal a truly functional training unit, comparable to a

workshop or laboratory in other disciplines, which presents itself as an example of current practice, encourages students' participation in its work and management, supplies demonstration collections for teaching use, and provides resources centre facilities for the continuous and constant development of teaching methods.

As part of its services to the profession the Leeds School publishes *Selected current periodical articles in librarianship and information science*, an annotated list, arranged under subject headings, of articles suitable for use within library education based on the journals subscribed to by the unit. At the time of writing this worthwhile current awareness bulletin has reached its 51st issue. The bulletin is circulated to several other libraries outside the Polytechnic and is valued by many librarians in the UK.

Whenever library practitioners take to discussing library education, it is not long before the concept of a teaching library, comparable to a teaching hospital, is floated. This comes round with monotonous regularity, although nobody ever seems to advocate a teaching building for architects, a demonstration court for lawyers, an experimental parish church for clergymen, a mock-up observatory for astronomers, or a foreign embassy complete with diplomats, terrorists, and hostages for the SAS to practise on. Nevertheless the idea has much to commend it. Taking advantage of its recent relocation, the Leeds School has closely involved the Study and Demonstration Unit in the course programmes.

Obvious possibilities inherent in library-based teaching like book selection exercises, the provision of case-study materials, the use of microform and audio-visual hardware, the demonstration of library furniture, library building, the use of different classification schemes, were all quickly called into play. Then a more ambitious project was embarked upon: an investigation into the feasibility of the library undertaking some of the functions of field-work in external libraries. The conclusion drawn from this research project is that on balance 'much experimental learning at present carried out in fieldwork libraries could be transferred to an internal laboratory/library'.[1] Other schools, lacking the same facility, may choose to continue to rely on the traditional hospitality of their regular placement libraries.

Changes in library school courses over the last fifteen years are reflected in the nature of the students attending them. No longer is the student body exclusively composed of full-time students engaged on two-year diploma, three-year degree, or one-year postgraduate courses. A variety of part-time courses has been introduced to meet the demands of the profession: qualified librarians who through historical accident had no opportunity to take a degree course can now take advantage of modular courses, specifically designed to meet their needs, available at a consortium of polytechnic library schools all prepared to build upon modules already completed elsewhere should an individual's career progression require an enforced move to a different part of the country. Professionally unqualified postgraduates, reluctant to give up a full-time library post to attend library school, or unable to secure one of the severely rationed Department of Education and Science bursaries, can also now obtain their professional diploma by part-time study. Higher degrees, either by research or by taught courses with a strong practical element, are available at a gradually increasing number of schools.

Quite clearly there is no longer a recognizable species labelled typical library school student, or, for that matter a prototype library school lecturer. Inhabitants of contemporary British library schools range from sixth form school leavers who may perhaps have helped out a time or two in the school library in wet lunch hours, older undergraduates with or without full-time library experience, postgraduates in a similar position, perhaps attending a course on release from their library post one day a week, to senior professionally qualified librarians returning to academic studies on a Master's course. Some may be research students and a few in all these categories may be from overseas. All of them place a different type of demand on the library school's collections, with part-time students perhaps the biggest headache in administrative terms. It is becoming increasingly noticeable that even the part-time student occupying a library post experiences difficulty in obtaining the books he requires from his own library. Where staff libraries continue to exist, and it is a reasonable assumption that many have disappeared, they are at best static or moribund, and it is a matter of chance whether they are accessible to staff who work at some distance from a headquarters library. Consequently they rely on the library school to meet their needs which can be both urgent and multifarious. For this reason one or two library schools retain their own British Library Lending Division request forms, or a London Library or National Book League institutional membership, although in most instances these latter are more probably used by staff rather than students.

Security problems with regard to library materials should be negligible almost to the point of non-existence in the library schools. Professional discipline should ensure that the minimum of regulation necessary for the common good, be readily and sympathetically observed but, regrettably, this is not always the case. The consciences of a few embryonic librarians are as elastic as those of their fellows in other departments when it comes to surreptitiously removing books and journals for what can only be described as quintessential private study. Even more inexplicable are the library school students who think so little of their chosen profession that they can bring themselves to extract chapters from books or articles from bound volumes of periodicals purely for their own personal convenience. Less heinous in nature is the disappearance of sets of Dewey at certain times of the year, but admiration at the physical accomplishment of removal is tempered by the knowledge that the missing sets do not invariably reappear once the examinations are over. And even when books are legitimately borrowed and charged out in conventional manner they can still be extremely dilatory in returning. Simon Francis, Head of Library Services, Polytechnic of North London, remarked upon this phenomenon in his *Annual Report* 1980–1. Writing on the 15% increase in overdue notices dispatched he notes that 'Members of the School of Librarianship have the unenviable distinction of being the worst offenders but then the cobbler's children are always unshod'. We can all share his puzzled bewilderment. What hope for the rest of mankind if the library school library can't get its books back on time? Lecturers are as culpable as any – the rows of books they keep for months on end in their offices, more often than not precisely those most in demand by students, even when funds are available for their own desk copies, bear unimpeachable witness to their guilt!

The position of the polytechnic librarian *via-à-vis* the library school libraries is a little invidious and certainly not one to be envied. From where he sits he sees independent collections not under his direct control housed in a department within the institution, financed in at least one case from polytechnic library funds. On a professional level he might justifiably argue that the very existence of such collections transgresses the principles of academic librarianship which presumably the department concerned is inculcating in its students. He also sees up to 25 qualified librarians squatting on his doorstep, all of whom are likely to have their own views not only on the library provision to their own department but also on all other conceivable matters of library service and policy.

Close involvement of the polytechnic librarian and of the head of department of librarianship in each other's affairs, the librarian (and other senior library staff) perhaps taking part in the teaching programme, the head of department sitting on the library committee giving support when needed, both ex-officio members of the academic board, ensure that the two men at the top effectively march in step. In two instances, the Polytechnic Librarian at Liverpool, and the Head of Readers' Services at Manchester, the present holders of these appointments were themselves senior library school staff in a previous incarnation. Joint participation in research proposals and the use of each other's computer hardware and systems, a subject librarian regularly liaising with the library school in book ordering, and not least the cordial personal relationships of staff at all levels, have contributed in immeasureable degree to avoiding what might otherwise have developed into a sad and unnecessary conflict of academic and professional interests.

Paradoxically, the situation now is that many polytechnic library staff, always willing to respond to calls for assistance from the library school, are fast reaching the point where they may be in danger of neglecting their normal, day-to-day, routine duties. It is deceptively easy to accede to constant requests from lecturers to bring their students to inspect library operations at first hand at the expense of allowing less enticing work to pile up for a morrow that somehow never arrives. Added together, the hours spent with library school students can total a forbidding number per week and, at a time when posts are being lost, and when the library service is under very real pressure, this must give senior management serious grounds for concern. Library school staff, desperately anxious to refute suggestions that their courses are too theoretical, can all unwittingly put far too heavy a load on their friends and colleagues in the library who find themselves taking on more and more responsibilities. . . . It is not exactly a vicious circle, but it is one which needs a close watch if regrettable misunderstandings are not to occur.

The inconvenient necessity for polytechnic library staff to provide a library service to the whole polytechnic explains why so many library schools have formed their own special collections for practical instruction. No doubt, as the advocates of the teaching library vision would agree, it would be immensely beneficial for budding librarians to gain constant practical experience in a large working library. The trouble is that the numbers involved present practical difficulties. Other library users, for example, have a right to expect some measure of continuity in service provided by experienced staff and not by inevitably hesitant, tentative, self-conscious, and apprehensive groups of library school students. Screening off parts of the library for practical tuition and demonstrations is a more realistic possibility but, apart from the confidence boosting knowledge that the venue is an actual library, what difference is there between this and a similar demonstration unit, more conveniently accessible every day of the week, in departmental accommodation?

The question follows whether it would be either feasible or desirable for a combined professional staff to run the library and the library school in one smooth coordinated operation. Conceivably this would be possible if higher education in this country could start afresh in some miraculous new dawn. Unfortunately the tradition of higher education outside the universities is now almost a century old and the obstacles preventing such a radical new approach are all too evident. At a mundane level there would likely be intractable union opposition to a merger of library and library school. Libraries would certainly harbour deep suspicions that the local educational authority would regard such a move as a heaven-sent opportunity for 'rationalization' which in concrete terms would spell redundancies. Work experience for students would in fact provide an almost bottomless reservoir of semi-skilled labour to disguise frozen vacancies on the cheap. Perhaps union fears could be proved groundless, perhaps local education authorities might take an enlightened view, but the recent track record of both unions and local government in library affairs is not one to justify extravagant optimism. Educationally, practising and teaching by the same members of staff, working in closely knit teams, is undeniably an attractive concept, but it would demand superhuman individuals willing and able to undertake such an exacting dual role. Practising librarians coming into library schools for a 'one-off' expert lecture, or even a series of lectures, is one thing, but doing and talking at the same time over a long period is quite a different proposition.

Within the national library scene the polytechnic library school libraries may occupy an inconspicuous niche but they are by no means entirely lost to sight. None of them have reached, or indeed are likely to reach, a stage whereby they are designated back-up libraries in the national inter-lending system. Nevertheless, at times, their specialized stock can be made more easily available to the profession than the immense resources of the British Library's Lending Division or Library Association Library. There are instances in the writer's experience when this has undoubtedly been so: a public library sent its van to pick up the latest edition of Dewey when urgently required; a deputy university librarian researched his latest book in the library school's library; another university library sent along two of its junior assistants preparing for Library Association examinations. Instances not exactly earth shattering in themselves but indicative of the value of the library school's collections. News arrives that one famous city reference library has been forced by current budgeting constraints to cancel its long-standing subscriptions to a number of librarianship journals. Whether or not this decision was influenced by the knowledge that these journals were available elsewhere in the city remains to be discovered, but it needs no special ability with a crystal ball to foresee circumstances in which the library schools' holdings will be increasingly exploited by librarians in their immediate neighbourhood. Allied to continuing education in the form of part-time and short courses, the active participation of staff and students in professional affairs, the availability of their premises for Library Association group and branch meetings, this could lead to the library schools' libraries developing into community libraries for the library profession at large.

What then of the future? In these troubled and uncertain times it is wise and prudent not to be too dogmatic about anything but, clearly, contraction rather than expansion is the order of the day and the polytechnics cannot expect to return to the youthful vigour, full bloom, and prosperity of the early seventies. So far as the departments and schools of library and information studies are concerned it looks more and more improbable that they will ever be in a position to expand their various laboratory collections to a point where they might reasonably demand their own separate library. Even if sufficient space were available, and that particular 'if' is getting bigger as every term passes, ambitious departments would very quickly come to grief when it came to the question of library staff. With early retirements constantly being urged, there is obviously little chance of special staff being appointed. Similarly, no polytechnic librarian in the foreseeable future stands the remotest chance of finding himself with the staff resources to man an independent departmental library. No doubt most library schools would prefer to establish their own separate library despite the brave face put on about students familiarizing themselves with the total stock of an integrated polytechnic library and the advantages it offers from a subject bibliography point of view, but the most they can realistically hope to achieve is a modest increase in departmental resources to strengthen their specialist collections supporting developing areas of the curriculum. Beyond that, optimism degenerates into wishful thinking.

REFERENCE

1   Prytherch, R J 'The laboratory/library: further work on an internal teaching and working library unit in a school of librarianship'. *Journal of Librarianship* 14 (3) July 1982. 204–15.

Part 3
THE LIBRARIANSHIP

15

Staffing: Policy and Problems

C M Turner

Few college libraries, whether they are large polytechnic systems with 50 to 60 staff or small 'one-man-band' operations, are without some sort of so-called staffing problem. 'Staffing' however is an umbrella term for several different though related problems in the college library. There may be a staff shortage due to an insufficient establishment or to unfilled, or for financial reasons unfillable, vacancies. Such staff as there are may be inappropriately graded, usually a euphemism for 'underpaid', causing discontent and difficulty in recruiting or retaining people of the right calibre.

Alternatively, the library may have an unsatisfactory staffing structure; too often a hotch-potch of roles and responsibilities is created when colleges are amalgamated. Disparate and often distant elements may have been hastily thrown together in order to avoid closure, with little consideration of how the resulting aggregation will operate as a systematic whole.

Of course, there are also problems associated with the management of the staff themselves: inadequate selection procedures, the inevitable but unavoidable selection error, or the character who has been around since the year dot and is as inflexible as the foundations. These can all be sources of friction between staff and of frustration for the college librarian. These problems can however be mitigated by the management practices of the college librarian. Too often, especially in the smaller library, the pressures of simply manning the issue/enquiry desk, or controlling the shelving and/or cataloguing backlog, mean that staff management is neglected. One must beware of becoming too busy 'running' the library to devote any time to 'managing' it.

Staff development and training is yet another potential source of difficulty. The twin constraints of money and inadequate staffing levels reduce opportunities for attendance at professional meetings, courses, and conferences. In another context, the spread of 'new technology' emphasizes the need for suitable training if the technology's potential is to be exploited without attendant disasters. In addition, the Library Association itself places demands on the employing library to provide a programme of professional training for younger staff.

The Library Association's restructuring of professional qualifications places the responsibility on employing institutions to provide in-service training for junior qualified staff. Broadly speaking, the Association requires that a candidate for Licentiateship should have a one year programme of training under the supervision of a Chartered Librarian. This should comprise guided reading, counselling, on the job training, short courses internal and external, attendance at meetings and courses, and projects. The candidate is required to keep a diary or logbook of these activities. This programme will force all organizations to look carefully at their training programmes, but all but the very smallest institutions should be able to undertake such training. This training requirement, coming as it does from the professional association, can be used by the chief librarian to press for more training resources from his college management.

Another aspect of training is that related specifically to a particular task or range of tasks, and is normally associated either with induction of new staff or with the adoption of new technologies and working methods. Too often this element is overlooked, sometimes with disastrous consequences. Lack of understanding and even hostility to new methods due to lack of proper training and preparation can render the best of systems unworkable.

Staffing: Policy and Problems

Even with a staff of only two or three, the college librarian has a responsibility to maintain motivation, assist with personal and professional development, provide some incentive and, if possible, reward, for good performance, in short to provide the maximum level of job satisfaction for his staff. Quite apart from the benefit to staff as individuals, a justifiable end in itself, staff with a high level of motivation and job satisfaction will be more likely to provide a high quality of service to the college.

These responsibilities are, if anything, even more important in times of financial restraint. The rate of staff turnover is likely to be artificially and undesirably low, with a consequent decline in opportunities for career development through promotion and job change. In addition, restricted budgets mean that innovation within the service is more difficult, though not by any means impossible. (It may be argued that identifying, implementing, and managing appropriate innovation within existing resource envelopes is in fact one of the principal challenges facing librarians, and indeed all public sector management, at present.) There are a number of strategies which the college librarian can adopt in order to manage staff effectively, even within severely limited resources.

A deliberate policy of involving staff in the decision-making process is a significant factor in maintaining motivation. Quite apart from the obvious but often neglected fact that people who actually do a job are likely to have useful views on ways of modifying and improving procedures, participation gives staff the feeling that they have something to contribute to the organization in addition to obedience to instructions and the following of procedure, and that they have some control over their working environment.

For personal and professional development, there are, traditionally, external conferences, courses, and meetings; but these cost money. Many colleges, however, seek to provide staff development from within their own resources, and the librarian should ensure that his staff have the opportunity to attend college based courses where relevant; wordprocessing, microcomputing, introductory accounting, and courses in education itself are all germane to the librarian's job.

Personal development can be derived also from participation in the work of committees of the Library Association's groups and branches, or from involvement in trade union activities, including the growth area of health and safety. Such involvement can benefit both individual and library, and do not draw cash from a slender budget. Although in rare cases individuals can become over-committed, it is generally recognized that those members of staff most active in external professional business tend also to be those most dynamic in the college work situation.

It is both a necessity and a duty for a professional person to continue to develop his professional education and awareness throughout his career. Any librarian with responsibility for staff must try to ensure that his staff have and accept opportunity to keep themselves up to date with professional developments in some logical and structured manner. The employing institution can only benefit from the improvement in motivation and contribution that derives from a staff development programme.

Professional isolation is a problem of which most librarians, particularly in smaller colleges, are acutely aware. In addition, in such colleges, it is all too easy to become almost exclusively concerned with the daily round. It is essential that staff develop-ment opportunity be generated to combat these tendencies.

The problem of providing tangible rewards for staff in recogni-tion of particularly good performance is perhaps the most intract-able. Promotions, regradings, or even accelerated increments are often ruled out by strict cash limits and/or inflexible out-of-college administrative procedures, and the process of trying for any of these may raise expectations only to frustrate them. This may prove counter-productive. Conversely, however, if the chief librarian does not attempt this sort of exercise when it is justified, his staff will feel that he is not working for them, and is not appreciative of their efforts. It must remain a matter for individual judgment in particular circumstances as to whether and how far a chief librarian should proceed in this area, but the responsibility for doing so when circumstances merit it is a real one, to be pursued actively and positively.

Performance can also be rewarded with additional responsibility. This may look like 'squeezing the lemon till the pips squeak', and there are obvious limits to such a policy. In situations where people's abilities are evidently under-utilized, however, this avenue may prove fruitful. Lack of job mobility may have trapped a person in a post for too long, a member of staff may have outstripped the requirements of this post; it is important that such cases are recognized and that people are given opportunity to develop their potential.

The college librarian must manage his staff on a day-to-day basis in such a way as to get the best from them and to do the best for them in their college's particular situation. In order to tackle those problems of staffing levels and gradings which too often form a constricting framework for operations, he must adopt a rigorous and analytical approach.

The Library Association's *College Libraries: Guidelines for professional service and resource provision*[1] – known as the *Guidelines* – is based to a significant extent on good contemporary practice. For the majority, they provide target solutions at which to aim, and they form the basis for the advice and assistance which the Library Association gives to members, employers, and trade unions alike.

The *Guidelines* propose basic levels of staffing dependent on the size and type of the parent institution. They favour the academic role and grading of professional librarians, and state clearly and forcibly the wisdom of proper staff development and training programmes. The *Guidelines* are supported by the detailed *College Libraries Policy Statement* produced by the National Association of Teachers in Further and Higher Education (NATFHE).[2] They enjoy a wide degree of acceptance and support throughout the profession.

Such evidence as is available, however, would suggest that general practice in colleges is some way from the *Guidelines*, especially in the area of staffing. Guidelines, unless mandatory, by their very nature should be in the van of professional theory and practice: to be otherwise would be pointless. However, in some instances, the gap between guidelines and practice is so wide as to present serious problems, particularly for those wishing to make use of them to argue for improved resources.

The main sources of information on general practice in staffing and grading are: the Library Association's Academic Library Staffing and Grading Census,[3] last conducted in 1978 and due again in 1984; the annual staffing survey carried out by the Council of Polytechnic Librarians (COPOL);[4] occasional surveys such as those conducted by NATFHE's Libraries Section in 1980, and by the Colleges of Further and Higher Education (CoFHE) group of the Library Association in 1982. The DES's biennial *Statistics of libraries in major establishments of further education in England, Wales and Northern Ireland*[5] covers staffing levels rather than gradings, but is extremely valuable not only for its staffing figures, but also for additional information on funding and stock levels. This series was last produced in 1979–80. Despite its unique position and its consequently enormous value, its future is very uncertain due to the review and consequent cutback of government statistical services conducted during 1981.

Lomas has done some detailed analysis of the 1979–80 DES statistics[6] and has taken some care to eliminate the obviously incorrect figures which have appeared in the series from time to time and which have tended to corrupt the summary figures. His analysis shows the following ratios of library staff to full-time equivalent student population:

Polytechnics	1:86.6
Institutions of Higher Education	1:90.8
Colleges of Further Education	1:422.2
Others	1:223.6

The Library Association *Guidelines* recommend, for colleges engaged principally in advanced work, a ratio of 1:80, scaling down to 1:120 for colleges with a small proportion of advanced work. For further education the recommended ratios are between 1:200 and 1:250, subject to a basic complement of four staff which is the minimum considered necessary to operate a library service. According to my own analysis of the DES statistics, approximately one third of non-polytechnic libraries have less than the recommended minimum of four staff.

Obviously, it is possible to 'prove' many things from statistics, but the evidence does suggest that there is a very considerable gap, particularly in the further education sector, between what the profession considers to be appropriate staffing levels, and the reality. Accepting that the Library Association *Guidelines* on both staffing and services are based largely upon good practice and professional consensus, then it would seem clear that staffing is one of the major constraints upon the proper development and exploitation of college libraries.

Can the publication of guidelines by the professional body or policy statements by a concerned trade union help to remedy this situation? A great part of the answer lies in how these documents are used by individuals and organizations.

As suggested earlier, the further and higher education sector of the UK's education system covers a very wide range of institutions. This situation is yet further complicated by differing views over what constitutes a library. In recent years the term 'resource centre' (or similar) has been added to, or sometimes replaced, the term 'library'. The learning resources concept of college libraries has gained wide acceptance within the profession, though college managements have been slower to embrace the new thinking. However, there is now a definite trend towards a broader view of libraries, with the result that some college libraries offer primarily traditional, print based services, while others have a much broader range of interests and collections.

A brief description of my own library department, in a college of further education, may serve to illustrate the staffing implications of this wider, learning resources concept.

'Educational Resources' comprises the libraries (ours is a split-site college), and the educational technology and reprographic units. In practice therefore, the acquisition and/or creation, storage, dissemination, and exploitation of teaching and learning materials are united in one department. Staffing consists of librarians, audio-visual and reprographics technicians, library assistants, and clerical/secretarial assistants. We are of course under-staffed and underpaid! The service is for the most part centred physically around the libraries as the main contact point for users and the major storage facility for finished materials. In practice, it is important that all staff have some understanding of the range of services offered and of the basic technicalities of the various operations. Technicians, who often act as first line consultants in the creation of resources, need to understand possible alternative sources of ready-made materials and of some of the ways in which materials might be stored and retrieved. Librarians on the other hand should know about basic production techniques and the potential of the various items of equipment available. Achievement of these goals depends on selecting staff with the right degree of flexibility in their approach, and on staff training. The individual who likes to identify his or her defined area of responsibility and concern and to concentrate on that to the exclusion of all else is a positive handicap.

As librarian responsible for managing such a department, I am in a position which, though increasingly common in further and higher education, is probably unique to that sector of education. Although the 'new technology' is well established in libraries, making for a greater technical awareness in the profession at large, it is not unreasonable to assert that the management of a library-associated educational technology and reprographic service, based on the application of technology to achieve specific educational objectives, does not fall within the scope of traditional librarianship and is certainly not provided for in present education for librarianship. Nevertheless, it is a challenge which an increasing number of librarians are facing, and it is likely that more will face it in the future. It is vital that the challenge be accepted if college library services are not to be subsumed into a resources service run, for example, by a subject teacher with educational technology expertise, rather than by a librarian, whose approach to and understanding of information and its use make him the natural leader of educational resource services.

Whatever the policy regarding learning resources in the individual college, the variety of possibilities and of degrees of integration make for a still wider range of institutions and circumstances in the further and higher education sector. Again one may question the applicability of general guidelines given such a diverse background. Again I suggest that the question is not *whether* guidelines are applicable but *how* they are applied.

The various aspects of staffing – grading, staffing levels, structures, training, etc in the individual college library cannot be quantified absolutely by reference to a general standard. The librarian who simply extracts a staffing figure or a grading recommendation and goes to his principal with the 'it says here I should have 10.6 staff and I've only got 3.7' approach is unlikely to make much headway. The *Guidelines* offer much more advice than this. That advice is derived from two fundamental truths about staffing. First, the quantity of staff can only be determined and argued for on the basis of the quantity of work actually done. Second, grading of staff can only be determined and argued for on the basis of the nature and quality of the work done, that is the duties and responsibilities of the job. There is widespread misunderstanding of this point, not just amongst college librarians, although it may seem more prevalent in that sector. There appears to be an underlying assumption that one is paid for merely *being* a college librarian. The truth is that one is paid for what one does, not for what one is, or for what one thinks one should be doing if only one had the staff, book fund etc, etc.

The various aspects of staffing cannot be treated in isolation any more than staffing guidelines can be used and applied on their own out of context. Grading, staff levels, structures, and training are interrelated and should be dealt with as such by a properly integrated staffing policy. Identifying this should commence with determination of the range and volume of tasks to be performed. From this, the quantity of staff, the gradings, and the training needs can be identified and a suitable structure developed. Whilst forming the basis for a method of determining staffing policy, this task analysis cannot itself be conducted in a vacuum. One should continually ask: 'Why is it necessary to perform this task?' in order to provide a rationale for each activity. A staffing policy built on assumptions which cannot be readily and coherently justified will collapse like a house of cards when questioned by those who hold the purse strings.

The exercise of questioning activities should lead naturally to the real starting point, not only for staffing policy, but for the whole range of library policy; the identification of an agreed set of objectives for the library service. Staffing policy should be derived from the objectives of the library service within the parent institution. In practice it is likely that the library with no explicit and agreed objectives is likely to be staffed and resourced according to vague, often conflicting implicit objectives buried in the subconscious of college management. The most common implied objective probably goes no further than the feeling that academic institutions should

211

have a library, and that libraries are rooms with books in! What the college should expect to gain from the library will rarely have been considered in rigorous and specific terms.

Establishing a set of objectives and agreeing them with college management will help to clarify attitudes within the institution. Furthermore, it is a step towards making college management more conscious of the library *and more demanding of it* – always the first step towards improving resources. Objectives are an essential tool for the librarian in determining staffing policy and in arguing for the resources necessary to implement that policy.

The following objectives will serve as an illustrative example of this process. They are not revolutionary, nor are they regarded as immutable or definitive. Objectives should always be subject to review and modification in the light of changing circumstances if they are not to become a straightjacket and a restraint on innovation and development. It is too easy for the college librarian to become enmeshed in day-to-day concerns and to lose sight of the fact that the library must be a responsible and dynamic system if it is to serve the college effectively. The knowledge that the service is constantly under review, and that modifications are actively encouraged by the chief librarian is a stimulus to staff and is itself a significant factor in maintaining morale, motivation, and high levels of contribution.

1   To ensure the availability of learning resources necessary to support the academic life of the college by:
1.1   Acquisition and production of appropriate materials.
1.2   Provision of flexible loan and reference services.
1.3   Provision of equipment necessary to access non-print materials.
1.4   Provision of access to national and international collections of materials and information.

2   To ensure the effective exploitation of learning resources by:
2.1   Production of printed guides and publicity.
2.2   Programmes of tuition both formal and informal for staff and students covering library use, information retrieval, research techniques, use and application of educational technology.

2.3 Provision of current awareness and SDI services etc.

2.4 Formal and informal participation in academic planning and development, and routine course administration.

2.5 Provision of advice and consultancy service on bibliographic and information systems and educational technology systems.

3 To ensure the efficiency of the library service by:

3.1 The general management of the service by the chief librarian as part of the college senior management.

3.2 Staff management, training, and development.

3.3 Financial management and control.

Having agreed a set of objectives along these or similar lines with college management, it is possible to break these down into specific tasks and to group the tasks together according to function: librarian, technician, library assistant, etc, and according to physical location in, for example, a split- or multi-site operation. At this point one may arrive at several lists similar to those given below. They are not intended to be exhaustive, merely illustrative.

1 Librarian's tasks:

1.1 Teaching: ie developing, constructing, and implementing relevant programmes of instruction for groups and/or individuals.

1.2 Stock development and maintenance, in conjunction with course planning teams and individual teaching staff.

1.3 Development of flexible loan policies to meet particular needs.

1.4 Development of special collections and services for particular categories of users.

1.5 Cataloguing, classification, and indexing of collections.

1.6 General user advice.

2 Library Assistant's tasks:

2.1 Issue and return of stock.

2.2 Maintenance of loan records.

2.3 Shelving

2.4 Book processing.

2.5 Maintenance of stationery stocks and records.

2.6 Maintenance of periodical receipts and stock records.

3   Technician's tasks:
3.1   Maintenance of equipment.
3.2   Issue and return of equipment.
3.3   Assistance and instruction in use of equipment and related software.
3.4   Production of specified learning materials.
3.5   Acquisition and maintenance of materials stocks, eg blank tapes, film, reprographic supplies etc.

Clearly, the numbers of staff required to perform these tasks, and the organizational framework, will depend on the size and type of the institution and on the number of sites to be serviced.

At this point, survey data, policy statements, and guidelines relating to staffing can be utilized to good effect, both in determining the quantity of staff required and the appropriate gradings and conditions of service to be used.

The Library Association's *Guidelines* on staffing levels relate the quantity of staff to the full-time equivalent student numbers and the level of advanced work in the institution; it is therefore possible to derive a target figure for staffing levels in the individual institution. It cannot be emphasized too strongly that these staffing figures are not absolute. They are indications of the numbers of staff necessary to provide the range of services outlined elsewhere in the document. If the agreed objectives of the individual institution do not encompass the full range of services envisaged in the *Guidelines* then the staffing target should be modified accordingly.

Having determined the number of staff appropriate to the institution with regard to the factors outlined above, it is possible to group tasks together to make up individual job descriptions. Below is a description of the sort of job which an experienced Chartered Librarian may expect to find himself doing in a college library. This is not a formal job description, but an attempt to give the flavour of the work involved.

> Responsibilities are centred around a course or group of courses, depending on the size of the institution. The librarian should be fully involved in the course management structure, thus getting to know staff and students, and course structure and content. He should understand the pattern of coursework

and the nature and content of the student's set work. Thus he will be able to advise on the best means of resourcing the course with learning materials. He should contribute to the design and amendment of course structure in so far as it is affected by the availability of different types of learning materials and library services.

Armed with this knowledge, the librarian will be in a position to select materials and build collections appropriate to course needs. He will be able to develop special collections and services such as news cuttings, trade literature, short loan collections, SDI and current awareness services, and should be in a position to influence the patterns of demand made on inevitably limited resources.

The librarian should also have a tutorial function related to all courses. In conjunction with the course team, he will devise a programme of instruction designed to familiarize students with the materials and services available and to give the students the skills necessary to make best use of these according to the needs of their course. This may range from the completion of simple assignments and the use of the catalogue to advance research techniques.

Depending on the policy of the library, our librarian may be responsible for the cataloguing and classification of materials relating to his courses and will almost certainly be expected to undertake periods of duty at the readers' advice desk. He may also have line management responsibilities, perhaps in charge of a site library, as well as duties involving staff supervision and training, and some financial planning.

In practice, there will be variations from this model. In small institutions, and at the small sites of larger colleges, there will inevitably be a blurring of the distinctions between the librarian's tasks and those of the library assistant. Some of the routine work will fall upon the librarian, and the assistant may have to deal with readers' enquiries to the best of his ability. Some semi-professional work, such as inter-library loans and bibliographic checking, may be allocated to either. Conversely, in larger institutions there will be a greater tendency towards specialization. Cataloguing and classification may be done by a centralized unit, perhaps linked to an outside automated cataloguing cooperative. The handling of non-print media may be in a separate section, and staffing and administration may be dealt with by one or two individuals.

It is here that the chief librarian's assessments of individuals' aptitudes and capabilities must be taken into consideration. High sounding objectives and task analyses notwithstanding, square pegs won't work in round holes. Few librarians will be in the happy position of having resources to fulfil all objectives totally. The chief librarian must determine priorities, and in doing so, should have regard for the quality and experience of his staff resources, as well as their quantity. He would be wise to play to his strengths, and would serve his college better by doing so. Thus, the emphasis given to reader services in a library in contrast to technical and/or bibliographic services may well be influenced, not only by demand, but also by existing staff capabilities and experience. A change in personnel may well suggest a change in service emphasis.

These variations notwithstanding, the essential nature of the professional librarian's role in a college is the provision of a service designed to meet specific *educational* objectives. The librarian himself must be as much an educationist as a librarian to function effectively.

Having defined the nature of the job, appropriate gradings and conditions of service can now be established. Broadly speaking, there are two types of salary and conditions of service schemes operating in college libraries in the UK. These are the local government scheme, known as NJC, and the academic scheme, known as Burnham. (Scotland has its own variations on both schemes but the basic principle of division is the same.) The Inner London Education Authority (ILEA) has its own system derived from the NJC scheme. There are wide differences in the two types, both in salaries and in conditions of service: under Burnham, the salary for the basic grade, Lecturer I, currently (1983) runs from £5,649 to £9,735 by 15 increments; attendance at college is required for 30 hours per week minimum over a 38–week teaching year; under NJC, the basic grade for a Chartered Librarian (Scale 4) runs from £6,264 to £7,005 by 4 increments; the working week is 37 hours with a 47-week year. The last full-scale census of gradings in the further and higher education sector was conducted by the Library Association in 1978. Of the 1,384 professional posts surveyed in England and Wales, excluding ILEA, 58% of posts were on the NJC scheme and a further 15% were 'hybrid' posts – that is paid according to Burnham but with NJC conditions of service.

The Library Association together with the National Association of Teachers in Further and Higher Education (NATFHE), the union responsible for negotiating the Burnham scheme, have for many years been in favour of Burnham salaries and conditions of service for all professional library staff in further and higher education. There has been opposition to this policy from NALGO, the union responsible for the NJC scheme and the one which negotiates for librarians in public libraries. NALGO regard themselves as the rightful representatives of all librarians in the local government sector irrespective of the nature of their parent institution, and seem unable to acept that librarians have (and welcome) an academic role in education. One should perhaps not expect a union to accept a policy which would result in loss of membership. Both NALGO and NATFHE are opposed to hybrid posts, and have agreed that such posts should be systematically reviewed and 'where the duties of a post predominantly involve an educational function the appropriate salary and conditions of service arrangements are those applicable to teachers'. There are, however, no guidelines for assessment, leaving the criteria for 'educational function' to be determined locally. Clearly, the onus is on individuals to make their case.

The task analysis described above leaves little doubt as to the fundamentally educational role of the college librarian, and the individual who has conducted a similar exercise and agreed his role with the college management, and is actually performing these tasks, will do no harm to his chances of obtaining an appropriate grading.

It would be wrong to believe that inter-union rivalry is the only reason why more college librarians are not treated as academic staff. In some instances, the problem lies with the librarians themselves, who may have a very restricted view of their role in the college. Occasionally, individual librarians are hardly to be blamed for this. There are a not insignificant number of chief college librarians on the minimum librarian's grade – and in some extreme cases in non-professional grades. These people are likely to be young, inexperienced, and ill-equipped to deal with the circumstances in which they find themselves. Obviously, in such cases college management has an imperfect view of the library's function in the college. That view will tend to be reinforced by the quality of staff they are able to recruit.

Petty considerations of 'status' for its own sake and the purely material questions of salary and hours worked are not the sole factors in the issue (though the differences are very great). It is the experience of librarians that academic status carries with it access to information and decision making that is vital to the development of the library as a power for academic good in the college. Furthermore, such surveys as have been carried out indicate that those colleges with the better libraries tend to have librarians on academic scales. *Verb sap*: McElroy *et al*[7] and Revill[8] have recently explored this area in greater detail.

The problem of inadequate gradings, and therefore of inexperienced staff, tends to arise particularly in smaller colleges. But the qualities required of a chief librarian, experience, maturity, commitment, and educational understanding, are basically the same irrespective of college size. Volume, rather than nature of activity, varies with college size. By appointing their librarians to appropriate posts, small colleges would effect immediate improvement in the quality of staff attracted, and provide incentive for librarians to seek a career in the smaller institution, rather than using it merely as a stepping stone along a career path.

There are other problems over the applicability of academic conditions of service in libraries. These conditions of service were designed originally for staff whose work consisted of classroom teaching and the preparation and marking of work. Hence the 30-hour week and the 38-week year. No college library can function properly if the professional staff work a 30-hour week and a 38-week year. Professional responsibility and the needs of the service should dictate the hours worked and leave taken, as it does for college management. This is a tenable view when considering senior library staff, but it may be difficult to convince college management that all professional staff will be so responsible.

Staffing: Policy and Problems

In universities professional library staff are regarded as academics, are members of the same union, and have the same pay scales. Conditions of service vary according to the academic roles played within the institution. If this pattern could be developed in colleges, then a considerable step forward would have been made.

In the final analysis the remedy is in the hands of the librarian himself, and in his own self perception. If he goes out to meet his colleagues as equal in his own mind, he will in the vast majority of cases be accepted as such. There is no magic solution to the salaries and conditions of service maze, but a structure such as the one outlined above, and an argument rooted firmly in the work actually carried out, is the only viable way to make progress.

To return in closing to broader discussion of staffing policy as a whole, the next stage after identifying target staffing levels and gradings is to develop an appropriate structure or organization. Such an organization does not or should not have a life of its own imposed on the service from above. If the task analysis has been carried out carefully and the tasks grouped sensibly into individual posts, then a structure should emerge naturally from the groupings of posts. There will of course be several possible groupings, and some will be dictated by physical considerations such as the number of sites to be served, or the availability of space.

It is important that the structure is clear and understood by those working within it. Lines of responsibility should be clear and must not allocate responsibilities without the power to fulfil them. The structure should not be rigid, preventing individuals from using their initiative and contributing to the service as a whole. Most important, it should where possible allow individuals to see a career development path within the service.

Staffing is a problem area for the college library, presenting a range of difficulties to which there are no quick and easy solutions. These difficulties will however become unsurmountable if staffing issues are treated in isolation. The staffing policy of any library is only meaningful if it is designed to fulfil the overall aims and objectives of the library service. A credible staffing policy can contribute significantly towards identifying the source of problems and may provide the means of arriving at solutions.

REFERENCES

1   Library Association *College libraries: guidelines for professional service and resource provision*. Third Edition, Library Association, 1982.
2   National Association of Teachers in Further and Higher Education College libraries: a policy statement. NATFHE, 1982.
3   Library Association *Census of staff establishments in libraries in universities, higher and further academic institutions*. Library Association, 1978.
4   Council of Polytechnic Librarians *Staffing survey*. COPOL.
5   Department of Education and Science *Statistics of libraries in major establishments of further education in England, Wales and Northern Ireland* 1979–80. The Department, 1981.
6   Lomas, T 'College library statistics.' *Library Association Colleges of Further and Higher Education Group Bulletin* 34, Summer 1982, 3–4.
7   McElroy, A R Swallow, K B and Harrison, C T 'Realistic (that is, academic) gradings mean better libraries'. *Library Association Record* 83 (3) March 1981. 136–139.
8   Revill, D H 'Academic librarians in colleges of further and higher education'. *Journal of Librarianship* 13 (2) April 1981. 104–118.

16

Selection, Management and Exploitation of Stock

J Gordon Brewer

The concept of library stock – that is, the physical collection of information-bearing media assembled for use – is rightly regarded as central to any understanding of the nature and function of libraries. It is at the heart of virtually every dictionary definition of the word 'library', and the image the word creates is essentially of shelves filled with books. This is the most obvious and visible expression of what a library is, and its *raison d'être*. Indeed, most librarians questioned about their libraries will refer to the size of the stock before referring to the staff or enumerating the services provided. Yet when pressed, these same librarians would admit that they could not assess the quality or effectiveness of a library from perusal of the stock alone, crucial as this is, and that the staffing and other factors play an equally important role in determining a library's 'quality': '. . . libraries will, in the last analysis, be assessed on the basis of the *impact that library distributed material has on the user.*'[1] The stock itself is in this sense not a major indicator of library performance, except in terms of its actual use and the extent to which it satisfies the requirements of readers. To divorce discussion of stock from that of reader services is both superficial, and logically impossible.

Implicit in the approach of this chapter is the belief that the more fundamental aspects of stock selection, management and exploitation do not lie within the area of technical and/or bibliographic services. To view library stock in this way represents a significant change from the traditional emphasis on the materials themselves and on the process of collection building which was once the central feature of academic librarianship, certainly in higher education. This is of course not an entirely new point of view, but is the result of gradually changing perceptions in the profession over a number of years which are neatly summarized in one of the recommendations of a major recent report from the Library and Information Services Council (LISC): '. . . it is in our view desirable that libraries and information services should move more purposefully from a mainly "holdings" strategy requiring the accumulation of large stocks towards a mainly "access" strategy in which emphasis is placed on the efficient procurement of material and information as required'.[2]

The important element in stock management, then, is not so much the stock itself but its deployment for use, the efforts made to ensure it is used effectively, and the rationale which underlies the processes of selection, organization, and exploitation. Following this premise, attention is focussed here on the interface between the stock and the library user rather than the technical aspects of acquisition and stock control procedures. Although the routines established for this must obviously be efficient and adequate to meet institutional objectives, no attempt is made in this paper to give guidance on *how* this should be done. Apart from the obvious point that local circumstances (notably the scale of operation involved and the staff and other resources available) lead to a wide variety of solutions, this is an area of extremely rapid change. The increasing availability of relatively inexpensive microprocessing equipment and the development of software, both commercially and by enterprising librarians, means that any guidance attempted would rapidly be superseded by technological advances. The days when computer applications in the housekeeping routines of stock management were the preserve of larger library systems are fortunately over, and the recent literature contains many examples of the use of microcomputers in college libraries. These applications cover virtually all technical aspects of stock management, from acquisiton,[3] through cataloguing[4] and serials systems,[5] to circulation control.[6]

A further principle which is implicit in the following discussion of library stock, and in the definition which was attempted in the opening sentence, is that both the nature of the media and its format are largely irrelevant. Taken literally, this would perhaps suggest that no attention need be paid to the problems of physical storage of non-print media, or to the provision of appropriate playback facilities, or to the various other particular difficulties (in cataloguing, or in terms of copyright, for instance) which attend audio-visual materials in the library. These problems are, of course, real ones, but they belong also in the category of 'technical' considerations and will be referred to only briefly in passing. The important point to be stressed is that although this chapter is concerned principally with traditional library stock (books, periodicals, and other printed materials), the distinction between different media in the library is a practical rather than a philosophical one. The days are long past when it was necessary for innovators such as Richard Fothergill to argue the case for the multimedia library in education.[7]

However, although this aspect of the debate, which centred on the stock itself, is now largely over, discussion of the broader and more significant considerations of the stock/user interface is still very much alive. As has already been indicated, it is this aspect of stock management which should be the primary concern of college librarians in the 1980s, and the most obvious manifestation of this is the development of the resource centre concept. Any attempt to equate 'learning resources' solely with non-print media is patently ludicrous, although one does occasionally still hear this done; books have always been simply the most traditional of resources for teaching and learning, which explains the centrality of the library (at least in theory!) in all institutions of further and higher education. The relationship between library stock and the further extension of the library's role into that of a Learning Resources Centre (LRC) is well expressed by Margaret Lattimore:

> . . . it seems likely that in many cases libraries will form the nucleus from which the LRC will evolve, particularly when a library has already developed along progressive lines. . . . Nevertheless, despite . . . progress made through the acceptance

of the new media as the proper concern of librarianship, it seems obvious that much more will be required of librarians in the future if the educational processes are to be fully supported. A greater understanding of the relationship between teaching and the use of resources will be necessary, *particularly in respect of the selection and exploitation of learning resources.*[8] (my italics)

A theoretical model linking stock selection, management and exploitation which shows the distinction between the technical/bibliographic and the reader services orientation of these aspects of college library work is shown in Figure 1. The cycle begins, obviously, with the selection of new material, ends with the

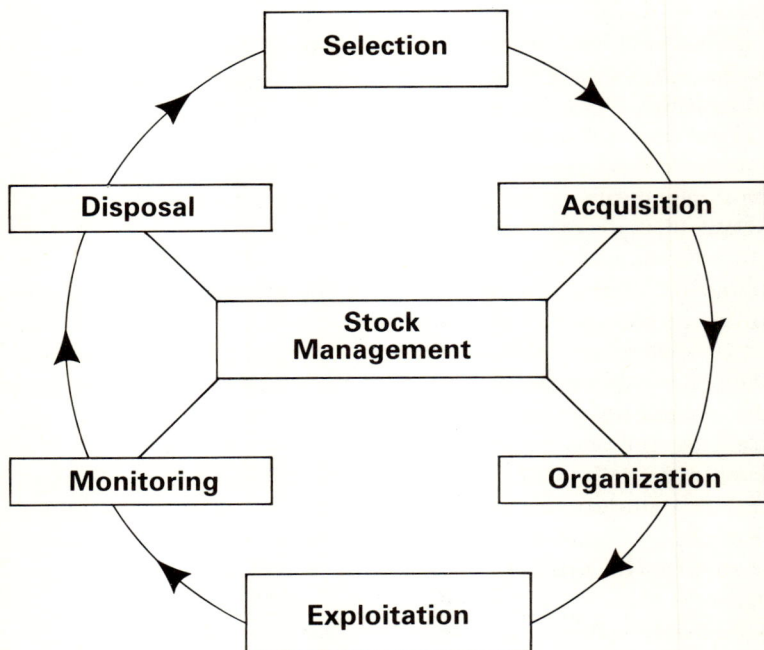

Figure 1: The stock management cycle.

disposal of outdated or redundant stock, and forms a continuous process with no fixed or predetermined time-scale. At two points (*selection* and *exploitation*) the task of the college librarian is above all concerned with user interaction. The other operations which complete the circle *acquisition, organization, monitoring,* and *disposal*) are largely technical processes in which the librarian's attention is directed to the stock itself, and these four elements are seen as the principal components of a formal scheme of stock management. In the remainder of this paper the broad principles involved in the six activities of this cyclic process will be discussed in their natural sequence.

SELECTION

Librarianship textbooks typically stress the necessity of building a 'balanced' stock, without stating explicitly what this means. It may actually be a genuine requirement in the case of a large public library with a broadly based readership, but it is certainly not so for the college library. In a college, it is not balance which is important but coincidence with the requirements of a specific group of users, largely teaching staff and students, and the range of work undertaken in that college. In this, as in other crucial respects, college librarians have more in common with their special library colleagues than with the public library service. One initial problem of definition, then, is that of identifying what these readers' particular requirements are, and it is useful in this context to note the distinction made by Line[9] between 'needs', 'demands', and 'use'. Both use and demand are to some extent measurable, or at least observable, while actual 'need' (which may be unarticulated and unappreciated by the readers themselves) is obviously greater than both. It is however this broader concept, by definition difficult to specify with precision, which must guide the selection of library stock.

The only way to ensure that needs can be properly identified is for the librarian to make stock selection a matter of close liaison with library users; to recognize that it is in fact a 'reader service'. This is particularly important if *needs*, as well as expressed *demands*, are to be adequately met. The recent Library Association *Guidelines* for college libraries[10] acknowledges both of these points in its initial statement on stock selection: '. . . the stock of the library will normally be selected by professional librarians in cooperation with teaching staff and students. It will be chosen to satisfy the demands made by students and teachers and to meet their educational needs'.

This is a very carefully constructed statement, not only recognizing the distinction between demand and need and the principle of cooperative selection, but also placing the ultimate responsibility on professional library staff. This is an important, and in some colleges, a contentious issue. There are institutions in which the funds for book purchase are divided on a departmental basis and teaching staff in the departments undertake the bulk of the selection themselves; indeed there are extreme examples where librarians feel almost unable to order materials in certain subject fields without offending their teaching colleagues. This is a ridiculous situation, and ultimately leads to inefficient use of resources and a stock totally 'unbalanced' even in terms of evident institutional need. Professional librarians should control the book fund, having an ultimate say in all decisions to purchase, but should consistently make use of the advice and expertise of teachers, who are experts in their subject fields.

The mechanics of achieving this cooperation can take various forms, formal and informal, although perhaps the most common practice (in larger libraries anyway) is through a subject specialist staff structure, or individuals (within either the library or the academic departments) with a designated liaison responsibility. This consultation with teachers would include also, of course, the forwarding of advertising materials received by the library for forthcoming publications, and the routine use of course reading lists and handouts as the basis of minimum stock requirements. Involvement of students in the selection process is rather more difficult to organize, but communication channels can sometimes be established via student representatives on course committees or as a by-product of the library's teaching programme; and the library should certainly remain open to suggestions for purchase from any quarter.

The selection of a stock appropriate to institutional needs involves important general decisions of principle in two areas. Firstly, in terms of the range of material held, some guidelines must be established on different media, on the subject coverage required, and on academic level. As has already been suggested, there is no doubt about the importance of non-print learning materials and the only question remaining really concerns institutional policy on their deployment. Although the development of libraries as multimedia collections is a natural one, and is well established nationally, in those few remaining colleges where the print/non-print distinction is still maintained the librarian has no alternative (at least in the short term) but to work within the local policy framework. It goes without saying that where audio-visual items are held within the library, the hardware implications must not be neglected. The minimum subject spread is naturally dictated by the range of courses offered in the college, but the librarian may wish to supplement this with items of general interest (current affairs, popular hobbies, recreational fiction) if resources permit. This, however, cannot be afforded priority, and policy in this area may depend also on the accessibility and adequacy of local public libraries.

More importantly, there are problems over level. Many colleges in further education and public sector higher education offer an enormous range of courses, from vocational preparation (including the new Youth Training Scheme) through craft and technician training and GCE, to undergraduate work with its research implications. Advanced periodicals bought in support of the latter are totally irrelevant for both teachers and students on non-advanced courses, yet in some colleges may account for as much as 40% of library expenditure. Conversely, the library has an equal obligation to provide resources (often audio-visual items, incidentally) appropriate for use with students at the other end of the academic spectrum.

There is unfortunately no answer to these problems, and the librarian must balance priorities and balance the budget. Above all, though, he or she must constantly remain aware of the effects of decisions made among these conflicting needs, to ensure that all groups of users receive fair treatment. A particularly difficult aspect of the provision for higher level courses is the need to satisfy the various validating bodies, notably CNAA. Such organizations are not concerned with balance and the internal allocation of resources, but only with the support available for their own area of work. Again, the librarian is in a delicate 'political' situation which must be judged subjectively. It is not really possible to give guidance on these issues, which call for a great deal of skill and local knowledge.

The second question of principle concerns the size of the stock, and its depth. The Library Association *Guidelines*[10] suggest approximate numbers of volumes related to college size (FTE students) and the amount of advanced work undertaken. These are perhaps as good as any. It is only possible to generalize such figures within very broad limits; the important concept, however, is that there is actually an *optimum* size for a college library. It is wrong to presume indefinite growth at a uniform rate, and reasonable to predict slow steady expansion once the optimum size has been reached, subject obviously to any change in institutional circumstances such as recruitment, teaching methods, or range of courses. Within the library stock, parallel questions must be raised and answered in respect of the depth of coverage in particular areas, and in terms of breadth versus depth. The most common small-scale example of the latter problem is the issue of multiple copies. Is it better to stock twenty copies of a heavily requested and recommended textbook or fewer copies of a greater variety of alternative sources? Again, there are no right answers, and the solutions as ever lie in compromise following widespread consultation with colleagues and library users, and making full use of the various monitoring procedures available, as described later in this chapter.

ACQUISITION

Most library materials, obviously, are acquired by purchase from commercial suppliers. Exceptions are donations, which should always be assessed critically and only accepted if there is clearly evidence that they will be used. Ordering and payment routines are beyond the scope of this paper and will be dictated by local circumstances, but must clearly be set up carefully to run smoothly and efficiently to ensure that at each stage it is possible to ascertain the status of each item outstanding, to obtain urgent requirements quickly, and to avoid bottlenecks and delays as far as possible. Some librarians appear to find the adoption of 'commercial' attitudes surprisingly difficult, but this is an essential ingredient of efficient acquisition. It is necessary to be aware of pricing policy in the case of periodicals where there is no uniformity among agents; to keep a watchful eye on foreign exchange rates; to weigh carefully the merits of paperback versus hardback; to chase booksellers about overdue orders and insist on receiving adequate reports on outstanding items; and to monitor the quality of service (especially delivery times) provided by different suppliers. The differences in quality of service are often most evident in the willingness of booksellers to undertake aspects of routine servicing (insertion of date labels, ownership stamps, security devices etc, and providing plastic jackets), and both this willingness and the costs involved must be taken into account when making comparison. All this demands an utterly practical and sometimes a tough attitude, and always an appreciation of the economic realities of the situation.

It is implicit in this approach that it is generally a mistake to rely exclusively on one supplier, and it also emphasizes how very important it is to develop good working (but definitely *commercial*) relationships with booksellers. It is worth operating a library licence in most college libraries, not simply in order to obtain the 10% discount but because it is appropriate to the role of the college in the local community to be able to offer at least reference facilities to members of the public. This rarely leads to heavy demands from 'external' users and is good for the image of the institution locally. A further important question surrounds the support which it is appropriate to give to a local bookshop, or perhaps one which operates within the college. The latter in particular might involve a moral obligation, but it is essential to avoid any contractual link which inhibits the right of the library to select the suppliers who provide the best service. Some local authorities' central purchasing agreements can make this very difficult, or impossible, but the librarian's priority in seeking to avoid or circumvent this situation in the best interests of the library service is inescapable.

A second common acquisition problem in colleges is the private enterprise of lecturers who obtain books and invoices themselves from various sources, often in response to direct mail advertising from publishers, and then present them to the library for payment. This too should be discouraged; not only can it lead to overpricing (resulting from loss of discount, addition of postal charges, etc) but it can lead to further complications where, for instance, a book obtained in this way is in fact already on order, or even in stock. Dealing with lecturers who operate like this is of course a fairly delicate matter, to be handled with tact and diplomacy.

Obtaining materials from internal college sources is an often neglected area of acquisitions work. Increasingly, however, it is likely that the most useful learning materials for many students (particularly on lower level courses) will be locally produced, and often in non-print formats). Off-air recordings of educational broadcasts, college produced video or slide-tape programmes, and audio tutorials or multimedia kits devised by teaching staff may all be usefully acquired by the library and used in it for private study. Once a policy in this area is established it is necessary to set up a system whereby such items may be acquired automatically and promptly; this presents no problems provided that good working relationships exist with the teachers involved, but the initiative may well have to come first from the library. This is an area in which a substantial effort is now needed, and which would yield great benefit both to the library and to its users.

ORGANIZATION

The use of the term 'organization' in the Figure 1 model is perhaps not adequate to describe the next stage in the process, and it is difficult to distinguish clearly between this and 'exploitation'. The distinction made here is essentially, however, between a passive and an active approach to library stock. Organization concerns the initial arrangement of materials ready for access by readers, and includes shelf arrangement, the place of special collections, and the setting of appropriate loan regulations, while exploitation involves the further and continuing efforts which the library must make to bring materials and users together, to create an awareness of what is available and to ensure that the optimum ongoing benefit is obtained from the stock. One of the main problems college libraries experience in terms of traditional library organization is that they all too often assume both motivation and a knowledge of systems on the part of both students and staff, which are not always present. This is perhaps particularly true of orthodox cataloguing/classific-ation systems, which despite their apparent simplicity and ration-ality to a professional librarian can be very confusing and not particularly helpful to the uninitiated. In these areas it is now possible (and desirable) for colleges to make use of national data bases through membership of cooperatives or by use of BLAISE services, greatly reducing the need for staff time to be spent on these activities locally. The price that is paid for this, however, can be considerable, financially and in the loss of sensitivity to local priorities and emphases in particular courses, in effect creating obstacles to access by those unable or unwilling to cope with the system. These problems must be reconciled with the undoubted advantages of centralized services, especially in the context of auto-mation. The overriding objective, as in all stock management, is to make library materials as readily available as possible.

This aim can be furthered by the selective use of special collec-tions. Most colleges concerned with teacher education will have 'teaching practice' collections of materials for students to take out into schools, and others will have collections of local information. Multi-site institutions usually find it necessary to maintain special collections in particular subject fields for use by students and staff whose courses take place at locations remote from the main college library. There are both dangers and advantages in all this of which the librarian must be aware, but in general the situation is unavoid-able and stems from college rather than library policy. Within larger library services, however, it is worth considering the deliberate creation of subject-based, or perhaps course-based special collec-tions as a means of simplifying access for particular groups of readers, provided that this does not conflict seriously with the more general responsibility to provide for all members of the college. Audio-visual materials and the question of their integration into the general library stock is a further problem which most often results in the establishment of a special collection. While this is unsatisfactory in a philosophical sense, the noise and distraction created by playback equipment and the sheer cost of an integrated approach to the storage of software generally preclude the ideal of print and non-print items being physically housed together.

Most library stock should be for loan wherever possible, and restrictions placed on this aspect of the library's service should be kept to a minimum. For many people, a library is a source of materials for loan rather than a place for study, and this preference should be respected. Loan periods should be the object of careful thought in the light of institutional circumstances, the particular problems of part-time or mature students and the demands of college courses, and should be kept as flexible as possible. There must be provision for reservation of items not immediately available, and ideally there should be photocopying facilities to help cope with the problem of material which really must be retained for reference use only. Linking the question of lending services with that of special collections is the very common use of 'short-loan' or 'tied-book' collections, often on closed access. This does enable materials in very heavy demand, either permanently or temporarily, to be made available to a large number of readers over a short period, and it is an inevitable result of the teaching style on some courses. It is an idea which can be extremely successful in meeting specified demand, but is also open to abuse; usage must be monitored carefully, and it is important to ensure that readers do not come to rely totally on the often very narrow range of materials included in such collections, to the exclusion of the broader range available in the stock as a whole.

EXPLOITATION

While the organization of stock within the library – both its physical layout and the arrangements made for access and for loan – should clearly be designed to make its use as simple as possible, this is not likely to result in optimum use unless further efforts are made to make readers aware of the potential resources available to them. At its simplest level, this means providing adequate shelf guides, layout plans, and directional signs. These should be well produced and professional in appearance, and their exact wording and location needs careful thought. Reynolds and Barrett[11] have produced a good modern practical guide to techniques and design concepts. It is easy to neglect this essentially very simple task, but it is valuable to seek expert assistance from visual aids staff or from the Art Department and to ensure that the job is properly done. We live in a self-service age, and the library should as far as possible conform to this model.

In additition to such fixed guiding, attention must be paid to the production of suitable publicity material. In both areas it is useful to try to envisage the situation of a student or a new member of staff faced with a bewildering, if not overwhelming, variety and volume of resource material without previous knowledge of the systems used for indexing or even, initially, much awareness of physical layout. What would be most useful in these circumstances? To be effective, publicity material should originate in a clear and objective assessment of the situation obtaining at the interface between the stock and the user. Publicity efforts normally include leaflets, book lists, (including accession lists) and displays, and could usefully be planned and implemented in conjunction with teaching staff rather than in totally independent action. The timing and subject matter can in this way be related to actual need and become an element in the teaching programme, closely related to the curriculum of particular courses.

More important, however, than both of these aspects of stock exploitation, is the human element implicit in the library's staff structure. The staff must know the stock and be able to guide readers both in response to specific requests for detailed information and in a more general, advisory capacity. To achieve this, reference points should be strategically located within the library and library staff must become actively involved in the teaching programme of the college. This last point is perhaps the most important of all: the stock of an academic library is only exploited in the interests of the academic work of staff and students, in the process of teaching and learning.

'The absence of the closest links between library and teaching staff can result in failures in the library regardless of the efficiency of library staff and the standard of provision. For success an academic library requires a working partnership with academic staff. It is the quality of the library staff, not simply the quantity of books or even the size of the bookfund, which ensures the success or otherwise of the library'.[12]

In other words, effective stock exploitation is largely dependent on library staff and their relationships with academic colleagues. The most direct way in which this academic involvement can take place is via the teaching process itself. This is not simply a reiteration of the case, argued so strongly by many librarians throughout the 1970s, for library instruction or user education; the case for that approach, which gave librarians an excuse for allowing their systems to become over-sophisticated and less user-orientated than they should be, has perhaps been overstated. The tendency now is for greater breadth, including elements of study skills and communication skills which fortunately bring the librarian more into contact with academic colleagues. This is by far the most effective method of alerting readers to the potential of the resources in the library's stock, and ensuring that it is fully exploited. It is perhaps particularly important (and certainly it is very evident) in the case of the smallest college libraries, where it is relatively easier to develop a really close relationship between the librarian and the readers. In this situation the personal assistance of a well-informed professional librarian is far more effective than the most elaborate systems of signs and plans.

MONITORING

Monitoring the use of stock is one of the most difficult problems faced by staff in libraries of all kinds. Apart from the intrinsic technical obstacles involved in collecting usage data on a very large number of individual items (which may be referred to without being borrowed, and borrowed without being read!), there is a more fundamental issue. While some of the data collection problems may be solved eventually as a spin-off from computerized circulation control, there is no way of making allowances for unpredictable user attitudes and behaviour. As Orr[13] has pointed out, both the conceptual problems and the practicalities of any kind of objective monitoring or evaluation of library collections without disrupting the service are enormous. Accepting these limitations on the data available for monitoring, the responsibility for accepting some kind of regular assessment of use remains, however imperfect the techniques may be.

The most common practice employed in such stock editing is the simple and routine examination of the date labels in books, which provides a rough guide to borrowing, if not to actual use. All college librarians should maintain a regular programme of such checking, working round the stock in a planned and systematic way, using both the frequency and the date of issue to determine whether each volume is still earning its place on the shelves. To this may be added the evidence collected from the reservations system and from inter-library loan requests. It is useful also to encourage readers to make suggestions for additional copies where deficiencies exist by instituting a clear and simple procedure by which this can be done without embarrassment – via a suggestion box, for example.

Particular attention should be paid to monitoring the use of any closed access collections such as of books available only on request for short-term loan. Books in such collections are in one sense less accessible than they should be, and it is important that they are only restricted in this way while demand makes the restriction necessary. There is a tendency, even where library policy is for items to be so restricted only on a temporary basis, for short loan collections to become permanent, despite the fact that monitoring use is easier than in an open access situation.

The use of periodicals poses rather greater problems. Many journals are used principally for reference and for their news content, for which loan is unnecessary even when library policy would allow them to be borrowed. A single article can easily be read within the library, or a photocopy taken, leaving no visible evidence of use. Solutions which have been attempted generally rely on the reader recording the use of a periodical issue by marking a card or slip attached to it, or returning it to a member of staff rather than to its place on the shelves. Any system of this kind obviously provides only minimum statistics of use and is certainly not adequate guidance when major decisions involving possible cancellation of subscriptions are contemplated. A carefully constructed questionnaire survey of readers provides a much better solution, although this is time-consuming and is inclined to lead to exaggerated evidence of use; also, of course, it can only be an occasional, rather than a regular, survey. Another way of ascertaining the level of use is unilaterally to cancel subscriptions to titles judged by library staff to be superfluous, and to wait for reader reaction(!); however, such a procedure must be used with caution as it is extremely damaging to public relations if many mistakes are made.

DISPOSAL

Virtually all stock added to college libraries should be regarded as disposable. There is no tradition of archival storage like that of the universities which resulted in such an outcry when the Atkinson report floated the concept of the self-renewing library.[14] It should perhaps be remarked that 'self-renewing' is not a particularly apposite term: stock editing does not, unfortunately, look after itself, and books are not discarded unless the librarian makes the effort to monitor use and take decisions based on this. It is also worth noting that there are no useful or universal guidelines for the shelf life of books in particular subject areas, and there is no way, therefore, of automating the process. College librarians have to make similar decisions about their periodical holdings: some libraries retain and bind only a very small number of the titles to which they subscribe. Some titles will be retained for a fixed period (five years, one year, six months) while in some cases only a current issue is kept available. Again there are no objective rules about this, individual judgments being made on the basis of demand and, of course, the shelf space available.

The attitude of teaching staff to the disposal of superseded library stock can be a major problem in colleges. For some reason (and this is not entirely blameworthy) many regard books as almost sacred, and deeply resent the librarian's utilitarian approach, which demands that books must justify their retention by regular use. One partial solution to this problem is to make discarded volumes available to teaching staff for their personal use, stressing that they are outdated if this is the case, and not allowing them to be given to students. It is particularly worthwhile to consider whether issues of periodicals, where long back-files are not needed in the library, might nevertheless be useful to individual teaching staff; much goodwill can be generated in this way. Alternative methods of disposal are via the British Library's gift and exchange scheme, by sale (worth trying if it is possible to recycle the cash raised back into the book fund), or simply by destruction. Sale may involve either disposal in bulk to a commercial dealer or the selling of individual items internally; although the latter has attraction in terms of publicity for the library service, careful thought should be given to the implications of allowing students to purchase out-of-date stock. In neither case (except perhaps the commercial sale of unwanted periodical runs, which will arise only infrequently) should substantial financial benefits be expected. Whatever method is used, discretion is important: the motives for discarding books are frequently misunderstood, and it can be extremely embarrassing if members of the college governing body, for example, unbriefed beforehand, discover apparently usable ex-library books in local second-hand booksellers! It is better to resort to shredding than risk such situations.

The success or failure of a college library's stock management, in all its phases from selection to disposal, can be difficult to evaluate formally. An attempt to achieve this has been made in respect of American academic libraries by Clapp and Jordan[15] using the simplest possible measure of overall collection size, but relating this mathematically to such factors as numbers of students and lecturers, range of courses taught, and aspects of the physical environment of the institution. The extensive literature on collection evaluation has been reviewed by Bonn[16], who identified and discussed six generally applicable methods:

1   compiling statistics on holdings, use, and expenditure;
2   checking lists, catalogues, and bibliographies;

3 obtaining user opinions;
4 direct observation (by subject experts);
5 applying published standards;
6 use of document delivery tests.

Bonn's conclusion stressed the importance of four recurring concepts from the literature which have considerable and obvious significance in the context of stock management:

1 The emphasis on library goals and objectives as the foundation for a library's selection or acquisition policy. . . .
2 The stress on quality and on user needs rather than on quantity and on basic lists alone as the decisive factors in building a collection. . . .
3 The realization that no library can ever be completely self-sufficient. . . .
4 The virtual necessity of having competent professional librarians in such strategic spots as selection and public service to ensure proper development and use of the library's collection.[16]

His last point returns to the links suggested at the beginning of this chapter between stock selection and management and the whole concept of reader service; *development* of the collection cannot be divorced from *use*. The weakness in Bonn's analysis, in terms of college libraries, is his lack of reference to institutional goals, as opposed to those set by the library itself.

In particular, the college library stock must reflect local approaches to teaching and learning. There is a close relationship here between library stock management and the concept of the teacher as a manager of the learning environment, which is seen at its most developed in the context of resource-based learning systems.

Just as there can be many different styles of classroom management, so there can be many styles in the management of courses based on learning materials. Physical format (print, film, cassette) does not dictate the style of the message carried, materials can be devised to meet differences between learners in terms of level, coverage, sequencing (or routing), and the amount of visual, commentary, or practical work set up. Materials can then be retrieved selectively from a bank to meet diagnosed needs or remedy weaknesses.[17]

The role of the librarian in stock selection, management, and exploitation cannot be separated from this activity. Virtually all courses are to some extent 'resource-based' and the academic librarian's task is to cooperate and facilitate; to adopt a joint management responsibility, contributing his or her particular skills and expertise to that of the teacher to ensure that the library stock provides the most effective possible resource for learning.

REFERENCES

1   Blagden, J *Do we really need libraries?* Bingley, 1980.
2   Department of Education and Science and Office of Arts and Libraries *Working together within a national framework* (Report from the Library and Information Services Council) HMSO, 1981. Paragraph 15.
3   'A versatile PET'. *VINE* 40 October 1981. 26–29.
4   Baldwin, R 'The use of the BLAISE EDITOR at Garnett College Library'. *Catalogue and Index* 60 Spring 1981. 2–4.
5   McKay, D J and Alexander, R A 'Bell College of Technology library's computer serials system'. *Program* 12 (3) July 1978. 139–152.
6   McKee, B 'Computerised circulation control: a case study of Solihull College of Technology'. *VINE* 44 August 1982. 46–50.
7   Fothergill, R 'Expanding the library'. *Education Libraries Bulletin* 46 Spring 1973. 1–7.
8   Lattimore, M I 'The learning resource centre' in Jefferson, G and Smith-Burnett, G C K (eds) *The college library: a collection of essays.* Bingley, 1978. 153–179.
9   Line, M B 'Draft definitions: information and library needs, wants, demands and uses'. *Aslib Proceedings* 26 (2) February 1974. 87.
10 Library Association *College libraries: guidelines for professional service and resource provision.* Third edition, Library Association, 1982.
11 Reynolds, L and Barrett, S *Signs and guiding for librarians.* Bingley, 1981.
12 Revill, D H 'Academic librarians in colleges of further and higher education'. *Journal of Librarianship* 13 (2) April 1981. 104–118.
13 Orr, R H 'Measuring the goodness of library services: a general

framework for considering quantitative measures'. *Journal of Documentation* 29 (3) September 1973. 315–332.

14 University Grants Committee 'Capital provision for university libraries: report of a working party'. (Atkinson Report) HMSO, 1976.

15 Clapp, V W and Jordan, R T 'Quantitative criteria for the adequacy of academic library collections'. *College and Research Libraries* 26 (5) September 1965. 371–380.

16 Bonn, G 'Evaluation of the collection'. *Library Trends* 22 (3) January 1974. 265–304.

17 Noble, P *Resource-based learning in post-compulsory education.* Kogan Page, 1980. 16.

17

Finance

D H Revill

In the final analysis all resources are cash. Money buys buildings, staff, and stock in order to provide library services. As O'Connor observes: 'Several years ago finance received little attention but with rampant developments outside the library world in other sectors we have seen the risk of importance of this function.'[1]

For the librarian the task becomes a cycle of obtaining resources, allocating them to sections, functions, and formats, controlling expenditure, obtaining information on the effectiveness of programmes or expenditures, and using this information to justify the current and future use of the same or more resources.

The cycle is represented in Figure 1. This chapter will explore this cycle, beginning with the librarian's justification for resources.

JUSTIFYING SUPPORT

The librarian must first understand the bases on which the college budget is prepared. Each department (and hopefully the library will be regarded as an independent department) may submit estimates. Estimates may have to be approved by a library committee. The totals for the college may be referred to the academic board and thence to the governing body. Discussions take place with the local authority.

LOCAL   INSTITUTION LIBRARY
AUTHORITY

Credibility of ⟵— Justification ⟵— Justification of
justification   resource demand   STOCK CONTROL

RESOURCES   Feedback ⟵   —Data

                 SERVICES/USE

       Internal   Library's internal
COLLEGE   allocation to allocation by site,
INPUTS   departments of format, programme
     ⟶ the institution ⟶etc.

           LIBRARY INPUTS——⎤ OUTPUTS

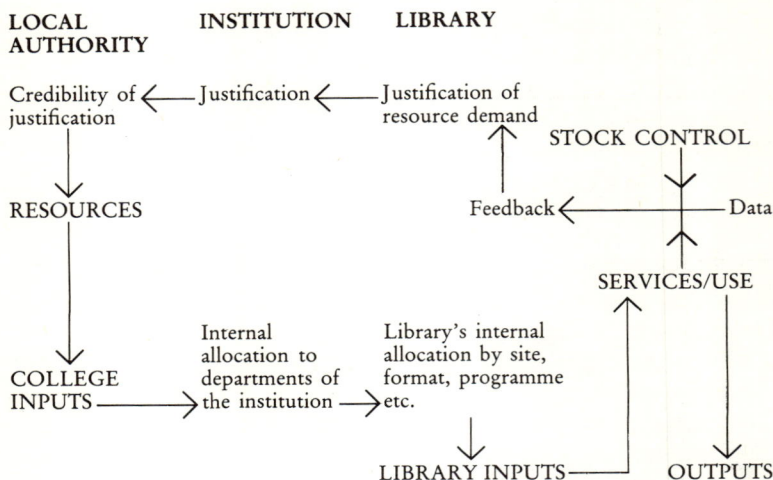

Figure 1: The college library's finance cycle.

Budgets for college departments may be derived, at least in part, by formulae based on student numbers, unit costs, norms or simply on last year's figures plus inflation. If this is the case then little effort may be required – unless one needs to change the formulae.

While student numbers have a strong influence on the amount of money the library receives, there is a danger in being tied too closely to student enrolments. The various conversion formulae (eg for part-time or post-graduate students to full-time equivalents) may seriously misrepresent the use made of the library. A more important determinant is the number of academic programmes to be supported and their level.

Determining one's budget by 'last year plus inflation' can be to the benefit of the library if one starts from a reasonable base line. Some libraries have succeeded in inflation-proofing their book funds by this means. The inflation increment may be based on the retail price index or a more specific index relating to book and journal prices. The trick is to adopt the most favourable figure or method, and ideally, to be able to change it according to circumstances. However, caution is necessary. Published figures of costs per subject such as those issued by the Library Association and the

Centre for Library and Information Management (CLAIM) may differ substantially from one's own experience.[2, 3, 4]

Institutions could adopt zero-based budgeting or Planning Programming Budgeting Systems (PPBS). Zero-base budgeting is based on the premise that one starts afresh each year. Sargent and Crowe provide excellent outlines of the procedures.[5, 6] PPBS, or variants of it, have been adopted by some local authorities yet both tend to be rare. Nevertheless PPBS is a useful technique which could be adopted *within* an institution.[7] It would particularly suit the librarian who has analysed his operations and, perhaps, employed a managerial style based on objectives.

Unfortunately the line-item budget still tends to predominate in local government. Weinburg observed: '. . . the present method of allocating funds to book buying, buildings, salaries and capital equipment . . . is improper because it is arbitrary with respect to the objective of supplying information'.[8]

Increasingly, college librarians are regarding their book funds as 'access funds' rather than simply for the acquisition of materials. So we may find inter-library loans and online services subsumed under it. One could further observe that the line-item budget is also of little value if one's objectives relate to sites, subjects, client groups, or programmes.

Staffing costs, based on present numbers, may be calculated centrally. The librarian's task is to remind senior management of new staff proposals, regradings, and special circumstances so that they can be taken into account in estimates. However, with present pressures on local government, regradings or new staff may be totally out of the question. One may not even be allowed to submit estimates based on establishments. An 'allowance' may be deducted to take into account 'frozen' posts, and 'normal' delays in filling posts.

OBJECTIVES

Of great importance in the pursuit of funds is the library's statement of aims and objectives. If the librarian can get such statements endorsed by the college they become the starting point for his justifications. The library budget is the vehicle that explicitly states the library's priorities, displays much of the information needed to control the organization, and, in retrospect, provides one way to analyse and evaluate the library's operations. Newman notes: '. . . through the use of carefully documented studies based on analytical evaluation of various services and functions, library budgets will be able to compete successfully with other institutional budgets'.[9] Having a reputation for critical self-study can do no harm in establishing credibility with college authorities.

There are many other ways in which to derive or justify the book fund. Comparisons with other libraries or professional standards can be used. Both are somewhat suspect. Being below average could be seen as a sign of good management, or an economy of scale, rather than poor provision. Professional standards are doubtful, even if of interest to librarians. They are devised by interested parties and may be attacked on those grounds. Those produced by teachers' organizations may be more powerful. The librarian will bring such standards to the attention of his college but will not base his whole case on them.

NEW COURSES

Some colleges may make special efforts to discover the likely demands on library resources arising from new course proposals and new developments in existing courses. The trick then is to have these future costs incorporated into one's financial allocation. Several problems arise here. Academic staff may under-estimate the costs of library materials; few will realise the implications for library staffing. Principals may argue that, other than for an entirely new subject not represented in the library, some areas are always in decline or sufficiently well provided for to allow the present budget to meet the new demands. In other words a reallocation of priorities is all that is necessary. As Martin observes, librarians have generally managed 'to squeeze together enough money to provide some resources, a response which is the equivalent of cutting one's own throat to provide someone else with a blood transfusion'.[10]

Existing 'course needs' is a stronger, because internal, argument.

However, these may be hard both to identify and to justify. One department's needs may be seen as extravagant or unrealistic by others. For those colleges having advanced level courses validated by the Council for National Academic Awards (CNAA), the various criticisms and reports on one's library produced by the Council can be powerful weapons. CNAA submissions may provide a further basis for justification. Book lists are included in the course descriptions. Some of these lists may be merely illustrative, others more exhaustive. Checking the lists against one's present holdings may reveal a deficiency which can be quoted.

It may be possible, for example by getting a development plan endorsed by the college, to adopt numeric measures of adequacy. The number of volumes per full-time equivalent student in stock or added per year, can appear to be plausible bases for internal standards at which to aim.

Other less tangible influences exist. One's reputation with the finance officer and senior management people responsible for resources has a lot to do with the slice of the cake one eventually obtains. Competence must be demonstrated in ways other than the purely professional. Many seemingly small things contribute to a reputation for being sound.

A further, overall, problem may exist. The library is there to meet the needs of the institution it serves. However, the individuals who express these needs may have low expectations of the service, so presenting the librarian with a dilemma. How is he to demonstrate the potential of the library in order to raise expectations? An injection of funds may be necessary first. Supply often creates its own demand, hence the library can be seen by many administrators as a bottomless pit – we can spend whatever we are given.

The budget as agreed within the institution eventually proceeds to the next hurdle – the local education authority (LEA).

LOCAL GOVERNMENT

Detailed justifications may not be necessary if simple methods are adopted by the LEA or institution. Indeed, increasingly there appears to be little use in providing detailed justifications, as an institution's funding tends to be handed down from above rather than being built up from below. Everyone may go through a painstaking exercise to little avail. 'Rate rationing' takes place. The council decides what rate increase is politically acceptable and then hands down budgets to departments. The amounts spent are unlikely to be related to need or to what can be achieved.

The system of local government finance is something of a jungle. For example, there are no rewards for economy. If one does not spend one's entire budget, it is likely that a reduced amount will be allocated for the next year, regardless of the reasons for the underspending or future needs. Some authorities, recognizing the 'end of year' problem where departments order prematurely or purchase items which are something of a luxury, 'claw back' the cash. There is then an undignified backwards leap-frogging as the spenders discover the new rules and order earlier each year. If one does make savings they may be retained centrally either in the institution or in the local authority. Those who save may receive no benefit. Another absurdity is a planning cycle based on one financial year and the further complication that the academic year differs. Other examples are 'price events' and the sometimes arbitrary distinctions between revenue and capital expenditure.

The principal 'price event' is that of extra resources being made available towards the end of the financial year. The likelihood of this 'topping-up' is uncertain, therefore one cannot rely on it. It is usually unwise to turn down cash, one's altruism will not be rewarded, but one must be aware of the effect of large, uncertain, injections on one's technical services. Planning is thrown out of gear by these events.

The distinctions made between capital and revenue expenditure can also lead to inefficiencies. There is a strong case for treating the book stock as a capital rather than a revenue item. Capital costs are intended to produce future benefit. Present book usage is itself a result of past spending – the accumulation of stock. Admittedly it appears that new stock accounts for a disproportionate degree of current use but the argument is still valid. Hamburg enlarges on this point.[11] If book funds were treated as capital it would be possible to amortize the expenditure and calculate the amount needed to preserve the present value of the stock.

Apart from the difficulties outlined above there may be a more fundamental problem to overcome. Differences in understanding, objectives, and sympathies between the various parties are not uncommon. The LEA may regard the college's demands as ambitious, whereas CNAA, as the degree-awarding body, may see them as only moderate in comparison with other institutions with which it deals.

Differences may also be apparent at the next and highest level in the chain – central government.

CENTRAL GOVERNMENT

Colleges of further and higher education obtain their funds from central government via local government. Small colleges, with no advanced work, are supported from the local rate income – itself supported by central government through the Rate Support Grant (RSG).

The complexities and, indeed, crudities in the financial systems are exemplified by the recent history of advanced work supported from the 'pool'. Figure 2 shows the relationships between central and local government and the polytechnics.

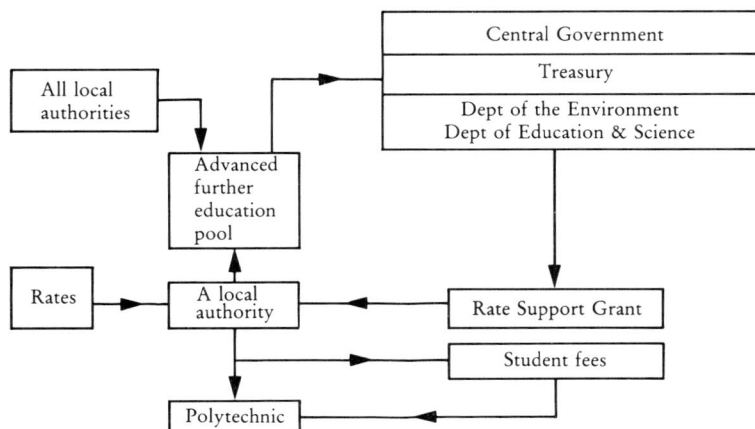

Figure 2: The financing of non-university higher education in England and Wales.

All local authorities pay into the 'pool' and draw from it according to the extent to which they provide facilities for advanced courses. The local authority receives income from the rating system on properties in its area. The rates are themselves supplemented by RSG. A local authority gives grants to students to attend colleges. The students pay fees to the institutions they attend. Thus the principal sources of finance for a polytechnic are income from the pool, student fees, and support directly via the rates for any budgetary deficiencies.

When the total sums claimed by local authorities with advanced work was known, the Pooling Committee divided it between all local authorities. As the government wished to reduce public expenditure it 'capped' the pool for 1980/1 and has announced cuts in future years regardless of the fact that the capacity exists to meet a greater demand for places and raise the age participation rate in further and higher education.[12] Confusion followed this precipitate action. A Study Group on the Management of the Advanced Further Education Pool was formed in order to investigate alternative methods including the use of unit costs. Shortly afterwards, in January 1982, following many years of discussion, and indeed argument, over an appropriate body to control the polytechnics, an Interim Committee for Local Authority Higher Education was established. Popularly known as the 'National Advisory Body' (NAB), it is a kind of poor man's University Grants Committee dominated by the civil service and the local authority associations. NAB advises the Secretary of State for Education and Science on resource allocation, student numbers and, increasingly, course provision.

A local authority will find it increasingly difficult to supplement advanced work in its colleges using rates income. The RSG contribution by central to local government has been reduced progressively from 61% to 56% (in 1982/3). It may be further reduced. Local authorities have to work to financial targets set by central government. Penalties, in the form of loss of grant, are imposed for exceeding targets. The uncertainty over funding, the expectations of further severe reductions, coupled with the restrictions imposed on colleges in the use of funds have serious consequences, not least for their libraries.

INABILITY TO OPTIMIZE THE MIX

Eventually the LEA receives a budget which it then dispenses to its constituent parts. The college allocates internally to its departments. The librarian's budget will be fairly tightly constrained – divided into staff costs, book fund, equipment and so on. The librarian needs freedom to react to changing circumstances. Present financial controls do not adequately allow for this. Yet our political masters are mostly and properly concerned with overall expenditure and should not be too concerned that we employ two more library assistants rather than buy 1,000 books more. However they do tend to interfere in detail. Martin has spelled out the problem:

> A department or college is principally concerned with teaching and therefore has a budget which is almost entirely composed of personnel costs. These costs can be related to enrolment projections; and, while there may be unhappiness over inability to expand a teaching program, in general the intention is to provide enough teachers to teach the courses to be offered. By contrast, a library is concerned with a very wide range of services, whose volume it is unable to control (perhaps even to predict) and with a very substantial purchasing program for materials. The interactions of the several portions of a library budget are complex and sometimes unpredictable, requiring a greater degree of flexibility than most other administrative areas. Relationships between student enrolment and library use cannot be reduced to a formula.[10]

Dunworth and Cook argue that being allowed x staff, y clerical assistants, and z technicians gives no latitude in optimizing the mix. For this reason, leaving individual academic units the maximum possible freedom in the allocation of their total resources, rather than imposing a rigid pattern from above through the device of detailed budget heads, would contribute to a more responsible use of resources.[13] Microeconomic theory supports this view. It suggests that if a given output can be achieved by varying mixes of certain inputs then one favours that input factor which is, or is becoming, relatively cheap in comparison with others.

In our case one could argue that useful services are provided by staff, stock, equipment, and buildings. One could vary these quite considerably to achieve similar results. For example as staff costs rise one may automate the issue system; as journal costs rise one may depend more on (staffed) inter-library loans. The problem is that relativities between factors may not persist over time whereas once one builds a building or employs a new staff member one cannot easily reverse the process. Moore discusses the possibilities.[14] Thus the librarian is constrained. He may know perfectly well that the book fund is exceeding his staff's capacity to deal with it yet he may not be allowed to switch resources to staff (even if temporary staff), or to capital equipment. Some controls are still necessary to prevent people using the entire budget to raise their own salaries. But the power to approve changes should be at the college level. More effective decisions could be made.

Each college will have some mechanism for allocating resources internally. One may receive whatever was justified in the estimates or a pro rata share if a reduction in the budget has been imposed. The role of the principal or director of the institution is vital in this respect. Even in better times some principals in (smaller?) colleges had an inordinate influence on resource allocation. It was not unusual for the librarian not to be a member of the academic board.[15] The librarian may lack the rank or position in the formal structure to influence events.

The relative standing of the library through the librarian is, in these circumstances, of great importance. The centrality of the library (social, educational, physical) may not be sufficient to protect it. Its all-pervasiveness and philosophy of assistance to all may not be sufficient to give it any power. Therefore the librarian must seek allies. The humanities departments, for example, may see the library as their laboratories and argue in its favour. The power structure, however, may be otherwise.

ALLOCATION WITHIN THE LIBRARY

In due course the library will receive its budget. Libraries differ widely in the extent to which committees are involved in matters of expenditure. With any luck the librarian will have the authority to allocate funds to sections, services, or functions within the library. This independence is worth preserving. He may be assisted by library staff either as individuals, or as part of a participative management or committee structure.

In their turn, site or subject librarians may have considerable freedom to apportion sums to the disciplines they serve. One should not expect trust from above if one cannot confer trust below. Student numbers and relative costs are important determinants of what subjects receive, but additional factors such as known deficiencies, new courses, actual usage, publishing, and supply patterns must also be taken into account.

It is advisable to allocate to subject areas rather than teaching departments lest the latter begin to regard the money as theirs. Where subjects and departments are more or less coextensive political problems can emerge. Fine judgment is necessary in order to balance the degree of autonomy necessary with informing and involving the staff of teaching departments. One problem is that some teaching staff may pursue their own interests to the detriment of undergraduates. Academic staff do not, generally, see the other side of the equation – the use made of materials in the library. The librarian's neutral stance and pervasive role should be sufficient protection for all. It is up to the librarian to generate trust in this respect.

Formulae for allocations to subject areas have been used, but there appears to have been a return to the use of professional judgment in view of the arbitrary nature of various weightings and values used in formulae and the multiplicity of factors which could be taken into account.

However, what should one do if one has an uninterested department or one which makes little use of the library? Their teaching methods may be such as to make few demands on the library. This raises the question of whether the librarian should try to equalize the standard of provision given to all departments or whether he should simply feed strengths. The author's inclination would be to prefer the latter. Those departments that make use of the library would, in this case, receive proportionately more. It is to be hoped that the others will become aware of the disparity and change their ways. Perhaps one can use student dissatisfaction to bring pressure to bear. Unfortunately students may not be vocal. They may not be required to use the library by academic staff. So the failure is perpetuated as attitudes are communicated.

BUDGETARY CONTROL

The financial system is a system of control. As their institutions suffer reductions in income, libraries come under greater scrutiny. However, as they may account for less than 5% of the college budget, any reductions in support will save little for the college but do serious damage to the library. The economist's principle of 'the importance of being unimportant' *may* work to our advantage. We *may* preserve a low profile and be left alone while more important budgets are scrutinized. But. . . .

As money becomes tighter there is a tendency for librarians to assume greater control – and for their masters to assume greater control over them! Conversely teaching departments, whose demands were once virtually automatically satisfied, may attempt to gain greater control of all funds concerning their disciplines. It is here that the support of the library committee and the principal or director become essential.

Ideally the librarian should be free to purchase how and where he determines. Unfortunately obstacles are likely to be erected in his path. Interference can occur from principals (who may like to see what everyone is ordering), educational auditors (who will query 'unusual' or expensive items), and central purchasing units (who may try to get higher discounts). Only by having a degree of freedom can the librarian reduce costs, for example by following Urquhart's advice to buy ahead where possible (eg inter-library loan forms, three-year subscriptions).[16]

Further difficulties may be faced in the form of very specific ordering systems to which one must conform. In these days of tele-ordering, ISBNs and online services, the pre-typed order in multiple copies is an anachronism.

PRODUCTIVITY

Libraries grow. A 6% growth per year in costs will double them in twelve years. Librarians *must* find ways to raise their productivity, otherwise libraries may outstrip their institutions' capacity (not to mention their willingness!) to support them.[17] At the moment, being regarded as cost-effective is practically synonymous with being under-resourced. One of the ways to raise productivity is to increase the value of capital resources per staff member via automation and computerization. However this needs large injections of cash to start the process. Thus a paradox results. We need to be cost conscious and use modern financial techniques. Decision trees, indifference curves, discounted cash flow, are relevant techniques seldom used, one suspects, by librarians. We must also be aware that what we do individually adds up to collective action which may affect the national, even international, information system. King gives one example in discussing the costs of borrowing rather than purchasing periodicals,[18] the Royal Society provides another.[19]

Despite the above we should not be too concerned about the limitations of present performance measures. Committees, lay politicians, and non-librarians generally may be quite satisfied with conventional measures.

INCOME

With all these preassures librarians may devote more attention to the generation of income – from fines to book sales and charges for online services. Cash might also be obtained for special projects from the Manpower Services Commission. Burman has thoroughly explored the possibilities.[20] Beware, however, the danger of the funding body which cuts the total amount earned from the library's initial funding level.

CONCLUSION

The librarian has to prove effectiveness in the use of resources. He has to acquire feedback data on the consequences of his actions in order to justify his services to the institution and the LEA. The same or similar data are also necessary strictly from an internal point of view in order to manage the library better.

The financial system, coupled with the vagaries of local control mediated by varying national policies, has produced considerable variation in institutional and library support.[15, 21, 22] Yet one must retain some optimism. Cuts in public spending may not be entirely disastrous. The 'trimmer and leaner' argument could apply. As De Gennaro points out, the librarian *may* acquire the power to cut inessentials, carry out long desired pruning, and 'implement the bold changes . . . that really make a difference in the long run'.[23]

REFERENCES

1 O'Connor, M J *Research in library management* (British Library Research and Development Department Report 5550) BLRDD, 1980. 24.
2 'Average book prices'. *Library Association Record* 83 (11) November 1981. 531.
3 'Periodical prices'. *Library Association Record* 84 (5) May 1982. 184–5.
4 Cooper, A and Hart, M *Average prices of British academic books 1982*. (CLAIM Report No 21) Centre for Library and Information Management, 1982.
5 Sargent, C W 'Zero-base budgeting and the library'. *Bulletin of the Medical Library Association* 66 (1) January 1978. 31–5.
6 Crowe, W J 'Zero-base budgeting for libraries: a second look'. *College and Research Libraries* 43 (1) January 1982. 47—50.
7 Fazar, W 'Program planning and budgeting theory'. *Special Libraries* 60 (7) September 1969. 423–33.
8 Weinburg, C B 'The university library: analysis and proposals'. *Management Science* 21 (2) October 1974. 135.
9 Newman, G C 'Budgetary trends in small private liberal arts college libraries' in Miller, W and Rockwood, D S (eds) *College librarianship*. Scarecrow Press, 1981. 47–64.
10 Martin, M S *Budgetary control in academic libraries*. JAI Press, 1978.
11 Hamburg, M *et al Library planning and decision making systems*. MIT Press, 1974. 25–6.
12 *The Government's expenditure plans 1981–82 to 1983–84* Cmnd. 8175. HMSO, 1981. 106.
13 Dunworth, H and Cook, R 'Can universities be made more efficient?' *Times Higher Education Supplement*. 200 22 August 1975. 11.

14   Moore, N 'Economics in library management' in Holroyd, G (ed) *Studies in library management.* (Vol 4) Bingley, 1977. 120–137.

15   Department of Education and Science *Statistics of libraries in major establishments of further education in England, Wales and Northern Ireland. 1979/80.* Department of Education and Science, 1981. (71% were members of their academic boards compared with 67% in 1975/76.)

16   Urquhart, J A 'Balancing the library budget' in Woodworth, D P (ed) *Economics of serial management.* Proceedings of the 2nd Blackwells' Periodicals Conference, Trinity College, Oxford, 23–24 March 1977. Loughborough Technical College, School of Librarianship. 95.

17   Baumol, W J and Marcus, M *Economics of academic libraries.* American Council on Education, 1976.

18   King, D 'Pricing policies in academic libraries'. *Library Trends* 28 (1) Summer 1979. 47–62.

19   Royal Society *A study of the scientific information system in the United Kingdom.* (British Library Research and Development Report No 5626) Royal Society, 1981.

20   Burman, C 'Charging for library services'. *Library Association, University College and Research Section Newsletter. July 1982. 6–11.*

21   *Council of Polytechnic Librarians statistics of polytechnic libraries 1980–81.* COPOL, March 1982.

22   Lomas, T 'College library statistics'. *Library Association, Colleges of Further and Higher Education Section Bulletin* (34) Summer 1982. 3–4.

23   De Gennaro, R 'Matching commitments to needs and resources'. *Journal of Academic Librarianship* 7 (1) March 1981. 13.

18

Reader Services: for Students, Teachers, and Management

Nigel Ford

I wasn't certain whether my own ideas would be applicable. I hadn't thought about it. . . . I disagreed about some things, but I didn't put this in. . . . It's a game. You need the mark. You can't be daring or show your own ideas.

I whizzed through the essay and was just sort of feeling for help, saying 'Can I use this? Can I use that?' But I didn't really – I should have thought more about whether it was fairytale or not. I don't think I thought too much about it.

Reading all this research . . . is a waste of time. I'll never use it. But if that's the way they want to judge us, that's what I'll give them.

Quotations from students at the same college, using the same library, in interviews for a study reported in detail elsewhere.[1] Their courses made extensive use of modern teaching methods, with a large element of independent library oriented study coupled with expert and individualized tuition from teaching staff. They all obtained the qualification for which they were working. They all spent long hours in a new, well stocked, and well equipped multimedia library. They searched for, found, used, and quoted books and journals. They came to the enquiry desk with queries that were answered. But were their 'information needs' satisfied? How well did 'reader services' cope?

There are two answers to this question. At one level, that which librarians have often tended to regard as reader services, 'the marriage of circulation control and information services, chaperoned by inter-library loans',[2] have performed well. These students came to the library; were able to find a large number and a wide range of printed and audio-visual information sources; study them in comfortable and well lit surroundings; borrow certain of them to study at home; photocopy others; find details of, and borrow on inter-library loan, yet more.

Reader services as defined above did all that was asked of them. But what of reader services in a wider sense? How far did the library, through its services, help them to 'free curiosity; to permit individuals to go charging off in new directions dictated by their own interests; to unleash a sense of enquiry; to open everything to questioning and exploration; to recognize that everything is in process of change. . . .'[3]

Rogers' idea of desirable learning aims may seem somewhat idealistic. Yet I think they were a fair way towards being achieved by other students from the same batch of interviews, on the same courses, using the same library resources and services:

> I mean, I regard the journal . . . or the book, as a point of view, and the tutors as a point of view – you've got to make up your own mind about its importance for you in your particular situation. . . . I tried to relate what was said in the texts to my knowledge and ideas. . . . I've also tested out, in a sense, my own particular prejudices, ideas, preconceptions – call them what you like – against those in the literature. . . . The danger is that you start doing it for them and not yourself. . . . I'm not denying that (the qualification) is a nice thing to have, but were it a Z.Q. or whatever . . . it's all the same to me.

> I don't think I can put anything down in an essay unless I believe it. I have to take in the information, digest it and bring

it out. . . . It's just a question of absorbing it and making decisions about it. . . . Whether I personally consider the groups used in the research were valid; whether I can compare one lot of research with another. . . .'

The main areas I sought to explore and work on concerned my school. I'm not afraid to go back and say 'I don't agree with that – what about this? You haven't thought about that'.

These readers were served (and in my view served well) by reader services, but reader services in a wider context. For these students, the pieces of the jigsaw – the library, teaching methods learning aims and objectives, and their own needs, goals, abilities, and preferences – all fitted together to form a coherent and harmonious picture.

Clearly, the learning jigsaws of some students fit together harmoniously. Not so with others. The library is one of the jigsaw pieces, yet it would be foolish to extol the virtues of one piece as being particularly well cut, finely shaped, and superbly finished, if it did not combine effectively with all the other pieces. Harris[2] is of the opinion that 'Reader services should be a description of the whole library operation'. I would go further, and insist that reader services should be a description of the whole library operation *as it interacts with and responds to the whole learning operation*. If individuals' learning jigsaws do indeed differ, then the library piece and the learning pieces must somehow bend, flex and adapt to each other in order to fit. Reader services are about this process.

Within this broader context, we must approach the problem of service to readers from the point of view of what we know about the learner and the learning tasks on which he is engaged.

At a basic level, it is an axiom of modern learning theories that the meaningfulness of learning depends on the extent to which new information can be successfully linked to the learner's existing knowledge stored in memory.[4] Such a principle underlies approaches to teaching from Skinner's[5] advocacy of small steps and careful sequencing in 'programmed learning' to Ausubel's[6] proposed 'advance organizers', in which linking bridges are laid between new information to be learned and the learner's existing knowledge, and to Pask's[7] stressing of the importance in learning of analogies, by which the unknown is learned via the known.

At this basic level, reader services must provide information about the library and its often bewildering array and arrangement of information sources and services in a way which is intelligible to readers. There has been much activity recently in the relatively simple aspects of basic library orientation and reference finding. In many college libraries, algorithms and other forms of guide have been developed, along with user education programmes using a variety of media designed to familiarize the learner with such things as catalogues and how they work. However, the problem is that we may provide an internally coherent and consistent system (equally, because of the considerable amounts of time and expertise necessary to produce and maintain, say, an effective subject index, many of us may not!), yet this may not necessarily enmesh with students' perhaps limited, even eccentric, searching abilities and strategies.

To continue the example of subject access to information – one of the key services to readers beyond those relating to basic author/title reference finding and document delivery – the new student may be taught to locate the catalogue and be aware of how to use it, yet may not have the librarian's experience and dexterity of mind if, for example he has to search under 'attendance' having found no entry under 'truancy'. Many librarians may not appreciate the mental and linguistic agility, which they themselves have developed to a high degree, required to translate information needs into a set of disciplined and restricted index terms. Will the young college student perceiving the problem of, say, the frustrations and difficulties encountered by people in wheelchairs trying to get in and out of public buildings necessarily search an index under terms like 'disabled', 'access' and the like? He may well prefer, ludicrously from the librarian's point of view, terms like 'difficulties', 'frustrations' or even 'getting in and out'. In the main, we simply do not know the extent to which our systems of subject access enmesh or fail to enmesh with our users' cognitive and linguistic repertoires.

To compound the problems, in many libraries cataloguing staff are less than generous when making added subject headings and cross references. Lack of time has also too often meant the abandonment of a thorough and ongoing review and updating of

indexing languages and cross referencing systems. Automated cataloguing systems are making subject access via Library of Congress
(and less commonly PRECIS) subject headings possible for many
polytechnic and a number of smaller college libraries.[8] However,
to what extent are subject headings – whether produced locally,
cooperatively or centrally – based on anything more than terms
used in documents and librarians' intuitive appraisals of what terms
and combinations of terms users (or more probably, they themselves!) are likely to use in their searching? How successfully do
such languages enmesh with users' existing knowledge and expression? The answer may differ considerably from college to college,
and from one student group to another. Yet how many college
libraries conduct systematic (which can nevertheless be small-scale)
investigations into the effectiveness or otherwise of the subject
access they provide to their readers? How many conduct such
investigations even into the extent to which their readers find what
they want on the shelves, whether by subject or author/title access?
Statistics of enquiries and complaints are crude measures of this
aspect of reader services. Oiling the squeaky wheel may in certain
contexts be an effective way of maintaining a service, but in this
context many faulty wheels do not squeak (or speak), none less so
than the wheel which has long since fallen off.

But to equate reader services with facilitating readers' acquisition
of the information sources they request is to underestimate the
complexity of the task and duty of providing services to readers
within an educational context. At one level, we must of course
draw on what we know of the reader in order to improve the
library's internal systems and services – 'reader services' in a paro-
chial sense. However, in terms of giving services to readers in a
wider sense, we must also concern ourselves with the complexities
of a broader view of the learning operation.

The student at college works in the context of a number of interacting variables: teaching methods, learning aims and objectives,
the student's own abilities, study styles, attitudes, motivational
orientations, and goals, formal assessment procedures. All of these
factors help to shape the information needs which it is the library's
task to help resolve. Information needs may be thought of as a gap

in the jigsaw which takes its shape from these surrounding pieces. At one level, reader services are about helping students find pieces to fill the gap and complete the picture. At another level, reader services must be about determining what the picture should be. In other words, the library, as well as responding in relatively passive mode to information needs as shaped by factors such as teaching methods, aims and objectives, and assessment procedures, should also have a more active contribution in helping to determine the nature and role of these factors. In so far as these factors may be far more influential in determining the nature of student learning and information needs than even superb library facilities (which may be *necessary* but not *sufficient*), failure of our concept of reader services to encompass them may restrict our activities to tinkering with the paintwork when we should be helping to redesign the car. For the library has a great potential role in curriculum development, and a duty to exercise it. What greater service to readers than that of improving the effectiveness and quality of the learning in which they are engaged?

To satisfy information needs in more than a superficial sense, information with which the student comes into contact must meet certain requirements besides being intelligible.[9] Students may have distinct differences in the way they study and build up knowledge. If they are forced into another mould, their learning may be less effective. New information may be understood yet discarded if it clashes too harshly with attitudes, beliefs, or the student's stage of intellectual development. Assessment procedures may in some cases instil an extrinsic attitude to study. A student may switch off and go through the motions of learning (often successfully in terms of formal assessment) but with little personal meaning and possibly little chance of remembering and using what has been 'learned' in the longer term.[10]

Ford[11] has drawn attention to the possible effects on learning of assessment procedures, the integration of learning aims and methods with students' attitudes, belief systems, and self-determined goals, and has drawn out implications for librarianship of differences in students' stages of intellectual development and the way they go about studying and learning.[12, 13] These implications centre on differences in the extent and type of structuring of information which is likely to be most effective, and on the extent to which the student is presented with a number of alternative and often conflicting views on the same subject – the raw material of 'critical thinking'.

The library's contribution to learning has not received much empirical investigation. I would argue that this role is broad and complex, and includes both passive and more active aspects. The library has a valuable role to play in providing what a lecturer could – only less efficiently – provide. The library is open for longer hours than a lecturer may be available. Information prescribed by a lecturer may be available for self-paced study in a variety of media, some of which (including print) may allow complex interaction between student and information. The growth in multi-media resource-based learning in colleges illustrates this function well.

However, as well as influencing *how* students learn, the library has an important role in determining *what* students learn. As well as facilitating learning which is determined and structured for students by their teachers, the library has the equally, if not more important, educational role of promoting autonomous learning – an important aim of tertiary education with a long pedigree, matched only by imprecision in definition. The relationship between autonomy as an aim or outcome in education, and autonomy as a method of achieving autonomy as an aim, is complex, and not as simple as many exponents of independent and resource-based learning may lead us to believe.[14] I am not arguing for bandwagoning campaigns for students' independent library use in pursuit of autonomy. What I am arguing is that we should review the provision and opportunities in our colleges for students to develop autonomous learning. I use this term to include three aspects:

1 The ability to 'find out' relatively independently in order to update and extend knowledge outside the context of a formal educational course. The growing importance and recognition of this educational aim is well documented.[13]

2 Awareness of and an ability to cope with a variety of different views and approaches to a problem or area of study – or 'relativistic reasoning' as Perry[15] has termed it – in terms of perceiving

the need for and being able to develop an 'own view' instead of relying on 'authority' views.

3 An intrinsic valuing of what is learned, as opposed to learning primarily in response to relatively extrinsic rewards or punishments.

The library, and librarians, are at the 'sharp end' of the vast, prolifically increasing and relatively unstructured volume of information. The interface between student and this level and type of information has traditionally been the teacher. He has selected and predigested information, making it available through his teaching, more recently by means of the library or resource centre in the form of lists of prescribed reading, and increasingly, listening and viewing. But if we are to promote autonomous learning, increasingly the information-learner interface must become library reader services, the whole process monitored, guided, and evaluated by teachers. Students must move towards instigating and planning their own study areas and activities in negotiation with teaching staff.[13]

Clearly, predigestion and structuring, as well as the teaching of the core content of basic building blocks and underlying principles in a subject are important components of learning.[16] And the development of skills in 'learning to learn' and 'relativistic reasoning' will not be well served by unthinkingly pitching students into the stormy seas of unstructured information on their own. Again, predigestion and structuring, with subsequent progressive destructuring would seem to be desirable.[17] However, the ultimate objective of any small scale, sheltered, and predigested teaching of information handling skills and relativistic reasoning must the unleashing of the student into the reality of the information explosion, represented in the main by the library and interpreted via 'reader services'. The role of the library and its staff, particularly at relatively advanced stages, is paramount.

The third strand of 'autonomous learning' which permeates the development of knowledge and skills is the extent to which learning is intrinsically valued. The library has an important role here. 'Library learning' can make learning meaningful in so far as it can allow learners to pursue, to a far greater extent than otherwise, their own particular areas of interest. If externally imposed selection of areas and problems to be studied, as well as the way in which they are studied, engenders an extrinsic orientation to study, then the student may switch off from learning as a personally meaningful activity, and may not value, retain, and apply what he has learned once the qualification being sought has been obtained. If the library has a role in promoting more intrinsic learning, then this is a reader service of value.

We are dealing here with the whole structuring of student courses: how this build-up of knowledge, based on information, is organized; the amount of independence students should have, and be allowed to develop, in deciding on areas of study; the extent to which, and the ways in which, information is structured for them; how learning is assessed. A major influence may be not superb library facilities or personalized reader services in a narrow sense, but phenomena that many may feel to be outside the library's concern: forms of assessment, course design, and curriculum development within the college.

Many librarians may feel that students' learning as a concern of study and investigation is a province of specialist educational technology organizations (which may themselves come within the learning resources organization of the college). The library's role is that of storing, organizing, publicizing, and arranging access to information sources, which may well include the products of the educational technology department or unit. How the information is used, and for what purpose, is the concern of course designers and teaching staff, as are patterns and methods of assessment. The library's task is to serve these patterns and to advise particularly on the feasibility, from an organizational point of view, of their realization.

However, if reader services are, as I suggest, about facilitating, the fit of the library component into the complex jigsaw of factors affecting the student's learning, then librarians must act as members of a team of people with various skills and concerns, all geared to facilitating and improving students' learning. This team will include educational technologists, counsellors, curriculum developers, and teachers. They must be involved in research as well as development based on the research of others outside the college. What we do not know about the learner far outweighs what we do know; arguably, important aspects of the learner that we need to know relate to him in a local context (as opposed to universal features identifiable in the study of samples of students in other environments).

I would go further, and suggest that not only must reader services extend to a librarian's membership of and work on a team, but that his contribution to that team's work is a key one. Librarians have a distinctive point of view, a distinctive contribution to learning; there are specific types of learning aims and objectives to which they are particularly oriented. These aims and objectives are particularly related to 'autonomous learning' as I have defined it. A central reader services aim must be to represent the need for such intrinsic, long term, and high level learning aims, particularly if these are under-represented within a college. But could they be?

In a small survey, Ford[1] found evidence of students 'going through the motions' of learning – passing their courses but perceiving little value in what they had learned except as a means to the end of obtaining a qualification. Many of these students were student teachers from whom one would have expected a high level of application of what had been learned, in a teaching situation. In a large scale survey of higher education students, Entwistle[18] identified three distinct groups of students characterized by different approaches to study. One group was intrinsically motivated, and geared their learning to obtaining deep personally meaningful understanding. However, a second group was achievement oriented, gearing their studies to achieving success. As with the first group, they tended to do well in examinations. A third group was extrinsically motivated, seemingly by a 'fear of failure', geared to reproducing information without understanding it at a deep level. Even so, many of this group still performed well in examinations.

The characteristic of gearing study to extrinsic assessment rather than intrinsic personal interest in the subject has also been identified in Eraut's[17] 'course-focussed', and to some extent in Miller and Parlett's[19] 'cue-seeking' approaches to study. Hazell[20] reports a widespread feeling of 'pointlessness' felt by students in relation to their experiences in higher education. Brennan and Percy,[21] reviewing British and American studies, conclude that there is some measure of agreement that students' intellectual/academic expectations, while remaining comparatively high, are rarely met. Students claim to be expecting 'challenge', 'stimulus', 'relevance', from academic work, but later report that they are not receiving it. There is also some support for the notion that, at least in the context of professional courses such as teacher education, what is 'learned' on a course often fails to be applied outside the course. McNamara and Desforges[22] note that 'preparations, contrary to or divergent from current professional practices appear to be "washed out" within a short period of the student leaving training'.

Professor John Merritt,[23] writing generally of courses in education, concludes: 'The majority of students revert to their former methods within a relatively short time. Much of what is learned is simply forgotten, and what is left tends, very often, to fall on stony ground. This cannot be regarded as a fault of the students – we must accept this as a basic flaw in course design.'

I have argued elsewhere that neither assessment procedures[9] nor the way in which the academic work of librarians is measured and credited[24] are particularly well geared to the needs of teaching and learning or to the development of autonomous learning as defined here, despite its increasing importance. The librarian has a key role in improving both the 'how' and the 'what' of student learning. By virtue of their work and background, librarians may be less likely than many others to undervalue autonomous learning, or to let such undervaluing go unnoticed.

In background and expertise, subject experts, educational technologists, and others have often been concerned with bringing learners into contact with the information they need in a relatively narrow context of small amounts of highly structured information. By comparison, the librarian has been concerned with relatively large amounts of relatively unstructured information. Subject experts may often face the information explosion within a limited context. Some may even prefer and be able to extract a relatively unchanging core of subject matter which they can teach without needing to face the storm of information. But the librarian's expertise lies in his overview of individual subjects, the interrelationships between them, the relationship between new information and old, the extent and control of the information explosion. In other words, it is possible for some to ignore the overview and minimize the need to help students develop autonomy in their learning. Yet to the librarian this is a central concern. Lecturers may be expert in French, business studies, or computing – the librarian is expert at handling information within the context of the information explosion. In many ways the library stands for autonomous learning. Particularly if (as is possible) this vital aim in education is undervalued in a college then who better than the librarian to champion this cause. But to do so he must be involved in policy making at the highest level. In such a case he is giving a service to readers *par excellence.*

In this context, 'reader services' takes on a dynamic and far-reaching role. But if representation is necessary on key committees, where discussion and decision making takes place in relation to learning aims and objectives, assessment, teaching methods, study skills, staff and curriculum development, it is not of itself sufficient to ensure an effective service to readers through improving the effectiveness and quality of their learning. It is all too easy to sit on committees waiting to hear of developments which may affect library services. But to be a prime mover and an active force within the college requires knowledge, expertise, and a commitment to ongoing research in collaboration with others concerned with the investigation and improvement of student learning. These considerations must influence the selection of staff, their status, and conditions of service. They must be allowed opportunity for study and research on at least an equal footing with their subject teaching colleagues, particularly in relation to time and opportunity, college support, study leave, and the like.

Much can be done to improve the quality of learning. Important if awkward questions must be asked and answered. How does the library contribute to learning? How effective in terms of learning are certain print and audio-visual resources? What is the effect on learning of different ways of deploying them? What should be the balance between learning specific subject content and learning how to learn? How can the library best facilitate both these aims? What are the effects, desirable and detrimental, of assessment procedures? How do these measure the achievement of autonomous learning? To what extent do readers find what they want in the library? To what extent is what they *want* what they *need*? How effective is the learning that goes on in the college? How can we measure effectiveness?

Such questions can only be answered – indeed, can only realistically be asked – within an environment supportive of and open to the results of research. Librarians havs a poor track record when it comes to research – using it or conducting it.[25, 26] Many colleges have a poor track record of allowing them opportunity to conduct or even attempt research. Yet the role of research and development, and within it the role of the librarian, in the improvement of learning is a key one and is likely to increase in importance in the future.

Effective reader services depend on the quality of a library's stock, information services, circulation control, inter-library loans, cataloguing and classification, and a myriad other tasks. But despite this, and despite agreed quality in each of these areas, 'students, in short, may receive their degrees and diplomas without developing intellectually at all – simply having become "well-informed bores" – or without acquiring that flexibility of thinking and method of attack on issues that Robbins saw as a main aim of higher education.'[27]

Only by extending the concept of 'reader services' to encompass the whole learning experience, the interaction of learner with information at many levels and in many contexts, and by extending their own activities to encompass the study, practice, and application of systematic investigation (whether small- or large-scale, 'illuminative' or 'scientific', in-house or in a wider context), can librarians hope to play their part in the development of more effective learning, and in this way provide a real 'service to readers'.

REFERENCES

1 Ford, N 'Levels of understanding and the personal acceptance of information in higher education'. *Studies in Higher Education* 5 (1) 1980. 63–70.

2 Harris, K 'Organisational structures' in Jefferson G and Smith-Burnett G C K (eds) *The college library*. London, Bingley, 1978. 78–94, 84.

3 Rogers, C *Freedom to learn*. Merrill, 1969. 105–6.

4 Johnson, R E 'Meaning in complex learning'. *Review of Educational Research* 45 1975. 425–459.

5 Skinner, B *Science and human behaviour*. Macmillan, 1953.

6 Ausubel, D P 'The use of advance organizers in learning and retention of meaningful material'. *Journal of Educational Psychology* 51 1960. 267–272.

7 Pask, G 'Conversational techniques in the study and practice of education'. *British Journal of Educational Psychology* 46 1976. 12–25.

8 Seal, A W *Automated cataloguing in the UK: a guide to services*. Bath, Centre for Catalogue Research, Bath University Library, 1980.

9 Ford, N 'Relating "information needs" to learner characteristics in higher education'. *Journal of Documentation* 36 1980. 99–114.

10 Ford, N 'Study strategies, orientations and "personal meaningfulness" in higher education'. *British Journal of Educational Technology* 10 1979. 143–160.

11 Ford, N 'Recent approaches to the study and teaching of "effective learning" in higher education.' *Review of Educational Research* 51 2 1981. 345–377.

12 Ford, N 'Cognitive psychology and "library learning".' *Journal of Librarianship* 11 (1). 1979. 25–38.

13 Ford, N 'Towards a model of "library learning" in educational systems'. *Journal of Librarianship* 11 (4) 1979. 247–260.

14 Boud, D (ed) *Developing student autonomy in learning*. Kogan Page, 1981.

15 Perry, W G *Intellectual and ethical development in the college years: a scheme*. Holt, Rinehart and Winston, 1970.

16 Baron, J 'Some theories of college instruction'. *Higher Education* 4 1975. 149–172.

17 Eraut, M 'Should curriculum decisions be made "for" or "by" the independent learning?' in Furniss B S and Parsonage, J R (eds) *Independent learning in teritary science education*. London, Thames Polytechnic, 1975. 1–17.

18 Entwistle, N, Hanley, M and Hounsell, D 'Identifying distinctive approaches to studying'. *Higher Education* 8 1979. 365–380.

19 Miller, C M L and Parlett, M *Up to the mark*. Society for Research into Higher Education, 1974.

20 Hazell, J 'The problem of pointlessness – a challenge for counselling'. *British Journal of Guidance and Counselling* 4 (2) 1976. 156–170.

21 Brennan, J and Percy, K. 'Sociological perspectives on teaching and learning in higher education'. *Higher Education Bulletin* 3 (2) 1975. 107–126.

22 McNamara, D and Desforges, C 'Social sciences, teacher education and the objectification of craft knowledge'. *British Journal of Teacher Education* 4 (1) 1978. 17–36.

23 Merritt, J E 'Standards of reading and in-service education: some harsh realities'. *Reading Education – UK* 2 1977. 16–22.

24 Ford, N 'Academic and non-academic roles in teaching and learning: a problem for librarians'. *Journal of Further and Higher Education* 5 (1) 1981. 24–29.

25 Roberts, N 'Review of Heriksen, T IRFIS 3'. *CRUS News* 9 1980. 17–18.

26 Dain, P 'The profession and the professors'. *Library Journal* 105 1980. 1701.

27 Wilson, J D *Student learning in higher education*. Croom Helm, 1981. 165.

19

User Education

Ian Malley

lthough there are common elements in the practice of user
education throughout tertiary education in the UK, there
has been a tendency, in the 1960s and 1970s at least, to
consider user education in the polytechnics and universities as an
area separate from user education in colleges of higher and further
education and colleges of technology, etc. Polytechnic and university user education has developed in close association, chiefly
through the influence of bodies like the Standing Conference on
National and University Libraries (SCONUL) and the Council of
Polytechnic Librarians (COPOL), and particularly through
cooperative agencies such as the SCONUL Tape-Slide Group
which drew its membership from both bodies. The other colleges
have of necessity developed outside this association, frequently
with little discernible cooperation between one another. Whether
the division between the two areas is artificial and whether the
continued separation is desirable are moot points, but this chapter
will discuss activity in the polytechnics separately from work in
the various types of further education college. It is not only practical and convenient to do so, but it enables one to highlight some
special features which apply particularly to these colleges.

COLLEGE LIBRARIES

The colleges comprise a rather amorphous group of institutions, yet they have certain features which, although not entirely shared by every college, are sufficiently common to warrant discussion before user education itself is examined in any detail.

To begin with, considering the small numbers of professional librarians employed in most of these colleges, one must express surprise that any user education programmes are to be found in their libraries at all. Only exceptionally does the number of staff in any one library reach double figures, and in a substantial percentage of cases there are only one or two professional librarians on the staff. They have, of course, a primary responsibility to organize and administer a library service for staff and students (with enrolments ranging from hundreds to several thousands) and this demands a range of services in addition to user education. It says much therefore for their commitment to the principle of user education that so much time and manpower resources are made available to it.

However, one must qualify this statement by emphasizing the dual responsibility of many of the professional librarians in the colleges. Often designated tutor-librarians, their duties involve partly the provision of a professional library service, and partly teaching in the parent institution. In some cases this is formalized by their placement on the Burnham (*ie* teaching; for a full discussion, see Chapter 15) scale or some equivalent grading which demands that a proportion of their time is spent teaching. It would be unfair to suggest that their placement on these scales stimulates or underwrites the programmes of user education, or even that the programmes are inspired by the hope that they will be recognized as an entrée to such scales, but it is a factor that might be kept in mind. At any rate, it is a factor that sometimes pushes user education into the politics of college libraries and their parent institutions.

Where tutor-librarians have a teaching function, that teaching may not be user education alone – a certain amount of subject teaching in the curriculum may be required also. Librarians, individually and collectively however, have fought to avoid being used as 'makeweight' teachers in general studies, communications, and other subjects, and have argued strenuously that they have a specialist teaching role of their own, in user education, subject bibliography, use of information, and like areas. This can have an important influence on user education. If the librarian is teaching what the institution understands to be an academic discipline he or she will be recognized as a teacher by both students and other academic staff: thus any programme of user education will have a certain automatic and fairly secure standing because the tutor-librarian has the status of a teacher. Furthermore, the tutor-librarian, with a sound knowledge of the requirements of the curriculum (and now, increasingly, of some academic subjects), will be able to offer and present more meaningful and appropriate programmes of user education. This then enables the programme to fulfil the great credos of user education: that it should be relevant to the parent course and correctly timed to take advantage of student interest and need.

Finally, the inclusion of user education in many colleges has been made more easy and acceptable by the implicit or explicit recognition that library and information skills should be an integral and vital component in the courses of TEC, BEC, SCOTEC, SCOTBEC, etc. There is no blanket requirement for user education in these courses, nor is the precise nature of the skills spelled out, so professional librarians in colleges may still have a difficult task to persuade colleges and to determine content. Yet the widespread admission of the necessity for these skills gives the college librarian a valuable opportunity to provide formal user education in the curriculum – an opportunity rarely open to librarians in other areas of user education apart from the polytechnics.

The description of current activity in colleges that follows elaborates the features of college user education that have just been discussed, and is based on the results of a recent survey of user education programmes in colleges in the UK organized by the author in his capacity as British Library Information Officer for User Education. Although the survey attempted to be comprehensive, returns were no more than 30% of the questionnaires distributed (the results were gathered by a postal questionnaire). Nevertheless, enough information has been gathered to offer a useful if not complete picture of the present situation.

LIBRARY ORIENTATION IN COLLEGE LIBRARIES

As in other institutions of further and higher education, initial orientation to the library is common to most colleges. The range of techniques employed in this orientation is as wide as in polytechnics and universities; lectures, seminars, tours, audio-visual introductions, library guides, etc, but there are some differences in emphasis and content.

Firstly, audio-visual introductions are uncommon. The chief reason for this would appear to be lack of money, and perhaps other resources, for the production of this sort of presentation, although it may lie too in the attitude that A-V is not a very effective way of orienting the user. A 1981 survey indicated that only 25.3% of the responding colleges used audio-visual media, while the relevant percentages for polytechnics and universities were 66.6% and 61% respectively.[1] One of the strongest arguments for the use of audio-visual introductions to the library is that a large intake of students can be covered. By this criterion, many colleges could easily justify their use, because from a sample of 50 colleges in the recent college survey, 22% had student populations of 3,000–5,000 and a further 22% had student populations of 5,000+.

Secondly, library guides seem to be less common, shorter, and less well produced than in the other sectors. Again, the probable reason is lack of money and of the sophisticated reprographic equipment and support personnel common in larger institutions.

The above two types of orientation are relatively passive forms of teaching: seminars, tours, etc are more active and are preferred by most colleges. This preference is reflected in the frequent accompaniment of exercises or questionnaires in college library orientation. Though they are rarely stated, there are other possible, sound reasons for this. Firstly, unlike other sectors of tertiary education, the orientation is often timetabled and compulsory, even part of a course requirement. Secondly, many courses may be at a non-advanced level, with a concomitant need to determine how much knowledge has been absorbed in the orientation programme before proceeding with other instruction. It is felt too, that students may benefit from an orientation programme which introduces them directly and personally to a member of the library staff, thus putting a familiar face on what may seem to some of them a remote, unfamiliar, and even daunting organization. In the colleges' survey mentioned earlier, some librarians remarked upon students' literacy and numeracy problems, extending even to the use of the alphabet.

USER EDUCATION IN COLLEGES BEYOND INITIAL ORIENTATION

The point where library orientation ends and more advanced user education begins is frequently unclear, more so in the colleges than in the polytechnics and universities. There is a tendency for many formal programmes to follow the initial orientation fairly quickly, and there are sometimes imperceptible differences in the level of the techniques and skills taught. This lack of apparent division between orientation and instruction is no bad thing. In fact, librarians invariably advocate continuity in user education as very desirable, and stress that there should be an easy transition from orientation to advanced instruction. Universities, and to a lesser extent polytechnics, rarely achieve this because there is often a gap of almost two years between initial orientation and the advanced instruction which is likely to be linked to large projects prepared in the final year of the students' course.

It is useful to pursue the contrast with universities and polytechnics in assessing the influence of the vocational nature of college courses. In the universities in particular, where courses are often more 'academic' than 'vocational', there is a tendency for the advanced instruction to become equally academic. The research skills offered are certainly geared to the specialized research projects that take up so much time in the student's final year. Sadly, however, skills which are tied too closely to the literature of their course subject can rarely be applied after university unless students proceed in the research field. On the other hand, the colleges, with their high proportion of vocational courses, tend to offer a more non-academic, practical, problem-solving approach – an approach which must begin early in the course and be continued throughout the course and beyond. This is a constraining and guiding discipline for the college librarian. Anything not obviously related to vocational courses and student needs is clearly redundant.

Another factor which gears college user education programmes to students' courses is the fact that they are often a compulsory, timetabled part of the course. They are thus open to the inspection of other academic staff. Many of the programmes are planned and prepared in cooperation with faculty. Whether or not this faculty cooperation is the cause or the result, the fact is that user education programmes are in most cases timetabled on the curriculum and formally linked to courses. The colleges survey showed that in the case of the non-orientation programmes, 80% were timetabled, and 60% were a formal part of the student's course (usually in TEC and BEC courses). For those who advocate this formula for user education, this is encouraging, although it must be qualified by the fact that very few of these programmes were directly assessed or examinable. Furthermore it must be pointed out that only 90 (or approximately 30%) of the libraries who replied had such a programme of advanced instruction. There is still a long way to go before this type of instruction becomes widely accepted. Nevertheless, the present position is promising, and certainly better than the situation which obtains in the polytechnics and universities.

The length of the programmes varies from one to, in one case, 30 units, but most are one to three units long. Perhaps length is not as important as the fact that most are linked to academic subjects (business studies, engineering, art and design, etc). This, combined with the faculty cooperation noted above, would seem to indicate that the old charge, frequently made, that library classes are usually linked to liberal studies or general studies courses is no longer valid. It also confirms that non-advanced technical subjects no longer rely simply on lectures and handouts, rather than on the use of library resources. Coursework at all levels in the colleges incorporates project work just as much as in the polytechnics and universities.

A point of current concern in user education circles is the relationship between study skills and library skills. It would seem that in colleges, study skills, in its accepted definition of notetaking, examination techniques, etc, are rarely included in user education programmes. Although they are commonly taught in colleges, they are generally the province of general studies lecturers; this would seem to block the prospect of that amalgamation of study skills with library skills which is so strongly advocated in the schools. Yet it is interesting to note that in the survey, many librarians identified or even confused study skills with aspects of library skills. Perhaps this perceived relationship will in the long term bring these skills together in some association. For the present, they are separately taught for the most part, and are likely to remain so while other academic staff want to retain their teaching interests in existing courses and disciplines.

Some instances were reported where librarians were not permitted to teach advanced library skills, this being the responsibility of other teaching staff. While it is remotely possible that there may be advantages in this, one cannot help feeling that the librarians were excluded because they were not designated as tutor-librarians and that other teaching staff were defending their allocation of teaching hours. Team teaching of advanced user education, with a librarian and a subject specialist cooperating on a course, and each contributing his special knowledge and skills to the students, is a totally different matter, and a technique of proven worth.

The fact that professional librarians are few in number in many college libraries means that library skills programmes in colleges are more carefully coordinated than in universities and polytechnics. Generally, only one or two professionals are involved in the teaching, and they know exactly the full scope and extent of their programmes. This awareness brings coordination and hence the prospect of sound planning, well illustrated by the frequent existence of detailed course outlines, course objectives etc.

POLYTECHNIC LIBRARIES

Some would argue that user education in higher education in the UK has made most progress in the polytechnics. As they emerged with the technological universities in the 1960s and 1970s, they were certainly at the forefront of user education developments, and they have continued to develop strongly along parallel lines with this type of university; some have even been more innovative.

Although they are generally associated with universities in terms of user education, they owe much to their antecedents as colleges of art, commerce, technology, etc, which were similar to the present-day colleges of further and higher education. The polytechnics have much in common with the colleges; funding, the proportion of part-time to full-time students (about one third), diplomas or certificates awarded (TEC, BEC, CNAA, etc), the range of vocational studies. These points of similarity would lead one to expect that their pattern of user education would be similar to that of the colleges, and there are indeed some similarities with colleges in user education. However, points of difference between the polytechnics and colleges make the style and content of their user education programmes more akin to the universities. It is therefore valuable to explore differences and similarities between polytechnics and colleges, and between polytechnics and universities.

Crucially, there is the size of the polytechnics' libraries. On their establishment, most polytechnics inherited several college libraries and several sites. This meant a network of libraries and of professional librarians. These not inconsiderable library stock and manpower resources brought them nearer to the scale of the newly-established university libraries, and they now contrast strongly with the relatively small libraries and the small number of professional librarians in the colleges of further and higher education.

The greater size of library stocks and the greater number of professional librarians made it possible to introduce a degree of subject specialization in the management of the polytechnic libraries, though perhaps not to the extent obtaining in some universities. Wherever there is a commitment to user education in a polytechnic, it tends to be strongly subject oriented, this being regarded as essential to relevant and successful user education. There is a danger that such a philosophy produces more 'academic' programmes of user education, but the fact that a high percentage of courses in polytechnics are vocational has modified this tendency. At the same time, the subject specialist structure allows user education to escape from the narrow restrictiveness that permits 'separate' library instruction units which may sometimes be remote from the course subjects. Though larger than their further and higher education college counterparts, the polytechnic libraries were still small enough to maintain good contact with the faculty and the staff – a relationship which valuably assists any programmes that might be developed.

It is important to note the role of some staff in certain of the polytechnics. In the 1950s and 1960s the post of tutor-librarian emerged in many colleges (with a role still similar to the present-day colleges). As the polytechnic absorbed some of these colleges they acquired these tutor-librarians, who had a recognized role in teaching and a commitment to user education in particular. The polytechnics benefited from their help and awareness of what was required, and thus had a sound basis for user education.

Larger library collections and larger library staffs demand and bring more money to the library, and although any allocation of financial resources to user education on the library balance sheet may seem low, there are enough resources materially to affect the programmes. The most obvious manifestation of this in the polytechnic libraries (as in the university libraries) is the printed and audio-visual teaching aids. Many polytechnics produce a wide range of subject and information guides, and several audio-visual subject guides. Whereas a college library might produce a single tape-slide or videotape introduction to the library, a polytechnic may produce several. Polytechnic libraries, even with relatively large complements of staff, have found it necessary to produce many audio-visual, 'mass-teaching' aids (at the orientation level and above), even when their student populations are not substantially higher than those of the larger colleges. Student numbers, it seems, are not the overriding *raison d'être* for such productions in the UK, either currently or in the past.

Briefly then, the present profile of user education in polytechnics is that they have built on the useful features of user education in colleges, and have benefited from the advantages of larger scale, without going too far along the path taken by universities. Compared to the several hundred colleges of further education, there are only 30 polytechnics, yet there is no comprehensive survey of user education activity to draw upon. Considering their relatively small number and their undoubted importance in the UK tertiary education system, this may seem surprising, but one of the difficulties of organizing such a survey is the variety of sites, and therefore activity, within individual polytechnic libraries; data collection is not easy.

LIBRARY ORIENTATION IN POLYTECHNIC LIBRARIES

Almost every technique of introducing the student to the library is in use in polytechnic libraries; virtually every library attempts some form of orientation. Practical work, in the form of question sheets and other exercises, is not often used in association with orientation.

Although it may be infrequently timetabled, orientation is often arranged in consultation with the academic faculty. Guided tours, as in the colleges, are still the most popular method, but various self-instructional methods (including self-guided tours) are common. Tape-slide and videotape media, which are basically self-instructional (though often not used in that mode) are widespread; common to all the libraries is the library guide. Undoubtedly, the polytechnic libraries have led the way in the variety and the quality of their production. Substantial sums have been spent on them and they have sometimes made excellent use of the expertise of graphic designers employed in the polytechnics. Present financial constraints do not seem to have affected the quantity and quality of printed orientational material.

USER EDUCATION IN POLYTECHNICS BEYOND INITIAL ORIENTATION

Advanced instruction, or bibliographic instruction as it is often called, is the more substantial form of user education in the polytechnic libraries. Unlike the colleges' pattern, this instruction follows much later in the students' course, usually in the second and/or third year. This is a matter of some concern to most of the librarians, because more continuity would be preferred, not least because when the advanced instruction is offered, students remark that they wish it had been earlier. There is a dilemma here: if the advanced instruction (and it can be very advanced) is given too early, the students at the first stages of their course cannot see its relevance. Timing is therefore of major importance, and the librarians have to seek opportunity actively.

That opportunity is usually the projects and dissertations undertaken by students in their second and third years. These demand a considerable amount of independent study and call for a number of information-handling skills as well as knowledge of the subject literature in the library. The need is real and is felt by students, teaching staff, and librarians. There is little of that artificiality in the instruction provided by the librarians which can exist when programmes are timetabled into courses as independent units.

Without these projects it is doubtful if polytechnic (or for that matter university) library user education would have developed as far as it has done, because although CNAA validating panels insist that user education should be written into degree syllabuses (30–40% of all polytechnic courses are CNAA-validated), it is accepted more in spirit than in practice. Only a handful of polytechnics have CNAA courses which include units on information skills, and not many more polytechnic libraries have been able to get user education written into the overall aims of the library service. Yet there is not a tremendous concern on the part of librarians to remedy this formally, because they know that their existing project-related approach to the work is highly relevant to the needs of the students. Moreover, the pressure of timetable space is unlikely to persuade lecturers to permit substantially more information skills in the timetable, even though they might be sympathetic to the need for them.

Programmes of advanced instruction tend to vary from one to four hours in length, and most are on a voluntary basis. Lectures and seminars are usual, but are often supplemented by audio-visual and printed aids, in which polytechnic libraries have been very active. These subject guides to the literature often include an analysis of the literature search process, though a large number are simply annotated lists of reference material (including abstracting and indexing services). The audio-visual formats include tape-slides, audiotapes and videotapes, and for this reason can be used in a self-instructional mode by the students. There is little evidence, however, that they are used independently; they seem to be more popular when they are included in seminars.

CURRENT TRENDS AND FUTURE DIRECTIONS

It is difficult to perceive any particular trends in the user education in the college and polytechnic sectors. The acceptance of library skills, in TEC and BEC courses in particular, seems likely to continue to increase. Both the polytechnics and the colleges teach such courses, but so far the college libraries have made more progress than the polytechnics in successfully adding library skills units. Tutor-librarians in further and higher education colleges appear to be more closely connected with the courses than their counterparts (sometimes designated academic librarians) in polytechnics. One might surmise that if more publicity were given in the professional library literature to these course-related programmes then, by example, there would be more effort on the part of the librarians. For the college libraries it is interesting to speculate on the value and impact of a relatively recent publication describing some of the TEC and BEC library modules,[2] as well as the outline syllabus put forward for TEC and BEC modules.[3]

Recently there has been a move towards remodelling user education as information skills, and including within this umbrella term study skills, learning skills, and communication skills, as well as library skills. This is a promising development, although it is fraught with political problems both in polytechnics and colleges, where some of these skills may already be the province of other teaching staff in the institution. It suggests that library skills are part and parcel of the education process and that they should not be treated in isolation, which is often how they have been regarded by students and staff. Already, some polytechnic libraries have developed study skills programmes within their user education activity. The prospects for college libraries are less auspicious, because sometimes library skills have been taught within study skills modules, rather than vice versa. Nevertheless, whoever teaches the broader concept of information skills, the long-term successful future for this re-named set of skills would appear to lie in the colleges.

As far as new techniques are concerned one tends to think immediately of online searching. So far, work in this sphere has concentrated on promoting online search services rather than teaching online information skills, the reason being that the services are still relatively expensive and the skilled intermediary approach makes more efficient use of the facility. The polytechnics are ahead of the further and higher education colleges in this field, for the simple reason that online facilities are rarely found in the colleges. With the very small library budgets found in most further and higher education colleges, this situation is unlikely to change in the near future.

What of other information technology? It was encouraging to find in the colleges' survey mention of instruction in the use of PRESTEL. The same might be said of attempts to use videotext systems for library orientation in polytechnic libraries. While admiring this enterprise in adopting new teaching techniques, it should be noted that this is still at a very preliminary stage, and may be still an expression of a continuing attempt to 'dress up' user education and present it in a more palatable way. User education has not been short of such innovation since the 1960s. (This is not to suggest that it is anything but professionally commendable on the part of any teacher to present his or her courses in the most acceptable form.) Perhaps in the present period of continuing financial restraint, consolidation of user education should be the keyword, rather than innovation, yet, given the current governmental and industrial awareness of and interest in information technology, it is rather disappointing to see so little sign of its introduction in information skills courses and user education programmes. If we are to educate people for an information society, when better to start than in the wake of Information Technology Year (1982); where better to start than in the varied information stores of the library?

User Education
REFERENCES

1 Malley, I and Moys, S *Survey of audiovisual programmes produced for user education in UK academic libraries.* Loughborough, INFUSE Publications, 1982.
2 Library Association and Colleges of Further and Higher Education Group. *Examples in library work for TEC and BEC courses.* (CoFHE occasional publications no 5). Library Association, Colleges of Further and Higher Education Group, 1980.
3 'Outline syllabus for BEC and TEC modules for non-librarianship students'. *Library Association: Colleges of Technology and Further Education Section: Bulletin,* 22 Summer 1978. 10–12.

20

Audio Visual Materials in the College Library

Simon R Bradford

If the phrase 'a machine for living', which Le Corbusier used to describe a house, has been accepted as providing some insight into how domestic architecture can be analysed, then similarly a college can be described as a machine for learning and the library as one of its major motive powers. This rather grandiose description is not as overstated as it may seem when it comes to dealing with an account or analysis of audio-visual materials in the college library, as one of the central themes must unfortunately be the distinctions still made between audio-visual materials and other stock. This is historically and practically inevitable, but it is extremely important that all materials in the library are seen as contributing to the common objective of providing a service to that educative process which is the college's business. The machine analogy can be pursued further; the book, the periodical, the map, the videocassette, or the slide can all be reduced to a commonality; they are all cogs in the machine for learning, carrying information to their readers or users.

In order to discuss the role, function, development, value, and special problems associated with audio-visual materials, their nature, and boundaries, require definition. A common term applied to them is 'non-book material', but a conflict is immediately apparent here. Everything that is not a book is not necessarily what is understood by the term 'audio-visual'. Some plainly textual material could fall into this category: the display of a computer file online, a periodical on microfilm, are both non-book material. The original term audio-visual is equally ill-defined. It is wider in some respects and it becomes difficult, theoretically, to exclude the customary fiche catalogue or, more seriously, the book itself! This difficulty is seldom very important as the particular stock of any one college library tends to reflect the specialist academic courses taught and the special nature of audio-visual materials is usually self-evident. But a large institution with a broad range of faculties may have significant stocks of many or all of the various media that need discussion.

One clumsy sentence may go some way towards defining the boundaries of the material under discussion here. Audio-visual materials are characterized by the need to provide machinery to interpret them and/or by the need to provide special storage facilities, and/or by the need to employ different husbandry techniques in the cataloguing, classification, and indexing of the stock and in its delivery to the user.

Librarianship, or indeed any profession, and, more particularly, any service, is involved with balancing apparently incompatible needs. Before detailing the range of audio-visual materials and some of the specific problems associated with them, it is worth listing some of the balancing acts which are common to most and which underlie the day-to-day administrative problems which confront audio-visual librarians.

The first is that many of the materials which form the collections are used in two quite different and conflicting ways; they may be used as teaching aids in lectures and seminars; they are also used as part of individual study programmes by both staff and students.

Another such balancing act involves the boundaries which evolve between librarians and technical support staff. In most instances, though ill-equipped by training (and probably by inclination), the librarian is involved in teaching people how to use quite complex machines, and inevitably will be expected to fault-find on a limited scale, limited only by how 'correct' (in demarcation terms) and at the same time how helpful he is prepared to be. This balance can be tilted as far as having the librarian contribute to the production of software where precedent and concern for quality control are strong.

Another choice that has to be considered is the degree of integration of the material with the traditional book stock, although in most college libraries there are determinants at work which militate against much choice in the matter. These will become apparent below when some historical factors are considered.

More flexibility is available to the librarian when dealing with other means of administering the stock. For example, the question of closed or open access can be examined in relation to a non-integrated audio-visual collection in response to changing demands and pressures brought about by such everyday considerations as increased numbers of users or fewer library staff. The amount of physical space available is a further contributory factor.

Another conflict is that between the large, unified, multi-disciplinary site library and the need to operate within a multi-site institution where the needs of each site library will be closely associated with the work of a small number of disciplines or even a single discipline. The effect of these positions on the audio-visual material in the library may be extreme. On the one hand, one has a broad range of media which can be easily integrated both with the bibliographic tools available, and physically on the shelves, storage problems notwithstanding, and essentially treated similarly to all other stock. On the other hand, on a single discipline site, one tends to find that the material is concentrated in only one or two media and therefore the case for differentiation becomes much stronger.

The historical process whereby a collection of audio-visual material has grown up is liable to have created precedents and customs in the way the material is used which pre-empt some of the decisions that should properly be made by the librarian. Most common of these is the growth of a collection inside an academic department with little or no reference to the library. Seen purely as a direct teaching aid by academic staff, the implications for other use and the storage/cataloguing/retrieval problems have often been ignored until these collections (for example of videocassettes or slides) have reached a very significant size. In recent years, a number of such collections have then been passed into college libraries. Considerations of staffing, and/or the deteriorating order of the collection, are often the spur. Because their prime function remains to provide direct support to the teaching programmes, and because the needs of lecturers in specific subject areas are claimed to be paramount, the first effect is liable to be that there is no possibility for integration with existing library stock in any broad sense. They can be seen as an extra commitment undertaken by the library, but few librarians would hesitate to seek their inclusion in the library. The strings that are invariably attached to such 'bequests' are subject to attrition only over a period of time. The simple fact of being able to make the information they contain available to a broader range of users with whatever degree of effort and/or difficulty is reason enough for their inclusion in the college library.

An equally strong historical factor is the creation of a new library, whether from the amalgamation of smaller existing ones, or to serve a new establishment. This is perhaps difficult to believe in the present climate, but such things did happen in the not too distant past! This may give the librarian the opportunity of starting afresh, and integration of the whole stock has some real meaning. It is unlikely that this would entail total identity of treatment of all materials, for the reasons outlined in the initial definition of the term 'audio-visual', but access to the information via cataloguing and indexing tools can be put on an equal footing, and the layout of the building can be planned so that the various special storage needs and viewing or playback facilities can be coordinated. The relationship between technical staff (responsible for the showing of material and in many cases for the manufacture of some of the software), the library and its staff, and their relative siting can be properly planned. Ideally, they should work in close proximity, and in the best of worlds they should share, at local level and at the rarefied heights of senior college management, a common management structure.

The standing of audio-visual materials will be further affected by the backing that has been given to this aspect of librarianship in the particular institution over the years. In many cases, this will be the most crucial factor, in that the importance attached by senior librarians to the audio-visual will be directly reflected in its availability and the quality of its provision. This is not simply confined to the proportion of the book fund allocated to the audio-visual but affects also the level at which library staff with specific responsibility for the material are appointed. With regard to the division of the book fund, some institutions skim off a certain amount at source and direct this to the audio-visual collection, while others divide between faculties or subject areas and leave any division by medium to subject specialist librarians. This particular dichotomy is reflected in the staff within libraries who are actually responsible for audio-visual material. Some institutions have specialist audio-visual librarians, in others the audio-visual is subsumed by subject specialists whose responsibility is to provide all stock in a certain subject area.

Advantages and disadvantages are to be found in both styles of funding and staffing. The advantage for the thesis that all materials within the library are cogs in the same learning machine lies obviously with funding and staffing not being differentiated, and in the ideal world (or the progressive institution!), this system must be the correct one. However, in the model described previously, inheritance of collections from academic departments, or in multi-site operation, the choice is less clear. Similarly, it is less clear in the initial stages of building up resources in audio-visual materials against a background of librarianly resistance to 'gadgets'; here the only effective tool to promote the growth of the materials in the library is to allocate specific staff and funding. Once again it is a question of balancing various pressures, and generalized rules are irrelevant to the particular needs of the plethora of different institutions described collectively as colleges.

Any descriptive account of the actual materials available to the library which fall into the definition outlined earlier must necessarily be sketchy and must omit some categories of material, such is the scope now available and in use in college libraries. These faults will certainly be apparent in the outline account that follows.

One of the first audio-visual materials common in libraries was the photographic print, collections of which, for various purposes, figure in many college libraries. This medium demonstrates two of the problems facing the librarian. One is common to all librarians; the conflict between the intrinsic value of the article itself and the possible value of the information it contains. The second is more pertinent to audio-visual librarians. In common with many of the media described later, its ideal storage and preservation environment is not very hospitable to human beings and to browsing. Many of these (ie photographic prints!) survive best at low temperature, constant humidity, and no light. In order to make use of them, some compromise must be reached.

Most colleges with courses in art will have within their libraries an illustrations collection. The need for this is expressed by all art students in the library; a voracious appetite for images which relate to their work. Most libraries answer this with a rather primitive weapon. Pictures cut from magazines, newspapers, redundant books, or whatever source they can command are mounted on cardboard and filed in some order in a filing cabinet. This order may or may not resemble something one might learn at library school! If it does indeed correspond to anything recognizable, it will probably be a subject headings list. Development in the storage and retrieval of visual information in other fields have great implications for the trusty illustrations file but for largely financial reasons have made little or no impact as yet.

Similarly, other forms of printed (book and non-book) material are collected where they relate to the specific needs of particular areas of study; for example a variety of teaching aids for use by student teachers on teaching practice in schools may be available.

Slides are also important in colleges with art courses, as they are in those teaching medical sciences, geography and many other subject areas. Some slide collections in college libraries are very large, running to several hundred thousand slides. This obviously militates against most forms of integration within the library. There is no such constraint on more modest holdings when in the form of sets they may be interfiled with books on the shelves.

Maps too require specific treatment, particularly in terms of storage, and are found in substantial numbers in any college teaching geography or allied subjects. In many cases, however, they do not figure largely in the library, as the academic departments still retain many collections.

At one time the tape slide presentation was seen as the 'up and coming' new technique for self teaching; this has been overtaken by the videocassette, but there are still many useful sets available in a broad range of subjects, and they still have considerable advantages as far as cost and ease of production are concerned.

Films are another long-serving tool in the educative process found in some college libraries, although the problems associated with viewing tend to mean that they are either the basis of a special collection to cater for the needs of an institution where film studies are central, or they are few in number and inappropriately held in the library.

The same cannot be said of videocassettes however, which are rapidly becoming central to the operations of the audio-visual librarian, supplanting many of the more traditional tools. Until recently the mainstay of these collections has been the off-air recordings of material transmitted in connection with those Open University courses which relate to courses taught by the college. Now, commercially produced programmes for educational purposes are becoming available in greater numbers and over a much wider range of disciplines. Videocassettes have many advantages for the librarian. They are easy to handle and store, being conveniently uniform in size; they are easy, even attractive, to use; although they eventually wear out they are not easily susceptible to casual damage. An added attraction is that off-air recorded material can be erased and the tape reused. This however leads directly to the major drawback, one common to all software which may be in the library and which is photographed and/or recorded within the institution.

Space does not allow elaborate discussion here of the issue of copyright, but because of the inadequacy and ill-defined complexity of the present (1982) law, it is an issue which can cause many headaches for librarians who are concerned with audio-visual material. It need not concern the librarian who simply purchases commercially available video and/or audiocassettes or slides, though even at this level he may encounter some difficulty, as a retailer may freely supply a videocassette to a library which has as its first frame 'for home use only'. A headache this may be – but what a simple one compared with the housing in the library of material, for classroom use, recorded off-air by a technician in response to requests from academic colleagues, and whose legality a child might question! Whilst some teaching staff may be prepared to ignore a legal quagmire in the short term, a librarian is ill-advised to be so cavalier. Yet public catalogues of library holdings containing examples of such material exist in some colleges, though most treat the problem in different ways. This problem is not associated only with the videocassette, nor, to be fair, only with audio-visual material within the library.

Audio material alone takes many forms, with large collections of both music and the spoken word in many college libraries, particularly those teaching courses related to the performing arts. Again, in such institutions, their sheer size, notwithstanding storage and administrative considerations, tend to designate them as separate collections within libraries. In the better endowed colleges records may be kept as master copies, with taped copies being used to perform the everyday tasks, as these are far less susceptible to casual damage.

The above represents the broad range of different media currently to be found alongside the books and periodicals in many college libraries, but it is worth examining two specific examples of developing areas which illustrate what this era of educational technology may have to offer. Any librarian who is involved with the storage and dissemination of visual information, be it currently on slides, illustrations or photographs is liable to be affected in the future by one or both of these, unless they are superseded in their turn.

The first is the microfiche containing high quality colour and/or black and white illustrations. This is already in use and expanding fast. It allows one to store about eighty pictures in good quality colour on a single standard sized microfiche. The implication for the arrangement of images is in itself important, as one may be able to give a reader one fiche containing good reproductions of all the major works of a painter, or an architect, or the visual arts of a particular decade. They can be projected to groups in class or used by individuals. They may have accompanying 'hard copy' notes. The storage, handling, and retrieval are minimal compared with conventional systems.

The second example is the development of the videodisc linked to the computer. The science fiction element here is more striking and as yet examples are not in use, but the system will, theoretically, be able to store many thousands of images on each disc, each accessible according to any particular sort of enquiry one may wish to program the computer to accept, and no doubt within microseconds!

There is more material that can be classed as 'audio-visual' (that is, composed of sounds or pictures) in college libraries than in most other sorts of library, but the clarity and unity of purpose that can be seen to underlie the institution (and hence the library, its servant) make it easier to see that this material is an integral part of the 'teaching-learning machine'. It is a very important part of these libraries and increasing in importance as, at a time of financial stringency when cost-effectiveness is the criterion of survival, its efficacy in reaching large numbers of users and efficiency in transmitting information cannot be ignored.

The superficial day-to-day problems are in many cases very different from those presented by other library stock, but the real problem, of how to achieve the best service, is the same; it may be that to classify ten thousand records by Dewey so as to present a conformity with the book stock would be a nonsense, but the considerations of classification are equally relevant in constructing a scheme or adapting an existing one to match the needs of the stock, as in the consideration of how and what to apply in terms of classification to the books.

It may be that, because of the various specialisms developing within libraries, librarians are not trained readily to accept and adopt every one of these, but staff with a thorough knowledge and understanding of the broader considerations of the profession are more useful than a mixed collection of specialists with no common ground; ill-integrated librarians to perpetuate ill-integrated libraries.

The audio-visual demands inclusion and integration in our libraries, by virtue of its range, variety, and intrinsic worth, and by virtue of its appeal to student and educationist alike. The audio-visual demands sympathetic librarianship from informed and receptive librarians.

21

The Roles of New Technology

Douglas Anderson

During recent years there has been a rapid growth of college library automation, based largely on mainframe and mini-computers, either featuring independent, in-house applications or utilizing the facilities offered by library cooperatives. Unfortunately, as college librarians are only too well aware, increasing financial pressure has seen dramatic reductions in the funding of many college libraries, enforcing radical rethinking of their services, particularly in relation to automation and its implications. However, coincidentally and perhaps ironically, there has been considerable emphasis, most significantly by central government, on 'information technology' and its potential, primarily through the microcomputer in its many different guises.

This chapter will overview the possible applications of 'new technology' in the college library whilst bearing in mind that new developments in this area are occurring continually, making any attempt at comprehensive coverage inadvisable!

What then does the concept 'information' or 'new' technology represent? The Department of Industry has defined it as: 'the acquisition, processing, storage and dissemination of local, pictorial, textual, and numerical information by a microelectronics-based combination of computing and telecommunication'.[1]

Considering we've had the telephone since 1876 and the digital computer since the 1940s, there must be some reason why we now have the ubiquitous new technology! The major reasons are first, the development of microelectronics and the convergence of technologies in computing and communication to provide public networks capable of providing data transmission links between computer-based equipment, eg mainframe, mini-, and microcomputers, and second, various applications such as videotex, word processing, facsimile transmission, telesoftware, electronic journals, and data base access, which are represented in the above definition and fall within the scope of the college library's operations. The college library is a committed agent in the application of new technology, both in housekeeping and information retrieval, acting as a central referral point for staff and student access to networked data.

THE MICROCOMPUTER

Any overview of the applications of new technology and its core concept the microcomputer (micro) should consider the place of the micro as a link in the wider communication chain with the ability to interface with other computer-based equipment and to provide computing power of a much higher order than the 'stand alone' machine. Until recently, an inherent problem of micro use has been the lack of adequate data storage facilities; most floppy disc systems cannot handle enough records to make certain library operations worthwhile. This is one of a number of factors to be considered when differentiating between mainframe, mini-, and microcomputers. Such differentiation is rapidly becoming obsolete because of developments such as videodisc application for mass storage in the micro.[2] One such development, the Winchester hard disc, already offers more than 30 times the capacity of an equivalent sized floppy disc, with an access speed ten times that of the floppy system *and* the provision of multiple terminal access.

To further illustrate the point, one micro on the market in 1982, the DEC LSI 11/23, has one million characters of primary memory, uses a 96 million character removable disc drive, and can support up to 16 terminals at any one time![3] The rate of change in this field is so rapid that it is said, 'If you can make it, it's obsolete!'

While they do not have the same high information processing

speed of mainframe computers, micros are beginning to offer impressive, economic computer power to the college library and also, importantly, the facility of direct interaction for interrogating data files without the need to consult data processing professionals or other intermediaries, should appropriate software be available. Economy and autonomy through new technology!

Clearly, because of the continual increase in mass storage and the ability to interface micros with other computer-based systems, any overview should not be restricted to in-house applications of an independent stand alone micro system, but rather should consider housekeeping and information retrieval functions in the college library, utilizing the micro additionally in a hybrid system in the role of an intelligent terminal, creating and storing data as required online from mainframes or minicomputers such as, for example, those of DIALOG, BLAISE-LINE or PRESTEL. Within the role of intelligent terminal is the micro's application as word processor,[4] either via applications software or as a dedicated machine for in-house and externally linked library operations necessitating, for example, the input, editing, formatting, storing, sorting, display, and transmission of data.

COMMUNICATIONS

Within the meaning of new technology, the major development parallel to computer microelectronics is the development of communications technology, particularly public data communication networks for sending and receiving data at high speed and comparatively low cost. Telecommunications software has been developed to the point whereby most computers can now communicate with each other.

Such development is necessary for the library to connect with external service computers located throughout the world and offering data files of value to the college library and its users, *eg* DIALOG and SDC in California, Questel in Paris, ECHO in Luxembourg, BLAISE-LINE in Harlow, Blackwell's in Oxford, and Woolstons and Blunt's in Nottingham.

To access external files, the college library may utilize the British

Telecom public data Packet Switched Network (PSS), which is linked to packet switched networks in many other countries and allows the user to connect with the network by means of a terminal coupled with a modem and a 'local' telephone number, *eg* Edinburgh, Manchester, Birmingham. These local nodes allow libraries to access remote files via PSS and other similar and interlinked networks, such as Euronet, and Tymnet and Telenet in the United States, at an economic rate and at a high speed of data transfer. Linking with the Euronet network, for example, gives the college library access to a number of host computers throughout the European Community, supporting bibliographic and factual data bases, with access via a local node to keep telecommunications costs down. Economies can be further effected in the library by interfacing the micro to the network as an intelligent terminal for storage and subsequent local manipulation and output of search results. Future communication channels to remote files will include cable multi-channel television facilities.

APPLICATIONS

The new technology amalgam of computing and telecommunications offers many areas of application in the college library with novel ideas continuously reflected in the literature. However, it would be useful to consider applications within the major functions of housekeeping and information retrieval which form the backbone of the college library service. Applications such as data base access, distance learning facilities, and online catalogues would provide students with first hand experience of using new technology within the college library, and familiarizing them with its potential in libraries, demonstrating possibilities and limitations of computer systems, and complementing the college's computer appreciation courses amongst others. The Library Association has recently recognized these opportunities and supports them in a recent policy statement:[5]

Information technology is a further area to which professional librarians must contribute. If students are to be taught something of the 'new technology', they must receive from professional librarians some insight into methods of structuring, organising and handling information.

Students must not only be given some understanding of microprocessor-controlled systems, they must also be given first-hand experience of using them. The library . . . is an excellent place for the student to meet and use the microcomputer at work, on a real job, rather than the necessarily artificial environment of the laboratory or classroom.

Housekeeping applications may be taken to include cataloguing, circulation control, acquisitions systems, serials control, inter-library loans, in-service training, user education, production of reports, bulletins, directories, and management information for decision making. Many of these applications could be integrated to form a total system either in-house or alternatively by subscribing to one of the library cooperatives which are making a major impact on cataloguing in the United Kingdom, and which generally offer, or plan to offer, such services as integrated acquisitions, circulation, and inter-library loan facilities, eg BLCMP (Library Services) Ltd, SWALCAP, SCOLCAP, LASER, and OCLC Europe.

Integrated computer packages can be purchased off the shelf for in-house applications from those developing the software, whether institution or computer manufacturer, eg for mainframe or mini-computer use – ASSASSIN, STATUS, and CAIRS, described in a special issue of *Program* on library software packages,[6] and the GEAC 8000 System used by the Polytechnic of the South Bank[7,8] amongst others. Alternatively, the college library can develop its own integrated system in-house, based on a mainframe or minicomputer, and designed to meet the specific needs of its own users. An example of this approach is that of Teesside Polytechnic Library, integrating acquisition, cataloguing, and lending functions on the library's PRIME 250 computer, and observing local rules and local formats as deliberate policy.[9]

Although a considerable amount of data base management software exists for micros,[10] generally speaking there would be storage problems for all but the smallest files in attempting to develop an integrated system on a stand-alone machine, albeit there will be major enhancements in the near future. The micro could of course be interfaced with a mainframe or mini, as previously mentioned, to act as an intelligent terminal in a hybrid system of online and batch processing.

Integration of library applications utilizing the new technology may be an ultimate aim of many college libraries but the majority have still to reach this goal, applying automation in a rather more piecemeal fashion to specific functions within housekeeping and information retrieval, tasks which will now be considered individually, bearing in mind the availability of computing and telecommunications support.

CATALOGUING

Historically and logically, the automated catalogue file is the central essential file of stock on which other library applications can be based through further exploitation. New technology has provided facilities for online, remote, shared cataloguing, accessing, and supplying records through various sources, eg the established library cooperatives and the British Library's BLAISE-LINE system. The concept of shared cataloguing assumes common bibliographic standards acceptable to all, so that libraries can utilize each other's records with confidence. The philosophy of shared cataloguing is the elimination of duplication of effort, transferring rather than re-creating catalogue data, whilst maintaining quality of data in the file both in centrally produced records and those input by member libraries. New technology is supplying the opportunity for immediacy of data transfer either to or from the cooperative's remote location, eg BLAISE-LINE in Harlow, SCOLCAP in Edinburgh, or LASER in London, with the means to edit records to meet individual requirements and create local structured catalogues in the desired output formats using computer-based equipment, including word processors.

New technology also offers the college library the facility to produce an independent, in-house catalogue, perhaps using the micro in the form of a word processor to reproduce and reformat entries on catalogue cards, and perhaps ignoring the move towards utilizing centrally produced, definitive records with their resulting potential for resource sharing through union catalogues and interlending.

Centrally produced records forming the British Library Bibliographic Services Division (BLBSD) UK MARC and the Library of Congress' LCMARC files are available online and offline through BLBSD's BLAISE-LINE system, where a selective record service allows the college library to transfer selected records to its own computer for subsequent manipulation in-house or to transfer appropriate records to the BLAISE LOCAS service, via the BLAISE EDITOR function, for record conversion to suit the college library's local requirements and for subsequent catalogue production by BLBSD on behalf of the college library. Examples of libraries utilizing BLBSD services outside the cooperatives include Garnet College Library, where the entire cataloguing operation is dedicated to online working through BLAISE-LINE,[11] and Robert Gordon's Institue of Technology Library, which subscribes to the BLBSD Selective Record Service offline for the local creation of COM catalogues and to support an integrated book ordering system in-house using the Institute's DEC-2050 mainframe computer. BLBSD also offers a micro-based catalogue and information retrieval software package, CORTEX, used by several BLAISE LOCAS libraries in their preparation and derivation of catalogue records.

Although there is a small but growing incursion of stand-alone library software packages, the major influence is that of the cooperatives, offering access to large data bases which record the holdings of member libraries through cumulations based on the centrally produced standard MARC II communications format records of UK MARC, LCMARC, and Extra MARC Material (EMMA) records supplied by the member libraries themselves. The college library can link its terminal (intelligent or non-intelligent) or computer to the cooperative's computer by means of a local node and the PSS network for online access.

It would be useful at this point to consider a brief outline of the major cooperatives in the UK,[12] each of which offers a shared computer resource and a shared data base, initially to support cataloguing, but with considerable potential for other applications, some of which are already being realized by the cooperatives and by the British Library.

BLCMP (Library Services Ltd) offers a data base representing items held by its 35 members, including 16 polytechnic libraries. Significantly, the cooperative's files contain over 650,000 Extra-MARC records, to which a further 140,000 EMMA records are added each year. In addition to online cataloguing, BLCMP offers an online acquisitions service and a circulation control system (CIRCO).

SCOLCAP will offer online cataloguing and acquisitions systems to its 21 members, including three college libraries, with a data base of over 700,000 records, to which approximately 180,000 records are added each year. SCOLCAP uses the British Library's BLAISE LOCAS service for the production of members' catalogues on COM.

SWALCAP's 17 members, including six polytechnic libraries have access to 250,000 EMMA records on the data base, with online cataloguing and circulation systems available. SWALCAP allows member libraries to create their own local versions of any master records, and to maintain separate files, recognizing the need for flexibility amongst its members whilst attempting to maintain cataloguing standards.

LASER offers online cataloguing and interlending services based on their data base of 1.23 million bibliographic records.

BLAISE LOCAS is the popular catalogue production service offered by BLBSD, utilizing current and retrospective UKMARC and LCMARC files, supplemented by locally created EMMA records as in the other cooperatives, and accessed either in batch or online through BLAISE-LINE. As mentioned earlier, the SCOLCAP members have their catalogues produced by BLAISE LOCAS, as do three individual polytechnic libraries and 13 Inner London Education Authority (ILEA) colleges of further and higher education, amongst many others. The ILEA colleges have formed a library consortium (ILEA LOCAS User Group) based on BLAISE LOCAS, producing a union catalogue as well as individual local library catalogues, mostly offline, but with some colleges using online working via BLAISE-LINE and BLAISE EDITOR. Each member has complete control over its own records.

OCLC Europe markets the services of its American parent company OCLC Inc with its data base of over 8 million records and its membership of over 3,000 libraries, mostly located in the United States. The data base is situated in Ohio, with UK access via a dedicated telecommunications network. In addition to shared cataloguing, the cooperative offers serials control, acquisition, and circulation control systems, along with its major feature, an online inter-library lending facility.[13]

Proposals have been published regarding the establishment of a UK Library Database System (UKLDS)[14] by 1984 to provide for online access to a single data base of both cataloguing and location records, created primarily by the British Library and the UK library automation cooperatives as an enhanced partner to BLAISE-LINE. Initially, the data base is expected to include current UK MARC formatted standard records from the following sources, with the possibility of including certain retrospective records, ie those created before UKLDS's operation:

1   UK library automation cooperatives; BLCMP (Library Services) Ltd, LASER, SCOLCAP, SWALCAP.
2   UK MARC and LC MARC.
3   BL Lending Division monograph stock catalogue.
4   BL Reference Division catalogues.

Other libraries will be encouraged to participate in the provision of records, eg BLAISE LOCAS libraries, contributing to an estimated total of over 4 million records online in one single, coherent file and supporting cataloguing, reference and interlending activities through terminal or computer-to-computer access.

CIRCULATION CONTROL

As indicated earlier, BLCMP (Library Services) Ltd, SWALCAP, and OCLC Europe offer circulation control facilities, as do many software houses and computer manufacturers, with the additional or integrated utilization of specialist data collection devices such as those of Telepen, Plessey, and ALS.[15] College libraries can, of course, develop their own in-house systems for use on mainframe, minicomputer, or micro, either online, offline, or as a hybrid. McKee[16] reports on the 'do-it-yourself' system used at Solihull College of Technology Library, based on the College's PDP 11/03 minicomputer. Whilst an autonomous, online system clearly offers the ideal in stock control, with immediacy of access for record interrogation and updating, offline and hybrid systems also have their place in college libraries, relative to the library's needs. Useful discussion of the offline versus online decision is offered by Young,[17] whilst the problems to be considered in establishing a circulation system, such as maintenance, training, and liability of system supplier, are outlined by Boss[18] and remind us that new technology is no panacea; libraries must be aware of possible drawbacks.

ACQUISITIONS SYSTEMS

New technology offers the possibility of online access to booksellers' remotely held files for ordering college library material. A number of library suppliers' computers can be contacted via the public telephone network, eg Blackwell's BOOKLINE system and their PERLINE online serials service, Askew's service in Preston, and Woolston and Blunt's LIBTEL online book enquiry and ordering system. Additionally, BLCMP (Library Services) Ltd and SCOLCAP offer acquisitions system facilities to member libraries. There could be future scope for library suppliers to provide relevant compatible software to college libraries, so enabling them to access their files online with resulting benefits for both parties. However, acquisition systems are generally the least standardized of all library operations and any software package must, as a result, be easily modifiable to individual library requirements.

Word processing facilities are most useful in this area, providing the multiple copies necessary either for a more traditional approach or as hard copy records relating to word processor/supplier online access. The word processor additionally allows interrogation of its own acquisitions files (created in-house and/or downloaded from the supplier) from many access points such as author, requester, date, and with inbuilt functions such an automatic order 'hastening', budgetary controls, foreign currency conversion to sterling equivalents, and integration with circulation control to order automatically additional copies of heavily used items.

In addition to acquisitions systems, the college library can apply word processing facilities to many other tasks, either via a dedicated machine or through applications software on the computer. Particularly appropriate library tasks are those that necessitate the mundane and repetitive manipulation of text, such as report writing, compilation of directories, students' reading lists and bulletins, preparing input for a data base, and reformatting references from an online search.

The proceedings of the American Library and Information Technology Association Institute in 1980[19] provide useful material relating to the area of automated acquisitions systems and includes a substantial bibliography.[20]

EDUCATION AND TRAINING

New technology has a significant role within education and training, particularly by providing facilities for interactive self-learning through software applications on the micro in many subject areas of the college curriculum. Such applications can cut across departmental boundaries, resulting in piecemeal acquisition of equipment and software by separate college departments and possibly creating problems of incompatibility if overall control is not undertaken by the college administration. A central college library register or catalogue of new technology hardware and software and its location within the college is essential. Additional to and complementing departmental facilities, the library can offer a central referral point for videotex, micros, and their associated software which could be considered part of the library's resources with a potential value to all college personnel. The requirements of computer-assisted instruction through distance and open learning endorse the need for central library facilities in new technology, for Open University and Open Tech students amongst the many others utilizing this growing area of non-traditional study technique.

The library can also supply staff trained in the conventions of operating systems such as non-bibliographic data bases and view-data for possible integration with the teaching needs of the college. Online interaction with non-bibliographic data bases for example is particularly important in the economics and business education field, where students often require data for project work, and where such data could be provided by the library staff accessing remote files. Lee and Miller[21] report on the practice of Lake Forest College Library in the United States where undergraduates are instructed in the use of computer searching as an introduction to 'methods of information retrieval which will be standard in tomorrow's world'.

New technology also has application to the education and training of staff within college libraries themselves. The recently introduced Licentiateship scheme of the Library Association places the onus for training new professional entrants squarely on the shoulders of the supervising librarian through a training programme which must be acceptable to the Library Association.

Viewdata and especially the micro are applications which can help in this training programme, particularly in the provision of simulations and emulations of external data files and their idiosyncracies, where 'real time' training costs could be very high. PRESTEL for example, hosts British Library frames which are helpful in understanding the BLAISE system,[22] the University of London's Central Information Services has produced, amongst others, *DIALOG with PET*, a series of programs for use on a PET micro and designed to teach various aspects of DIALOG searching, and *MICROBLAISE* which is designed to aid potential BLAISE users.[23] There are many micro based software packages available to the college library and of value within internal training programmes.

MANAGEMENT INFORMATION

In an integrated automated system it is possible to obtain statistical data for management control as a by-product of the operations undertaken by the computer. Quantitative data relating to counts, times, costs, ratios, and percentages are of great importance to the college library and the computer's inbuilt facility to 'numbercrunch' is of value in this area. Questions such as the number of items acquired, the time taken to acquire an item, the percentage of particular groups of readers using the library, the circulation per capita per department, budget allocations and predictions, ie statistics on narrowly or broadly defined areas, can be provided by the system and are invaluable to the librarian trying to monitor the college library service.

INFORMATION RETRIEVAL

New technology provides for exciting developments in the area of information retrieval, particularly in relation to data access through external files and national/international communication networks, facilitating linkage with an estimated figure of over 1,000 unique data bases from a UK-located terminal.[24] Although the main emphasis in this area is random access online, there is still a need for college libraries to produce printed subject indexes for multiple use or as a supplement to the online facility. The computer is particularly apt at generating subject indexes of some quality within the broad descriptor of 'string indexing', where an input master index entry is manipulated according to specifications to produce multiple entries, inter-filed and often with syntax. Examples of 'string indexing' include SLIC, KWIC, Double KWIC, NEPHIS, and PRECIS, each of which offers the college library particular potential in particular situations. No one technique necessarily helps with all the problems of information access, especially of access to composite subjects with their major problem of scatter in large files, because of interposed elements in index strings, a problem overcome by random access but generally present in printed indexes.[25] Many software packages are available commercially for use on the micro, enabling the college library to import relatively sophisticated techniques for index production.[26]

DATA BASE ACCESS

As already indicated, the college library has access to many external data bases located throughout the world. Additionally, the library can create its own in-house data base(s) with locally produced files, by utilizing one of the many data base management packages which offer the same basic retrieval facilities as the external online data base services. Alternatively, the library can develop its own software designed for its own needs and with adequate in-house storage capacity, a major consideration whether using commercially produced or in-house software. Robert Gordon's Institute of Technology Library is an example of a college library in the latter category, with the college mainframe computer maintaining online data bases of selected library holdings in subject areas such as oil technology, communications, and architecture, with multi-site access and printed index support in the form of dual dictionaries. Burton's directory[10] lists a number of college libraries with in-house micro based data bases.

The computer offers dramatic search benefits whether accessing in-house or external files, removing the traditional restrictions of a linear search as would be necessitated in searching printed abstract or indexing services. Benefits include post-coordinate and pre-coordinate searching, truncation, Boolean logic, free-text searching, multi-dimensional searching, and selective dissemination of information. Additionally, the trends towards full text storage in data bases makes possible the provision of text as well as citations as a result of searching, changing the college librarian's role in the retrieval process.

The application of new technology to data base access is providing for three types of retrieval – reference/citation retrieval, data retrieval, and document retrieval.

REFERENCE/CITATION RETRIEVAL

The computer/telecommunications facilities of new technology provide immediate and remote access to current and retrospective bibliographic data bases concerned with most areas of recorded knowledge. Major vendors of these files include DIALOG Information Services, System Development Corporation, the British Library, Infoline, and Bibliographic Retrieval Services (BRS), offering access to files such as *Science Citation Index, UK MARC,*

Oceanic Abstracts, Sociological Abstracts, etc, and realistically equalizing access to recorded knowledge for all libraries, albeit incurring variant telecommunications costs. The search facilities provided by the data base vendors vary between base and operator, each with its idiosyncracies. For example, *Chemical Abstracts* has special search features compared with *Sociological Abstracts*; DIALOG's command language differs from that of the British Library's BLAISE service. The problem of online telecommunications costs and the lack of a common command language between vendors can be overcome to a certain extent by using a micro in the college library to act as an intelligent terminal linked to these external services, storing predetermined search strategies and logging-in protocols for later high speed transmission, and also storing any data retrieved from external sources for subsequent manipulation offline with consideration for user requirements.[27] Additionally, there would be considerable advantage in storing a single search language in the micro for automatic translation into the command set appropriate to the service accessed.[28]

The data received in response to interrogation of these bibliographic files can be printed online at the college library terminal, printed offline on a high speed printer at source and then mailed to the college, or transferred into computer store as indicated above, for further processing as required. Such further processing may include contacting the British Library Lending Division (BLLD) for inter-library loan facilities based on the citations retrieved. BLLD offers an automatic document request service from a library's computer terminal, from within a network through PSS, online as part of the BLAISE service to libraries, or online through DIALOG's DIALORDER facility. Leicester Polytechnic Library has developed a micro/mainframe interface for this purpose, with their PET micro transmitting batches of requests direct to BLLD's computer after initial editing and checking on the micro.[29]

DATA RETRIEVAL

Non-bibliographic data bases are available from many sources, including videotex services and some of the vendors of bibliographic files. The data offered relate to areas such as business information (prices, statistics etc), general information (encyclopaedias, directories), legal information, and information for manufacturers (standards, regulations), all with emphasis on currency.

Videotex provides the college library with access to broadcast teletext systems, eg BBC's CEEFAX, IBA's ORACLE, and also online viewdata systems, eg British Telecom's PRESTEL system, France's TELETEL system, and Kingston-upon-Thames Library Services' KINGTEL system. Viewdata systems are major information sources, with an estimated 50 million frames available within 13 operational European systems,[30] not including the many private viewdata systems which could be of additional value to the college library. PRESTEL is networked in the UK such that a college library might be (hopefully) in close proximity to a local node for economic access. This network has been extended with connection to third party computers through Gateway techniques,[31] allowing the library to link with other viewdata systems and with data base vendors such as those within the Euronet network, whilst still utilizing the basic viewdata hardware used to access PRESTEL. PRESTEL offers college libraries the facility to become information providers either directly or, perhaps more realistically in economic terms, under the umbrella of a body such as LASER or the Council for Educational Technology (CET), publishing information in the form of frames within the system for dissemination to all PRESTEL users, or alternatively, within a closed user group for selective use. Some private viewdata systems involve college libraries and educational data, with others planned for the future. Kingston Polytechnic Library, for example, contributes to the KINGTEL system while Leicester Polytechnic Library is planning an internal viewdata system.[29] The Scottish Council for Educational Technology (SCET) private viewdata system hosts a data base called MICROTEL which contains information on microelectronics in Scottish education, information such as computer programs available in specific subject areas, types of microelectronic equipment in use in the non-university sector, and details of courses in microelectronics and computing.

The micro has almost all the hardware necessary to act as a viewdata terminal, requiring only a modem or acoustic coupler plus the relevant software to interface with PRESTEL for example. The micro can act as an intelligent terminal with storage and editing facilities for capture, transfer, and manipulation of data, and with the potential to input data to the system.

Telesoftware is a significant educational development involving viewdata and the micro, whereby computer programs and their accompanying descriptions can be transferred (downloaded) from a central computer to a user's micro through the viewdata facility to provide the lecturer or student in his own college environment with the means to browse through a library of software, select a program, and have it transmitted and stored on disc within a few minutes for immediate use on a micro. Telesoftware provides college staff and students with a convenient and rapid method of determining, on a regular basis if necessary, what software is available on a given topic and of obtaining the chosen program(s) without delay. The micro(s) in the college library would again offer a central referral point for this service, extending the library's resources in a rapidly developing area. This area of software provision suffers from the lack of a materiography and standardization of 'bibliographic' description, drawbacks which could be overcome by the creation of a national software library capable of handling numerous simultaneous requests by remote telesoftware users and offering standardized online records for information retrieval purposes. Both CET[32] and SCET are undertaking pioneer work in the area of telesoftware provision for educational establishments. SCET's private viewdata system is used to download programs held centrally by the Scottish Microelectronics Development Programme to a variety of micros in Scottish schools and colleges. Software has been developed by CET for a number of micros, making PRESTEL downloading of telesoftware a practical possibility for many college libraries.

Online data bases and viewdata facilities are also providing for the electronic journal, whereby the college library can access journal articles as full text files, complementing the extensive secondary literature search facilities provided by online vendors and with the future potential of linking traditional secondary system search results with the full text of selected articles held in a primary data base. Already, BRS are offering selected Elsevier biomedical journals online, with a total of 50,000 primary journal pages per annum available as full text electronic journals.[33]

An example of a private network offering the electronic journal is the British Library Research and Development Department (BLRDD) funded BLEND System[34] (Birmingham and Loughborough Electronic Network Development), with educational institutions operating an electronic communications network whereby research papers can be entered, referred in closed cycle, and, following amendment, made available to all subscribers. The scope of the BLEND project includes extension of the electronic journal concept to that of computer conferencing as a medium of communication between research workers. The college library's role in this area could once again be that of central referral point for interactive information transfer and receipt in relation to the electronic journal. Computer conferencing with its necessary technology allows meetings to go to research workers, lecturers etc rather than having researchers, lecturers etc travel to meetings. There are obvious savings in travel and staff time, but such is the expenditure required in communications hardware at present that no one college could justify this facility, other than on a rented, cooperative basis such as is offered by British Telecom.

New technology also offers the college library sophisticated copying, printing, duplication, and other information transfer facilities through developments such as micrographics, electronic mail, optical character recognition, electronic printing, and facsimile transmission.[35] Facsimile transmission facilities provide for the retrieval of documents from remote sources via the telecommunications networks and specialized hardware, offering full-text articles to users, albeit at considerable cost to the library. An example of this facility is DIALOG's ABI/Inform database where facsimile transmission to a UK library from DIALOG in the US would cost about $100 for a six page article. Although costly, new technology in this example provides an immediate data transfer service of which, like other applications, the college library should be aware and which it may consider necessary either directly or through an intermediary with the appropriate facilities.

CONCLUSION

New technology offers considerable application in the college library, with major implications for cost and levels of service. Librarians must, of course, continue to consider user needs within any service; bibliographic standards and principles must be maintained in record descriptions such as catalogue entries and bibliographies; improvements in library resources generally should be sought whether with the aid of new technology or not. New technology is not a panacea. There is still a need for the library with a bibliographic catalogue to observe the main entry for collocative purposes if any hard copy output is produced – only multiple terminal provision for all and simultaneous access to online random access catalogues will realistically dispense with this need. Although computer searching permits retrieval on terms occurring in titles, abstracts etc, librarians should not lose sight of the continuing need for classification in the college library to provide collocated and structured material on shelves and in catalogues for open access and browsing requirements, arguably still the principal mode of library use by the majority of readers. Classification and subject indexes are complementary with or without new technology. Online bibliographic data bases generally offer high recall results with the reciprocal lack of precision; they tend towards non-standardization of authors' names with resulting search problems, and their general lack of retrospective coverage could be a disadvantage to the college library. PRESTEL's tree indexing structure is cumbersome and has been criticized with a view to its improvement for information retrieval purposes.[36] New technology applications are analogous to the emperor's new clothes in some situations, but their potential contribution to the extension of resources and library operations in college libraries generally cannot be underestimated. The library's ability to utilize external data files is of major importance, equalizing access to recorded knowledge for the user irrespective of the location or scale of resources of the individual library. Additionally, by subscribing to relevant software, the library is able to import technical expertise to provide services both in housekeeping and information retrieval previously unattainable, although perhaps highly desirable to the college library's function.

REFERENCES

1 Department of Industry *Information technology: the age of electronic information*. DOI, 1981. 3.

2 Horder, A *Videodiscs: their application to information storage and retrieval*. Second edition, NRDC, 1981.

3 *Small Computers in Libraries* 2 (6) June 1982. 4.

4 Whitehead, J B 'Developments in word processing systems and their applications to information needs'. *Aslib Proceedings* 32 (3) March 1980. 118–133.

5 Library Association *College libraries: guidelines for professional service and resource provision*. Third edition, Library Association, 1982. 28.

6 *Program* 16 (3) July 1982.

7 Botten, D A 'The GEAC 800 system at the Polytechnic of the South Bank'. *Program* 16 (2) April 1982. 67–77.

8 Hawes, D F W and Botten, D A *Library Automation at the Polytechnic of the South Bank*. Library Association, 1983.

9 'Teal being hatched on Teesside'. *VINE* 43 May 1982. 31–3.

10 Burton, P F *Microcomputer applications in libraries and information retrieval: a directory of users*. Leith Nautical College, 1981.

11 Baldwin, R 'The use of BLAISE EDITOR at Garnet College Library'. *Catalogue and Index* 60 Spring 1981. 2–4.

12 Bakewell, K G B 'The UK library networks and the Cooperative Automation Group'. *Aslib Proceedings* 34 (6/7), June/July 1982. 301–309.

13 British Library. *Ad hoc working party on union catalogues. Report.* British Library, 1982. 18.

14 'Towards a national database'. *Library Association Record* 84 (9) September 1982. 293–294.

15 Rowley, J E *Computers in libraries*. Bingley, 1980. 129–144.

16 McKee, R 'Computerised circulation control: a case study of Solihull College of Technology'. *VINE* 44 August 1982. 46–50.

17 Young, R C 'United Kingdom computer-based loans systems: a review'. *Program* 9 (3) July 1975. 102–114.

18 Boss, R W 'Negotiating an automated circulation system: the librarian's viewpoint' in *Clinic on Library Applications of Data Processing*. University of Illinois, 1977. University of Illinois, 1978. 54–65.

19 'Automated acquistion systems: papers presented at the LITA Institute'. *Journal of Library Automation* 13 (3) September 1980 and 13 (4) December 1980.

20 Heyman, B L 'Automated acquisitions: a bibliography'. *Journal of Library Automation* 13 (4) December 1980. 260–264.

21 Lee, J H and Miller, A H 'Introducing online database searching in

the small academic library'. *Journal of Academic Librarianship* 7 (1) March 1981. 14–22.

22 King, S V 'A BLAISE programmed instruction course on PRESTEL' in *Proceedings of the 4th International Online Information Meeting*, London, 9–11 December 1980. Learned Information, 1981. 435–445.

23 Anderson, D 'Online access in public libraries: education and training aspects' in *Proceedings of the Scottish Library Association Conference*, Peebles, 3–6 May 1982. SLA, 1982. 73–79.

24 *DIANE News* 27 July/August 1982. 7.

25 Sharp, J R *Some fundamentals of information retrieval.* (Chapter 4) Deutsch, 1965.

26 Armstrong, C *Software for printed indexes: a guide.* Aslib, 1981.

27 Petrie, J H and Cowie, J 'A microcomputer based terminal for assisting online information retrieval'. *Journal of Information Science* 4 (1) 1982. 61–64.

28 Williams, P W 'Microprocessor assisted terminals for online information systems' in *Proceedings of the 3rd International Online Information Meeting*, London, 4–6 December 1979. Learned Information, 1980. 139–146.

29 Adams, R 'Leicester Polytechnic Library's PET solution'. *VINE* (44) August 1982. 41–45.

30 *DIANE News* (27) July/August 1982. 7.

31 Horne, C 'Gateway – an enhancement of PRESTEL'. *Aslib Proceedings* 34 (5) May 1982. 266–270.

32 Brown, M 'A viewdata telesoftware system for education' in *Proceedings of the 4th International Online Information Meeting*, London, 9–11 December 1980. Learned Information, 1981. 115–118.

33 'Electronic publishing'. *Communication Technology Impact* 4 (3) June 1982. 1–2.

34 'Experimental electronic communication network'. *British Library Research Reviews* (1) May 1981. 1–2.

35 Morgan, T J *Word processing and office printing.* NRCD, Hertford, 1981.

36 Maynes, E S *PRESTEL in use.* National Consumer Council, 1982.

22

College Librarianship in Continental Europe

Gordon Harris

urope, though small in area, is culturally and ideologically
diverse. Its individual states and groupings continue, even
in the East, to display proud distinctiveness. These differences are to be found as much in higher and further education as
in politics and eating habits. Indeed, any attempt to harmonize
vocational training seems doomed to failure.[1] The continent could
be seen as a microcosm of the planet: capitalist, socialist, and
developing. I stop the allusion at this point for fear of making
further specious comparisons. It is nevertheless true that patterns
of provision for education and library services vary widely over
the continent.

To give an accurate survey of the continent is not easy. One
problem is the uneven nature of the information available. Western
Europe not only has its butter mountains and wine lakes, but it
also has its constantly erupting information volcanoes. Yet even
here there are barren areas. For example, why should there be
so little information available about France's rapidly modernizing
library and information services in the sector under consideration
when other countries are virtually over-described? Although the
lack of statistics in higher education mentioned by Altbach[2] does
not constitute quite such a basic problem in Europe as in the
Third World, figures are still often unavailable, more often non-
comparable, and have to be analysed carefully when compiled in

eastern Europe. Moreover, higher education outside the universities is summarized under varying terms through the continent, and the numbers of part-time students in post-secondary education is recorded inconsistently or even ignored completely. This obviously has a fogging effect on the subject focus of this book. Comparisons thus have to be made with caution.

The general picture of higher education on the continent is one of deceleration and pessimism. While there are exciting innovations in some areas, a crisis situation continues to dominate. High unemployment throughout most of western Europe, coupled with accelerating technological change, has brought about a need for retraining; consequently the proportion of students outside the 18 to 21 years age band is generally rising. But higher education no longer enjoys the unprecedented surge of investment of the 1960s. The European Centre for Higher Education[3] reckons that student population growth was high until 1970 but has since fallen substantially; high rates of growth tend to persist in areas such as eastern Europe, where the base was still small when growth in the western democracies had reached its peak. During the 1970s, retraction was partly due to the declining population of persons of school-leaving age. Table 1 illustrates this decline in western Europe, and its effect on expansion in higher education is shown in Table 2.

Now the same decline in population of student age is forecast again: there will be a decrease, according to Lervik,[5] after a peak in 1985.

The difficulties experienced by newly qualified young people when trying to enter the job market spring substantially from the world recession, the irrelevance to wealth production of much of what they have been studying, and the unwillingness of higher educational establishments, notably the universities, to make courses more vocational. Lervik[5] estimates that 50% of graduates in western Europe depend on employment in the public sector; on the whole the higher education system has not adapted to applications in small and medium-size enterprises in the private sector.

The demand for graduates started to fall in the early 1970s. This was noticed first in France because French graduates are overwhelmingly dependent on public sector employment. As investment in jobs in this sector fell, opportunities for graduates

Table 1: Average annual compound growth rate of population of the relevant age group for new entrants to higher education.

	1965–70	1965–75	1970–75
Belgium	1.4	1.5	1.7
Denmark	–2.1	–1.3	–0.5
Finland	1.9	0.3	–1.3
France	4.4	2.1	–0.2
Germany, West	2.9	1.6	0.4
Italy	3.0	0.7	–1.5
Netherlands	0.7	0.5	0.3
United Kingdom	–2.3	–0.9	0.6

Source: *Educational statistics in OECD countries.* OECD, 1981[4], Table 50.

Table 2: Average annual compound growth rate of new entrants to higher education.

	1965–70	1965–75	1970–75
Belgium	6.7	6.0	5.2
Denmark	–	–	7.0
Finland	0.9	2.7	4.5
France	4.0	2.3	0.6
Germany, West	–	–	4.8
Italy	12.9	8.7	4.6
Netherlands	–	–	8.7
United Kingdom	6.5	4.9	3.3

Source: *Educational statistics in OECD countries*, OECD, 1981,[4] Table 49.

fell, demand for university places fell. French universities stopped growing in 1971.[6] Similarly in the Netherlands, the government has stressed that not all graduates can be absorbed by public service.[7] The accompanying saturation of the professions in many countries led to low status and low pay for newly qualified persons. The paradox is that the need for qualifications to advance in a profession and in a career continued to increase.

Added to this is an imbalance within western Europe of higher educational resources, the south being generally less well provided for. The Council of Europe is attempting to transfer resources, for example between West Germany and Spain.[5]

The chasm between academically-based institutions of higher education and the world of commerce and industry has contributed to the lessening of confidence in the universities. But while the universities tended to stagnate through the 1970s the growth rate of other higher educational establishments has been greater.[8] It is not surprising therefore that, although (as Table 3 indicates) the growth rate in student numbers in France, Italy, Norway, Sweden and Switzerland declined after the 1960s boom, the overall number of people in higher education in all countries by 1975 was still an enormous increase over 1970.

As might be expected, the structure of post-secondary non-university education varies tremendously throughout the continent. In West Germany, young people can enter company apprenticeships and go on day-release to technical colleges; in Sweden children stay on at secondary school for vocational training; in Holland academic work and practical skills are intertwined from the early years in secondary school. In most countries there is an attempt to maintain a strict balance between college- and company-based training. Curricula in the colleges tend to be under much greater governmental control than in the United Kingdom. The consequent slackening of autonomy in continental college management permeates through to the institutions' libraries.

The great divide in status between universities and the rest of post-secondary education is evident. Indeed Brosan's indictment is directed to the continent as much as to the UK.[9]

> The universities carry out, nobly, the ideal: the non-university institutions do the pragmatic work, ignobly. This dichotomy and lack of diversity, which is at present in Europe as it is to some extent in the UK, gives rise to substantial strains, to lack of efficiency in resource allocation, and inhibits all sorts of technological and social progress.

There have nevertheless been innovations in this uneasy relationship. The binary system might reign in Britain (apart from such

Table 3: Student numbers in higher education per 1000 of
population.

	1965*	1970**	1975**
Austria	680	803	1286
Belgium	888	1296	1630
Bulgaria	1220	1170	1474
Czechoslovakia	1024	913	1048
Denmark	1010	1542	2179
Finland	841	1298	1639
France	1049	1581	1970
Germany, East	440	1776	2291
Germany, West	632	830	1684
Greece	678	975	1296
Hungary	503	778	1020
Italy	583	1283	1749
Netherlands	1209	1774	2108
Norway	525	1291	1663
Poland	800	1218	1692
Portugal	376	581	846
Rumania	686	746	775
Spain	417	666	1518
Sweden	888	1756	1985
Switzerland	554	821	1010
United Kingdom	579	1084	1308
USSR	1674	1878	1908
Yugoslavia	948	1282	1850

* Source: *Statistical Yearbook 1970*. UNESCO, 1971, Table 2.12.[10]
** Source: *Statistical Yearbook 1980*. UNESCO, 1970, Table
3.10.[11]

rationalizations as the 1983 merger of the New University of Ulster
with Ulster Polytechnic) but the concept of the 'Polyversity' has
risen in the West German *Gesamthochschule*, and also in Denmark:
in this scheme both sectors are more integrated, they receive more
or less equal esteem, and students pass freely from one sector to
the other. There is however less autonomy from government than

has usually been enjoyed by universities. The 'Combined Development' model exhibits greater ease of student transfer but status of and investment in each sector is still not equal; this is seen in the District Colleges of Norway and in France's *Instituts Universitaires de Technologie* (IUT). Universities on the continent are not on the whole as highly selective as those in the UK. Indeed, students in France are often rejected by highly selective technical institutes and go to university as a second choice.[9]

The proportion of young people entering non-university higher education varies substantially over the continent. The traditional importance attached to vocational education in the Low Countries and Scandinavia is illustrated by Table 4. The Table shows the increase in popularity of college (or equivalent) education in the 1970s, despite in some cases a static or even falling population of student age.

Table 4 also shows the massive Soviet input in non-university higher education, and the figure shown does not include part-time, distance, and correspondence students. The importance accorded to technical, non-university, training in eastern Europe is demonstrated by the university/non-university numbers in Table 5. The heavy emphasis put on the role of universities in higher education in the Mediterranean countries is also shown.

Figures produced by Jallade[16] indicate a much lower *and more slowly growing* increase in higher education investment in eastern Europe.

Although the total student numbers in the countries of eastern Europe compare reasonably with countries of similar size in western Europe, expenditure on higher education is lower, as Table 7 illustrates. It can only be concluded that expenditure on libraries in higher education establishments must also be low.

The socialist countries tend to draw fewer students than do the western countries from their total populations, as shown in Table 3. Countries outside COMECON on average attract 1,627 students from 100,000 of the total population; the number for the COMECON countries is 1,458. It is difficult to draw conclusions on the youth or maturity of students in west and east because of widely differing (and non-existent) figures for the countries concerned (see Table 7).

Table 4: Annual entry to non-university higher education as percentage of relevant age group, 1970 and 1976.

Country		New entrants (000's)	Age spread	Population of age spread (000's)	% of new entrants from age spread
Austria	1970	3.9	18–20	97.0	4.02
	1976	5.7		112.1	5.08
Belgium	1970	23.4	18–20	142.6	16.41
	1976	31.7		152.3	20.81
Denmark	1970	10.7	19–21	75.3	14.21
	1976	15.0		74.2	20.22
Finland	1970	6.8	19–21	86.3	7.88
	1976	8.1		80.3	10.09
France	1970	53.7	18–20	843.4	6.37
	1976	75.3		844.3	8.92
Germany, W	1970	44.0	19–21	821.7	5.36
	1976	49.1		873.7	5.62
Hungary*	1970	–	18–22	–	6.30
	1976	–		–	6.90
	1980	–		–	9.20
Italy	1970	6.0	19–21	808.7	0.74
	1976	9.1		800.6	1.14
Netherlands	1970	22.0	18–20	222.0	9.91
	1976	39.4		234.4	16.81
Spain	1970	29.9	17–19	526.2	5.68
	1976	15.2		598.8	2.54
UK	1970	74.4	18–19	765.0	9.73
	1976	76.7		549.0	13.97
USSR**	1975	481.1	–	–	–
Yugoslavia	1970	87.1	18–20	385.9	22.57
	1976	101.0		392.7	25.72

Source: OECD *Educational statistics in OECD countries*. OECD, 1981, Tables 52 and 55.[5]

* Figures pertain to *all* higher education in Hungary. Source: *Statistical pocketbook of Hungary*. Budapest, 1981.[12]

** Source: *Narodnoe khozyaistvo SSSR, v 1979 g*. Moscow. 498.[13]

Table 5: Total students in university and non-university establishments of higher education, 1974–77 (000's)

Country	Total full time students in university higher education				Total full time students in non-university higher education			
	1974	1975	1976	1977	1974	1975	1976	1977
Belgium	81.0	83.4	86.9	–	71.1	74.8	77.5	–
Czechoslovakia*	–	–	–	68.6	–	–	–	128.0
Denmark	60.8	63.5	66.6	–	32.6	32.7	31.7	–
Finland	68.1	73.7	76.8	76.7	18.3	20.0	21.8	22.4
France	807.9	840.8	871.3	870.7	167.2	174.3	175.4	177.5
Germany, W	641.2	675.3	698.9	724.2	145.5	160.7	173.0	181.4
Italy	911.0	960.2	995.9	–	19.2	22.1	24.8	–
Netherlands	112.5	120.2	129.2	137.4	97.4	111.2	118.4	123.8
Norway	39.2	40.8	40.6	39.3	29.2	29.4	30.3	30.5
Portugal	45.7	55.3	69.1	66.3	11.8	16.2	17.1	15.6
Spain	446.4	505.7	567.8	645.9	30.0	42.9	46.9	43.7
Sweden	108.6	110.0	113.0	–	25.9	25.5	26.1	–
Switzerland	50.7	52.6	54.2	55.9	–	–	18.2	18.8
UK	323.1	343.1	345.2	–	174.5	171.7	170.7	–
USSR**	561.3	565.9	–	–	1977.3	2062.2	–	–
Yugoslavia	67.7	–	–	–	160.6	–	–	–

Source: OECD *Educational statistics in OECD countries*. OECD, 1981. Tables 18 and 20.[4]
* Figures are for 1980. Source: *Statistická ročenka Československé Socialistické Republiky 1981*. Prague, 1981, 577, 578.[14]
** Source: *Narodnoe obrazovanie nauka i kul'tura v SSSR: statisticheskii sbornik 1977*. Moscow, 1977.[15]

Table 6: Annual percentage growth rate in expenditure on higher education (at 1970 US $ prices).

	1965–70	1970–75
Western Europe	11.1	9.8
Eastern Europe	7.8	4.4

Source: Jallade, J–P 'Expenditure on higher education in Europe'. *European Journal of Education*, 15 (1) 1980. 38.[16]

Despite the generally poorer showing of eastern Eruope as a whole, it should be noted that Poland and the Soviet Union have a well established and significant base as far as higher education is concerned.

Table 7: Expenditure on higher education (HE).

	Total FT enrolled in HE (000s)	Total spent on HE (US$m)[4]	% GNP on HE[4]	% education budget on HE[4]	Annual % increase in HE budget
	(1976)[1]	(1975)	(1975)	(1975)	(1965–77)
Austria	105.1	334	0.9	15.4	20.0
Belgium	164.4	599	1.0	15.4	19.3
Denmark	98.3	592	1.7	20.3	15.8
France	1046.7	1629	0.5	13.6	12.0
Germany, W	871.9	3204	0.8	14.8	10.1
Italy	1020.7	1131	0.7	13.0	20.0
Netherlands	247.6	1833	2.2	27.4	17.2
Norway	70.9	260	0.9	13.1	16.5
Spain	614.7	210	0.2	14.9	15.8
Sweden	139.1	569	0.8	12.3	13.9
Switzerland	72.4	506	0.9	17.7	9.7
UK	524.9	2322	1.2	19.0	–
Bulgaria	71.9[3]	97	0.7	11.9	10.0
Czechoslovakia	136.0[3]	672	1.0	21.0	7.8
Germany, E	104.0[3]	895	1.2	21.0	2.5
Hungary	64.7[3]	506	1.1	22.2	7.1
Poland	307.0[3]	384	0.9	25.4	9.7
Rumania	149.0[3]	317	–	13.4	4.4
USSR	2861.0[2]	5296[5]	1.0[5]	13.4[5]	11.8[5]
Yugoslavia	257.3	259	0.8	15.4	22.5

1 Source: OECD *Educational statistics in OECD countries.* OECD, 1981. Table 16.[4]
2 Source: *Narodnoe obrazovanie, nauka i kul'tura v SSSR: statisticheskii sbornik 1977.* Moscow, 1977. 214.[15]
3 Source: *Statisticheskii ezhegodnik stran-chlenov Soveta ekonomicheskoi Vzaimo-pomschchi 1979.* Moscow, 1979. 467.[17] (Figures are for 1978).
4 Source: Jallade. [16]
5 Source: UNESCO *Statistical Yearbook 1978–79.* UNESCO, 1980. Tables 6.1 and 6.3[18]

Table 8: Percentage of 20 year-olds in higher education in 1975.

Denmark	11.4	Bulgaria	12.0
France	15.4	Hungary	9.6
Germany, W	9.4	Poland	12.0
Greece	14.0	Rumania	5.2
Norway	9.8	Yugoslavia	14.9
Portugal	6.7		
Spain	13.3		
Sweden	10.1		

Source: European Centre for Higher Education *Access to higher education in Europe.* UNESCO, 1981, 16–19.[3]

FRANCE

It is now explicit French policy to activate higher education to serve the economy. France must develop products that are marketable to survive the harsh conditions facing western Europe over the past decade. Tournier[19] sees this policy resulting in an end to the old order in the higher education structure, with the *grandes écoles* being elevated to university level and having their research programmes enriched as the need for the future managerial class to have experience of practical applied research methods comes to be realized.

Another result of the greater interest shown by central government in higher education (as an investment) is the retraining and the continuing education programme. A 1968 law established that permanent education must be one of the principal concerns of the universities, and the proportion of firms' salaries bills devoted to training and retraining must reach targets specified in the Industrial Acts of 1971. This ensures vigorous provision for apprentices who study for the *Certificat d'aptitude professionnelle* or the *Certificat d'études professionnelles*. Those willing to qualify at a further level in technical studies take courses lasting two or three years leading to the *Brevet d'études professionnelles*. Higher up the scale in vocational education are institutions which reach university level – the *Instituts universitaires de technologie* (IUTs); the above-mentioned *grandes écoles* which offer non-university education in applied disciplines with relatively prestigious three year courses; the *Instituts nationaux polytechniques* which were founded in 1970 in Grenoble, Nancy, and Toulouse; and the *Instituts d'administration d'enterprises* (business schools).

Government investment in manpower training through further and higher educational institutions is impressive. In 1977, 2.8 million workers were in training schemes. The cost was borne by the state to the tune of 3,500,000,000 FF and by the statutory (see above) contributions of employers (7,500,000,000 FF). Of these workers in training, 21% or 588,000 took courses at tertiary level – a figure almost competing with that of full-time students at that level: 865,000.[5]

Despite the growth in numbers and status of the non-university sector, the 77 universities have managed to retain their aura of prestige. Despite the eruptions and strikes of 1968, 1970, 1973, 1976 and 1979 when the universities were brought to a standstill, they attract the more highly academically qualified of the nation's youth. This élite is in a position to gain degrees that are more valuable in the job market than those available elsewhere.[6] At least until the sudden elevation of Mitterand to power, the system has remained traditional.

Academic libraries in France are active and enthusiastic, but not in the sense that an Anglo-Saxon librarian might readily understand. Although higher educational establishments normally have libraries, some well established, they have not necessarily gone through the professionalization encountered in Britian. There is a much greater link in France with documentation, computerization, and research methods. An emphasis on library management or 'housekeeping' is not so easily perceived.

The emphasis tends to be very much on the future, and developments do not always seem to be in the hands of librarians. This is not to say that librarians are inactive: union catalogues of periodicals are produced (such as the one for 528 centres in the Grenoble region and the AGAPE system at Nice); inter-library loans are rising; the problem of copyright is being tackled; library use instruction and readers' services are being pursued as at the School of Business Studies in Paris (CESA). But a great emphasis is laid on the librarian as a documentalist and bibliographer rather than as library manager. This trend is evident in many of the activities of the Bibliothèques Universitaires et Bibliothèques Specialisées section of the Association des Bibliothécaires Français. This professional group is concerning itself in depth with the documentation and retrieval aspects of academic library work. Strong pressure has come from government to modernize information services and to invest in computerization of information retrieval. In 1978 the Agence Universitaire de Documentation et d'Information Scientifiques et Techniques (AUDIST) was established to create data banks and to train librarians and students in automated retrieval procedures. The ability of students to cope with the new technology in the 'information society' desired by the French government is seen as a priority and training schemes in online techniques

for students are being recommended by the Mission Interministéri-
elle d'Information Scientifique et Technique.

BELGIUM

A traditional élite role for universities survived the 1970s in Belgium
as in France. They conserve their very high academic standards by
continuing to attract those who perform well in academic subjects
at secondary school. While this status quo lives on there has been
a sharp deceleration in university enrolment. The boom of the
1960s meant that graduate output doubled from 1962/6 to 1966/70.
This 9% growth rate slumped after 1971 to a now stable 2%.[6]
Accompanying this is a steadily increasing proportion of students
who opt for vocational courses in the colleges (36% in 1971/2, 40%
in 1975/6) and who reject the high academic standards, significant
failure rate, and deteriorating job prospects.

Since 1970 the non-university sector has been divided basically
into colleges of technology, economics, agriculture, paramedical
science, social work, art, and teacher training. In 1977 an Act
established 23 'industrial colleges' to give training in construction,
mechanical engineering, electrical engineering, nuclear science,
textiles and agriculture.

The colleges diversified courses and offered routes into the
professions and working life. Ironically their very success in attracting the 'mass' market of students increased their respectability and
they started to attract more academically qualified staff. This
created problems of cooperation between the technically experienced but academically unqualified staff on the one hand and the
newly academically related staff on the other. As a result, training
became more academic and less practical.[20]

The Library of Liège Law School typifies the more traditional
library which has nevertheless adopted modern methods. Founded
in 1929, it holds 250,000 volumes, concentrating mainly on Belgian
law, and acquiring also legal material from France and the EEC.
It has produced by computer since 1971 a bibliography of legal
books and articles published in Belgium. The library is equipped

with several terminals which access a data base of references to parliamentary papers and collective labour agreements.

NETHERLANDS

Dutch librarians display dissatisfaction with the provision made for college libraries. These serve the institutions of *hoger beroepsonderwijs* which provide practical courses on a further education basis, and the *hogescholen* which teach at university level. Deficiencies are pointed out in staff training, book selection, user education, and funding. In 1979 the Centraal Bureau voor Statistiek reported that two-thirds of staff in academic and special libraries were unqualified. In the same year it was reported that Dutch library school libraries were critically under-resourced: while American and Swedish libraries had book stocks of 100 volumes per student, Dutch libraries had 18; American libraries provided five seats, Holland one seat, for every ten students. Government funding was obviously not high enough for the libraries to reach proper standards. Another survey in 1979 showed that less than 50% of recently graduated students could do an effective literature search in their own subject; the government strongly recommended in 1980 that library instruction be given to students entering the new information age. The profession has itself recognized this need and recommends an academic role for the college librarian in training students in the use of reference works, periodicals, and audio-visual material.[21] The State Library Advisory Council has itself supported this goal, adding that college libraries should take on the role of information centre, should acquire more non-monograph items such as reports, conference proceedings, and audio-visual material, and make this stock more accessible. Whether these calls for improvement will be accompanied by improved funding remains to be seen.

FEDERAL REPUBLIC OF GERMANY

Higher education in West Germany is, comparatively speaking, marked by growth and flexibility. In 1975 the country was educating 665,000 students (20% of the age cohort) and by 1985 hoped to have one million students (22–24% of the cohort). The number of students was only slightly short of one million in 1979. These are dispersed in a system very roughly comparable to the British binary. There are 66 *Universitäten* and *Technischen Universitäten*, while the *Fachhochschulen*, which were previously schools of engineering, approximate loosely to British polytechnics and attract about 20% of the student population. These are accompanied in this 'public sector' by 18 colleges of education and 26 colleges of art and music. The significant additions to this set-up are the eight *Gesamthochschulen* which are 'comprehensive' in the UK sense of the term and attempt to combine the best of both sectors by conferring degrees and other awards in a large array of subjects. The need for awareness of other vocations amongst a workforce which may now work in several professions per lifetime forms the rationale for this multi-faceted structure. In all these institutions the Federal government is building a community service function, ie research capacity which can provide consultancy and thus earn income.

In library provision the universities tend to retain their privileged status. The special collection of 10,000 school textbooks for example at the Education Department library of the University of Nuremberg, Erlangen, would seem an almost irrelevant luxury to the hard-pressed libraries of the colleges of education. Although advances have been made (eg the development of the 'integrated library' concept whereby several subject libraries combine under one central administration) there is still a great need for investment and professionalization. Even the integrated system, though rational in the eyes of a college administration, can pose problems of alienation: information on services and stock in one part may be unknown in another; centralized data processing can make the local staff feel uninvolved with the flow of material.[22, 23]

Professional groupings exist and play an active part in gathering data to present their case to their masters who decide on resource allocation.[24] Not only is provision inadequate, say the college librarians, but the staff structure and their job descriptions are vague and inefficient.

Such is the financial stringency in all academic library develop-

ment that the concept of the self-renewing library, largely rejected
by librarians in Britain, was suggested in the late 70s. Libraries
were told that they must be prepared to withdraw stock for storage
at local, regional, or national level. Many librarians said that more
funds would only be forthcoming if a massive public relations
exercise were staged to enhance the poor image of the librarian.
Indeed, in many of the lower level technical schools, what libraries
exist simply coast along under the eye of a lecturer, as no qualified
librarian's post is ever created.[25] A breakthrough was made in 1979
when new university laws affected the constitutional position of
the *Fachhochschul*-libraries. Under this provision they have the
right to plan their budget expenditure and staff development.
Activities such as book selection, however, are still very much in
the hands of teaching staff.

SWITZERLAND AND AUSTRIA

Apart from its universities Switzerland has various other institutions at the higher level: two Federal Institutes of Technology at
Zurich and Lausanne, 23 higher technical schools (the *ETS*), 21
colleges for teacher education, and 105 para-medical schools.[26]
Library provision for staff alone at the Lausanne Federal Institute
of Technology is impressive: 2,000 monographs, 1,000 periodicals,
a collection of articles on higher education and psychology, films,
videotapes, subject retrieval by optical coincidence cards. Students
may use and borrow from this collection too.[50] An online classified
catalogue may be found in the National Technical University
Library in Zurich.[28] This system, the Electronic Documentation
and Information System (EDIS–1) has been in operation since 1976
when the library's catalogue was converted into machine-readable
form.

The relatively modern and well-financed scene in Switzerland,
where the consultancy role of higher education is valued, is
reflected to some extent in Austria where there is a substantial body
of legislation for the development of academic libraries. In practice
this determination to develop is seen in the Mining and Metallurgy
Institute (the *Montanistische Hochschule*) where two 10-year plans[29]

were put into operation between 1958 and 1978 to modernize the library: the closed store was expanded, staff increased, the conservation of rare material was put into action, and technology such as telex, photocopying, microforms, and audio-visual material were brought into a traditional library that had been established in 1840.

SOUTHERN EUROPE

As Humphreys[30] notes, the advances in library science seen in North America and northern Europe have passed southern Europe by. Apart from the influence of scattered British Council libraries, and until the Library Association's initiatives for bi-lateral cooperation in the early 1980s, academic librarians in particular have retained the roles of keeper and student of rare books and manuscripts. Humphreys indicates further the passivity of librarianship in this region; it has not only remained uninfluenced by the north, it has had virtually no influence on the outside world either.

This trend follows the general pattern of division between the poor south and affluent north. Portugal, for example, is classified by the World Bank as a developing country. Its higher education system, traditionally – and still today – dominated by the old universities in the cities, became 'binary' in 1973 when new universities were established to provide short vocational courses for the rural population, to improve teacher education and to forge links with industry. Yugoslavia, with centrifugal tendencies in government to contend with as well, relies substantially on external agencies for development in academic library practice.[31]

Most observers see widespread deficiencies in Italian academic libraries. The designation of *università* to virtually any higher education institution poses problems of definition. Apart from the 29 state universities there are six *istituti universitari* (which nevertheless have only one faculty) and nine *istituti liberi* (also sometimes referred to as *università*). In the 'public sector' are two *politecnici statali* which teach engineering and architecture, and four *magisteri* for teacher education. Within this structure Italy has a large number of students who have to cope with a library provision that is castigated by the Italian library profession itself. Many of their complaints were expressed at a seminar in Turin in March 1980. Librarians have had a particularly poor image.

Until 1961 the university libraries were staffed by administrative or teaching staff and any 'librarian' posts that were created specifically were for subordinate positions. Although the situation has improved, the parent institutions do not provide the resources for library services that match the contact teaching programme. Serrai[32] maintains that the libraries are not integrated into the institutions, and that even though book provision and library services are hopelessly inadequate for teaching requirements, the teaching staff do not themselves recognize the need for radical library reform. Beattie[33] concludes that much greater investment is required at both national and regional levels. Education libraries are ill-equipped to aid teacher training, although this training itself contains little educational theory or teaching practice. The libraries and resource centres also have limited opening hours, partly because of funding restrictions on salaries and because library staff have other jobs in the afternoons, so a full day's service cannot be provided.

SCANDINAVIA

The professionalism of Nordic library practice is a byword even among the most xenophobic of Anglo-Saxon librarians. This professionalism is most noticeable in the public library networks, and college libraries have not (except in Sweden) developed quite so well.

Denmark

Outside the five universities there are fourteen institutes of higher education, or *hojere Laereanstalter*, which provide vocational training in physiotherapy, engineering, librarianship, journalism, midwifery, and teacher education amongst others. A development on the university side is the *universitetscenter* – there are two at Roskilde and Aalborg – where social work courses are offered.

Extra post-school training is provided by the *teknikum*, and the folk high school (these schools have been operating since 1840).

While these institutions possess a sound library base, there is much to develop. Many colleges have traditionally relied substantially on the public libraries for book provision. Danish librarians are pressing for stronger collections and for a common policy of appointing qualified personnel in colleges and in senior secondary schools.

Norway

The same sort of relationship with public libraries has tended to persist in Norway as college libraries were not developed fast enough and students put a great strain on public library provision. This problem did not affect the higher level institutions so badly, such as those colleges awarding degrees, the State Veterinary College in Oslo, and the State College of Business Administration in Bergen.

Sweden

'The most radical in Western Europe' is Premfors'[34] description of Sweden's higher education system. Forged in 1968, that *annus mirabilis* of educational self-determination, the concept of comprehensive higher education became law in 1975. This reform was proposed by the Education Commission (known as U68) in a setting of public debate and wide consultation with the groups and unions involved. The overthrowing of university élite status was a remarkable demonstration of the power of national consensus and participation.[35] A National Board of Universities and Colleges (*UHA*) was established to plan higher education provision with reference to training and professional studies rather than to scholarly pursuits, with common admission rules for all institutions and added provision for people over 25.

It would be interesting to compare carefully the development of college libraries through the 1970s with those of other countries in the same period where universities retained their dominant role. It is nevertheless clear that Swedish college libraries are generally superior to those of most of Europe in professionalization, book provision, technical services, and user education. The development of services at the Royal Institute of Technology Library combines the automation-centred approach of France with the people-centred approach of the UK and US: information services to industry (similar to HERTIS in the UK); research into unsatisfied requests for books; compilation of a bibliographic data base in mechanical engineering (MechEn); an online information retrieval system called 3RIP. One of its most admirable features is an ongoing link with Portugal,[36] with a programme of introducing modern concepts of information science to Portuguese research and development.

Finland

As in Norway and Denmark, the position of the academic library in the national system is a subject for debate. The admission of the general public to academic libraries has proceeded without extra resources, library grants being assessed by the parent institutions solely on the number of students enrolled. With the problem also probably occurring in reverse as well, it is not surprising that there is constant pressure for academic and public librarians to cooperate, and formulate workable systems.

POLAND

Across the Baltic in Poland – indeed in most of eastern Europe – there is a heightened awareness of an information-geared society combined with library plant that is under-resourced by western standards.

The Polish student population outside the universities is substantial, and is rising slowly as a proportion of all students (69% in 1975/6 to 71% in 1979/80), with as many students in the higher technical schools or *wyższe szkoły techniczne* as in the universities.[37] User education for all these students amounts to rather more than the occasional library tour. Engineering students at the Politechnika Wroclawska have special training in scientific and technical information systems, while SDI profiles are maintained for the teaching staff. At Bydgoszcz the curriculum for all courses at the Academy of Agricultural Technology covers the organization of information in economics as well as in science and technology. Then there is further study incorporating the application of bibliographical and information work to the course and vocation being pursued. Even teaching staff do not escape the campaign to inculcate a knowledge of information provision! Here, as in many other socialist countries, the need for continuous education among professionals is recognized and dealt with at the initial training stage; the absence of such officially inspired training at further and higher levels in Britain[38] means that professionals are often cut off from sources of new information and throughout their lives are left with a level of knowledge acquired in their teens or twenties.

GERMAN DEMOCRATIC REPUBLIC

In comparing the higher education systems of the GDR and Yugoslavia, Geoffrey Giles concludes that while the disintegrating momentum of nationalism of Yugoslavia may be responsible for the considerable autonomy of institutions, the grip of the party and bureaucracy in the GDR has produced dependent and uniform institutions.[39] Ironically this grip may have favoured library development in East German colleges because standards of library provision have been imposed from without rather than within.

Dependence and deference – particularly with regard to aid, advice, and sustenance from the Soviet Union – are to be found in most areas of East German life, and libraries are no exception. The relationship is normally seen as cooperation, which is to be expected in a community of states.

Internally, control is exerted from the government ministry through various channels, eg from the Ministry of Education through the Central Library of the Academy of Pedagogical Sciences, or through the parent institutions themselves affecting finally the library of the teacher education college or the teachers'

centre media centre. Such control, even to the extent of making a
new cataloguing code (named *RAK*) compulsory in all libraries in
1977, may seem strange or unacceptable to members of the profession in Britain, but it does after all follow that pattern of curriculum
control common in many countries of western (as well as eastern)
Europe but anathema in Britain. In East German college libraries
even user education (about the most variegated and optional of
library activities in the West) is handed down from above. Guidelines were published in 1978 and provide for a standardized
programme of instruction throughout the student's college career.[40]

There is nevertheless debate on such subjects as decentralization
of colleges' book collections and open access. Professional organizations flourish, and cooperate with the appropriate Ministry. The
Arbeitskreises der Hochschulbibliotheken (College Libraries
Working Group) has developed from an informal *ad hoc* gathering
in 1959 to an articulate assembly which formulates policy and
operates in close consultation with the Ministry of Higher Education. No doubt pressure is exerted in both directions. The
Working Group has various aims: the provision of literature to
students, contribution to the communist education of students,
the growth of information services, the rationalization of library
routines, and the winning of continuous education and training for
library staffs.

As in Poland, library user education is considered an important
part of the college curriculum and is designed to perfect information
handling techniques for the professional life as well for the duration
of the course.[41] User education is backed up by SDI for students
as well as staff in many colleges.

Libraries of the *Hochschulen* are expected to provide information
according to the needs of the region, as are the British polytechnics,
and to cooperate with public libraries and information networks in
the area. Overall planning of documentation provision among
various centres is not always as efficient as might be expected;
librarians are often critical of government ministries falling short
in this respect. The concentration of power and authority in the
ministries presumably makes the system top-heavy and renders
librarians impotent and frustrated.

CZECHOSLOVAKIA

College libraries operate under the direction of the appropriate Central Library in the region, and the regional board of the Czechoslovak Scientific and Technical Society. Most colleges include compulsory lectures on library use in their first-year timetable.

There are signs that libraries are having difficulty in keeping up with the growth of educational activity. Librarians have called for increased investments.[42, 43] Book supplies do not satisfy the demand from students and staff; western material swallows an ever greater share of the budget because of soaring book prices; and staff turnover is high because salaries hardly changed through the 1970s. All the while, extra-mural, postgraduate, and part-time studies expand. The profession calls for more realistic book funds so that more current material such as conference proceedings and periodicals may be acquired; staff time must be better used by introducing centralized cataloguing more widely, and libraries should have longer opening hours and better buildings, and advances should be made in the more modern activities: bibliographical services, photocopying, and computerization of housekeeping routines.

HUNGARY, RUMANIA, AND BULGARIA

The technical training sector in Hungarian higher education has grown substantially since the late 1960s and follows the German *Ingenieurschule* tradition. One third of non-university students pursue technical courses; one quarter are engaged in teacher training; nearly a half of all students in technical colleges are part-time or correspondence students, a tendency also noticeable in the Soviet Union. The hand of the state is again evident in the management of colleges. Selection and admission of students is guided by the manpower requirements specified in the economic plan, as well as by a stated policy of positive discrimination in favour of the offspring of working-class families.[44] Intervention in library management goes beyond recommendation and takes the form of decree. This may result, as we have seen in the case of the GDR,

in the strengthening of the library, because library provision standards are imposed on the college by the Ministry of Culture. A
Council of College Library Leaders (the *Egyetemi Könyvtárigaz-
gatók Tanácsának*) meets as a professional ginger group and works
in cooperation with the ministries.

Emphasis on user education is noticeable too, in Rumania. It is
seen not just as a means of finding one's way around a library for
three years but, in the form of information training, as an essential
part of technical education. It trains engineers to think systematically and to adopt an investigative and innovative outlook for life.

The same philosophy holds in Bulgaria, where user education is
part of a whole package of standards handed down by the Communist Party Central Committee. These requirements have been taken
up by librarians and used in the struggle for more funding and
better facilities. Academic libraries are on the whole much less
sophisticated than in the west, and there is a general feeling among
librarians that they have put up with too much for too long. On
top of the need for good technical services there is a desire to
build up good subject collections, but inadequate hard currency
allowances militate against improvements in this area. Some libraries however, sound impressive. For example the Library of the
Vasil Kolarov School of Agriculture has provided an SDI service to
staff for over ten years; this has been enhanced by a computerized
retrieval system, which now accesses AGRIS and BIOSIS.

SOVIET UNION

After 11 years in general school young people may move on to
secondary special educational institutions or to vocational schools.
Beyond that level they may enter a higher educational institution,
or *vuz (vysshee uchebnoe zavedenie)*. The *vuzy* had nearly three
million full-time new students enrolled by the end of the 1970s,
and over two million part-time.[45] The *vuzy* cover all sectors of
higher education in a unified approach reminiscent of Sweden's.
Within this category come (a) the universities, (b) the institutes
(which provide training in a single field, eg agriculture, law, drama)
and (c) the polytechnics (which offer a broader base for study).

Courses can last between four and six years and lead to a degree
or *diplom*.

Within these institutions librarians are asserting themselves more
than in the past as they realize what they can offer to the teaching
process and to the academic community generally. This outward-
looking thrust became particularly apparent in the 1976–80 Five
Year Plan. Current awareness bulletins, SDI, user education have
all come into prominence, and Avalova suggests more activities,
such as raising cultural standards by introducing students to works
of fiction, careers guidance, training in study methods, even speed-
reading schemes.[46] Another public relations method is the 'Information Day' or 'Library Day'. At the Kalinin Polytechnic in Lenin-
grad, Library Days are held for particular departments so that
teaching staff can be introduced to documentation and information
services in their subject. It is interesting to note that Library Days
were introduced in the polytechnic because teaching staff did not
pay sufficient attention to Library Committee minutes![47]

There is a constant drive for improvement in efficiency in library
routines. Some polytechnics have a *metodicheskii sovet* or council
for methodology whose members (mostly librarians) plan the routines of junior staff. Monitoring of work performance by these
grades is common and is done through questionnaires and work
diaries. New staff are supervized closely and part of their training
involves attendance at lectures organized by the unions and the
party to raise their political awareness. The need to streamline
routines is particularly acute when many of these institutions
operate over a very large number of sites, and acquisitions and
book processing have to be centralized. A tremendous amount of
effort seems to go into analysing and raising productivity, and it is
surprising that automation is not mentioned more. For example, a
thorough enquiry into the labour effectiveness of catalogue card
production at Kuibyshev Polytechnic Library surveyed hand-
written, typed, and duplicated cards but not computer-generated
cards, let alone COM.[48] Some libraries attempt mechanization by
inventing their own equipment: the Malinovsky Armoured Troops
Academy Library ingeniously produced a hectograph for duplicat-
ing cards, put together a special machine for spine labelling, and

installed their own horizontal conveyor between the depository and the Lending Department.[49]

Soviet librarianship has nevertheless much to offer the west in enthusiasm and ideas. Apart from the user education and public relations exercises mentioned above, there is the concept of socialist competition. Libraries compete in numbers of users, number of loans, frequency of use etc. This quantitative approach may be reminiscent of the worst excesses of socialist planning, but libraries are also judged on the quality of their promotion and publicity.

CONCLUSION

This all-too-brief survey of college libraries in continental Europe displays a wide variety of library practices and emphases. Nevertheless certain trends are discernible.

The declining fortunes of higher education in the west have made college librarians search for more economic ways of doing things and learn how to fight off staff cuts imposed by the college, or indirectly by the local authority or government ministry. Standards in southern Europe are generally low and rising only slowly. In some respects the academic libraries in the socialist countries have standards to be respected; they operate in a library economy that might have been familiar in the west 30 years ago, with little technological advance to assist their pursuit of efficiency, and staffed mainly by poorly-paid women with little political influence in the system. But they do attempt to provide a service for enormous numbers of students.

In the north-west of the continent technological advance is much more rapid as the over-production of librarians ensures a high level of professionalism and computerization becomes ever cheaper. It is difficult to foresee a synthesis of all these trends over the continent, but the level of service can be enhanced by a variety of factors. Strong professional associations and specialist groups are essential in pressing for standards to be accepted and fulfilled. Existing national statutory standards are invaluable as a base which can be defended, cited, and built upon. Standards imposed or recommended externally on higher educational institutions or ministries by supra-governmental bodies (the economic communities in both east and west, the Council of Europe, and global bodies like Unesco and IFLA) present a challenge to administrators as well as librarians. The international agencies have a great responsibility, in southern Europe in particular, for they are often the only channels through which innovation can enter an introverted national structure.

REFERENCES

1 Gwyn, R 'Towards a European policy for initial teacher education: scope and constraints'. *European Journal of Education* 14 (4) 1979. 359–368.
2 Altbach, P *Comparative higher education*. Mansell, 1979.
3 European Centre for Higher Education. *Access to higher education in Europe*. Unesco, 1981. 16–19.
4 OECD *Education statistics in OECD countries* (Various tables) OECD, 1981.
5 Lervik, H 'The future of European higher education'. *Coombe Lodge Report* 13 (2) 1980. Further Education Staff College, 1980. 512–530.
6 Geiger, R 'The changing demand for higher education in the 70s: adaptations within three national systems'. *Higher Education* 9 (3) 1980. 255–276.
7 Neave, G 'On wolves and crises'. *Paedagogica Europaea* (13) 1978. 11–35.
8 Musnik, I 'Student flows in higher education 1970–1977'. *Paedagogica Europaea* (13) 1978. 37–70.
9 Brosan, G S in *Higher education and the EEC*. North East London Polytechnic, 1973.
10 Unesco *Statistical yearbook 1970*. Unesco, 1971.
11 Unesco *Statistical yearbook 1980*. Unesco, 1981.
12 *Statistical pocketbook of Hungary*, Budapest, 1981.
13 *Narodnoe Khozyaistvo SSSR v 1979 g*. 498.
14 *Statistická ročenka Československé Socialistiké Republiky 1981*. 577–8.
15 *Narodnoe obrazovanie, nauka i kultura v SSSR: statisticheskii sbornik*. 1977.
16 Jallade, J-P 'Expenditure on higher education in Europe: past trends and future prospects' *European Journal of Education* 15 (1) 1980. 35–48.
17 *Statisticheskii ezhegodnik stran-chlenov soveta Ekonomicheskoi Vzaimopomoshchi 1979*.
18 Unesco *Statistical yearbook 1978–79*. Unesco, 1980.

19 Tournier, M 'Towards a transformation of the French educational system in the 1980s?' *Comparative Education* 16 (3) October 1980. 281–290.

20 Van Vaek, G and Van Daele, H 'Non-university higher technical education in Belgium'. *European Journal of Education* 14 (1) 1979. 25–36.

21 Schaafsma, C 'De HBO-bibliothecaris als informatiespecialist (The College of Higher Professional Education librarian as an information specialist)'. *Open* 11 (5) May 1979. 248–253.

22 Barton, W 'Über Schwachstellen einschichtiger Bibliothekssysteme (The weaknesses of the integrated library system)'. *Mitteilungsblatt (Verband der Bibliotheken des Landes Nordrhein-Westfalen)*, 28 (4) December 1978. 320–332.

23 Böhm, P 'Die Struktur der integrrierten Hochschulbibliothek (The integrated college library)'. *Zeitschrift für Bibliothekswesen und Bibliographie* 26 (6) 1979. 461–473.

24 Klein, H 'Fragebogenaktion Fachhochschulbibliotheken (Technical college library questionnaire)'. *Zeitschrift für Bibliothekswesen und Bibliographie* 25 (3), 1978. 204–209.

25 Heinzel, W 'Mediothekserfahrungen (Media centres)'. *Schulbibliothek Aktuell* (2) 1979. 127–134.

26 Crausaz, R 'Higher education in Switzerland'. *European Journal of Education*, 14 (1) March 1979. 37–57.

27 Kellner, E 'Die Deutschen Musikbibliotheken und die Bibliotheken der Musikhochschulen (The German music libraries and music college libraries)'. *Forum Musikbibliothek* (4) 1980. 39–54.

28 Walser, M 'Das Programmsystem EDIS–1 für Online-Sachrecherchen nach der DK im Katalog der Bibliothek der Eidgenössischen Technischen Hochschule Zürich (The EDIS-1 for subject searching at the National Technical College, Zurich)'. *Nachrichten für Dokumentation* 31 (4/5) September 1980. 193–197.

29 Sika, P 'Zur neueren Entwicklung der Universitätsbibliothek der Montanuniversitat Leoben, 1958–1978. (Development of the Mining & Metallurgy Institute Library)'. *Biblos* 27 (3) 1978. 275–281.

30 Humphreys, K W *The crisis for academic libraries in southern Europe.* University of Coimbra, 1978.

31 Slajpah, M 'Education of students as users of scientific and technical information in Yugoslavia'. In *Developing library effectiveness for the next decade*. Chalmers University of Technology, 1978. 181–185.

32 Serrai, A 'Le biblioteche universitarie italiane: un caso di arretratezza e di oscurantismo (Italian university libraries: a case of backwardness and obscurantism)'. *Associazione Italiana Biblioteche – Bolletino d'Informazioni* 20 (3) 1980. 73–89.

33 Beattie, N 'Education libraries in Italy: a reader's view'. *Education Libraries Bulletin* 23 (3) Autumn 1980. 24–28.

College Librarianship in Continental Europe

College Librarianship in Continental Europe

23

College Librarianship in North America

John Lubans Jr and Dennis Klappersack

The community college is a recent educational phenomenon in the milieu of college and university campuses. The library or Learning Resources Center (LRC) as it is known in the USA, represents quite well, in microcosm, the differences between the community college and the traditional university campus. To a large extent the LRC epitomizes the ongoing evolution of the community college's role in education. The differences are to be seen in services provided, hours of operation, types of staffing, book and media collections, and the users served, both faculty and students. This chapter analyzes the overall setting in which the LRC is located, and describes the LRC and its role in helping to fulfil the educational purpose of the community college.

SOME STATISTICS

At the turn of the century there were eight junior colleges in the United States, each serving about 100 people. Today there are 1,193 institutions, the vast majority being public or tax supported (925 to be exact, versus 268 privately financed community colleges), serving a student body of over 4.7 million. What is even more remarkable about this expansion is that much of it began in the post-Sputnik days of the early 1960s. In 1963 there were 850,000 students enrolled in 634 community colleges. Twenty years later, the student numbers have quintupled and the number of institutions has nearly doubled.

There are basically four types of programmes to be found at these two-year institutions in the United States: two-year associate degree; vocational-technical; two-year college transfer programme; community colleges emphasizing continuing education. Often a single community college may incorporate two or three of the above in its goals as a higher educational institution.

A college may offer an Associate of the Arts (AA) degree to students who complete requirements stipulated for graduation and the resulting certification or licensing in a career field. The required courses in the liberal arts AA-for-transfer are usually equivalent to the freshman and sophomore course work found in many four-year schools, and thereby allow a student full credit for two years of college level work and, upon transfer to a four year school, immediate entrance to classes at the third year or junior level. Often, the two-year AA degree will qualify and train a person for immediate job entry such as court reporter, library technician, or photographer, thus coinciding with the objectives of vocational-technical schools.

'Vo-tech' schools (frequently a part of a general community college) offer training in skilled or semi-professional work. On-the-job training (OJT), apprenticeship programmes, and work experience are often an important aspect of this schooling, which has close ties with industry and potential employers.

Continuing education programmes remain the most difficult to 'type'. They are now readily found in most community colleges and may encompass a wide range of credit or non-credit courses from personnel management to a weekly offering in 'interior design for the home', an example of a personal enrichment course.

A closer look at student numbers reveals another major difference between the traditional, four-years-or-more colleges and universities, and the community college. About 1.8 million or 61% of the community college students are part-time, and nearly all of these are 'commuters', that is, they do not live on campus. In comparison, the universities have a part-time enrolment of 24% while four-year colleges have 32%. This of course suggests differences among these student groups which will be explored later. Another statistic, largely unexplored, is the nature of the four million non-credit enrolment, ie those people making selections from the multi-tudinous listing of 'self-help' or personal enrichment programmes from aerobic dance, to car care, to pottery.

WHY COMMUNITY COLLEGES? SOME THEORIES

As the above suggests, a great deal of diversified activity is going on in the community college setting. Change is a constant in most organizations but is not probably as unremitting as that found in the community college. One suspects that the growth and develop-ment of the community college is not something carefully planned in anticipation of predicted societal and educational shifts. Rather it appears that the community college and its LRC respond, because they have the ability and the institutional flexibility to react to the major, often sudden, demands placed on them. Several variables can be suggested as influential in the upsurge of activity and the variety of responses required:

Technology

Whirlwind developments in technology have created a need for skilled technicians at all levels. Industry has begun to look toward the community colleges as a training base for many workers, eg laboratory technicians, for whom otherwise industry would have to develop its own training programmes at great expense. As the technological demands continue to grow and diversify the community college has sought to establish a firm basis for providing the needed service.

One method of accomplishing this is the setting up of industrial advisory panels to make recommendations on curricula and outcomes, and to guide the educational process in producing an employable graduate. Examples can be found where the community college has gone out into industry and provided training to update skills, unlike the traditional technical institute notion of students coming to a classroom after work.

Flexibility

In terms of hours, location, class size, curriculum, methods of instruction, and instructors, flexibility is a useful term in describing what community colleges do and how they do it in responding to the needs of technology. Programmes have often been tailored for the convenience of the student rather than that of the instructor or the college. Such programmes are strictly goal oriented and ignore any educational outcomes other than that of providing the student with the information and skills needed, whether to overhaul a jet engine or to fight an oil fire.

Remedial Education

Secondary education appears to be producing people who are ill-prepared for the labour market. Many recent high school graduates have neither the basic skills of reading nor those of basic numeracy. Older adults wanting to advance from an entry level position find the opportunity to master the necessary basic skills in the community college. 'Open admissions' (ie the indiscriminate enrolment of students), followed by the realization that many so admitted were functionally illiterate, has resulted in intensive programmes in basic skills development. This recognition of educational failure and the programmes developed in response to it have made the community college the leader in remedying this serious problem. Community colleges have accepted a major share in reversing the trend of illiteracy in the various academic skills.

If a mechanic cannot read directions to repair a brake master cylinder, then either he or she learns to do this by imitating someone else, or by learning to read at a level adequate to understand printed directions. If a supervisor's language skills are poor, then the college can attempt to correct this through a programme for improving such skills. Also, numerous people who have failed to achieve the high school diploma have a second chance provided through the Graduate Equivalency Degree (GED) offered by many community colleges. This prepares the individual for other courses of study in the curriculum or may qualify them immediately for jobs demanding a high school diploma.

A search of the educational research literature under terms such as 'curriculum reform' and 'basic skills in higher education' turns up a dozen or more recent entries for community college programmes but only one or two for the traditional colleges and universities. The remediation problem seems to be on the community college's doorstep. As to how much it should be a matter of improving the high school system and its curriculum and graduation requirements or parental responsibility is worth discussing. In the meantime the community college has taken on the problem and is trying to improve the individual.

'Minorities' in the workforce

Changes in society have led to major demands on the community college, eg women entering the workforce because economic and other societal pressures require couples to work. This has resulted in a large number of women, previously unemployed, interested in acquiring saleable skills in the labour market. Community colleges have responded not only with traditional programmes such as secretarial skills, but also with programmes in small business management, office management, etc. Many racial minorities have not been able, for a variety of reasons, largely financial, to take advantage of traditional education with its extensive requirements of full time study in residence on campus in a variety of subjects. People from the lower socio-economic strata have wanted, out of necessity, programmes that would make them into wage earners in a short time. It is moot if they would have preferred a traditional liberal arts education – they could not afford it and would be less likely to have learned in the groves of academe to be a welder, or carpenter, or green keeper, or petrochemical technician.

The job oriented aspect of the community college's courses, its open admissions policy, flexible scheduling (part-time, evenings, weekends), self-paced instruction and importantly, low tuition, give it a practical appeal to people with limited budgets seeking to swim up the economic mainstream. Refugees from Vietnam and other non-English-speaking groups seize upon the community college as their ticket to employment. Programmes training workers for direct placement in a particular type of employment will attract students interested in improving their economic situation. At the same time, corporations needing certain types of trained workers happily encourage the often symbiotic relationship between college and business. For example when draughtsmen are needed, industry may turn to the college and guarantee work for all of its graduates in draughtsmanship, regardless of ethnicity.

The Not-so-Leisured Society

One might wonder how, if couples all work, there is any time for leisure learning. Working at leisure may be a better phrase, at least in the USA. However, incongruous as it may seem on the surface, there is a demand for leisure type education: four million enrolments take place each year.

This may be a result of broadening individual horizons, such as a woman, recently returned to work, becoming aware of other opportunities and experiences beyond the home. The homemaker contemplating a return to the workforce, perhaps in opposition to a spouse, may opt to venture forth in community college evening classes, something relatively non-threatening to the traditionalist household. One young female executive says that for her, it is basically a matter of taking charge of one's life, a view that reverses long held assumptions in the USA for women and to a certain extent for men as well.

Often the continuing education aspect is stressed in the types of courses taken for non-credit. Here examples are languages and financial investment or business law, which may enhance one's career. (In fact, an employer may legally require the employee to take a specialized course.) Other courses taken, such as upholstery techniques, or watercolours, or working with stained-glass windows, may be largely avocational, but not without some exploration by the individual of new career possibilities.

The retired person (often now 55 years and up) has increasingly turned to the community college to explore a variety of subjects for pleasure and profit. Some community colleges offer tuition fees reductions for senior citizens. The concept of life-long learning is evident daily in community colleges. Also, of late, the craze for physical fitness has produced a rash of exercise classes for all age groups supplementing many existing physical fitness programmes already operated by the YMCA, YWCA, and those in the private sector.

THE STUDENTS

Although it is difficult to generalize about a diverse student body which is taking anything from a 'mini' course of one to several weeks' duration to a full traditional course load of 12–15 semester hours of work, several salient points have emerged and may be said to epitomize this group.

To a very large extent the community college student is much more goal oriented than the traditional student. The broader concept of acquiring an education that covers a wide spectrum of disciplines and provides one with a blueprint for one's life has been largely replaced by a very specific need to acquire a skill or a family of skills that will qualify one for placement in a certain industry. The key words describing this approach are *specific* and *useful*. The student very frequently has a clear idea of what he wants or needs to know to meet his specific objectives and will disregard courses that are not germane to these objectives.

This shift in attitude about what education is expected to provide has produced a highly motivated student body. Students enrolling in community colleges are generally 5–10 years older than traditional college students (28–33 as opposed to 18–23), the vast majority work on a full-time basis in addition to attending classes, and most have substantial family responsibilities as well. Thus the time the student spends at the college is fairly limited and perforce concentrated.

For the instructor and the librarian these students present a number of opportunities. Very often highly motivated, the students are eager to learn both in the classroom and in the library. They present an ideal audience, are receptive and appreciative, and generally gratifying to work with.

Because of their diverse backgrounds and very specific objectives they present a number of unique problems as well. A large majority of community college students are individuals who are returning to school after a break in their education ranging from one to 20 or more years. Their exposure to the classroom and the general learning process is not current, and they may require a 're-entry' period in order to benefit from coursework. Unfortunately, this is not apparent to many who return to college with unrealistic expectations of what they can accomplish within a short period of time. This factor, coupled with a narrow focus on what courses or programmes they wish to pursue, often leads to frustration, failure, and dropout from college. Indeed, the retention rate, the proportion of students who successfully complete a course of study, is lower at community colleges than at any other type of institution of higher education in the USA, and attrition rates often exceed 50%.

This situation has forced the community college to focus a great deal of attention on providing resources that will increase the students' chances for success in the classroom and thus encourage their continued status as students. In the classroom this has engendered a number of new and creative approaches to teaching, and in the library it has encouraged the librarian to develop new techniques and strategies for meeting the needs of these students. In many respects this situation has placed the community college librarian at the forefront of innovation in the library community and has made the LRC an exciting and vital place to work.

THE LEARNING RESOURCE CENTER (LRC): INNOVATIONS AND DIFFERENCES

Generally the main requirement for the librarian at community college level has revolved around the need to modify traditional approaches or techniques to meet the specific and in some cases unique needs of the community college student and faculty. This has led to innovation and a shift in emphasis in a number of specific areas.

Faculty and librarians

At college and university campuses there is usually some interest on the part of librarians in working closely with faculty to achieve the library's goals related to collection development and to improve on and increase library use. In reality, what should be a natural partnership must often be worked at arduously by librarians with minimal results. Seemingly traditional divisions, perhaps due to each group's specialization and the relative stability of the curriculum, contribute to the difficulty of crossing over and exchanging views. A common, redeeming assumption is made that even if the faculty are not visible they really do know about libraries and their use.

In the community college it can be observed that a different climate prevails.

First, no assumption can be made that they, the teachers, should know better than not to use the library. They may in fact have never used a library, by choice or otherwise, in their experience. Second, the programme is ever changing and there is no restricting, extensive tradition. One rarely hears 'We've always done it this way' as a ready-made excuse for not trying out an idea. These reasons promote a willingness among community college faculty and librarians to interact readily.

Another factor contributing to the interrelationship is the specialized nature of many courses for which library resources do not exist in the usual channels. Also, there is the newness of many course offerings and the requirement to teach different levels of students in the same class with multiple methods. All of the above contribute to the close collegiate interaction with faculty found at most community colleges.

In the instance of the specialized course, books may not exist or the books that are available may be at too high a level. It is then up to the librarian, in league with the instructor, to seek out relevant course materials that may support classroom needs. These may be in the form of training manuals only available through a particular industry or society, and available to the LRC only after much cajoling and wheedling to obtain them, perhaps with the help of an instructor from that industry. Future good working relationships can result from the joint effort in acquiring materials.

Because many of the faculty are drawn from industry, they may be new to teaching and may, as a result of minimal teaching experience, be willing to look to the LRC for help in getting their message across to a class, especially when such help is offered in the form of pre-packaged, time-saving media. Unlike the university campus where a film may be used occasionally, the community college classroom will feature several per semester, along with assignments to view tape-slides or videocassettes in the LRC.

Another important consideration in this regard has been the level of materials provided by the library. Students without recent academic experience or poor preparation are frequently confronted with the situation of having to absorb information at a level that is above their grasp. While the sources may well be standard or definitive, they are of little use if they cannot provide information at a level the student can readily absorb. This has led to an increasing awareness that information must be provided on a number of levels, from elementary to advanced, to enable students to progress at the pace that is most fruitful for them.

One community college, recognizing that people learn in different ways, produces a series of classes in several media formats for self-paced instruction in the mode most preferred by the individual. In other words, several 'generic books' on the same topic are provided. While this may be a luxurious extreme, variations on this idea are to be found in the community colleges' producing and placing media programmes in the LRC to augment and allow for student review of the classroom presentation. Since the LRC may be involved in producing the media programme or at least 'retailing' it, a close working relationship with the teacher is expected.

The remedial needs of many students have also made the faculty open to non-traditional ways of educating learners. If a class of student auto-mechanics is barely literate, a realia of a carburettor may help them learn more quickly than a workbook with a picture of a carburettor. Teaching composition to minimally skilled students or recent immigrants will require some recourse to media to get a teaching message across. In the case of the foreign born, the LRC may be able to help the English as a Second Language instructor locate vernacular teaching materials. Further along, the LRC may provide foreign language materials to help students gain, on their own, an understanding of course materials through media or books in their first language.

Visual display is an important concept to keep in mind in the design if point-of-use instructional units for library services. For example, where a printed text may contain a full, single-spaced, typed explanation on how to go about using a microfiche catalogue, it will not have the learning effect of a poster of a series of snapshots showing how something works which a foreign student or semi-literate person can grasp quickly.

Another force bringing teacher and librarian together is the often sophisticated equipment used in classrooms to 'play' the software. The librarian is counted on as being the expert adviser, video technician, or projectionist. At the same time those faculty wanting some degree of expertise in the use of such equipment in their classrooms are often willing to attend a workshop or a tutorial on how to trouble-shoot the equipment whenever problems do come up.

At the community college, curriculum committees will often include a librarian as the learning resources representative. As such, one can see that the potential influence of the library viewpoint can be significant, especially regarding library skills.

Outreach programmes are required, often launched by the LRC staff, to help students floundering in a subject area where the faculty are totally unfamiliar with library resources or, in the extreme, need to be dissuaded from a popular vo-tech faculty delusion of protecting sacrosanct library resources from greasy hands! This is a major concern with some of the trades such as building, welding, carpentry, or car repair, where unbeknownst to the instructor a wealth of media and other reasons exist why the student pouring a test slab of concrete could look at a film loop to remind him how to do it correctly, or someone repairing a brake lining can look into an automotive manual explaining how to do the job.

LRC: FORM FOLLOWS FUNCTION

As can be seen from the above discussion the LRC staff and their users are apt to make demands not readily fulfilled in a traditional library building. A recent analysis of community college LRCs illustrates how the community college administration through its LRC building and staff, has responded to student and faculty needs:

Table 1: Services provided in 28 LRC's (built 1979/81).

Service	Colleges
Library	27
AV Distribution	27
Graphics/Photographic Production	18
Audio Video Production	23
Reprographic Production	16
Audio Video Learning Laboratory	17
Learning Assistance Center	8
Career Information Center	10
Computer Assisted Instruction Terminal	8

Source: *Bowker Annual*, 1982, 276.

Twenty-seven have an area designated as a library. In it can be found books and journals and the conventional departments and their information handling functions: Circulation lends, Acquisitions acquires, Cataloguing indexes, and Reference interprets the collection. The other services listed are indicative of how the LRC differs from the other types of libraries. Audio-visual distribution, found in 27 of the 28 new LRCs, reflects the need to centralize and control the hardware used with the media software. Usually this service not only houses and sends the hardware to near or distant classroom locations but also sets it up for use and maintains it. Not infrequently, if the media is housed within the service department, it routinely cleans and repairs the software. For example, one library with an extensive 16mm film inventory cleans and repairs, as necessary, films after each use. Preview rooms are usually featured as part of this service since instructors need to review media for classroom use and/or purchase decision making.

Many of the LRCs feature production services in support of curricular needs. As mentioned above, many of the community college instructors, students, and courses of study are non-traditional and require specially tailored course materials. Since these may not be commercially available through the usual channels, it behoves many community colleges to produce their own software. Graphics/photographic production, audio/video production and reprographic production all relate to this seemingly unique need in the community college. It needs stressing that these services involve not just specialized equipment but require facilities, such as studios, and technicians and professional staff, to develop curricula and produce these materials for use by the LRC's clientele.

In recognition of the remedial needs of many of the students in regard to basic learning skills, eight of the new LRCs encompass learning assistance centres. Such centres include staff, materials, and equipment for improving reading, writing, and other skills. Relatedly, in recognition of the non-traditional student and the commitment of the LRC to mediated instruction, there are 17 audio/video learning laboratories in the new LRCs surveyed. These 'labs', of course provide seating and equipment for students to review course, or related software at their own pace of learning. The process here is one of individualized, self-paced instruction. The student requests the media and then, after instruction in the use of the equipment, plays it in a learning station equipped with the appropriate equipment such as a videocassette player, a film-loop projector, a slide-tape machine or a filmstrip/cassette player.

The eight LRCs listing computer assisted instruction terminals will be related functionally, if not physically, to the audio/video learning laboratory.

Lastly, the career information centre located in ten of the LRCs demonstrates the vocational counselling, job placement emphasis in the community college.

THE URBAN LRC: MANAGEMENT

Another issue, equally interesting, and, if anything, a more pressing problem than the difficulties involved in meeting the needs of a rapidly shifting, expanding and non-traditional student body is the logistical problem of managing the day-to-day operations of the contemporary urban community college library system. Before looking at this complex of problems more closely, several points need to be made.

The community college, as it evolved in the United States in recent years, is essentially an urban phenomenon. While there are some rural community colleges, these have retained their character over the years as either academic transfer institutions or agricultural/vocational training areas. It is the urban community college that was specifically established to meet the needs of students not served by established institutions, working adults, the academically unprepared, in areas of study not normally encountered in the traditional college setting.

Because the urban community college was specifically established to meet the needs of student groups not being met by other institutions, it has, in the interest of its own continued survival and expansion, found it necessary to be sensitive to those needs and to reflect changes as the nature of the potential student body shifts and as the economy changes and develops new or different needs.

Instructional sites, campuses, while retaining some traditional characteristics have become much more fluid than the traditional college campus of spacious lawns and ivied buildings. A site is established based upon demographic and economic needs rather than quietude and aesthetic principles. When those needs change the campus is discontinued or moved to reflect population or economic shifts.

Under these circumstances, the difficulties encountered in operating a library system are manifold. While it would be difficult to generalize about these problems, certain principles may be discerned. There is an overriding need for flexibility. Circumstances change constantly. Only by being ready to change with these circumstances can the library maintain its effectiveness. Large urban community college systems have often grown up rapidly and haphazardly over a short period of time. Communications and/or lines of authority, as a result, have tended to remain ambiguous, with the result that the library often has little forewarning of service contractions or expansions or policy shifts and must respond quickly. A 'crisis' approach to management is more the rule than the exception.

Perhaps the best way to illustrate a number of these issues is to look at the emergence of one of the more recent community college systems. While the situation may be unique, a number of the underlying circumstances and the responses to them govern the management of this type of system generally.

HOUSTON COMMUNITY COLLEGE SYSTEM

Houston Community College System (HCC) is located in the city of Houston, Texas, which has a population of over 3 million. Established in 1971 as an adjunct to the public (kindergarten to 12th grade) school system, the college experienced rapid growth over its first decade of existence and now maintains campuses at 20 locations within the city and offers courses at an additional 17 sites, reaching a total of 45,000 students. The library system has managed, barely, to keep pace with this growth and maintains an LRC at each of the established campuses. The problems, however, in establishing and maintaining resources and personnel for all of these sites have been enormous.

The approach taken in overcoming these problems has been to focus on the system as a whole rather than on individual campuses. Because of HCC's youth and rapid growth it has been impossible to develop an adequate collection at each site. In lieu of this, the library has focussed on building an overall system-wide collection of basic works and a collection of materials concentrated in the subject areas taught at each site. The central LRC retains an overall comprehensive collection and most of the media which are used to supplement the campus collections on a semester basis.

The catalogue for the HCC library system is published quarterly in microfiche format and lists all holdings throughout the system. These are available to students at any campus through an inter-site delivery service. A daily delivery system is maintained by the LRC to serve all campuses and to expedite interrelationships in the system by ensuring a timely response to specific needs. A complete circuit of the campuses by the delivery service covers 200 miles and delivers and picks up media, books, mail and equipment.

To enlarge the scope of the collection, borrowing agreements with other local institutions, such as the University of Houston, have been negotiated. When the resources of the college prove inadequate, the student is able to go to a number of other, more research oriented, institutions within the city and continue research there. User education programmes at the HCC LRC regularly stress the need and means to connect with other libraries in the city.

More problems have been involved in maintaining consistency of procedure and training and communications among the librarians and staff at the various sites. Because of the distances between sites, personal contact between the central LRC's staff and people at the outlying sites is limited, and supervision is restricted to occasional on-site visits. Moreover, the majority of the outlying sites are only open in the evening, to accommodate an adult, working student body. The librarians at these sites often hold full-time day positions in other libraries in addition to their responsibilities with HCC. In many cases these librarians find themselves switching from one type of user to another (public or school to college) and even from one classification scheme to another (Dewey Decimal to Library of Congress). While the problems inherent in this situation are not insurmountable, they are a difficult fact of life on a multi-site campus.

The on-site visits are designed to resolve particular problems that may arise at the outlying locations as well as to ensure that system-wide procedures are being implemented uniformly. These visits are supplemented by several in-service training sessions each year designed both to provide necessary information on policy and procedure and to afford an opportunity for the outlying staff to interact with each other and the central LRC staff, thus contributing to an overall sense of participation in the system as a whole.

To a large extent, however, each campus is an independent unit, and each campus librarian must be free to act independently in response to local circumstances and needs. While in some ways this may be viewed as a potential weakness, tending towards a disruption of the system-wide approach which is the most viable for a multi-campus system, it can also be seen as a great source of creative strength by giving considerable autonomy to branch librarians. As pointed out earlier, the success of the system has been largely dependent on its ability to maintain flexibility in the face of changing circumstances which may often be of a political nature. This is true at both system and campus levels. The campus librarians are encouraged to, and indeed must, act independently to be successful.

The recognition of the need for a great deal of freedom of action has also led to the evolution of a democratic style of management. The rapid development of the system soon made it apparent that no one individual or small administrative group had enough information – political, technical, or logistical – to make intelligent decisions concerning the operation of the system as a whole. As a result the participation of as many of the outlying librarians as possible was seen as necessary and mutually beneficial. Based on this perception, there is gradually developing a system of consultation and participation on the part of the librarians in all major decisions. The librarians themselves decide what portion of the materials budget to allocate for print and non-print materials, what percentage to devote to serials and periodicals, what types and levels of equipment are needed at the various sites, and what levels of staffing are needed at each location. Major decisions are arrived at in full staff meetings and generally reflect a consensus of opinion.

The result of this approach has proved beneficial on a number of levels. Because the staff play a major role in the decision-making process, they both understand the reasoning behind the decisions taken and have a great degree of interest in seeing the decisions successfully implemented. This encourages a broader view and interest in the operation of the system as a whole and encourages the staff to view situations intelligently and to develop solutions to problems or circumstances as they arise.

While not perfect, the system has shown the ability to grow and evolve to meet changing needs. Its one constant aim has been to meet student and instructor needs. To do this a high degree of flexibility and responsiveness to changing circumstances are the only guide to a successful approach. The system stands as an illustration of the need for non-traditional approaches to meet the needs of non-traditional library users in the community college.

APPENDIX: CANADIAN COMMUNITY COLLEGES

The authors' own US bias of experience shows through this chapter, which in its specifics has dealt exclusively with the community college scene in the USA. In fairness to this chapter's intended discussion about North America there follow some comments on those community colleges found in our neighbour to the north. From our view here in the USA, Canadian community colleges and their LRCs, while fewer in number, are similar to those in the United States in the following principal ways:

1 They are perceived as alternatives to a traditional university education, and they offer largely a technical and vocational training (ie semi-professional) and transfer opportunities to universities.

2 They are a recent phenomenon occurring during the 1960s in response to the philosophy that higher education should be available to a broader segment of society than under the traditional university system. In 1960 there were 29 community colleges with an enrolment of 9,000. In 1981 there were over six times this number with an enrolment of over 250,000.

3 Open admission is a concept endorsed in spirit by many of the Canadian community colleges; if not as open as the USA's colleges, they are at least flexible in their admission requirements, and tuition fees are lower than for university level education. These colleges profess flexibility not only in admissions but also in types of programmes (credit and non credit) and the class times offered to part-time and full-time students.

4 Similarly, the Learning Resource Centers in Canadian community colleges are comparable to those found in the USA.

5 The LRCs place emphasis on media for multiple uses such as class instruction and self-paced learning and are closely concerned with skills remediation of inadequately prepared students.

6 They rely heavily upon good collegiate relationships between faculty and librarians in addressing problems and in producing and retailing a mediated curriculum.

24

College Librarianship in Australia

Edward R Reid-Smith

THE COUNTRY

Australia is an ancient land some 3,000,000 square miles in area (UK 94,000 square miles, USA 3,500,000 square miles).[1] Distance and large areas of arid land form major barriers to communication between townships, so electrical and electronic media are important in solving problems of isolation. The island continent may be divided into four major regions: the central desert plains, the arid plateau, the highlands near the eastern coast extending roughly north-south across the country (highest point over 7,000 feet), and the narrow, sandy coastal plains.

Politically the country comprises six states (New South Wales, Queensland, South Australia, Tasmania, Victoria and Western Australia), the self-governing Northern Territory, and the Australian Capital Territory (the ACT, which is administered directly by the Commonwealth or Federal Government). Formerly the states were separate colonies, but in 1901 were federated into one country. However, 'states' rights' is a sensitive issue, and the demarcation of responsibilities between the central and the states' governments is closely monitored.

With an exceptionally low population density, just over four people per square mile (compared with about 587 in the UK and 64 in the USA), Australians may nevertheless be categorized as urban (75%) rather than rural (25%).[2, 3] Most people live in large cities or small townships on the coastal strip, and all capital cities of the states and the Northern Territory are ports. (The exception is the capital, Canberra, built as an administrative city in territory carved out of inland New South Wales as an alternative to Sydney and Melbourne.)

About 62% of the country's 14,616,000 population lives in the six state capital cities alone; the average density figure quoted above obscures the true situation.[2, 3] In reality, Australia consists of a few large cities, a scattering of small townships (especially in the southeastern states of New South Wales and Victoria), few of which have over 20,000 people, and vast areas which are either unsettled deserts or poor agricultural land with isolated homesteads. These properties may have thousands of hectares of unfenced land. Two-way radio and light aircraft are their normal means of communication.

Recent archaeological finds indicate the presence of human societies in Australia as long ago as 40,000 years, but today's inhabitants are overwhelmingly of European origin resulting from migration during the past 200 years. There are about 140,000 Aboriginals (a high percentage being of mixed race).[4] and considerable numbers of people of Chinese, Greek, Italian and other origin whose languages are in everyday use. The official language is English (or 'Strine'!) which is used at all levels of education.

THE EDUCATIONAL SYSTEM

In general, education in Australia is the responsibility of the individual states and of the Northern Territory government. However, the federal government does exercise direct control of education in the ACT, Norfolk Island, Christmas Island, and the Cocos (Keeling) Islands. As elsewhere in the world, there is an observable tendency for the Australian government to heed the calls for public accountability by issuing guidelines and occasionally, directives, when distributing funds for education. This is not yet seen as a serious problem, and indeed it is the occasional lack of compatibility between states' educational systems which causes slight difficulties.

In all states except New South Wales and South Australia there are single education departments which look after all levels of education. Both New South Wales and South Australia have an education department concerned with primary and secondary schooling, whilst another department is responsible for technical and further education (TAFE). The universities and colleges of advanced education (CAEs) are autonomous institutions established under acts of the appropriate state parliaments, though the meaning of 'autonomous' has been questioned, particularly in the case of the CAEs.

Primary and secondary education within states has some administrative and supportive input from regional education offices, which also help to convey local wishes and feelings to state education departments. At the same time, some of the disadvantages of purely local government provision of education are avoided. A UNESCO publication some years ago saw a number of distinct advantages in having centralized educational systems in a country such as Australia.

> The meeting of all [primary/secondary] educational costs from States finances has ensured a more even spread of facilities than could be achieved in any other way. The child living in an isolated or undeveloped district is not educationally handicapped as he commonly is in countries with decentralized control.[5]

Nevertheless, current popular opinion is that metropolitan schools have better facilities and educational standards than rural ones, and statewide examinations appear to support this to some extent.

Rather more contentious is the question of public funding of private schools. This is a political matter in that the Australian Labor party and trade unions such as the Teachers' Federation see such financing as depriving the public sector (ie government schools) of money, and subsidizing the higher salary earner. (Teachers in private schools belong to the Independent Teachers' Association, so there is a lack of workers' solidarity here.) On the other hand, no Labor government has withdrawn subsidies from private schools, and it may be argued that this support helps 'to protect the community against inefficient private schools'. It is also a religious matter in that the powerful Roman Catholic education lobby is concerned at both primary and secondary levels, though the Anglican and Presbyterian grammar schools also rely on federal funding to maintain the standards which see a high proportion of their students continuing on to universities and colleges.

Although parents may consider that the state schools are not so academically oriented as the Protestant schools (the various 'Scots' schools in particular), UNESCO has a more positive view of their contribution.

> Special measures have been taken to provide for the rural child. One-teacher schools are conducted on efficient lines, and teachers are specially trained for working in them. Methods of teaching isolated and hospitalized children by correspondence constitute Australia's major contribution to educational method.[5]

Similar innovation in distance education has been contributed by the tertiary education sector, though without utilizing the two-way radio system which is the sole daily link of many outback families. The world's first School of the Air began in 1949 from a studio in Alice Springs in the centre of Australia, and used a land-line to the local base of the Royal Flying Doctor Service, which maintained radio contact with isolated homesteads and communities. There are now twelve such schools covering about 1,500,000 square miles across the country, with a total enrolment of about 1,000 pupils.[6] One other service operated for a number of years and about 5,000 pupils have been taught by this means overall.

Many students have received primary education from the schools of the air and have then gone on to boarding schools in metropolitan cities. UNESCO saw that: 'State-wide courses of study, and the uniformity of teaching standards facilitate greatly the transfer of children from school to school. This is important in a country with considerable mobility of population.'[5]

Problems come with moving interstate, however, as curricula and methods vary quite considerably. A similar problem may face teachers moving interstate, in addition to practical matters such as non-transferability of superannuation. UNESCO believes that: 'Teachers as servants of a [state] government department are free from the petty politics of local government', though the unions may well think that teachers are not free from the greater politics of State and national governments.

Whereas tertiary education has experienced a proliferation of institutions during the past twenty years or so, a growth of the school bus service has enabled some rationalization in the other two sectors.

> The present trend towards consolidation through the closing of small rural schools and the provision of road transport has gone ahead more rapidly than in countries where local bodies have the final control. In general it is possible under favourable circumstances to introduce new methods and to disseminate ideas throughout the service much more rapidly than in the case of decentralized systems. . . . A variety of special services can be provided which would be impracticable for the small administrative unit. It may be doubted, for example, whether any other school system of corresponding size (both geographically and with respect to number of pupils) has a better developed research and guidance service than that possessed by one of the States.[5]

A comparison of the state-provided schools and the local government provided (or absent) library services supports this view.

State centralization is not seen by everyone as being beneficial however. Comments such as: 'An important barrier to progress appears to be the inbred nature of the teaching service of the State Education Departments', and 'The centralized administrative structure tends to exert a strong influence towards conformity, uniformity and stability', are common and by no means unjustified. Direct federal funding (from income tax sources) of such areas as school libraries, science facilities and tertiary education, has therefore been of more than a financial benefit.[7]

Central funding is particularly important for the colleges, a few of which are subject to denominational control (particularly so in teacher education) but none under local government auspices as in Britain. Federal government money has been given to colleges (through the states) and universities for capital works and recurrent expenditure, as well as to students in the forms of free tuition and means-tested grants under the Tertiary Education Assistance Scheme (TEAS).

States have set up boards to receive and allocate federal funds for tertiary education for courses which they themselves approve. This followed the central government's acceptance in 1965 of the Martin Committee's recommendations to establish CAEs. The national Tertiary Education Commission (TEC) is now taking a more active role in the rationalization of courses nationwide as states tend to allow proliferation. Librarians have criticized the acceptance of colleges' proposals to introduce new courses without ensuring adequate library resources and staff during the expansionist 1970s. However, once a state has approved a course of study at an appropriate level (2 year Associate Diploma, 3 year Diploma, 3 or 4 year degree, 1 year Graduate Diploma, and recently masters' degrees of about 2 years), acceptance by the central government has followed.

All approved courses are nationally accredited by the Australian Council on Awards in Advanced Education (ACAAE). The work done in Britain by the CNAA is thus shared in Australia between the states (examination of proposals with on-site visits) and the ACAAE (accreditation). However, the awards themselves are made in the names of the various individual CAEs as awards are in universities. As with polytechnics in Britain which they strongly resemble, the Australian CAEs offer mainly vocational courses with a strong practical application.

Colleges of technical and further education (TAFE) are also concerned with practical courses, but at the technician rather than the technological level. This is reflected in the awards given (certificates and Associate Diplomas) in the names of the states and not of the individual colleges. The work of the two college systems complement and sometimes overlap each other.

THE UNIVERSITIES

Tertiary or higher education in Australia generally follows the British pattern, though there are some important differences. There are nineteen institutions of university status established under individual acts of parliament, and receiving federal government funds. The Australian National University (ANU) being situated in Canberra, is funded directly by the federal government.

Table 1: Federal government expenditure on universities

(Year ending 30 June ($000,000s))[8]

	1977/8	1978/9	1979/80
ANU	67.9	75.6	81.2
Grants to States (Univs)	626.9	645.7	704.9
Total for universities	781.0	810.1	875.0
Total all education	2388.3	2522.7	2608.1
% for universities	32.7%	32.1%	33.5%

The federal government inaugurated a comprehensive programme of university expansion in 1957, a movement which lasted throughout the seemingly prosperous 1960s and ended in the early 1970s when the present period of economic difficulty was already apparent. The last university to be established was in fact Deakin in Victoria, based on existing colleges and destined to play an important part in distance education on the British Open University's model. The planned university in the Albury-Wodonga development area straddling the NSW and Victoria border disappeared in the 'razor-gang' financial trimming of 1981, and the Robinson University College in Broken Hill (Western NSW) is just being closed down by its parent University of New South Wales in Sydney.

COLLEGES OF ADVANCED EDUCATION

The federal government makes grants to states for allocation to CAEs, but funds directly the Canberra College of Advanced Education. It is of some interest to compare the Commonwealth outlays on higher education (Tables 1 and 2).

Table 2: Federal government expenditure on non-university higher education

(Year ending 30 June ($000,000s))[8]

	1977/8	1978/9	1979/80
Canberra CAE	16.7	15.2	17.3
Grants to States	449.5	481.7	497.2
Total other HE	526.3	562.2	583.2
Total all education	2388.3	2522.7	2608.1
% for non-university HE	22.0%	22.3%	22.4%

Altogether about 56% of the federal government's educational expenditure goes to the higher education sector, and of this rather more goes to the universities than to the colleges. There were about 40 CAEs in the 1970s, many of them multi-purpose, but a few single-purpose ones such as teachers' colleges, agricultural colleges etc.

'Because of their recent introduction and deliberate government policy and financing, CAE enrolments have been growing at a faster rate than university numbers; in 1969 some 32,000 students were enrolled. . . .'[9] Ten years later the number had increased to almost 500% of that figure, but there was a very high proportion of part-time students in the CAE system. Table 3 shows that full-time students accounted for only 49% of the total CAE enrolment in 1980, and this proportion decreased in 1981 and 1982.

It would seem that two factors are at work here. Firstly, academic drift is ensuring that older people are upgrading qualifications (eg professional to academic), or taking study for the first time whilst engaged in full-time employment or home duties. Secondly, the

Table 3: Students enrolled in CAEs[8]

(Actuals)

Year	Full-time	Part-time	External	All
1980	78,219	60,892	20,355	159,466
1979	82,125	56,368	17,174	155,667
1978	84,266	51,407	14,249	149,922

(Percentages)

Year	Full-time	Part-time	External	All
1980	49.0%	38.2%	12.8%	100%
1979	52.8%	36.2%	11.0%	100%
1978	56.2%	34.3%	9.5%	100%

worsening economic situation has encouraged people to take the increasingly scarce jobs first and then look for study facilities afterwards. This latter may be supported by the countrywide increase in the number of full-time applicants for college and university places in 1983 (and in those staying on at high schools for a further period). Employment opportunities are now so restricted that higher education is seen not only as increasingly essential in a technologically advanced society, but also as a viable alternative to the dole queue.

These overall figures, although indicating national trends, hide the individuality of the CAE system. Some of the colleges do not offer courses by external study (the distance education mode), and this tends to be true of metropolitan colleges. Other CAEs may have more than half of their enrolment as external students, and this may be particularly true of the larger regional CAEs which serve large inland areas. Nevertheless, students may be enrolled in any CAE from anywhere in Australia, and indeed overseas. The size of enrolment, however, does not necessarily indicate the contribution of graduates and diplomates to the workforce (Table 4), for the drop-out rate is high.

The growth of the external student participation has created a situation of concern not only to librarians in the colleges and universities themselves, but also in the public library networks. There has also been a corresponding increase in the number of part-time staff in the CAE and TAFE systems (Table 5), which appears to have gone unnoticed by CAE librarians.

Table 4: CAE students starting and completing courses[8]

	Starting	Completing
1980	63,757	–
1979	62,436	33,913
1978	62,243	33,263
1977	–	31,492

Table 5: Staff of colleges in 1980[8]

	Full-time	Part-time	Both
CAEs	8,927	1,312	10,239
TAFE	7,479	3,048	10,527

All states except South Australia witnessed an overall growth in the numbers of TAFE staff between 1979 and 1980. In the CAE sector there was a total increase of 2.8% 1978–1980, but this average hides the fact that this was slight (1.3%) for full-time and much greater (14.6%) for part-time staff.

Although the money allocated to higher education seems to be keeping up with rising costs, this is done at the expense of capital works which of course affects the building and expansion of libraries. Table 6 shows the central government funds given to the state of New South Wales since the period of financial stringency began in 1975. In 1980/1 there were six universities, 23 CAEs attracting Commonwealth grants (plus eight colleges awarding diplomas under the Higher Education Act of 1975 but not listed by the Commonwealth for grants) with 87 TAFE Colleges (26 metropolitan and 61 elsewhere) and 167 associated TAFE teaching centres.[10]

It will be seen that the CAEs have been particularly hard hit as regards building programmes at a time of expansion in student numbers. College of advanced education libraries have not been enlarged, library staff numbers have increased but slowly, and escalating costs of learning materials have posed immense problems in trying to bring library services up to standard.

Table 6: Commonwealth grants to New South Wales
(Year ending 30 June ($'000))[10]

Recurrent Expenditure

	1975	1976	1977	1978	1979	1980
TAFE	10,333	17,652	16,714	19,184	21,061	23,546
CAE	62,122	69,089	90,831	98,303	105,103	115,272
University	149,997	168,831	199,633	222,893	230,197	252,856
TOTAL	317,205	393,874	468,120	521,216	545,806	606,430

Capital Expenditure

	1975	1976	1977	1978	1979	1980
TAFE	5,859	8,919	12,262	15,162	19,279	28,054
CAE	41,197	23,716	27,200	11,866	20,070	12,087
University	22,526	21,754	17,553	17,910	21,840	25,353
TOTAL	146,584	104,350	112,293	105,944	120,143	111,770

OTHER COLLEGES

Mention has been made of recognized colleges granting awards to students but not receiving central government funding. These may nevertheless receive some state assistance but policy varies. In New South Wales, for example, there are eight such institutions: a college of physical education, an Adventist teachers' college now also offering other courses, a drama college, three theological colleges, and two Roman Catholic teachers' colleges which are outside the CAE system. All of these institutions are recognized under State laws however.

TECHNICAL AND FURTHER EDUCATION

Although the Commonwealth government took on full responsibility for funding CAEs in 1974 this is not the case with colleges of TAFE. Across Australia there are some 219 major TAFE institutions with 776 annexes, so that there is a presence even in quite small communities of perhaps only a few hundred people.[8] Many courses are offered by correspondence from headquarters in each state. The work concentrates on technician certificates but courses are also offered for the Higher School Certificate or equivalents and in the field of adult education.

Table 7: TAFE funding in New South Wales

(Year ending 30 June ($000))[10]

	1975	1976	1977	1978	1979	1980
Commonwealth	16,192	26,571	28,976	34,346	40,340	51,600
State	52,460	66,041	83,807	101,781	114,687	135,588

Although there has been a considerable expansion in TAFE funding as the NSW example indicates (Tables 6 and 7) the libraries still require some special attention and particularly with regard to staffing in the smaller colleges in rural areas.

The TAFE staffing situation has already been noted as far as academic staff are concerned (Table 5), but it is rather more difficult to detail the number of people studying in the system because of the varying length of courses. The number of TAFE enrolments in 1980 was given as almost one million across the country (Table 8), but the actual number of individual students must be less than this.

Table 8: TAFE enrolments (Australia) 1980[8]

Full-time	Part-time	External	Total
57,092	833,928	64,747	955,767

It may be claimed that as there is a TAFE concentration on practice rather than theory, there is less need for libraries in this sector than in the other colleges. It may also be claimed that with such a preponderance of non-full-time students the public library systems should be the mainstay for the majority of people. These arguments should be refuted. Although more cooperation between all publicly-funded libraries is essential, the TAFE colleges must acknowledge that they themselves have the prime responsibility for ensuring (if not always personally providing) adequate library services.

OFFICIAL REPORTS ON COLLEGES

The Murray Report

In 1957 the Committee on Australian Universities under the chairmanship of Sir K A H Murray (of the UGC in Britain) recorded the exceptionally high student non-completion rate of about 42%, and recommended a number of measures including emergency grants, an Australian UGC, university expansion, and a system of scholarships. The 1960s saw a considerable increase in the number of universities and students, and in the range of vocational courses at this level. This was accompanied by a narrowing of subjects studied and a diminishing of the general educational breadth of undergraduate studies.[11]

The Martin and Wark Reports

The federal government in 1961 authorized Sir Leslie Martin to investigate tertiary education, establishing the Committee on the Future of Tertiary Education in Australia. The committee's report appeared in 1964–5 and was widely criticized for its fragmentation and lack of clarity. Its main success was in persuading the federal government to fund technical training, but it failed to make any immediate impact in its objective of diversifying tertiary provision. In 1965 the Commonwealth Advisory Committee on Advanced Education was appointed with Dr I W Wark as chairman and its report included a recommendation that grants be made to states on a dollar-for-dollar basis to support non-university colleges of advanced education. It contained a whole chapter on libraries.[12]

Martin envisaged institutes of colleges formed from groups of existing technical colleges for sub-university study, whereas Wark proposed that CAEs should provide university-level courses. The former was effected only in Victoria, where college autonomy already existed, and the latter led to the establishment or upgrading of colleges in all states. It was mainly in these that the new professional library schools were established in the late 1960s and early

1970s, with a corresponding movement in the TAFE colleges in the later 1970s and early 1980s at library technician level.

The Swanson Report

By the time that the report of the Special Committee on Teacher Education appeared in 1973 there were already signs that a reduction in demand lay not many years ahead. As early as 1969 the then Federal Minister for Education, Malcolm Fraser (unseated following a long period as prime minister, as this chapter was being written), warned that: 'The introduction of teacher education into country Colleges of Advanced Education will provide the only means by which some of them can become viable tertiary institutions.'[13]

Some multi-purpose CAEs thrived because of the incorporation of strong teachers' colleges; some single-purpose CAEs such as teachers' colleges have been hard hit in the present decade, leading to amalgamation or threat of disestablishment.

The Australian Commission on Advanced Education had suggested standards for the development of CAE libraries, and the Special Committee found that the average of 37 volumes per student (range 27–46) in state teachers' colleges in the five mainland states would have to increase to an average of 60 volumes per student to meet these guidelines. The estimated growth was in fact to an average of 44 volumes by 1975 (range 38–51). Even such a moderate increase called not only for special finance of $1.25 million in the period 1973–5 for materials, but a further $0.25 million for additional staff. There was a planned increase of 45% in staffing in the triennium for teachers' college libraries, but the Swanson Report stressed the need to provide 'library services effectively and economically' by using students as well as part-time and temporary staff. Use of centralized cataloguing data was also recommended.[14]

The Kangan Report

The Australian Committee on Technical and Further Education under the chairmanship of M Kangan issued its Report in 1974, and as a direct consequence of its general acceptance by the federal government the allocation jumped from $28.6 million in the year 1973–4 to $96 million during the two years 1974–6.[11] Funds were recommended for extra staff for existing technical college libraries, for the training of professional and library technician staff, and for library resource materials and equipment. Priority in allocation of subsequent grants was to be given to colleges having full-time library staff: a form of encouragement which did not in fact lead to widespread appointments.

A major proposal was that each State should set up for TAFE external students 'a Central Resource Centre (CRC), which should contain a comprehensive variety and quantity of learning media that facilitate development in the individual'. These resources were to be available additionally to 'learners in industry and commerce and to non government as well as government educational institutions', and support the individual college library resource centres (LRC). Although the CRCs have not developed as planned, the TAFE libraries do place heavy emphasis on multimedia resources.

The Kangan Committee 'found that the (then) present libraries in technical colleges range in quality from mediocre to appalling', and it is still only a minority of colleges which have professional staff to develop the service (though regionalization has led to some improvements). It considered the position to be worse than that recorded in the 1966 *First Report* of the Commonwealth Advisory Committee on Advanced Education, and laid the major part of the blame on 'the relegation of libraries to a very low priority in the total teaching scheme' by managerial and teaching staff. Most colleges held fewer than two library books per student, and the Kangan Report firmly stated that: 'without a substantial increase in staffing at all levels – librarians, library technical assistants, clerks and typists, and media specialists – there is no prospect of any appreciable improvement in the standard of services offered by the LRCs to college staff and students'.

The report also recommended the establishment of bibliographic centres in each state to provide centralized acquisitions, cataloguing, union catalogues, and inter-library loan services. Library services and users were included in a survey of technical colleges but some difficulty was experienced as few accurate statistics were maintained. It is apparent that the Kangan Report is of considerable importance in the development of TAFE college libraries and is the basic document on which improvements during the past few years (and even current proposals) have been built.[15]

The Williams Report

The last of the great committee reports also looked at education from an economic viewpoint, but whereas the previous ones had been expansionist the Williams Report on education, training and employment looked firmly towards 'negative growth' across the whole spectrum from primary to tertiary. The exception was in the TAFE sector. Put succinctly, the report saw that 'in the next 20 years problems of growth will be less important and problems of rationalisation and co-ordination more important'.[28] It has much to say not only about education but also redundancy, not only training but overproduction. Its statistical tables range from teenage unemployment to higher degree students. More research studies were advocated, and it was recommended that consideration be given to tenured appointments being conditional on satisfactory completion of inservice programmes. Libraries as such rate little mention.

COLLEGE LIBRARY STANDARDS

In 1974 the Kangan Report noted the lack of standards for technical college libraries, and as a result of requests from college administrators and librarians it published some interim guidelines for developing library resource centres. These were actually formulated by the committee's two librarian advisers (Flowers and Brown), and covered spatial matters, book stock and serials subscriptions, and staffing. Although not pretending to scientific authoritativeness they did provide potentially attainable standards for TAFE libraries. To be too innovative and forward-looking could have discouraged their adoption, but in the event the state and regional librarians within the TAFE system have (within ever-present budgetary constraints) been able to develop some imaginative services.

Somewhat crudely the guidelines proposed that by 1981 unstaffed libraries in colleges having fewer than 1,000 students (individual enrolments) should have an interim five books per student. This then proceeded on an arbitrary scale:

> below 2,000 enrolments not less than 10,000 volumes
> 2,000 – 5,000 enrolments not less than 25,000 volumes
> 5,000 – 10,000 enrolments not less than 50,000 volumes
> for each additional 1,000, a minimum of 5,000 volumes

This to include not less than 1,000 reference volumes.

Somewhat optimistically the guidelines proposed 100 serial subscriptions for every 1,000 enrolments up to 10,000 students (minimum 100 subscriptions) and 5 subscriptions for each 100 enrolments thereafter. Naturally, no attempt was made at a policy based on subjects taught. Staffing (administrative and technical services, reader education and services, AV services, and office) were similarly based on the number of student enrolments.[15]

One of the problems with guidelines and standards is that they tend to concentrate on quantity, on the assumption that quality will follow. Library services may be seen in terms of numbers rather than as a very personal service between specialist (librarian, technician, information, or media workers) and client. The aim, certainly, is to 'raise standards' and it is notably difficult (though not impossible) to present standards of quality of service.

The matter of standards for TAFE libraries has been the subject of much discussion, and it has been pointed out that there is an essential difference between a guideline and a standard. Mitcheson suggests that the Flowers–Brown guidelines have been accepted as standards by virtue of their having been used in three planning exercises, two of which were applied.[16] He also revealed that the spatial section had used quite heavily the 1973 IFLA public library standards.[17] This is interesting in view of the claim that in some states administrators had dismissed the guidelines because they 'were based on university standards and were unrealistic for TAFE colleges' (Flowers is a university librarian though Brown is engaged in the TAFE sector). Certainly the guidelines paid little attention to audio-visual materials, which are so important in TAFE work today.[18]

In contrast to the TAFE colleges, the CAE sector has seen several attempts to establish quantitative standards. These range from a simplistic statement that the library should have a basic collection of 50,000 volumes plus an unspecified number of additional volumes (depending on the number of students and subjects),[19] to the impressively authoritative research-based proposals of Wainwright and Dean.[20] The first set of standards was published in the second Wark Report of 1969, and categorized five sizes of college by the number of FTE students. It mentioned only numbers of volumes and current periodical titles however.[21] The third Wark Report of 1972 proposed standards for the single purpose CAEs such as agriculture, art, and music, as also small isolated colleges. These all shared the feature of being extremely small, often having only one or two hundred students.[22] In the same year, the Library Association of Australia published standards which called for book stocks and serials greatly in excess of those previously proposed by government bodies, and in addition paid particular attention to non-book materials.[23] Indeed, it may be said that with the exception of the Wainwright-Dean recommendations, most standards appear to be derived from previous (usually overseas) editions, simply revised upwards.

Before leaving the question of standards, brief mention must be made of those for teachers' colleges which formerly were not part of the CAE sector. Taylor made some interesting suggestions in 1971 when he saw the need for the quantity of books to be based cumulatively on a basic stock of 25,000 volumes and five factors. These were student numbers, major and minor subject fields, minor optional topics, and the library's annual growth rate.[24] His suggestions may have no real validity but are much more imaginative than those issued the following year in Victoria, which again were mainly concerned with student numbers. They did, however, suggest 10% pa for replacements, and noted the need for non-book materials in addition.[25]

Much energy has been expended on quantitative guidelines and standards, and disappointment has been expressed that college libraries have not reached them. The blame for this has usually

been laid at the door of administrators whose low budget allocations show a lack of belief in the validity of standards proposed by
professional librarians. It has been suggested that the LAA should
produce authoritative standards, presumably in the hope that
educational administrators and governments will pay more attention to the proposals of individual librarians if issued under the
name of a corporate body. This does nothing to solve the basic
objection that the existing guidelines (other than those of Wainwright and Dean) are little more than guesswork. The bibliothecal
game of leap-frogging older standards is not in any sense the result
of professional expertise, and quite rightly does not impress the
taxpayer or the allocator of public funds.

COLLEGE LIBRARY STATISTICS

The literature of Australian college librarianship abounds with
complaints about the lack of reliable (or any) statistics, and the
difficulties in using those provided because of incompatibility. The
Kangan Report of 1974 noted that in technical colleges 'it was
obvious that many libraries do not keep accurate statistics, and in
many cases, information was not available'.[15] In 1976 a survey
encountered difficulties which 'point up the necessity for establishment of a standardized system of statistical reporting by the CAE
libraries in New South Wales', and recommended 'that the Higher
Education Board investigate establishing such a system in consultation with both the New South Wales CAEs and the Higher Education Boards in other States'.[26] It is clear, however, that the growth
in the quality of college library services has not kept pace with the
demands of the increasing numbers of students, let alone allowed
for a stimulation of library usage.[27]

The collection of statistics regarding colleges, and to some extent
their libraries, is now done through the appropriate state departments. However, the Williams report of 1979 found concerning
attrition that: 'The low quality of the statistical returns from many
of the colleges . . . were also disconcerting. Some of the returns
justified grave doubts about the accuracy of the statistics returned

to the Tertiary Education Commission. . . . Advanced education statistics are inadequate in accuracy and cover.'[28]

What was true of statistics concerning figures of enrolments and withdrawals (so important to good college planning and management) was probably equally true of library resources and usage.

In addition to the statistics published in the various surveys and government reports, an attempt has been made to collect academic library figures and issue them annually on a national basis.[29] These in turn have been used by the Tertiary Education Commission in its latest review, and it is worth extracting some figures illustrating the growth of 19 selected CAE libraries in New South Wales and Victoria.[30] (See Table 9)

Table 9: Growth of selected CAE libraries 1976–9

	1976	1978	1979	Annual %age change	
				1976–8	1978–9
Total volumes (000s)	3,315	4,415	4,879	+15.4	+10.5
Acquisitions: monographs	311	345	297	+ 5.3	−13.9
(000s)					
serials (000s)	70	76	81	+ 4.2	+ 6.6
Reader places	12,075	13,900	14,267	+ 7.3	+ 2.6
Library staff (FTE)	1,198	1,247	1,267	+ 2.0	+ 1.6
Loans (000s)	3,220	3,803	3,933	+ 8.7	+ 3.4
Average weekly hours open	61.4	63.7	64.3	+ 1.9	+ 0.9
Expenditure ($000,000s)	26.2	28.0	27.9	+ 3.4	− 0.4
Student enrolments	102,815	115,980	120,364	+ 6.2	+ 3.8
Academic Staff (FTE)	6,910	7,474	7,591	+ 4.0	+ 1.6

Some interesting changes are recorded for the period in question. In an inflationary period there had been a slight net increase in funding allocated by the individual colleges to their libraries, but a considerable decrease in purchasing power. This is reflected in the 1979 decrease in monographs acquired, though there is an interesting increase in the number of serials. Student enrolments and academic staff numbers were increasing at a faster rate than library staff. Non-academic staff are ignored in college library statistics and planning, and as such staff normally outnumber the teaching staff it would seem that libraries have an untapped pool of potential service here. What would be the effect of including in the library's budget bid a documented sum for information services to the principal's and the bursar's offices?

Australian statistics tend to be historical; we know quantitatively what has happened and the figures may seem to confirm what we felt in our bones regarding our ability to upgrade the quality of service. Yet are we right? What do the recorded 8.7% annual increase in loans 1976–8 and the 3.4% increase 1978–9 actually tell us about the libraries' contribution to the educational progress of our students and their integral place in the colleges?

INTEGRATION AND COOPERATION

Although various forms of networking have been preoccupying Australian college librarians for some years, there have also been a few experiments in closer cooperation and integration of systems and services which call for administrative rethinking. One of the most innovative forms of integration was suggested some years ago by Laurie Brown, then librarian of Moonee Valley regional service in Victoria and now state librarian of Tasmania. This concerned a growth area straddling the New South Wales and Victorian borders where the Hume Highway and the railway link between Sydney and Melbourne cross the River Murray which forms the boundary. The Albury-Wodonga Development Council still promotes and guides the government-assisted expansion of the two townships, though the economic climate has restricted the council's activities and postponed (or ruled out) the proposed university there. Needless to say, Brown's vision has not become a reality in this case.

The existing Upper Murray Regional Library service does cater for a number of local government bodies on both sides of the border, and is based in Albury. However it does not go as far as Brown's plan which was no less than the complete integration of all libraries in the twin towns under one administration. This would have had the effect of unifying the resources and services of the two major public libraries, the college of TAFE in Albury (the first purpose-built library in NSW outside the metropolitan area, which was opened in late 1980), Riverina College's study centre (now Albury-Wodonga campus) library, several school libraries, and special libraries such as that of the Health Commission. An important library established since his proposals is Clyde Cameron

College in Wodonga, run by the government-sponsored Trade Union Training Authority.

The difficulties of putting such a plan into operation are obvious, and may indeed have worsened in the intervening years. The public libraries are local government financed; the school libraries are serviced by their parent education departments in the two states; the Development Council is a joint federal and states project; special libraries are again under control of central government bodies; and the college of TAFE is part of the NSW government's responsibilities. Yet it is this very proliferation of provision within a restricted geographical area which makes Brown's report a desirable document. Moonee Valley was one of the earliest public libraries in Australia to take up computerization, and the growth of automated systems during the past decade has given a reality to the concept of library integration in areas such as this.

It is not surprising to find that Laurie Brown has worked tirelessly for a unified library service in Tasmania, and has achieved considerable success. One practical example of this occurred in April 1977 when the Robert Sticht Memorial Library was opened in Queenstown, when rebuilding allowed the incorporation of the municipal library with that of the West Coast Community College (at that time the Mount Lyell School of Mines and Industries). The education department provided the building in which the joint library is situated, with direct access for both public (street entrance) and TAFE college students and staff (linkway). Staffing and funding is provided by the State Library of Tasmania, and the new service operates as part of a 13-branch regional library system.[31]

Its slight physical separation from the college encourages use by the public (unlike the library of the Technical Institute in Nicosia, Cyprus, in which the present author assisted for a time in 1959, and which was housed in an upper floor with staircase access both inside for students and outside for the public). This is Australia's first example of an integrated college/public library, and may be seen as part of one man's vision rather than a definite nationwide movement.

Nevertheless, the availability of automated systems is making possible some practical integration and cooperation, even though

College Librarianship in Australia

complete administrative union cannot be achieved because of the various governmental interests involved. An example of this is the new joint service offered by Preston City Library and Preston College of TAFE in a district of Melbourne (Victoria). Since November 1981 the college library has been operating the AWA URICA Library System for reference enquiry, cataloguing and circulation. This year (1983) modules for acquisitions and periodicals are to be added, giving an online real time system over five campuses, each with terminals including one for public access at the main reference desk. The public library is joining the system on a cost-sharing basis, and there will be a joint stock of some 140,000 items. This common systems approach has developed from the reciprocal borrowing rights scheme in force since 1977, and close geographical proximity is an important factor.[32]

Common origins have no doubt assisted the close cooperation between Deakin University and the Gordon Technical College, both in Geelong (Victoria). Some book stock and periodicals in the university are available to the college students and staff,[33] and there is now a shared Data Phase circulation system. However, integration of systems between different levels of tertiary educational institutions in Australia is very much in its infancy. Some form of cooperation on similar levels is much less rare, and may be seen both within small geographical areas (such as the high density state capitals) and larger ones (such as states). Sharing automated systems becomes difficult for colleges hundreds of kilometres apart, but sharing of COM catalogues is now well developed. In the south-east there are two major schemes: CAVAL (Cooperative Action by Victorian Academic Libraries) and CLANN (College Library Activities Network in New South Wales).

A seminal research project was carried out by Elizabeth Stecher in Melbourne 1973–5, and basically asked whether COM was a cost-beneficial alternative to full print for library catalogues before online catalogues become available. The study found them to be acceptable on the grounds of cost, and also (with some reservations) acceptable to users.[34] This study was one of those examined by the Maguire-Peake proposal for the establishment of CLANN using the services of Libramatic Systems Pty Ltd, and the network is now an active cooperative of college libraries. The microfiche cata-

384

logues still suffer from the non-entry of many works held by participating libraries (sometimes in storage), but is assisting inter-library lending between institutions.[26]

MERGERS AND AMALGAMATIONS

Cooperation between libraries is one thing, but amalgamation of colleges presents quite different problems. The tables presented earlier in this chapter show the net growth in the CAE sector, hiding the fact that some institutions have merged. Especially since the date of these latest available statistics, there have been consider-able amalgamations throughout the country. At the end of 1981 the federal government announced the impending cessation of funding to some thirty CAEs which did not present satisfactory amalgamation plans by the end of 1982, but the election of the Labor government in 1983 has reversed this policy. Mergers have not necessarily been forced in this way, however, nor have they always resulted in fewer campuses.

The establishment of the early CAEs often depended on the incorporation of teachers' colleges, though this was usually a *de facto* growth of existing facilities rather than a *de jure* merging of institutions and libraries. However, by the mid-1970s genuine amalgamations were increasingly taking place, leading to rationaliz-ation of course offerings and library services on the various campuses. No doubt many of the problems experienced and solved in Australia are similar to those obtaining in Britain during the period of the creation of polytechnics from two or more colleges. In Australian cities this similarity may be more marked than in rural areas. One case reported from suburban Melbourne (Victoria) involved the merger in 1980 of a multi-purpose CAE (which also offered TAFE courses) and a primary teachers' college about four kilometres apart. Accommodation problems forced the transfer of a large department from the former to the latter, which involved the transfer of some 10,000 volumes and called for an initial harmonization of incompatible circulation policies.

Three major problems were identified which called for 'a substan-tial commitment of time and money': the selection of material to be transferred, the changing of library records, and handling and transportation. Selection was difficult because materials were used by different courses in some cases, and it was estimated that up to 60% of the material needed for the transferred department was also required by the main campus courses. Selection was estimated at $1.10 per volume (professional and clerical labour). Records were confusingly amended at a cost of $0.15 per record, by means of a temporary finding list linked to the main library's COM catalogue. The list was provided at each library on cards, and 'proved barely tolerable even in the short term'. Serials were interfiled but the incompatibilities forced the receiving library to house the trans-ferred books separately from its own collection; physical handling was estimated at about $0.20 per volume.[35]

Traumas of a somewhat different kind were experienced in Tasmania in 1981 when the CAE in Hobart was dissected, four departments following two previous ones to the university and the others being transferred to a CAE in the north of the island-state. The university library cautiously welcomed the CAEs extensive AV collection as its own was somewhat meagre, but the printed materials caused considerable problems for both the university and the northern CAE. Neither library could deal with superfluous duplicates or unwanted items. The university collection was increasingly on COM and classified by LC, whereas the old CAE stock was on catalogue cards and classified by Dewey. Cooperation between academic and library staff was essential for transfer of books to appropriate locations; kits and curriculum materials went to the new curriculum resource centre; subscriptions to serials were individually renewed as (and only if) appropriate. Planning and discussions lasted for some 18 months, costing many man hours. Selection, processing, and transfer of stock was also costly both in time and money; both had to be largely provided from normal resources.[36]

During the past few years there have been considerable campus upheavals following administrative mergers of colleges, particularly in South Australia but also notably in Western Australia and Victoria. In the political discussions little if any thought and money have been given to the implications for libraries. The college library staff concerned have had to cope with the situation, using often minimal help from hard-pressed college management. Despite changes in national government policy we can expect to see state governments looking on proposed mergers with some favour but little additional finance.

EXTERNAL STUDENTS

Tables 3 and 8 above indicate that in 1980 there were 85,102 enrolments as external students in the CAE and TAFE sectors alone, and together with distance education students at universities they pose a special problem (and opportunity) for library services. Although the Australian government decided against an Open University *per se*, there is in fact considerable though inadequate provision by many tertiary institutions scattered throughout the country. No institution teaches exclusively by the distance mode, though many do have only internal students. External students are 'at once even more dependent than other students on library services, and more difficult to supply with them'. In 1974 the Karmel Report noted the weakness of public library services, and their inability to provide for tertiary students to any great extent. Because of this the universities and colleges would have to make special provision for their external students.[37]

Experience shows that it requires very few requests from students to disrupt a state's inter-library lending (ILL) system, so that colleges must make immediate provision for access to required and recommended learning materials. A solution may be attempted in two ways: the provision of reprints of relevant pages from books and periodicals to accompany study guides on a non-returnable basis, and a liberal multiple copy provision and photocopy service by the college libraries, for postal lending. Free reprints are expensive but provide basic resources immediately; they also tend to 'spoon-feed' and discourage students from using other materials. Multiple copies and photocopies also add a financial burden, and introduce a delay in access though still quicker than the public library ILL service.

Photocopying raises the matter of copyright, and wise libraries will negotiate clearance in order to build up a small stock of frequently borrowed items. Many external students in fact live in the metropolitan cities, but this in itself is no guarantee of ready access to needed resources. However, many institutions will allow other students to use their libraries freely for reference, though often charging a fee for the 'privilege' of borrowing. Librarians who realize that all public funds come ultimately from the same taxpayers' pockets extend reciprocal borrowing rights; others fall back on the explanation that their own students must have priority, and that even they do not have sufficient resources. A more liberal attitude is slowly spreading however in the CAE library world,[38] though not apparently in the universities.

Few study centres have as yet been established, due to the small number of external students in any one township being enrolled in a particular course in any one institution.[39, 40] One solution (rarely applied) would be for a college to deposit on loan to local public libraries a selection of pertinent materials, and to encourage the libraries to buy works of more general use. Another would be for colleges to cooperate by collectively establishing study centres or deposit selections, a happy example of working together which has been developed in Queensland.

This still leaves very many students who are isolated. Even expensive airmail within the country can take ten days or more to be delivered, and there may not be a daily delivery in the suburbs of even moderately large towns. This lengthens the communication time for ILL services, as also for any special requests by an external student of his own college library. Materials supplied may reach the student too late for a particular assignment. We do not have a great deal of data on the usage of libraries by external students, though in one survey of mainly science students about 16% of respondents claimed that the nearest useful library was more than 100km away. Two thirds lived within 25 km. This of course is a subjective matter in that it records how students perceived the usefulness rather than the potential usefulness.[41]

The importance of a college's library to an external student depends very much on the area of residence and nearness to other useful libraries. Such students in large cities make much less use of their college library, though even here poor facilities may still make reliance on the institution necessary. Borrowing from friends tends to be very low, no doubt reflecting the isolation of many students (even though there may be other external students within a few kilometres, the probability is that they will be studying a different course or at least different level subjects). On the whole however, the subject notes and reprints may be the most important source for students, followed by buying one's own books, other libraries, and finally the college library.[42] This order may support the charges of spoon-feeding and lack of wide reading at undergraduate level to some extent, if students place heavy reliance on required reading. If external students of this category are not adventurous library users, and the institution still finds their achievements satisfactory (remembering that in Australia internal and external courses are almost identical in content and assessment), then perhaps responsibility for provision of learning resources should move more from the college library to the learning package.

One solution to the problems of storage and transport of books and periodicals for external students is microfiche, used by the University of South Africa for some years but abandoned (temporarily, it is understood) because of the problems in lending hardware. A similar project in Australia has met a similar fate, due in this case to a negative response from many of the publishers approached concerning copyright.[40] On the other hand, personal experience over several years has been that publishers of periodicals have almost always responded positively to requests for permission to reproduce articles for inclusion in books of readings accompanying notes, providing they are not sold to students. I made a practice of first writing to the authors concerned, who not only invariably consented (authorial vanity?) but often helpfully referred to other relevant literature. Little or nothing is being done regarding investigation of videotext accessed by computer or satellite, which could be of considerable relevance to colleges and their libraries in the next twenty years.

What is the answer to the problems of servicing external students in Australia in the immediate future? It is apparent that more cooperation between institutions may help, both at the library level for learning materials and at a college level to allow a student to enrol in certain subjects at more than one institution in order to facilitate access. Another approach may lie in the development of the library-college concept to counteract the existing tendency for administrative and academic staff to view distance learning as being merely an off-campus version of the normal on-campus programmes. An electronic or satellite library-college concept for external students is an exciting prospect for this author, at least.

CONCLUSION

Many of the topics of current concern to college librarians in Australia are similar to those elsewhere: networking and lessening purchasing power are familiar to colleagues the world over. Some older matters such as shortage of skilled staff are less pressing now in the sense that there is some over-production at professional and technician levels, though some specialisms are in short supply. Some problems such as servicing isolated external students are more likely to be Australian that British or American, though admittedly isolation is relative and not necessarily geographical.

The literature of Australian college librarianship is extensive though not vast, and many topics other than those mentioned in this chapter are exercising bibliothecal minds. Projects such as the TAFE Clearing House in the area of AV are occupying much time and effort to improve services.[43] ALARM 1981 (Australian Library Annual Reports on Microfiche) makes available the reports for that year of 23 CAEs out of the 45 or so in Australia. This is but one recent service to come from the library of Footscray Institute of Technology amongst many initiatives sponsored by the innovative Alan Bundy.[44] In recent years Nancy Lane has noted various preoccupations in college library reports (though some may be subjectively her own) such as computer applications, AV, periodicals, and reference services, during 1978. The following year she identified finance, amalgamations and closures, declining student numbers, and user services as being of concern in addition to those already mentioned for 1978.[45]

Within twenty years Australian college librarianship has moved from a plethora of encouraging government commissions each advocating bigger and better traditional college libraries, to a period of financial hardship and college closures. Colleges have seen spectacular growth followed by cutbacks, and a student population vacillating between job expansion and massive unemployment. Automation is here but still beyond the reach of many institutions. One thing is certain: the year 2000 will open on a different library world, and perhaps one in which Australian college libraries as we know them will have disappeared in a frenzy of activity.

REFERENCES

1 *Whitaker's Almanack, 1983.* Whitaker, 1982. 618, 707, 925.
2 *Statesman's Year Book 1982–1983.* Macmillan, 1982.
3 Kurtz, S (ed) *The New York Times Encyclopedia Almanac 1970.* New York Times, 1969.
4 *The World Book Encyclopedia*, Volume 1. 1977 edition.
5 Unesco *Compulsory education in Australia.* Unesco, 3rd ed, r.i., 1962.
6 Dodd, L 'Foreword' in Ashton, J *School of the Air*, Rigby, 1978.
7 Maclaine, A G 'The educational challenge of change', in Maclaine, A G and Selby-Smith, R *Fundamental issues in Australian education.* Novak, 1971.
8 Adapted from *Year Book Australia, No 66, 1982.* Australian Bureau of Statistics, 1982.
9 Jones, P E *Education in Australia.* Nelson, 1974.
10 *New South Wales Year Book, No 67, 1982.* Australian Bureau of Statistics, NSW Office, 1982.
11 Barcan, A *A history of Australian education.* OUP, 1980, 335–6.
12 Commonwealth Advisory Committee on Advanced Education *First Report.* (1st Wark Report). Canberra, Government Printer, 1966.
13 Australia, House of Representatives *Commonwealth Parliamentary Debates.* Vol 65, 1969. 189.
14 Australian Commission on Advanced Education *Teacher education: report of the Special Committee on Teacher Education.* (Swanson Report.) Canberra, Government Printer, 1973. 45–7.
15 Australian Committee on Technical and Further Education *TAFE in Australia: report on needs in technical and further education.* (Kangan Report). Canberra, AGPS, 1974. Vol. 1, 122, 125, 150–1, 153, 156–9; Vol 2, 8–10, 240–3.
16 Mitcheson, B 'Building standards for TAFE libraries' in Heinrich, E J (ed) *TAFE it from here.* Sydney, Library Association of Australia, 1980. 99–100, 102.
17 International Federation of Library Associations Section of Public

Libraries. *Standards for public libraries.* Munich, Verlag Dokumentation, 1973.

18 Good, J 'Standards for TAFE libraries: collections and staffing', in
    Heinrich E J (ed) *TAFE it from here.* Sydney, Library Association of
    Australia, 1980. 107, 112.

19 Victoria Institute of Colleges *Libraries in colleges of advanced educ-
    ation: a brief guide to their administration and function for the use of
    colleges and institutes affiliated with the Victoria Institute of Colleges.*
    Melbourne, VIC, 1971. 13. (There had, however, been an attempt by
    a group of college librarians some three years earlier to produce more
    definitive standards with a minimum book stock of 50,000 volumes
    (including serials) for 1,000 EFTS and a ratio of 50:1 (though small
    specialist colleges could have a minimum of 25,000 vols). These also
    included guidelines for duplication of prescribed and recommended
    reading. VIC Chief Librarians' Committee *Guidelines for college
    libraries with particular reference to libraries in colleges of advanced
    education affiliated with the Victoria Institute of Colleges.*
    (Melbourne, 1968).

20 Wainwright, E J and Dean, J E *Measures of adequacy for library
    collections in Australian colleges of advanced education.* Perth, WAIT,
    1976. *passim.*

21 Commonwealth Advisory Committee on Advanced Education *Second
    report* (2nd Wark Report.) Canberra, Government Printer, 1969.

22 Australian Commission on Advanced Education *Third report on
    advanced education.* (3rd Wark Report.) Canberra, AGPS, 1972.

23 Library Association of Australia: University and College Libraries
    Section *Draft standards for libraries of colleges of advanced education.*
    LAA, 1972.

24 Taylor, T K 'Progress and poverty in teachers' college libraries' in
    Library Association of Australia, *Proceedings of the 16th Biennial
    Conference held in Sydney, August 1971.* LAA, 1972. 449–51.
    (Compare these with the Clapp-Jordan formula of 1965.)

25 Victoria: Education Department: Advisory Committee on Teachers'
    College Libraries *Final Report.* The Department, 1972.

26 Maguire, C and Peake, D G *Report on investigation of the cataloguing
    requirements of New South Wales college of advanced education
    libraries.* 1976. 80–1.

27 McCulloch, G and Marginson, S *An examination of the decline in
    library facilities in Australian universities and colleges of advanced
    education.* Australian Union of Students, 1982. (A submission to
    the federal Minister for Education resulting from an investigation of
    academic libraries since 1975).

28 Committee of Inquiry into Education and Training *Education, train-
    ing and employment.* (Williams Report.) Canberra, AGPS, 1979. Vol
    1, 243, iv.

29   See for example: 'Australian and New Zealand university library statistics, 1977'. *Australian Academic & Research Libraries*, 9(3) September 1978, supplement (which includes CAEs); and 'Library statistics 1978', *AARL*, 10 (3) September 1979, supplement.

30   Steele, C 'The TEC report for the 1982–84 triennium'. *AARL* 12 (4) December 1981. 227–8.

31   *TAFEC News* (Newsletter of the Technical and Further Education Council of the Tertiary Education Commission). Number 11 October 1977. 3.

32   'College/public library shared automation'. *Australian Library News* 14 (2) March 1983. 7.

33   Bundy, A L (ed) *Directory of Australian academic libraries*. Footscray Institute of Technology, 1978. 18.

34   Stecher, E *Catalogue provision in libraries of colleges of advanced education*. Melbourne, RMIT, 1975.

35   Tweedie, C 'Transfer of library resources among merging institutions'. *AARL* 12(3) September 1981. 162–6.

36   Waters, D 'Problems of merging libraries'. *AARL* 12(3) September 1981. 167–173.

37   Committee on Open University *Open tertiary education in Australia: Report to the Universities Commission.* (Karmel Report.) Canberra, AGPS, 1975. 91.

38   Bundy, A L 'Inter-institutional personal borrowing rights'. *AARL* 9(1) March 1978. 13–21.

39   In 1978, eight CAEs had permanent or *ad hoc* study centres, many of which were in Queensland. See for example: Appleton, M and Meyers, N 'Distance education and the CIAE library: report on one planning survey'. *AARL* 10(4) December 1979. 247–9.

40   Store, R Crocker, C and McSwan, D 'Distance education and library services: planning and implementation in a small regional college'. *AARL* 9 (3) September 1978. 144–5. (Townsville CAE.)

41   Reid-Smith, E R *Results of a survey of residential schools held by Riverina College, September 1980*. Wagga Wagga, Riverina College of Advanced Education, Division of External Studies, 1981 8–9. (An unpublished analysis of 1,004 questionnaire returns completed throughout 1981 indicated 19.4% claiming to have no useful library within 100 km for the subjects then being studied externally. But this should not necessarily be taken as indicating a national figure).

42   Collis, M and Tolley, C. *Studying externally: the attitudes and experience of GIAE students*. Churchill, Victoria, Gippsland Institute of Advanced Education, 1979. 35–7.

43   Swinburne College of Technology. *National Union Catalogue of Audio Visual Materials*. Hawthorn, Victoria, 1979. 2912 on microfiche.

44 Bundy, A Letter in *AARL* 14(1) March 1983. 59. (Correcting a figure wrongly supplied to N Lane.)
45 Lane, N '1978 Australian CAE library reports'. *AARL* 11(4) December 1980. 229–31: 'CAE library reports for 1979'. *AARL* 12(4) December 1981. 222–6.

25

Some Trends in Further and Higher Education to 2000: the Libraries' Response

John Bate

The year 2000 is not very far ahead; not much time for any very startling changes. Everything likely to be happening then is already in embryo around us, if we had the wit to see it. The world of the 1980s was in embryo as long as 60 years ago – Communist revolution of 1917, retreat of colonialism (Irish Rebellion of 1916), radio and TV (BBC charter granted in the early 1920s), motoring for the masses, air travel, electronics and telecommunications, even the idea of the computer – they were all there in those leisurely, Bloomsbury, doomsbury years, when Joyce was handsomely subsidized by Harriet Weaver in Paris, and avoided Marcel Proust, and Diaghilev was bringing together painters, choreographers, musicians, and dancers in an unprecedented theatrical experience on the stages of Europe.

What then is present in our world that is going to shape the colleges of the year 2000? There are two fixed points that we can use to help locate the unknown embryos. First: human beings need to learn – we cannot proceed from birth to maturity without a long period of learning. Second: we all have leisure to occupy all our lives. The question that needs to be answered is: 'How will mankind be learning what he needs to know in the year 2000?' Will it be by the printed book? Will it be through lectures and exercises marked by a class teacher? How will we be choosing to spend our leisure?

Does the printed book have a future? This question was asked of Dr F W Ratcliffe, Librarian of Cambridge University, in a recent interview.[1] His answer was:

> Is that in doubt? The book, and I have said this on many occasions in the past, is probably the most important invention of Western Europe. In particular the format of the book, as far as I can see, has never been bettered, and I cannot see that it will be bettered. For transmitting information you need not rely entirely on the book, because you can put information into data banks; but for certain types of information, for relaxation and for all of those wonderful things that the book brings into your life, it will never disappear.

Good for Cambridge, and despite the videodisc and the resultant possibility of a bootlegged *Britannica* for £17 we can be sure this is true.

We have to remember that the literacy, numeracy, and oracy we demand of an educated person today was not considered necessary for a complete person in the past. Oracy was sufficient for thousands of years. William the Conqueror was illiterate and signed his name with a rather uneven Maltese cross. Moreover, the future of education is arguably a small matter when set against the vast question of mankind's future.

Jonathan Schell, a staff writer for *The New Yorker*, sets out the inescapable fact of 'the self-extinction of our species' being 'an act that, without quite admitting it to ourselves, we plan in certain circumstances to commit'. Paradoxically, it is an act that only an immensely complex and thorough-going educational system makes possible. But it is now not only possible, but even probable. Schell writes:[2]

> Once the strategic necessity of planning the deaths of hundreds of millions of people is accepted, we begin to live in a world in which morality and action inhabit two separate, closed realms. All strategic sense becomes moral nonsense and vice versa, and we are left with the choice of seeming to be either

strategic or moral idiots. . . . Strategic thinking refers to a reality that is supposed never to come into existence. Therefore, not only is morality deliberately divorced from 'thinking' but planning is divorced from action.

This is the world in which we live. What are society's expectations of the educational process? Are we expected in our schools and universities to continue to stoke up fuel for an eventual nuclear fire? Can we educate our youngsters in correct moral thinking, if the state which controls us, is, in ex-President Nixon's vivid phrase, guided by the 'Madman Theory' that only a President who appears to have taken leave of his senses will be obeyed? The appalling danger in which the world stands is so much greater than any other fact of life that 'the future of the printed word' seems a minor detail. By the year 2000 the nuclear monster that educated men have made may have destroyed life on this incomparably beautiful and fecund planet.

Perhaps, then, the first imponderable in a prognosis of what is likely to be the state of play in 20 years time is the very role of higher education in our society. The UK has always been chary of educating her people; waited 70 years after Germany before legislating for compulsory schooling; waited till 1944 to open the universities to the indigent, and until 1964 to enunciate the Robbins principle of 'courses of higher education available for all those who are qualified by ability and attainment to pursue them and who wish to do so'. This in itself a vague enough definition which, liberally interpreted, led to rash expense with very little to show for it. A hard core of academic dedication remains.

We know we have neglected vocational training when we measure our effort against that of our commercial rivals. We are anxious to catch up with them, but government seems reluctant to allow the education authorities to master-mind the exercise, preferring the untried mandarins of the newfangled Manpower Services Commission (MSC). The big question therefore is and will be: 'Are they up to the job?'

Librarians know their role and function is unchallenged in the ancient universities, and is welcomed and admired when imaginatively propagandized in the polytechnics, but in some schools and colleges 'education' itself is treated with suspicion and 'book' is a four letter word, the use of which is not to be encouraged. Despite these problems, and although books and magazines are now owned in greater numbers by a bigger percentage of the population than ever before in the UK, the British notoriously still buy fewer books than any other nation in Europe. MSC will need to be deluged with evidence of the contribution libraries can make to industrial training before they listen. The most effective approach is likely to be through the information providing function of libraries, which will give insight into the new technology, and access to videotext and online data bases and data banks for the students.

The creation of the National Advisory Body (NAB) as a basis for planning in the public (ie non-university) sector of higher education has increased the possibility of fruitful consultation between the universities and the polytechnics, and the CNAA system of course validation may yet be introduced into the universities. The chances of movement between courses will increase, so that students might be able to complete a degree after attending several institutions, even transferring across the binary divide. The whole education system, from primary school onwards, may become a responsibility of central government. Then the role of higher education could become that of achieving the objectives of government rather than to flourish freely according to academic custom. The conservatism innate in man, added to the weight of tradition in higher education, will make this change in role slow to become clear, but the essential policy decisions have already been made and are unlikely to be reversed.

Philip Hills, Director of the Primary Communications Research Centre at the University of Leicester, has edited a collection of papers[3] in which Maurice Line, Director-General of the British Library Lending Division, asks how inevitable are the changes which are possible if the new information technology is applied, and suggests that 'the vast majority of documents will be stored in electronic (chrysalis) form, but the majority of those used at any given time will be in their printed (butterfly) form'. Line also reminds us that whatever we do with the printed word in future, we have the uncounted billions of existing printed words to contend with, a great deal of which we shall need to make use of for a long time to come.

Dr Ratcliffe and Maurice Line, then, present strong arguments for a secure future for the book. It will be a future in which changes have taken place, eg publishers are adapting already to the needs for smaller runs of more specialist books (although marketing these products through the woefully inadequate booksellers of the UK no doubt limits sales to fewer copies than the potential demand).

Many changes in our educational system are clearly signalled in government reports and statistical returns. The chief of these is surely the deliberate switch of resources from university education to the training of 16–19 year olds. The creation of the Open Tech,[4] to be directed by Dr Tolley, recognized at Sheffield City Polytechnic for forging close links of many kinds with local industry, is an earnest of government's intentions. The influence of Tolley's vocational training efforts may well be to produce a much more vocationally based higher education system, in which some of the faculties of humanities will melt away to be replaced by schools of business management, a neglected area in higher education in this country, and the growth in higher education of such studies as catering and hotel-keeping, industrial engineering, applied physics, and office administration. Furthermore, highly qualified school leavers must be attracted to such studies in ever-increasing numbers. We need a diversion into careers in industry and commerce of those who seek the shelter of academe after achieving their clutches of 'A' grade passes at school.

Continuing education for changed responsibilities in mid-career, which the Open Tech proposals are meant to tackle, is the type of education most likely to be flourishing in the year 2000. The success of the Open University in providing an opportunity eagerly and successfully seized by older students, many of whom are in full-time employment, must cause serious questions to be asked of full-time tertiary education targetted almost entirely at school-leavers, so many of whom fail to complete their courses.

Whether this takes place depends on the image of industry and commerce. If its hard-sell, multi-national biased, consumer exploiting image is not modified by a more accurate and acceptable picture of industrial objectives and achievement, then the brightest of our students will not be drawn. Manufacturing industry, however, in common with agriculture, produces all that will sell with fewer people each year, despite trade union efforts to cling on to non-existent jobs. Why not? Does the human race wish to be chained to dull repetitive work? In the immediate pre-war period, a friend of mine with a double first in classics from Cambridge found a job selling oil with Shell, because all the men in that department of the company were classics men, whose days, when not actually selling oil, were spent in reading and discussing the works of Euripides, Plato, Virgil, and other favourite authors.

Class will tell; we shall always come back to the great minds and imaginations of civilization to study them and ponder over their works. Libraries must not abandon their task of preserving these works, and all the commentaries upon them. We shall perhaps in future become more aware of two distinct types of education, already plain to see, namely education for a definite purpose, such as the staffing of our hospitals, law courts, and other essential institutions, and education for the sake of knowledge, of understanding the human condition, of probing into the heart of reality. Information technology can marshal the resources at man's disposal with unrivalled efficiency for the former purpose, but for the latter, the printed book will suffice; it is not information which we need when we probe reality, but a free and yet disciplined imagination.

Some changes will take place because of the contraction of our population. By the year 2000 even government demographers who produced the most asinine predictions of an upturn in population growth by the end of the century, admit that the population of the western world is set for an absolute decline, so that by the middle of the 21st century it may be little more than half what it is today. Contraction of population on this scale will produce some devastating results. Consider all the houses that will never be needed, and which will crumble unsold, sheltering only insect and animal life.

The contracting school population as it works through the tertiary sector will cause mergers, closures, and fierce competition between institutions, unless government takes upon itself the long-term replanning of the whole educational system. Contemporary with this contraction in numbers will come the impact of information technology upon learning; videocassette presentation of course material; user-friendly interactive terminals where a student can sit and work through learning programmes at a speed to suit himself. The chore of teaching the basics will be eased; it will be possible to learn in the home; schools and colleges will be places for necessary social encounters, centres for organized 'happenings' which will involve the whole community, not just pupils or students. The library in such an educational environment will find itself being asked to satisfy a much wider range of demands. Just as education will escape from the strict institutional confines that shut off even neighbouring schools from much concourse with each other, and will become increasingly a part of the whole of society, so the library will be able to offer its resources not just to a small number of matriculated students and their teachers and supporting staff, but to the educational and informational needs of the whole of the local population.

Academic libraries therefore will need to become more adult, to lose the 'nanny' image and cooperate with the students in their learning programme, getting to know them much more closely than at present.

Although it is unlikely that new technology in the shape of learning packages, from videotapes and electronically controlled engineering kits to simple microcomputer floppy discs and old-fashioned tape-slide presentations, will ever seriously release teachers from the need to teach, nonetheless they have an effectiveness and impact which will lead to a more important role for collections of such material in the library.

The report commissioned by ex-President Carter from the Council on Environmental Quality[5] warns that over the whole world the:

> carrying capacity of the earth and the problem of sustaining the possibility of a decent life for the human beings that inhabit it are strained to the limit. Vigorous, determined new initiatives are needed if worsening poverty and human suffering, environmental degradation and international tension and conflict are to be prevented. An era of unprecedented cooperation and commitment is essential.

This environmentalist warning, taken in conjunction with the threat of the nuclear holocaust, may very well prompt the unprecedented cooperation that is called for, in which case libraries will find their resources being used as a base to spread knowledge more evenly over the earth's surface, with the emphasis on information technology, pairing of academic libraries in the Third World with those in the developed world, training of Third World librarians by periods of secondment to libraries in the developed world, in other words a much greater emphasis than heretofore on the training of librarians in the use of library systems. Non-professional staff in academic libraries today are grossly undertrained, compared, say, to the staff in medical laboratories. If the new syllabuses put forward by such technician training bodies as the Scottish Technical Education Council (SCOTEC) are accepted, the average technician in Scottish industry will have in the future a far better knowledge of how to use the stock of a big library than the average library assistant (although the academic libraries probably perform better in this respect than the public libraries).

Theophil M Otto[6] makes the extraordinary prediction that 'research in librarianship as a major function of future librarians was rated generally improbable but desirable'. Research is not only desirable, but vital to the future of librarianship, and Maurice Line[7] reminds us that:

> it is not difficult to detect a deep and widespread desire for a less competitive, less aggressive, less exploitative, and less polluted society – one less dominated by industry and the profit motive' which is perhaps responsible for a change in education where school children are 'less aggressive and self-seeking' and 'optimistic faith in technology is generally a thing of the past, except for those directly involved in technological developments'. At the very time that librarianship finds itself equipped with a new technology of tremendous potential, is the ethos of the age turning aside from the promises of technology?

Maurice Line prophesies a society in which there will be much greater leisure, and in which education will be adapted and developed towards this sort of society, and become 'de-institutionalized' or as Mrs Thatcher would say 'privatized', he adds:

A leisured society, educated to entertain itself and create, will produce more media, written, visual and aural. . . . The strange concept that appears to be held by many librarians that everything printed has permanent value and must be preserved while other communication media are largely disposable will become untenable.

It could be added that perhaps the most notable bibliographic feat of recent years has been the reconstruction of the six-hour 1927 film of Abel Gance, *Napoleon*, a task which occupied the devoted efforts of Kevin Brownlow for many years.

We shall have to find ways to occupy leisure which do not strain the limited supplies of fossil fuels, nor cause too much crowding on our transport systems, so we may imitate the Russians and build up 'Culture Parks' in our cities near our homes. The familiar but currently threatened humanities type of higher education may be reborn, if indeed it suffers a demise, in this milieu and the enormous popularity of fiction, a necessity, as Chesterton explained, will ensure the demand for librarians expert in the field.[8]

Paradoxically, it is the very technology that people are turning away from that is increasing the leisure of our society. The librarian will use videotext systems increasingly in the future to answer many enquiries; in fact, libraries may lose many enquiries to videotext sets in people's homes. The business librarians' loss in this way can be recovered by the librarian entering the field of information provision, that is the regular gathering and packaging of information for input into videotext services. These may be nationwide, as PRESTEL, or local, like the Edinburgh Multi-Access System (EMAS) system of the Edinburgh Regional Computing Centre. Librarians in academic libraries may also find themselves well placed to influence the development of the electronic journal, which is being researched quite extensively by various publishing firms. 'Dramatic shifts' in the nature of journal publication are forecast by the authors of recent articles.[9, 10] They point out that an 'electronic paper maintained by the authors will change over time, based on readership feedback, and only when the paper has obtained some level of "score" from its peer audience will it be likely to appear in some hard-copy collection'.

Thus hard copy journals will decrease in number, and the pressures on libraries for space, for money for subscriptions, and for staff to service the collections may also decrease.

To sum up, we see the beginning of a switch of educational resources from higher education to the more thorough training of those at the technician level, including non-professional staff in libraries; we see a vast increase not only in the time available for leisure, but in the value placed by ordinary individuals on leisure activities; against a background of an industrial society kept in being by information technology many of the arts and crafts of the pre-industrial era may return to favour, among them the book, as *objets d'art*.

Technology will influence the world of scientific and technical research so that videotext and electronic journal publication may become the norm for all that can be handled by such means; much learning may well be done by videotext of different kinds, and much research conducted by teams electronically linked, instead of their having to communicate, as at present, by meetings and the publication of papers in the learned journals.

Despite demographic forecasts, we predict a contracting population in the western world, and increasing contact with the under-developed world. The latter in its turn will gradually slow its rising flood of people. There may be an increasing desire of the highly developed to share their know-how with the less fortunate, rather than to pile the Pelion of affluence on top of the Ossa of a surfeit of education. The assault on Olympus may indeed be abandoned, so that mankind may settle for a less arrogant future. The dreadful alternative is there in all the newspaper headlines.

REFERENCES

1 Iles, A 'Ratcliffe in Camera' *Library Review* 31 (2) Summer 1982. 85–92.
2 Schell, H *The fate of the earth*. Cape, 1982.
3 Hills, P *The future of the printed word: the impact and the implications of the new communications technology*. Open University Press, 1982.

4 Manpower Services Commission *Open tech task group report.* Manpower Services Commission, 1982.

5 Council on Environmental Quality *Global 2000: report to the President.* The Council, 1980.

6 Otto, T M 'The academic librarian of the 21st century: public service and library education in the year 2000'; *Journal of Academic Librarianship* 8 (2) 1982. 85–8.

7 Line, M 'Libraries and information services in a part-technological society'. *Journal of Library Automation* 14(4) 1981. 252–268.

8 Mann, P H 'A browser's catalogue'. *New Library Review* 83 (988) October 1982. 143–45.

9 Turoff, M and Hiltz, S R 'The electronic journal: a progress report'. *Journal of the American Society for Information Science.* 33 (5) 1982. 195–202.

10 See most issues of *Communications Technology Impact.*

Glossary of Abbreviations and Acronyms used in the Text

AA	Associate of the Arts
AACR	Anglo-American Cataloguing Rules
ABLISS	Association of British Library and Information Science Schools
ACAAE	Australian Council on Awards in Advanced Education
ACT	Australian Capital Territory
AFE	Advanced Further Education
ALA	Associate of the Library Association
ALARM	Australian Library Annual Reports on Microfiche
ANS	Association of Navigation Schools
ANU	Australian National University
AP	Administrative and Professional
APTI	Association of Principals of Technical Institutions
ATCDE	Association of Teachers in Colleges and Departments of Education
ATTI	Association of Teachers in Technical Institutions (now NATFHE)
AUDIST	Agence universitaire de documentation et d'informations scientifiques et techniques
AV	Audio-visual

BBC	British Broadcasting Corporation
BEC	Business Education Council
BICBOC	Birmingham International Children's Book Collection
BL	British Library
BLAISE	British Library Automated Information Service
BLBSD	British Library Bibliographic Services Division
BLCMP	formerly Birmingham Libraries Cooperative Mechanization Project
BLEND	Birmingham and Loughborough Electronic Network Development
BLLD	British Library Lending Division
BLRD	British Library Reference Division
BRS	Bibliographic Retrieval Services Inc
BLRDD	British Library Research and Development Department
B/TEC	Business and Technician Education Council (forthcoming)
CAE	College of Advanced Education (in Australia)
CAL	Computer Assisted Learning
CAT	College of Advanced Technology
CAVAL	Co-operative Action by Victorian Academic Libraries (in Australia)
CCC	Consultative Committee on the Curriculum (Scotland)
CDP	Committee of Directors of Polytechnics
CET	Council for Educational Technology for the UK
CFE	College(s) of Further Education
CGLI	City and Guilds of London Institute
CI	Central Institution (in Scotland, a college funded directly by the Scottish Education Department)
CISE	Colleges, Institutes, and Schools of Education Group (of the Library Association) (now ELG)
CLAIM	Centre for Library and Information Management (at Loughborough University)
CLANN	College Libraries Activities Network, New South Wales
CNAA	Council for National Academic Awards

CoFHE	Colleges of Further and Higher Education Group (of the Library Association) (formerly CTFE)
COM	Computer Output Microform
COMECON	Council for Economic Mutual Assistance
COPOL	Council of Polytechnic Librarians
CRC	Central Resource Centre
CTFE	Colleges of Technology and Further Education Section (of the Library Association) (now CoFHE)
DATEC	Design and Art Technician Education Council
DES	Department of Education and Science
DIANE	Direct Information Access Network Europe
DipHE	Diploma in Higher Education
EDIS	Electronic Documentation and Information System
EEC	European Economic Community
EFL	English as a Foreign Language
ELG	Education Librarians Group (of the Library Association) (formerly CISE)
EMMA	Extra MARC Material
ESL	English as a Second Language
ESN	Educationally Subnormal
ET	Educational Technology/Technologist
FE	Further Education
FTE	Full Time Equivalent
GCE	General Certificate of Education
GED	Graduate Equivalency Degree
HE	Higher Education
HERTIS	Hertfordshire Information Service
HMI	Her Majesty's Inspector/Inspectorate (of education)
HNC	Higher National Certificate
HND	Higher National Diploma
IBA	Independent Broadcasting Authority
IFLA	International Federation of Library Associations
IHE	Institute of Higher Education
IIS	Institute of Information Scientists
ILEA	Inner London Education Authority

IMPI	Information Managers in the Pharmaceutical Industry
ISBN	International Standard Book Number
IT	Information Technology
IUT	Institut universitaire de technologie (in France)
KWIC	Keyword in Context
LA	Library Association
LASER	London and South Eastern Library Region
LC	Library of Congress
LEA	Local Education Authority
LIMB	Library Instruction Materials Bank
LISC	Library and Information Services Council
LLA	Licentiate of the Library Association
LOCAS	Local Cataloguing Service
LRC	Learning Resource Centre
LSSR	Library Staff: Student Ratio
MARC	Machine Readable Cataloguing
MLA	Marine Librarians Association
MSC	Manpower Services Commission
NAFE	Non-Advanced Further Education
NAB	National Advisory Body
NALGO	National and Local Government Officers Association
NATFHE	National Association of Teachers in Further and Higher Education (formerly ATTI)
NBL	National Book League
NEC	National Extension College
NEPHIS	Nested Phrase Indexing System
NJC	National Joint Council
NTI	New Training Initiative
OAL	Office of Arts and Libraries
OCLC	Online Computer Library Center (formerly Ohio College Library Center)
OECD	Organization for Economic Cooperation and Development
OJT	On the Job Training
ONC	Ordinary National Certificate
OND	Ordinary National Diploma

PPBS	Planning Programming Budgeting System
PRECIS	Preserved Context Index System
PSS	Packet Switched Network Service
RSA	Royal Society of Arts
RSG	Rate Support Grant
SCE	Scottish Certificate of Education
SCET	Scottish Council for Educational Technology
SCOLCAP	Scottish Libraries Cooperative Automation Project
SCONUL	Standing Conference of National and University Libraries
SCOTBEC	Scottish Business Education Council
SCOTEC	Scottish Technical Education Council
SCOTVEC	Scottish Vocational Education Council (forthcoming)
SDC	System Development Corporation
SDI	Selective Dissemination of Information
SED	Scottish Education Department
SFCLG	Sixth Form College Libraries Group
SLA	Scottish Library Association
SLIC	Selective Listing in Context
SSR	Staff: Student Ratio
SWALCAP	South West Academic Libraries Cooperative Automation Project
TAFE	Technical and Further Education (in Australia)
TEAS	Tertiary Education Assistance Scheme
TEC	Tertiary Education Commission (in Australia)
TEC	Technician Education Council
TOPS	Training Opportunities Scheme
UC&R	University, College, and Research Libraries Group (of the Library Association)
UCCA	Universities' Central Council on Admissions
UGC	University Grants Committee
UKLDS	United Kingdom Library Database System
Unesco	United Nations Educational, Scientific, and Cultural Organization
VoTech	Vocational/Technical college
WEA	Workers' Educational Association

WEEP   Work Experience on Employers' Premises
YOP   Youth Opportunities Programme
YTS   Youth Training Scheme

Index

K G B Bakewell

This is primarily a subject index, though authors of bibliographical references have been indexed if mentioned in the text. The index is arranged word by word.

Index

Index

Index

Index

Index

Index

William the Conqueror 396
Williams report 377, 380
Winchester hard disc 295
Wood, J. 155
Woolston Book Company 303
word processors 296, 303
Work Experience on Employers'
    Premises 103–104
Wright, G. 47
Wright, P. 181

YOP (Youth Opportunities) courses
    103

Young, R.C. 303
Youth Opportunities courses 103
Youth Training Scheme 104, 114
YTS (Youth Training Scheme) 104,
    114
Yugoslavia 330, 334
    expenditure on higher education 323
    student numbers 319, 321, 322, 323

zero-base budgeting 243
Zurich: National Technical University
    Library 329